WITHDRAWN
HARVARD LIBRARY
WITHDRAWN

The Silent God

By
Marjo C.A. Korpel
and
Johannes C. de Moor

BRILL

LEIDEN • BOSTON
2011

This book is printed on acid-free paper.

Library of Congress Cataloging-in-Publication Data

Korpel, Marjo C.A. (Marjo Christina Annette), 1958-
 The silent god / by Marjo C.A. Korpel, Johannes C. de Moor.
   p. cm.
 Includes bibliographical references and index.
 ISBN 978-90-04-20390-7 (hardback : alk. paper)
 1. God. 2. Hidden God. 3. Belief and doubt. I. Moor, Johannes C. de (Johannes Cornelis), 1935- II. Title.

 BL473.K67 2011
 212'.6—dc22

2011006138

ISBN 978 90 04 20390 7

Copyright 2011 by Koninklijke Brill NV, Leiden, The Netherlands.
Koninklijke Brill NV incorporates the imprints Brill, Hotei Publishing,
IDC Publishers, Martinus Nijhoff Publishers and VSP.

All rights reserved. No part of this publication may be reproduced, translated, stored in
a retrieval system, or transmitted in any form or by any means, electronic, mechanical,
photocopying, recording or otherwise, without prior written permission from the publisher.

Authorization to photocopy items for internal or personal use is granted by Koninklijke Brill NV
provided that the appropriate fees are paid directly to The Copyright Clearance Center,
222 Rosewood Drive, Suite 910, Danvers, MA 01923, USA.
Fees are subject to change.

CONTENTS

Preface xi

1. *The Silent God in Modernity* 1

1.1 Introduction 1
1.2 The Silent God in Modern Literature and Media 1
    1.2.1 Marie Louise Kaschnitz 2
    1.2.2 Jean-Paul Sartre 3
    1.2.3 Samuel Beckett 5
    1.2.4 Eli Wiesel 6
    1.2.5 Ingmar Bergman 8
    1.2.6 Endō Shūsaku 10
    1.2.7 Nathalie Sarraute 10
    1.2.8 Cormac McCarthy 12
    1.2.9 Patric Tavanti 13
1.3 Some Theologians and Philosophers 18
    1.3.1 Silent before the Silent 18
    1.3.2 Contemporary Theologians and Philosophers 20
        1.3.2.1 Karl Barth 20
        1.3.2.2 Kornelis Miskotte 22
        1.3.2.3 God Is Dead Movement 22
        1.3.2.4 John Paul II and Benedict XVI 23
        1.3.2.5 Emmanuel Levinas 24
        1.3.2.6 Rachel Muers 25
        1.3.2.7 Interim Conclusion 26
1.4 The Silent God in Agnosticism and Atheism 26
1.5 In Defense of a Silent God 26

CONTENTS

1.6 Critical Examination of Current Views 34
    1.6.1 Modern Literature and Media 34
    1.6.2 Contemporary Theologians and Philosophers 35
        1.6.2.1 Contemporary Christian Theologians 36
        1.6.2.2 Does a Silent God Require Silent Devotion? 41
        1.6.2.3 A New Theism? 47
        1.6.2.4 Is Atheism the Solution? 50
        1.6.2.5 Conclusion 53

2. *Prerequisites for a Fresh Investigation* 55

2.1 Defining the Scope of This Study 55
2.2 The Human Nature of Religious Language 59
    2.2.1 Metaphor in the Philosophy of Language 60
    2.2.2 Metaphor in Religious Language 64
    2.2.3 Religious Language: Conclusion 67

2.3 Silence Presupposes Speech 70
    2.3.1 Introduction 70
    2.3.2 Spaces Marking Rhetorical Silences 72

2.4 The Silent God: The Biblical Roots 74
2.5 The Silent God: The Biblical World 75
2.6 Why This Approach? 76

3 *Silence between Humans in Antiquity* 79

3.1 Introduction 79
3.2 Reasons for Silence between Humans 79
    3.2.1 Silence Because of Offenses 79
        3.2.1.1 In the Ancient Near East 80
        3.2.1.2 In the Bible 82

    3.2.2 Silence Because of Awe or Fear 84
        3.2.2.1 In the Ancient Near East 84
        3.2.2.2 In the Bible 86
    3.2.3 Silence Because of Forbearance or Prudence 87
        3.2.3.1 In the Ancient Near East 87
        3.2.3.2 In the Bible 90
    3.2.4 Silence Because of Incapacity 96
        3.2.4.1 In the Ancient Near East 96
        3.2.4.2 In the Bible 99
    3.2.5 Silence Because of Sleep 102
        3.2.5.1 In the Ancient Near East 102
        3.2.5.2 In the Bible 103
3.3 Conclusions on Silence between Humans 106

4. *How Did Man Address the Deity?* 111

4.1 Introduction 111
4.2 Songs and Prayers 113
    4.2.1 Songs and Prayers in the Ancient Near East 113
    4.2.2 Songs and Prayers in the Bible 115
4.3 Letters to Deities 116
    4.3.1 Letters to Deities in the Ancient Near East 116
    4.3.2 Letters to God in the Bible 117
4.4 Magic and Sorcery 117
    4.4.1 Magic and Sorcery in the Ancient Near East 117
    4.4.2 Magic and Sorcery in the Bible 118
4.5 Silence of Man before the Deity 119
    4.5.1 Silence Because of Offenses 118
        4.5.1.1 In the Ancient Near East 119
        4.5.1.2 In the Bible 119

  4.5.2 Silence Because of Awe of Fear 121
    4.5.2.1 In the Ancient Near East 121
    4.5.2.2 In the Bible 121
  4.5.3 Silence Because of Forbearance or Prudence 122
    4.5.3.1 In the Ancient Near East 122
    4.5.3.2 In the Bible 124
  4.5.4 Silence Because of Incapacity 130
    4.5.4.1 In the Ancient Near East 130
    4.5.4.2 In the Bible 132
  4.5.5 Silence Because of Sleep 134
    4.5.5.1 In the Ancient Near East 134
    4.5.5.2 In the Bible 135
4.6 Conclusions on Man Addressing the Deity 135

5. *How Did the Deity Address Man?* 139

5.1 Direct Communication between Deity and Man 140
  5.1.1 In the Ancient Near East 140
  5.1.2 In the Bible 148
5.2 Communication through Intermediaries 158
  5.2.1 Divine Intermediaries 159
    5.2.1.1 Lower Divine Intermediaries in the Ancient
       Near East 159
    5.2.1.2 Lower Divine Intermediaries in the Bible 162
  5.2.2 Human Intermediaries 166
    5.2.2.1 Prophets and Seers in the Ancient Near East 167
    5.2.2.2 Prophets and Seers in the Bible 180
    5.2.2.3 Scribes in the Ancient Near East 196
    5.2.2.4 Scribes in the Bible 204
5.3 Dreams, Visions, Oracles, Omina 210
  5.3.1 Dreams 212

        5.3.1.1 Dreams in the Ancient Near East 212
        5.3.1.2 Dreams in the Bible 215
    5.3.2 Visions 215
        5.3.2.1 Visions in the Ancient Near East 215
        5.3.2.2 Visions in the Bible 216
    5.3.3 Oracles and Omina 217
        5.3.3.1 Oracles and Omina in the Ancient Near East 217
        5.3.3.2 Oracles and Omina in the Bible 220
5.4 Conclusions on the Deity Addressing Man 224

6. *The Silent God* 231

6.1 The Silence of the Remote God 231
    6.1.1 In the Ancient Near East 231
    6.1.2 In the Bible 233
6.2 Broken Communication between God and Man 237
    6.2.1 Comprehensible Divine Silence 238
        6.2.1.1 Divine Silence Because of Offenses 238
            6.2.1.1a In the Ancient Near East 238
            6.2.1.1b In the Bible 239
        6.2.1.2 Divine Silence Because of Awe or Fear 245
            6.2.1.2a In the Ancient Near East 245
            6.2.1.2b In the Bible 246
        6.2.1.3 Divine Silence Because of Forbearance or Prudence 247
            6.2.1.3a In the Ancient Near East 247
            6.2.1.3b In the Bible 248
        6.2.1.4 Divine Silence Because of Incapacity 250
            6.2.1.4a In the Ancient Near East 250
            6.2.1.4b In the Bible 253
        6.2.1.5 Divine Silence Because of Sleep 255
            6.2.1.5.a In the Ancient Near East 255
            6.2.1.5.b In the Bible 258

  6.2.2 Incomprehensible Divine Silence 261
    6.2.2.1 In the Ancient Near East 261
    6.2.2.2 In the Bible 265
 6.3 Conclusions on Divine Silence 274

7. *Epilogue* 279

 7.1 Faith Talk 279
 7.2 God's Word in Human Guise 281
 7.3 Synergy 284
 7.4 Is Revelation Still Possible? 287
 7.5 Bearing Witness to a Silent God 289
 7.6 The Courage to Become a Witness 293
 7.7 The Integrity of Witnesses 294
 7.8 Theodicy 298
 7.9 Believers and Unbelievers 303

Abbreviations 307

Bibliography 309

Index of Subjects 349

Index of Texts 362

PREFACE

So much has been written about the silence of God that it seems hardly possible to put forward anything new. However, most of these publications are of a philosophical, systematical-theological or edifying nature. The biblical studies on the topic by professional exegetes are relatively rare. We do not imagine that we can do much better but in our opinion the broad historical background of the problem has been neglected too long. This has resulted in a distorted picture drawn by theologians and philosophers who were judging a past they did not know well enough to pronounce a balanced judgment on it. Yet it was this unrealistic picture that has contributed to deep skepticism, despair and agnosticism among many.

In this book we will try to let hear first of all the voices of others, from testimonies of our own recent past to the distant past of the first texts human beings ever wrote about the subject of a silent God. The subject is so all-encompassing that we do not imagine to have done more than skimming swiftly along a limited number of representative quotations, but we believe them to be sufficient to make our point.

We give all quotations in English, mostly following authoritative translations by others, but occasionally providing our own translations. If possible, we add a reference to the original text. Quotations should not be burdened by too much technical discussion so we confine ourselves to a few explanatory notes for non-specialists.

Obviously the subject of the silent God touches upon many other hotly debated topics, such as theodicy (the attempt to reconcile the existence of evil with the postulated goodness of God), deism, theism and atheism. Occasionally we will briefly comment on such adjacent matters, but our main concern is the question: what do people, in past and present, mean when they state that God is silent? This is something different from arguing that God is nonexistent, dead or absent. In these cases it is self-evident that God remains silent. The concept of a silent God, however, presupposes at least the possibility of a speaking God. So it will be necessary to also investigate how people conceptualized divine speech.

Unless explicitly stated otherwise, we use the terms 'man' and 'mankind' in an inclusive way.

Thanks are due to Bob Becking (Utrecht University) for several useful suggestions.

We thank Patric Tavanti (Berlin) for his permission to publish an English translation of his ballet play *Das Schweigen Gottes* (http://www.tavanti.de/schweigengottestext.html).

The Rijksmuseum in Amsterdam kindly granted us permission to publish a photograph of a painting by Cornelis Saftleven.

We thank the fine-art dealer Michael Kraut, Bleiburg/Kärnten, Österreich, for providing a photograph of the painting 'Non siamo gli ultimi' ('We are not the last ones') by Zoran Music and for his permission to use it on the cover of this book. From 1943-1945 Zoran Music was interned in the German destruction camp of Dachau. Between 1970-1975 he painted many canvasses entitled 'Non siamo gli ultimi', a kind of posthumous reply to a man who cried out shortly before he was hanged while the liberation of the camp in Auschwitz was already close at hand, 'Comrades, I am the last one'. All the horrible images of suffering in Dachau came back to Music when he realized three decades later that the hope of that man had been shattered. Suffering and killing continued on a worldwide scale, despite the Shoah. Zoran Music's painting on the cover powerfully expresses the conviction that mankind cannot afford to resign to God's silence vis-à-vis undeserved suffering.

We thank Liesbeth Hugenholtz, Acquisitions Editor at Brill's publishing house (Leiden), for her efficient and competent handling of the evaluation and printing process of the manuscript we submitted.

Finally we thank Janny de Moor who read the entire manuscript with a critical eye. Her comments and corrections have been extremely helpful. Her cheerful support and culinary art brightened many stages of this project.

The Authors

CHAPTER ONE

THE SILENT GOD IN MODERNITY

1.1 Introduction

The silence of God is a recurring theme in modern reflection.[1] It is not only addressed in theology, religious studies and philosophy, but also in literary fiction, film and theatre.[2] As Mark Taylor remarks, 'You cannot understand the world today if you do not understand religion' (Taylor 2007, XIII), even though an empty concept of transcendence is a characteristic of modernity (Friedrich 1956).

In this first chapter we give an overview of the ways in which people have handled the concept of a God who according to many believers may have spoken in the past, but is now silent. Why does he keep silent when humanity is hit by disaster? Why do so many ardent prayers remain unheard?

Or is it a misconception that God has spoken? Has he always been silent? And will he always remain silent? Because he does not exist, or is temporarily absent, or just indifferent?

1.2 The Silent God in Modern Literature and Media

In this section we discuss some poems, stage plays, movies and novels which illustrate how the silence of God in our age occupies the minds of artists and writers. Of course no more than a representative selection of relevant quotations can be presented here.

---

[1]Cf. Gillmayr-Bucher 2003, 317: 'Die lange gepflegte Kommunikation mit Gott ist verstummt, die traditionellen Formen sind unverständlich und damit unbrauchbar geworden' ('The communication with God that was kept up for so long has fallen silent, the traditional forms have become incomprehensible and hence obsolete'); Muers 2004, 25: 'The history and form of God's silence can ... be traced within the history of theology, particularly in modernity – within the ways of talking about God that have reduced God to silence.'; Sorace & Zimmerling 2007, 7: 'Die Epoche der Moderne, die im 20. Jahrhundert ihren Höhepunkt fand, ist vom "Schweigen Gottes" geprägt.' (The epoch of modernity which found its apogee in the 20th century is marked by the silence of God).

[2]To some extent these categories overlap. Especially French philosophers love to propagate their ideas in the form of stage plays.

1.2.1 *Marie Luise Kaschnitz*

In the post-war work of the German novelist and poet Marie Luise Kaschnitz the demolition of hitherto trusted religious concepts is painfully felt. She still talks to God, but experiences his remoteness as unbridgeable,[3]

> I started to talk to the Invisible.
> My tongue hit upon the awesome You,
> Feigning the intimacy of yore.
> But whom did I speak too? Whose ear
> Did I try to reach? Whose breast
> To touch – that of a Father?
> Father, you dying Giant,
> Perishing behind the Milky Flow,
> Father, you flickering of air,
> Twinkling from the fleeing star.[4]

Kaschnitz mingles the traditional mode of addressing God ('You', 'Father') with language vaguely resembling modern astronomical terminology. In this way she creates an impression of the enormous distance separating God and man since the discoveries of modern science. God is the 'Invisible', yet she perceives him as the last glimmer of a dying star.

In her view this remote God is responsible for all the sorrow, hurt and ruin in the world. If human beings call him to account, God does not answer,

> If one goes out to be judged, he finds no judge anymore.
> If one goes out to ask the elders, he does not get an answer.
> Break off you did the dialogue of old.
> If we ask what the purpose is,
> You remain silent.
> If we ask why so fast,
> You remain silent.[5]

---

[3] Cf. Kuschel 2001, 219-231.

[4] Our translation. German original: Kaschnitz 1957, 9. The first reading of this poem at the Lutheran academy of Tutzing in 1951 was met with perplexity.

[5] Our translation. German original: Kaschnitz 1957, 10.

Though God may have abandoned mankind, for Kaschnitz this is no reason to break off her dispute with him, although she raises the possibility that God might prefer human beings to reply to his silence with their own silence,

> Perhaps you do not even want to be mentioned.
> Once upon a time you fed on meat and blood,
> on hymns, on the singing
> Of the wheels. But now on silence.
> ...
> Our paralyzed tongues you prefer over
> The dancing flames of your pentecostal miracle.[6]

Her conclusion hints at certain modern dialectical theological concepts we will encounter later in this chapter,

> You will demand that we, the loveless of this earth,
> Are your love.
> The ugly ones your beauty,
> The restless your rest,
> The wordless your speech,
> The heavy your flight.
> ...
> But everyone will know: this is your last secret.
> Your remoteness is your closeness,
> Your being at the end your beginning,
> Your coldness your fire,
> Your indifference your wrath.[7]

1.2.2 Jean-Paul Sartre

In Jean-Paul Sartre's stage play *Le diable et le bon Dieu* (The Devil and the Good God) captain Goetz, who initially decided to do evil, comes to believe that God has illuminated him to do good. His opponent Nasty replies scornfully,

> When God is silent, you can make him say whatever you want.[8]

---

[6] Our translation. German original: Kaschnitz 1957, 13.
[7] Our translation. German original: Kaschnitz 1957, 17.
[8] Our translation. French original: Sartre 1951, 121.

Towards the end of the play Goetz addresses God,

> I am coming to you, Lord, I am coming, I walk in the night: give me your hand. Say, the night, that is you, isn't it? The night, the heartrending absence of everything! For you are the one who is present in the universal absence, the one who is heard when everything is silence, the one who is seen when nothing is seen anymore. O ancient night, great night from before there were living souls, night of not-knowing, night of disgrace and misfortune, cloak me, devour my foul body, glide between my soul and myself, and eat away at me.[9]

Somewhat later, when Goetz has seen that his attempts to do good have failed, he asks God why he has given mankind the desire to do good? Why not a longing to be evil? The following dialogue with the renegade priest Heinrich develops,

HEINRICH

Why do you pretend to talk to him? You know perfectly well that he will not reply.

GOETZ

And why this silence? Why is it that he who showed himself to the she-ass of the prophet[10] refuses to show himself to me?

HEINRICH

Because you do not count. Torture the weak or become a martyr, kiss the lips of a courtisane or those of a leper, die of deprivation or voluptuousness, God does not give a damn.

GOETZ

Who then counts?

HEINRICH

Nobody. Man is nothing. Do not feign surprise, you have always known this. [...] You have forced your voice to cover up God's silence. The commands you pretend to receive – you yourself are the one who sends them out.[11]

Goetz agrees,

---

[9] Our translation. French original: Sartre 1951, 209-210.
[10] Sartre refers to Num. 22:22-35.
[11] Our translation. French original: Sartre 1951, 236-237.

> I myself – you are quite right, Your Reverence. I alone. I pleaded, I begged for a sign – no reply. I sent messages to Heaven – no reply. Heaven does not even know my name. Every minute I asked myself what I might *be* in God's eyes. Now I know the answer: nothing. God does not see me, God does not hear me, God does not know me. Do you see that void over our heads? That's God. Do you see that breach in the gate? That's God. Do you see that hole in the ground? That's God again. The silence, that's God. The absence, that's God.[12]

A few lines further Goetz confesses with obvious relief that he believes God does not exist. But Heinrich admits that he does not really want to abandon his faith in God. 'Our Father who art in Heaven, I prefer to be judged by an infinite being rather than by my equals.'[13] Goetz ends where he started and becomes a cruel soldier again.

1.2.3 *Samuel Beckett*

In his famous tragicomedy *En attendant Godot* (Waiting for Godot)[14] Samuel Beckett relates the fuzzy dialogues between two tramps who are waiting for a personage called 'Godot'. Although Beckett himself in a letter to Michel Polac, dated January 1952, denied to know who this 'Godot' was,[15] it requires little imagination to see that the name is a thinly screened alias for 'God'. Twice the two men think that Pozzo, a strange human figure that crosses their path, is Godot but he denies it and the real Godot never appears and never speaks. His only message is delivered by a messenger boy: 'Mr Godot will not come this evening but surely tomorrow'.[16] This episode too is repeated later on with slight variations[17] and evidently the idea is that all this will hap-

---

[12] Our translation. French original: Sartre 1951, 237-238.

[13] Our translation. French original: Sartre 1951, 240.

[14] First French edition Beckett 1952; English version: Beckett 2004, first printed in 1954.

[15] 'I do not know who Godot is. I do not even know, especially not, if he exists. And I do not even know if those two who await him believe in him or not.' (our translation; original French text on the back-cover of the French edition).

[16] Beckett 2004, 43; French original: Beckett 1952, 66.

[17] Beckett 1952, 119-20.

pen over and over again. The play is interspersed with many long silences and in a confused monologue of Lucky, another character hiking by, the idea of a personal God is rejected because of his apparent apathy and aphasia.[18] Later on, when the messenger boy returns and announces again that Mr Godot will not come, one of the tramps asks what Mr Godot is doing. The boy replies: 'He does nothing, sir.'[19]

It is intriguing that till the very end of the play the tramps do not give up hope even though they know now that the chances of Godot still coming are slim. They decide to hang themselves the following morning 'unless Godot comes' and saves them.

1.2.4 Eli Wiesel

Obviously the Shoah, that most terrible and incomprehensible event of the twentieth century, prompted the question why God remained silent and did not protect the Jews, his chosen people.[20] One of the tormented attempts to describe the horrors of the German extermination camps is Elie Wiesel's *La nuit* (Night).[21] One day the inmates of the camp were forced to witness the hanging of three people, two adults and a child.

> The three condemned prisoners together stepped onto the chairs.
> In unison, the nooses were placed around their necks.
> 'Long live liberty!' shouted the two men.
> But the boy was silent.
> 'Where is merciful God, where is He?' someone behind me was asking.
> At the signal, the three chairs were tipped over.
> Total silence in the camp. On the horizon, the sun was setting.[22]

The young boy did not die immediately and the inmates of the camp had to witness his death agony.

---

[18] Becket 2004, 34-36; French original: Beckett 1952, 55.

[19] Becket 2004, 80; French original: Beckett 1952, 120.

[20] Cf. Jonas 1984, 41.

[21] Originally written in Yiddish (*Un di velt hot geshvign*, 'And the world remained silent'), it was finally published in abridged form in French by Les Éditions de Minuit in 1958. For the English translation we use Wiesel 2006, for the French edition Wiesel 2007.

[22] Wiesel 2006, 64. French text: Wiesel 2007, 124.

> Behind me, I heard the same man asking:
> 'For God's sake, where is God?'
> And from within me, I heard a voice answer:
> 'Where He is? This is where – hanging here from this gallows ...'[23]

That autumn, Wiesel was unable to praise God anymore during the celebration of Rosh Ha-Shanah, the Jewish New Year. He accused God, but at the same time felt terribly alone,

> But now, I no longer pleaded for anything. I was no longer able to lament. On the contrary, I felt very strong. I was the accuser, God the accused. My eyes had opened and I was alone, terribly alone in a world without God, without man. Without love or mercy.[24]

On Yom Kippur, the Day of Atonement, he could not bring himself to fast. 'I no longer accepted God's silence'.[25]

What such rebellious statements must have meant to a once observant Jewish young man becomes clear when one realizes that in Jewish worship the 'Days of Awe', originally the ten days from Rosh Hashanah through Yom Kippur, are days of prayer and repentance when the so-called *Selichos*, ingeniously composed poetical prayers pleading forgiveness, are recited daily. However, in both the Sephardic and Ashkenazic rites this period is expanded considerably. Ten times the supplicants implore God with heart-rending repetitions of the cry 'Answer us!'[26] But in Buna (Auschwitz III), God cloaked himself in silence ...

Later on, however, Wiesel prayed again to his silent God in whom he professed to believe no more. In his later writings he reestablishes his faith and admits to be firmly rooted in his people's memory and tradition. His commitment to the state of Israel is total.[27] Yet for Wiesel God's refusal to answer the cries of the victims of the Shoah remained incomprehensible (Boschki

---

[23] Wiesel 2006, 65. French text: Wiesel 2007, 124.
[24] Wiesel 2006, 79. French text: Wiesel 2007, 129.
[25] Wiesel 2006, 69. French text: Wiesel 2007, 131.
[26] For the Ashkenazic community, see for example Gold 1992, 42-43, 80-81, 120-121, 160-161, 200-201, 240-241, 280-281, 524-527, 596-597, 658-659.
[27] See, for example, Wiesel 1979/1986, and his Nobel Peace Prize Acceptance Speech, Wiesel 2006, 117-120.

2001). They were innocent children of his chosen people, so why did God keep silent?

1.2.5 *Ingmar Bergman*

For some time, the silence of God was also an obsession to the Swedish filmmaker Ingmar Bergman.[28] His movie *Det sjunde inseglet* (The Seventh Seal, 1957) starts with a quotation from Rev. 8:1 – the silence that falls when the Lamb opens the seventh seal. Death comes to fetch a crusader who has only just returned safely from a dangerous journey to the Holy Land. The nobleman succeeds in receiving a brief respite from Death by challenging him to play a chess match against him. Somewhat later the crusader goes to confession with a priest – who in reality is Death disguised as priest. He confesses that his heart is empty and that he only sees emptiness when he looks into a mirror. He wants knowledge of God. No faith, no suppositions, but true knowledge. 'Why is he hiding in a cloud of half promises and unseen miracles? Why am I unable to get rid of God? ... I want him to extend his hand to me, to show me his face and talk to me.' Death replies, 'But He is silent.'

Later on Bergman even devoted a special trilogy to the theme of the silent God. The name of the first film, *Såsom i en spegel* (As in a Mirror, 1961),[29] is evidently an allusion to 1 Cor. 13:12. Bergman wanted to point out two things by that title: here in our sublunary world man can never really come to know God, but love brings us closest to knowledge of God.

In an old mansion on the coast four people are together: a father who is a not very successful writer, a schizophrenic daughter and her husband, and the rather simple younger brother of the girl. One day she learns from the diary of her father that she is incurably ill. Her ailment grows worse by this frightening discovery and she starts to hear voices. She waits for God but He does not appear or answer her. Her brother tries to help her, but in a shipwreck she seduces him. After this incest she relapses totally and must be hospitalized. Towards the film's end she fi-

---

[28] Cf. Gibson 1969.
[29] English version also released under the title *Through a Glass Darkly*.

nally sees God, but he manifests himself as a loathsome spider. Her brother is ashamed before his father and tries to avoid him. Finally he confesses the intercourse with his sister and indicates that he wants to die. However, the father shows understanding and says, 'One must have something to go upon in life.' 'What then? God? Give me proof that He exists.' The father replies that God is present in all kinds of love, both in the good and in the bad kinds. God *is* love. This gives the boy some consolation.

The second movie of the trilogy was *Nattvardsgästerna* (The Communion Takers, 1963).[30] The film starts with a communion celebration in an almost empty parish church. Only five people come forward to partake in the celebration. The minister is a rigid man who has lost his wife four years earlier. He does not believe in God anymore and God's silence is the cause of his inability to help his parishioners adequately. A poor fisherman who fears the arrival of Chinese hordes possessing atomic bombs commits suicide when the minister instead of reassuring him professes his own powerlessness and disbelief. The clergyman fails as a witness of God.

There is a young schoolteacher, Martha, with whom he has had a two year long relationship, although he did not really love her. The parish disapproved strongly of it. The affair ended when he proved himself unable to pray for the hideous eczema on her hands. Although she had once said to him, 'God has never spoken, for He does not exist', she herself goes to a chapel to pray and is heard. From that moment on she realizes how strong her love for the clergyman is. She wants to help him and marry him. She writes all this down in a fat letter which in the film she reads out in a deeply moving monologue. But time and again he repels her. Finally he offends her cruelly to make clear that he does not want her. But just before he leaves the house he changes his mind and takes her with him to an even more empty service in another parish. Only the sexton and the organist are there, but since Martha is attending the service has to be held. The film ends rather abruptly, and it is unclear if her great love has won.

---

[30]English version also released under the title *Winter Light*.

The third movie *Tystnaden* (The Silence, 1963) is a monument of oppressive silence. Two sisters share the last weeks of one of them who has terminal cancer. The other has a very lonely small boy with her. A horrible muteness reigns between the three. Dialogues are often hardly audible. They talk and live past each other, although it is vaguely indicated that there existed a lesbian relationship between the two sisters. Although Bergman wanted to show that no communication is possible between people if God is silent, God is only once invoked in the film when the cancer patient prays, 'O God, let me die at home!' But of course no answer follows and she dies in a hotel.

1.2.6 *Endō Shūsaku*

A novel about the silence of God is Endō Shūsaku's *Chimmoku* (Silence), originally published in 1966.[31] Two 17th century Portuguese missionaries set out for Japan. They know that Christians are persecuted there, yet feel it their duty to support the few Christians remaining there. Soon they are captured and after much suffering required to apostatize. One refuses and joins other Christians in their death by drowning. The other, father Rodriguez who is the main subject of the book, is finally convinced by an earlier apostate, a father Ferreira, to give in and avoid cruel torture. Both become Japanese Buddhists and marry.

Time and again Endo's rationale is that God remains silent in the face of human suffering.[32] In the end Rodriguez imagines to hear Christ at long last speaking to him and instructing him to apostatize just as He himself, though blameless, carried his cross to share man's pain.[33] But the killing of other Christians continues, even if they do apostatize.

1.2.7 *Nathalie Sarraute*

Also a stage-play, initially a radio play, entitled *Le Silence* (The Silence) by Nathalie Sarraute[34] revolves round a silent main per-

---

[31] We use the English translation by W. Johnston (Endo 1976).

[32] Endo 1976, 96, 105, 153, 172-174, 194-195, 210, 222-223, 233, 265-267, 297-298.

[33] Endo 1976, 271.

[34] The original edition of the play appeared in 1967. We use the edition

sonage, a certain Jean-Pierre. Four unnamed women and two unnamed men discuss his offending taciturnity, all the more offending because they sometimes hear his smothered snickering. Apparently they see Jean-Pierre as a kind of Jesus. They themselves admit to be blind and deaf, like Jesus' audiences.[35] Time and again they beg, 'Have mercy on us', like the blind following Jesus.[36] They feel betrayed by Jean-Pierre's stubborn silence and reproach him for having thrown them into a state of utter confusion.

> [Female voice 1:] Hey, Jean-Pierre, aren't you flattered? You do not doubt [your right to do such a thing to people], isn't it?
> [Male voice 1:] Forgive them; for they know not what they do.[37]

As recognized by Rykner, this is an overt allusion to Luke 23:34. Couldn't Jean-Pierre reassure them?

> [Male voice 1, very serious:] You wish that you could reassure us, don't you? I'm sure you do... You would do it if you could ... Actually it would require so little. Even one word. One small word from you and we would feel delivered[38] ... One word only. A small remark, totally banal. I assure you, it doesn't matter what, but it would make all the difference. But it must be stronger than you, isn't it? You are 'walled in by your silence', aren't you? That's the way they put it, I believe...? One would like to escape but can't, is that it? Something is holding you back ... It's as in dreams...[39]

Soon after his company assumes that Jean-Pierre is too timid to speak up. Or that he feels embarrassed because of their insistence and ignorance, he who is pure like an angel and understands everything (Sarraute 1998, 37-41). Other hypotheses raised to explain Jean-Pierre's reticence are that he is afraid to say something

---

annotated by Arnaud Rykner (Sarraute 1998).

[35] Sarraute 1998, 28-29. Cf. Mt.13:13-17; 23:16-19.
[36] Sarraute 1998, 32-33. Cf. Mt. 9:27; 20:30-31 par.
[37] Our translation. French original: Sarraute 1998, 12.
[38] Rykner, in: Sarraute 1998, 87, refers to a formula pronounced just before communion in the Catholic mass liturgy. One might assume that this was inspired by Mt. 8:8 par.
[39] Our translation. French original: Sarraute 1998, 33.

stupid, or that he feels intellectually too superior to address imbeciles, or that he has something to hide, for example the seduction of a young girl who receives the suggestive nickname 'Martha'.

Eventually Jean-Pierre's silence seems to become contagious and the participants in the conversation try to observe absolute silence themselves – in vain. But nevertheless more and more silences are interspersed in their increasingly vague talks. When Mr. 1 pronounces an eulogy on Byzantine art in churches and chapels on the Balkan and mentions an authoritative work by a certain Labovic on the subject, Jean-Pierre suddenly joins in the conversation. He wants to know who this Labovic is and who has published the book. All rejoice that finally he has spoken. Yes, why wouldn't he be interested in Byzantine art? If this is how he wanted to break his silence? Jean-Pierre has fulfilled their wish and has uttered a total banality. Nothing mysterious about him, he is one of them.

1.2.8 *Cormac McCarthy*

In his terrifying novel *The Road* Cormac McCarthy describes a father and his young son roaming over the last remnants of an earth utterly destroyed by some unnamed disaster: 'Barren, silent, godless.'[40] They have to fight for their lives with the very few other survivors they meet on the road. The father is a kind of Job-figure. 'Then he just sat there holding the binoculars and watching the ashen daylight congeal over the land. He knew only that the child was his warrant. He said: If he is not the word of God God never spoke.' (McCarthy 2007, 3). Somewhat later he curses God,

> Then he just knelt in the ashes. He raised his face to the paling day. Are you there? he whispered. Will I see you at last? Have you a neck by which to throttle you? Have you a heart? Damn you eternally have you a soul? O God, he whispered. O God.[41]

---

[40] McCarthy 2007, 2. There is also a film version directed by John Hillcoat, 2009.
[41] McCarthy 2007, 10.

On the road father and son chance upon an old man in rags. They share their food with him and talk about their bleak future. The father asks the stranger,

> How would you know if you were the last man on earth? he said.
> I dont guess you would know it. You'd just be it.
> Nobody would know it.
> It wouldn't make any difference. When you die it's the same as if everybody else did too.
> I guess God would know it. Is that it?
> There is no God.
> No?
> There is no God and we are his prophets.[42]

At the end of the book there is a glimmer of hope. After his father has died miserably the boy finds another family to stay with and prays – not to God anymore, but to his father.[43]

1.2.9 *Patric Tavanti*

A recent ballet play entitled *Das Schweigen Gottes* (God's Silence) by Patric Tavanti lays the blame for God's silence entirely with mankind,

> SPEAKER:
> And God spoke ...
>
> BALLET DANCERS:[44]
> And God spoke ... and God spoke ... and God spoke ... and God spoke ... and God spoke ... God spoke ... God spoke ... God ... God ... spoke ...[45]
>
> SPEAKER:
> And God spoke ...
> but man did not listen to him.
>
> And God spoke to man ...
> and man listened to him, but did not understand.

---

[42] McCarthy 2007, 180-181.

[43] McCarthy 2007, 306. We are unconvinced by Patrick Horn's much more positive evaluation of McCarthy's novel (Horn 2009).

[44] In the German original the dancers are female.

[45] Tavanti clearly refers to the frequency of the formulae like 'Thus speaks the LORD' in the Bible.

And therefore God spoke so that man did understand him.
But man did not believe it.

BALLET DANCERS:
Why me?
Why so simple and clear?
That cannot be God.
I imagined that, it was not God who spoke to me.

SPEAKER:
And then God fell silent.
Man felt abandoned.

BALLET DANCERS:
Why do you do this to me?
Do not turn away from me.

SPEAKER:
Then God spoke: I do not turn away from you,
you only do not want to understand.

BALLET DANCERS:
I want, but I can't.
Do not speak to me alone,
nobody would believe it.

SPEAKER:
And God spoke to mankind ...
And everybody understood him – in his own way and manner.
Then man said to himself, he who speaks in so many different
ways cannot be only one.
There cannot be only one God, too many voices were heard.

BALLET DANCERS:
There cannot be only one God ...
He speaks in so many different ways to us ...
Not only one ...
Too many voices ...
Too differently ...
Not only one God ...
Too many ... many ... many ...

SPEAKER:
But God spoke to man, to reassure him:
There is only one God.[46]

---

[46] Reference to Deut. 6:4.

And man understood him – for his own benefit, and said now himself:

BALLET DANCERS:
There is only my God!
He spoke to me
and I have understood him!
Whoever says something different is a liar, it can only have been a false God who spoke to him.
Or he himself is a liar, to blind us.
He cannot belong to us anymore.

SPEAKER:
And God spoke again: Look, I invite you to unity.[47]

BALLET DANCERS:
Hear hear!

SPEAKER:
Was that someone calling?

BALLET DANCERS:
Now I know the truth.
I have heard it loud and clear, and I know the way
that leads us to unity with God and in God with us.

SPEAKER:
And thus spoke several others.
And furiously they pointed to each other and warned:

BALLET DANCERS:
Whoever says that he too knows the way, only leads us astray.
What separates us will be there to all eternity.

SPEAKER:
And look, man was separated then and remained separated – from himself, from God, from the other in God.
And only the possession of his truth remained for him, but he wasn't that sure about himself anymore.

He felt abandoned, confused and fear overwhelmed him so that he cried:

SPEAKER / BALLET DANCERS:
(*first mixed voices, then unisono*)

---

[47] Allusion to John 17:21-22.

O God, if you are the false one now?

(*Pause*)

Speaker:
What should God say to this?

Man, torn away, empty and troubled, wants an answer – and he gives it himself.

If only one truth leads to the one way that can give certainty about the goal, then only he can know the right one who is also the strongest. God is with him.

Thus he provides himself with the proof. Only one can gain the victory over all. Then there will be only one God and it will be his one, since he spoke to him it seems. The God who may remain, the victorious and only one, must also be the true one, so that man may know that he believes in the right belief. And so certain was man that he was right that he continued immediately: the victory which brings certainty will also bring me the unity. And whoever defends himself, him I simply slaughter. And he started slaughtering.

But God was silent and let man have his way,
who did hear, but could not listen,
who wanted to understand, but did not want to know.

In the stream of blood, shed for unity, truth and justice, everything drowned.
Merely the separation remained and became itself the iron truth of man who hacked around only more furiously and wildly slaughtered in order to finally experience the unity.
There was no victory, there only remained loneliness.

And then man cried one last time, almost a dying animal, full of bitterness and pain:

Ballet dancers:
And guilty is God alone, who spoke with me and took away my peace.

Speaker:
And God did not know what he could say then.

A ballet dancer:
Man felt himself very small

SPEAKER:
and God himself was no bigger now.

SPEAKER:
But when man – so weak and pitiable, so wounded and miserable, so without strength, courage and hope, so without one tear anymore – understood what he had unchained, he was left with nothing, left with nothing valuable.

In this empty silence he heard very softly, very hesitatingly, very shyly, a whisper.
And God spoke: You ... I ...

And man heard him and understood and said:

BALLET DANCERS:
Yes!

SPEAKER:
And then a new era started and the earth itself should become heaven.
And the Lord said: 'You shall love the Lord your God with all your heart, and with all your soul, and with all your mind.' This is the most important and first commandment. But the second is like it, 'You shall love your neighbor as yourself.'[48]

And thus heaven will be on earth. This is the greatest and most important promise!

But man remained his own neighbor.
And God was silent. What should he say anymore?

(*Black*)

Whoever can hear, let him hear.[49]

Apparently Tavanti proceeds from the assumption that it is humanity itself that has silenced God.

---

[48] Quotation from Mt. 22:37-39, itself a combination of Deut. 6:5 and Lev. 19:18.
[49] Tavanti 2008. Our translation. For the original German text see: http://www.tavanti.de/schweigengottestext.html. The last line hints at Mk 4:9.

1.3 Some Theologians and Philosophers

1.3.1 *Silent before the Silent*

Since God radically transcends the limits of human comprehension, an early response to the problem of God's silence has been that it is better for man to keep silent about him at all. Not even repeat what God would have said about himself in the Bible. In many religions of the world silent communication with the divine world is seen as a sublime form of pious worship. To the most pious virtues of the Coptic anchorites belonged absolute silence (Brunner-Traut 1979). Mystics like Gregory of Nazianze (*c.* 329-390), Evagrius of Pontus (*c.* 348-399), Pseudo-Dionysius Areopagita (5th century) and Meister Eckhart (*c.* 1260-1328) perceived that one cannot say anything definite about God.[50] If one tries nevertheless, it inevitably leads to contradictions and paradoxes, so that it would be wiser to keep silent about Him altogether. Only in absolute silence one may attain the experience of the mystic union with God.[51] Such mystics have deeply influenced great theologians like Augustine (354-430) and Thomas Aquinas (1225-1274) who have dominated modern discussions about 'God-talk'.

Similar ideas are found in medieval Judaism. Commenting on Ps. 19:2 the great Jewish scholar Moses Maimonides (*c.* 1135-1204) taught,

> ...whatever we utter with the intention of extolling and of praising Him, contains something that cannot be applied to God, and includes derogatory expressions: it is therefore more becoming to be silent, and to be content with intellectual reflection, as has been recommended by men of the highest culture, in the words "Commune with your own heart upon your bed, and be still" (Ps. iv. 4).[52]

---

[50] Cf. e.g. Blans 2000.

[51] See e.g. Caranfa 2004; Erickson 2007, 78; Armstrong 2009, 110-112, 123-129, 154-155.

[52] Maimonides 1904, 173. The reference is to Ps. 4:5[4].

On the basis of the apophatic or negative theology certain Christian monastic orders still restrict verbal communication to the absolute minimum. An example is the Order of the Reformed Cistercians of the Strict Observance (O.C.S.O.), a branch of the Roman Catholic Cistercians, founded by the converted courtier Armand de Rancé (1626-1700), who had governed the Cistercian abbey of La Trappe in France, which he transformed (1662) into a community practicing absolute silence. Although the rigid regulations have been moderated somewhat, silence is still strived after in the hundreds of Trappist cloisters all over the world.

Is keeping silent the best way of communication with a silent God? We live in a world full of noise.[53] So much noise that on airports, malls, in hospitals and factories silence centers are being created where people can find a few moments of quiet, inner reflection and prayer.[54]

People hanker for silence and simplicity. Silent meditation retreats have become exceedingly popular and handbooks on silent meditation sell well.[55] The success of a film like Philip Gröning's *Die grosse Stille* (Into Great Silence, 2006) about the Carthusian monks of La Grande Chartreuse in the French Alps shows a remarkable yearning for the simplicity of a life dominated by silence before the silent God. At first, silence appears to be a relative concept in this film, as there is a lot of noise: bell-ringing, clumping shoes on wooden floors, rain, thunder, cow-bells, rustling trees. Yet the prevailing silence is so deep that even the sound of a bumble-bee is experienced as a loud intrusion.

What the Carthusian order sees as its ideal is to join God in the silence and solitude of the hermit's cubicle. At the beginning and end of the film 1 Kgs 19:11-13 is quoted, a passage that seems to indicate that God is not present in storm, or earthquake, or fire, but in silence. We will return to this text later, but note here that the Carthusian monks are convinced that admitting God to speak

---

[53] Cf. Maitland 2009, 131-133.

[54] According to a 2008 survey in The Netherlands, there were about 250 enterprises that have opened facilities for employees who feel the need for quiet or prayer at work (Ajarai 2008). In many other countries similar initiatives exist, see for example http://www.christiansatwork.org.uk/.

[55] For example Gentili & Schnöller 1986.

his word in our hearts is the highest form of peaceful silence. They see silence as a way to overcome sufferings like blindless, illness or even the fear of death.

Of course Carthusian monks celebrate mass and chant their age-old hymns together. But only rarely are they allowed to engage in conversation with each other or to undertake short communal outings. The film shows how much they enjoy these occasions, especially the scene where they are frisking happily in the snow. This counterpoint demonstrates that a life in silence before God need not be dull or abnormal.

Also in certain Protestant circles silence is a regular part of the liturgy.[56] In the worship of the ecumenical Taizé community silence plays an important role[57] and several recent pietistic works advocate silence as an excellent way of communicating with the silent God in the noisy world we live in.[58]

1.3.2 *Contemporary Theologians and Philosophers*

Ever since Nietzsche proclaimed the death of God theologians and philosophers have tried to cope with the concept of a God who is silent like the dead. Some have tried to value this deep silence positively, as the real ground for faith. Others found this silence unbearable.

1.3.2.1 Karl Barth

According to Karl Barth, for example, God speaks while being silent. In his *Römerbrief*, the first edition of which appeared in 1919, he emphasizes the unknowability of God in his comment on Rom. 4:3-5,

> Beyond the line of death is God, substantial but without substance, essential without any essence, known as the unknown, speaking in his silence, merciful in His unapproachable holiness, demanding recognition as the One who supports everything, demanding obedience in his working alone, merciful in His judg-

---

[56]See e.g. Szuchewycz in: Jaworski 1997, 239-260. See now also Bittner 2009.
[57]http://www.taize.fr/ and Frère Roger 2005.
[58]Bentz 2007, 23-88.

ment. Because He is not man, He is the true Cause, the House which cannot be dissolved, the first and last Truth, the Creator and Redeemer and Lord of men. To men His ways appear always new, strangely distant, pre-eminent, beyond their horizon and possession.[59]

Elsewhere Barth states that any interpretation of the Word of God in a historical sense is false, because the Word of God remains silent if we treat it as human discourse,

> The Word of God hides and withdraws itself from the Church when the latter permits itself to regard and treat itself and its tradition or nature, or the being and history of mankind, as the source of its knowledge of God. The Word of God itself is silent, and yet it speaks even by its silence, when the Church wishes to hear only the human word of prophets and apostles as such and therefore the voice of a distant historical occurrence which does not really concern it or lay any obligation upon it. The Word of God itself veils itself in darkness when the Bible is interpreted with violent and capricious one-sidedness according to the promptings of various spirits instead of under the leading of its own Holy Spirit.[60]

In Barth's typical dialectical style he emphasizes God's freedom to speak or keep silent,

> God is free to deal in this way with creation. It is still His work and witness, though His silent witness. For His Word also implies His silence; what He says implies what He does not say; His Yes implies His No; His grace His judgment. His self-revelation as Creator also contains, as a true Word, His silence, No and judgment. Hence we must not be surprised if it is not identifiable with the Yes which we find in the created world.[61]

---

[59] Barth 1968, 120-121, slightly adapted by us to the German text of Barth 1940, 96.

[60] Barth, *ChD*, vol. 1/2, 684. Original German text: Barth, *KD*, Bd. 1/2, 767. A similar rejection of modern historical-critical biblical scholarship is found with followers of Barth, e.g. Miskotte 1967, 55, 106, 142, and more often. However, elsewhere Miskotte offers a more positive appreciation of the historic, oriental background of the Bible and critical scholarship, Miskotte 1967, 149-153. See also Levinas 1987, 191-200.

All this has to do with Barth's conviction that our everyday secular use of words is 'improper and merely pictorial use'. In so far as there is any appropriateness in our views, concepts and words they are not our property, but God's creation.[62]

1.3.2.2 Kornelis Miskotte

In his *Als de goden zwijgen* (When the Gods Are Silent) Kornelis Miskotte stated that the gods of paganism were not dead, but merely silent. 'That they never spoke is certain.'[63] Israel was the first nation to perceive that the gods of other nations were dumb gods (Ps. 115). The theophany of God in Israel sounded the death knell of religion.[64] Like Karl Barth, Miskotte emphasized that God speaks in the preaching of the Word of God, the whole Bible, including the New Testament.

1.3.2.3 God Is Dead Movement

The short-lived 'death of God' movement was a typical attempt to free theology from theism.[65] A 'dead' God cannot speak. Tom Milazzo summarizes the predicament of modern theologians well,

> But whether it is the road to Golgotha on which we walk, or the road to Babylon, or the road to Auschwitz, or the road that leads to our own death, only silence answers our prayer. In that silence, death casts its shadow over more than just our life. It casts its shadow over our faith as well. Where is God while we suffer and die? What are we to make of God's silence? Does God's silence speak of God's absence? Does God's silence speak of God's impotence? Or does God's silence speak of our murder

---

[61] Barth, *ChD*, vol. 3/1, 371-372. Original German: Barth, *KD*, Bd. 2/1, 425. See also 373: 'It is the revelation of God which, when He is silent and says No and exercises judgment, clouds the created world and wills to be honored in this too, demanding human complaint and accusation. But the revelation of God is as little bound up with the confining darkness of being as with its light. While it gives us cause for complaint and accusation, and places in our mouth a negative judgment on being, it does not in any sense consist in what creation can and does reveal in this way.' Original German: *KD*, Bd. 2/1, 427.

[62] Barth, *ChD*, vol. 2/1, 228-229.

[63] Miskotte 1967, 9. Original Dutch text: Miskotte 1956, 16.

[64] Miskotte 1956, 17, 25; Eng. translation: Miskotte 1967, 10, 19.

[65] For succinct overviews see Milazzo 1992, 151-157; Robbins 2007, 1-4; Taylor 2007, 199-205; Armstrong 2009, 289-330.

at the hands of God? Thus is the question of the reality of God inseparable from the question of what it means to be human in a world where all things die. In a world where all things die, if we cling to our faith despite or even because of the silence of God, though we might not deny God's existence, we must doubt that God's justice is absolute. We must doubt the sincerity, the efficacy, even the certainty, of God's love.[66]

For Milazzo and others[67] the hiddenness of God and his eternal silence is a paradox that cannot be resolved,

> Where is God while the innocent and the righteous die? Why has God chosen silence and absence? In the presence of God's silence and hiddenness, the paradox of our existence endures. As long as that paradox endures, the God of love seems inseparable from the God of death. Indeed, as long as that paradox endures, the shadow of death threatens to call into question all that is human. Once our humanity is called into question, so too is faith in God. Yet despite our death, despite the vanity of our existence, despite even the triumph of death, our faith stands.[68]

1.3.2.4 John Paul II and Benedict XVI

In an address to a general audience on Wednesday 11 December 2002 the then Pope John Paul II (Karol Jósef Woytiła) reflected on Jer. 14:17-21 and said,

> In fact, in addition to the sword and hunger, there is a greater tragedy, that of the silence of God who no longer reveals himself and seems to have retreated into his heaven, as if disgusted with humanity's actions.[69]

Of course the Pope did not leave it at that point and observed that 'God's silence was provoked by man's rejection. If people will convert and return to the Lord, God will also show himself ready to go out to meet and embrace them'. Can this age-old scheme of

---

[66] Milazzo 1992, x. See also p. 146.
[67] E.g. Terrien 1978; Balentine 1983.
[68] Milazzo 1992, 135.
[69] http://www.vatican.va/holy_father/john_paul_ii/audiences/2002/documents/hf_jp-ii_aud_20021211_en.html

sin – sanction – penance – remission still be applied confidently to the world at large?

In 2007 Benedict XVI (Joseph Ratzinger) wrote a meditation in which he pointed out that the death of God is part of the Christian tradition which is felt most painfully on Holy Saturday (Karsamstag), the day when Christ was in the grave. It is in this sense that Ratzinger valued God's silence positively,

> We need the darkness of God, we need the silence of God, to experience once again his greatness, the abyss of our nothingness which would be exposed if it were not there.[70]

No doubt such statements were meant well and many believers recognized their own feelings in them. Yet their ambiguousness may be confusing because the darkness and silence of God are presented as positive, even indispensable aspects of his being.

1.3.2.5 Emmanuel Levinas

In Zvi Kolitz's moving Yiddish fictional story about Yosl Rakover talking to God in the last days of the burning Jewish ghetto of Warsaw, the faithful Jew understandably reproaches God for having hidden his face from his chosen people. Yet he keeps believing in this God, preferring a revenging God over the 'God of Love' of the Christians (Kolitz 1999; 2008). The Jewish philosopher Emmanuel Levinas praises Kolitz for this attitude and writes,

> Man's true humanity and his powerful gentleness make their entrance into the world in the severe words of a demanding God; the spiritual does not impart itself in anything of substance; it is an absence. God manifests Himself not by incarnation but by absence. God manifests Himself not by incarnation but in the Law.[71]

The 'Law' is the Jewish Torah here. Levinas restricts the possibility of true humanity to the Jewish religion, at the same time equating the Jewish Law with divine absence. He explains this

---

[70]Our translation. German text:
http://diepresse.com/home/panorama/welt/religion/296271/index.do.

[71]Emmanuel Levinas, in: Kolitz 1999, 85.

more fully in several of his works, among them *Dieu, la Mort et le Temps* (God, Death, and Time),[72]

> ...God escapes objectification and is not even found in the I-Thou relationship; God is not the Thou [*Tu*] of an I, is neither dialogue nor in dialogue.[73]

And at the end,

> ...God is torn out of the objectivity of presence and out of being. He is no longer an object or an interlocutor in a dialogue. His distancing or his transcendence turns into my responsibility: the non-erotic *par excellence*![74]

For Levinas God is 'transcendent to the point of absence'.[75] A God who is absent and does not engage himself in dialogue is a silent God. And yet the same Levinas was a Talmudic scholar. It has rightly been observed that what Levinas intended was a new humanism which was rooted in biblical humanism (Purcell 2006, 36, 49-55).

1.3.2.6 Rachel Muers

The Quaker theologian Rachel Muers interprets God's silence positively as the patience of a listener (Muers 2001; 2004).

> Listening can be described as the act of "giving time" to allow the other's own possibilities for new speech to emerge – possibilities that are themselves in some sense given in and through the act of listening. The idea that God is patient, or that God "waits for" creation could, it would seem, allow the silence of God that grants responsibility to the world to be understood as coterminous with God's salvific action.[76]

This comes close to the positive view of the mystics we discussed earlier (Section 1.3.1).

---

[72]Levinas 1993; English translation used here: Levinas 2000.
[73]Levinas 2000, 203. Original French text: Levinas 1993, 232.
[74]Levinas 2000, 224. Original French text: Levinas 1993, 253.
[75]Levinas 2000, 224. Original French text: Levinas 1993, 253.
[76]Muers 2004, 94-95.

1.3.2.7 Interim Conclusion

The ambiguity with which leading theologians and philosophers of our day speak about the necessity of believing in a silent, absent, dead God who yet was or is able to speak may be confusing to laymen. Perhaps not to the theologians and philosophers themselves but it is a fact that many of them eventually loose their faith. Some disappear silently from the public debate, others have no objection to openly declare their inability to believe in an all-powerful speaking God anymore.

1.4 The Silent God in Agnosticism and Atheism

Ever since the Enlightenment the rationality principle made any form of non-empirical proof suspect and since religion can rarely, if ever, furnish that kind of evidence, agnosticism and atheism are gaining terrain among intellectuals worldwide.[77] In its strong form of a categorical denial of the existence of any transcendent being one might call 'God', atheism has vociferous advocates.[78] Sometimes this point of view is mitigated to 'Probably there's no God', as a recent slogan advertising atheism on public transport vehicles in many European countries ran. In Germany Christians hired an accompanying bus that posed the question: 'and if He really does exist ...'. The competition was friendly and incited lively discussions between the two groups. But it is evident that a speaking God is unacceptable in the framework of agnosticism and atheism.

1.5 In Defense of a Silent God

The silence of God as described in the previous section stands in stark contrast with recent attempts to deny that God is forever silent. Mostly these attempts are found in pietistic works that are often characterized by a highly autobiographical nature and not uncommonly start with a tragedy with which the author has been confronted in her or his personal life. The goal of this type of literature is theodicy – the attempt to justify God in the face

---

[77] For a brief history and evaluation, see Armstrong 2009, 240-261, 301-317.
[78] To mention only a few of them, Smith 1979; Everitt 2004; Dawkins 2007; Schulz 2008.

of apparent injustice or incomprehensible silence. At first some kind of crisis leads to angry questions like 'Why had this to happen?' The lack of a direct reply from God is experienced as an inexplicable and cruel silence.

Usually those who defend the silence of God derive their answers from Scripture. They do not seem to realize that this approach does in no way appeal to those who regard the Bible as a rather haphazardly collected bundle of writings from Antiquity that have very little bearing on our modern world. Moreover, these writers rarely take the trouble to check their interpretations with serious scholarship.

Several of these authors counsel patience, quoting biblical examples of prayers fulfilled only after a long period of suffering (Abraham and Sarah; Joseph; Naomi and Ruth; Hannah; Job). Only God is able to oversee history, human beings can perceive only fragments of it. Therefore, what seems injustice at present, may prove to be beneficial in the end. This kind of reasoning restores the author's faith in a good and merciful God and communication with him is resumed.[79]

Hope in salvation that is not yet seen is true hope (cf. Rom. 5:2-4; 8:24-25; 18:18-23). So if God is silent one should interpret that as a sign that he is pulling the wires in the wings,

> Silence is no indication that God doesn't care or that He is not interested. Silence simply means that He is up to something. When you can't hear from God, you should rejoice because something on the horizon is far greater than the challenge you are presently facing.[80]

Another type of theodicean argument is to invoke God's total freedom to choose whether or not to reply to prayers. In Wiesel's play *Le procès de Shamgorod* (English title: The Trial of God)[81] it is the devil, personified as 'Sam', who takes up the defense of God and states,

---

[79]Examples of this type of theodicean argument are found with Patterson 1991; Montgomery 2002; Allen 2005; Gire 2005; Bentz 2007; Sittser 2007.
[80]Montgomery 2002, 185. Similarly Clift George 2005, 19.
[81]Wiesel 1979.

> If God chooses not to answer, He must have his reasons. God is God, and his will is independent from ours–as is his reasoning.[82]

It is certainly not without reason that Wiesel attributes this acquiescent attitude to the devil. Others too affirm that not all evil in the world should be ascribed to God. Satan or the devil may be the cause.[83] One might be inclined to ask if God could not have restrained the devil? Is God less powerful than Satan? Faced with such challenging questions believers are fond to invoke the mysteriousness of the divine being. Gire, for example, relates the kidnapping of a woman on the parking lot of a supermarket. Daily he prays for her. But months later she appears to have been murdered by a sex maniac.

> If God is everywhere present, he saw what happened in that car. That he saw it and did nothing to stop it is the darkest and most unsettling mystery in the universe.[84]

What strikes us in such statements is the lack of precision and the deliberate exaggeration. First Gire poses a condition: '*If* God is present ... Already in the next sentence his doubt evaporates, 'he saw it'. How certain is Gire that God sees *everything*? Doesn't make such overstating God responsible for *all* evil in the world, despite Gire's conviction that it is the devil who should be held responsible? Yet he blames God for 'the darkest and most unsettling mystery in the universe'.

It is also common to lay the blame with the person complaining about God's silence. It is the deficiency of our God-talk, the idolatry of our human projections of God which causes him to withdraw from us.

> God deflects our attempts at control by withdrawing into silence, knowing that nothing gets to us like the failure of our speech.

---

[82] Wiesel 1986, 132. The original French text slightly diverges from the English translation: 'Si Dieu, béni soit-il, choisit de ne pas répondre, c'est qu'il a ses raisons. Dieu est Dieu, et sa volonté n'est pas dépendante de la nôtre.' (Wiesel 1979, 114). Similar reasoning with Clift George 2005, 22-24.

[83] Montgomery 2002, 24, 112; Clift George 2005, 2; Gire 2005, 49, 110, 184, 189

[84] Gire 2005. 8.

When we run out of words, then and perhaps only then can God be God.[85]

If God does not answer, we have to repair our belief system.[86] Despite God's silence we should value the experience of his presence when we pray (Rockwood 2004, 11, 13, 42-43). If we think that God is not capable of inflicting suffering on innocent people, we reduce his power and God isn't God anymore (Patterson 1991, 37-41, 50). If God does not answer your prayer in the way you hoped for, you may yet receive a different blessing.[87]

How does communication between God and man take place according to those who seek to explain God's silence? Man approaches God through prayer, preferably frequent prayer.[88] God answers either directly through the Holy Spirit,[89] or through others, human beings or angels, who act as faithful witnesses to God,[90] or through peace that is attained by solitude and allowing God to guide one's decisions.[91] God may answer through silence, like Jesus who remained silent when the Canaanite woman asked him to heal her daughter.[92] However, 'We should not allow the silence of God to silence *us*, not for long anyway.'[93]

Among the ingenious arguments to explain God's silence is the supposition that his heavenly host needs more time to conquer the forces of evil. Daniel, for example, had to wait for twenty-one days before his angel, with the help of the archangel Michael, was able to conquer his Persian opponent.[94]

According to others God's silence is the consequence of sins. Some apologetic works of this kind are quite old, but are still

---

[85] Brown Taylor 1998, 38-39.
[86] E.g. Montgomery 1999, 65; cf. Murphy-O'Connor 2003, 399.
[87] Rockwood 2004, 81; Sittser 2007, 175, 179, 193.
[88] Montgomery 2002, 8, 12, 27, 126; Allen 2005, 53; Gire 2005, 94-98, 102, 125.
[89] Allen 2005, 34, 108
[90] Allen 2005, 34, 59; Gire 2005, 33-44, 55-56, 62; Justice 2006, 33; Bentz 2007, 17-19.
[91] Allen 2005, 34, 75-95; Maitland 2009.
[92] Gire 2005, 123-124. As a matter of fact, Jesus' silence is mentioned only in Mt. 15:23. In the parallel account Mk 7:27 he answers immediately.
[93] Gire 2005, 125. Similarly Rockwood 2004, 19-21; Sittser 2007, 82-93.
[94] Dan. 10:4-13. Cf. Gire 2005, 56-57.

avidly read in fundamentalist circles. For example, Sir Robert Anderson's *The Silence of God*, which was first published in 1897, but was reprinted many times – the last edition we know of appeared in March 2010. For Anderson the arrival of Christ has been the ultimate answer to all our questions. The Cross of Christ marks the end of the time in which God was speaking and doing miracles. Because so many people rejected the Gospel – Anderson means specifically the Jews – God has chosen to remain silent. God could have used thunder and other punishments, but he just remains silent, until he will speak again on judgment day.[95] If we ask why God does not speak up nowadays, we do not see that the coming of Christ has been God's final answer. This answer can still be heard, but if we are just murmuring and sobbing, we do not see and hear it. God has spoken in the Bible and revelation is complete now. We have to bear disaster just as Paul did and take it as a boast, even enjoy it, for Christ's sake.[96]

According to some theologians calling God to account in ardent personal lament is impious or even blasphemous.[97] If so, Job, the authors of Lamentations, many Psalmists and prophets were impious blasphemers. Complaints against God have a legitimate place in faith talk.[98]

The Roman Catholic priest Charles Mœller launched a learned but utterly insensitive attack on writers who rejected theism because of the silence of God (Mœller 1958).

The Roman Catholic philosopher Gustave Thibon wrote a satyrical play *Vous serez comme des dieux* (You Will Be like Gods) in which he relates discussions between a few survivors of the destruction of our planet (Thibon 1959). All have lost their souls. Suffering, death and the old deities have been banned from their newly constructed world ('a city of light'). Human beings have become deities themselves. However, one of the main charac-

---

[95] Anderson 2008, 147.

[96] Anderson 2008, 154-155. Similarly, and also anti-Jewish, Brown Taylor 1998, 49-59, 72-73. See further Carse 1995, 9-11, 23, 32; Rockwood 2004, 27-31; Clift George 2005, 7-9; Sittser 2007, 38-39.

[97] See e.g. Fuchs 1982, 941-942; Westermann 1990, 78.

[98] Cf. Renkema 1998, 59-62; Bayer 2001; Berges 2003, esp. 1-19; Janowski 2003.

ters, Amanda, starts to have second thoughts about this abolition of the old world. At first she says to her fiancé Hélios,

> If I would have lived in the time of death and deities, I know that my life would have been nothing but prayer. Now however, I pray to you because the deities are dead. You will say yes, you will not be deaf or cruel like them.[99]

Later on Amanda slowly grows convinced that God still exists and that suffering and death should not have been abolished. A doctor Weber, her supervisor, sees this return to suffering, death and godhead as a very serious, contagious condition. However, his treatment of Amanda is unsuccessful. Her friend Stella worries about Amanda's belief in a God to whom she prays. The following dialogue develops,

AMANDA
We can pray to him without asking him anything. Perhaps we can give him everything. In the void. Without return. Without hope. Be the last courtier of an inert and dethroned king ...

STELLA
Pure absurdity ...

AMANDA
Pure prayer.

STELLA
All this is crazy. If God had existed, he would have reacted, would not have let it happen. He would not have permitted mankind to construct a false paradise veiling the truth for ever.

AMANDA
You do not know how far God's silence can go.

STELLA
Nothingness remaining silent ...[100]

After an encounter with her departed soul, Amanda prays to God and accepts death. Her example convinces Hélios, her parents and Stella to follow her. Dr Weber obliges by killing them all.

The new atheism of Richard Dawkins and his allies (Section 1.4) has come under attack from the side of other scientists like Anthony Flew (2008). Their theistic theology is no longer based on

---

[99] Our translation. Original French, Thibon 1959, 101.
[100] Our translation. Original French, Thibon 1959, 140.

revelation or tradition, but on natural phenomena which they believe to point directly to the existence of a superior Being responsible for the laws of nature and the existence of the universe. Especially Flew offers poignant quotations from great scientists like Charles Darwin, Albert Einstein, Werner Heisenberg, Erwin Schrödinger, Max Planck and many others who professed to be theists in this sense (Flew 2008, 95-112). Recent and well-informed refutations of the new atheists from the side of theologians are those of Gerhard Lohfink 2008 and Hans Kessler 2009.

Another fairly recent opponent of atheism is the French philosopher and writer Éric-Emmanuel Schmitt. In his play *Le visiteur* (The Visitor)[101] he arranges a meeting between an unknown stranger and the atheistic father of psychoanalysis Sigmund Freud.[102] Repeatedly Freud asks his visitor who he is, but the stranger remains silent.[103] The unknown visitor appears and disappears miraculously. He evidently knows all about Freud's past and future. Despite himself Freud sometimes considers the possibility that the stranger is a human incarnation of God and the latter accommodates him by assuming the fake name of Walter Oberseit.[104] In the end Freud acknowledges, 'You are almighty'. But his visitor replies,

> Well, actually, no, I'm not. The moment I made man free, I lost omnipotence, lost omniscience. I would have been able to control everything, and know everything in advance if I had constructed automata – mere machines.[105]

Freud's visitor explains that he has given man a free will to do either good or bad out of love. He even kneels before Freud and offers him his hand, but Freud is too embarrassed to take it.

For our study it is important to note that Schmitt appears to think that God can still address man in human shape and that this shape itself is relatively unimportant. When Freud asks 'Are

---

[101] Schmitt 1999; English translation Schmitt 2002.
[102] On Freud's 'atheism' see Oelmüller 1999, 112-114.
[103] Schmitt 1999, 144, 150, 154; Schmitt 2002, 82, 86, 89.
[104] Note the obvious play with German 'Oberseite' – the upper side.
[105] Schmitt 2002, 120. French original: Schmitt 1999, 201-202.

you Walter Oberseit, yes or no?' the stranger answers, 'I ought to say "no", but Walter Oberseit would say the same.'[106] 'Walter Oberseit' is an actor, a role in Schmitt's play. Freud believes in Walter Oberseit because he can see him, 'But who proves to you that Walter Oberseit exists?'[107]

In his novel *Oscar et la dame rose* (Oscar and the Lady in Pink) (2002) Schmitt explores the problem of the suffering and premature death of a boy who is ten years old and dying of cancer. His agnostic parents hardly dare to visit him anymore, but an old lady in a pink dress – the uniform of ladies who come in to spend time with sick children – visits him regularly and encourages him to write letters to God. The fact that she pretends to have been a famous wrestler, 'the Languedoc Strangler', impresses the boy very much. Yet Oscar hangs back at first,

> 'And why would I want to write to God?'
> 'You wouldn't feel so lonely.'
> 'Not so lonely with someone who doesn't exist?'
> 'Make him exist.'
> She leant over to me.
> 'Every time you believe in him, he'll exist a bit more.
> If you keep at it, he'll exist completely.
> Then, he'll do you good.'[108]

Every one of his last days Oscar writes a letter to God and relates what he has experienced. Through talking to God in his letters Oscar begins to realize that every day, even his last one, is worth to be lived. When the boy has died, the Lady in Pink herself writes a letter to God, thanking him for the hours she has spent with Oscar. She says, 'He helped me believe in you' and ends with a PS,

> For the last three days Oscar had a little sign on his bedside table. I think you should know. It said: 'Only God is allowed to wake me.'[109]

---

[106] Schmitt 2002, 114. French original: Schmitt 1999, 192.
[107] Schmitt 2002, 108; French original: Schmitt 1999, 183.
[108] Schmitt 2005, 11. Original French: Schmitt 2004a, 16.
[109] Schmitt 2005, 88. Original French: Schmitt 2004a, 94.

In the talks between Oscar and the old lady God shows himself through both of them who He is – a *good* God, even if it sometimes looks differently from our side. Oscar becomes someone who cares for others. His last days were not in vain: he has shown God to a sick girl, to a grumpy doctor, to his parents and to the Lady in Pink. Oscar became a witness of God.

1.6   Critical Examination of Current Views

Here we classify and critically examine some of the modern statements about the silence of God we have discussed in Section 1.2-5 above. This is necessary because it will appear that despite the enormous amount of literature on the subject of a silent God it is worthwhile to reconsider the origin and meaning of the concept of a silent deity.

1.6.1   *Modern Literature and Media*

Almost all writers and artists we reviewed in Section 1.2 above show a certain amount of bitterness about the faith they have lost. Most of them cannot be regarded as true atheists.[110] They are more concerned with human behavior and the absence of a divine response to that behavior than with the true atheist's categorical denial of God's existence.

On the other hand, theists who try to defend their faith against the criticism of agnostics and atheists clearly have trouble to deny that God's silence can be oppressing. Often they deny that any real dialogue with God is possible or express themselves in a frustratingly ambiguous or even contradictory way, to the effect that it is an unanswerable question if the Almighty does or does not reply to the cries of the helpless – both is in his power. In the end a man like Eli Wiesel arrives at an impasse,

> It is wrong to understand Auschwitz exclusively as a theological problem. Auschwitz was not brought about by God; it was brought about by human beings against other human beings. It is first and above all a human problem, human responsibility. However, it is also dishonest to leave God out. The tragedy is that

---

[110] For Sartre see e.g. Howells 1981. For Bergman see e.g. Gibson 1969. For Beckett, see e.g. Bryden 1998.

we can conceptualize Auschwitz neither with God, nor without God.[111]

Both parties, believers and non-believers, often refer to biblical notions about God, but they do so in a highly eclectic and sometimes naive manner, thus wittingly or unwittingly distorting the picture as a whole.

1.6.2 Contemporary Theologians and Philosophers

The modern captivation with the concept of a silent God is difficult to reconcile with the undeniable fact that the number of places in the Hebrew Bible where the silence of God is mentioned pales into insignificance compared to the number of ocurrences testifying to a speaking God:[112]

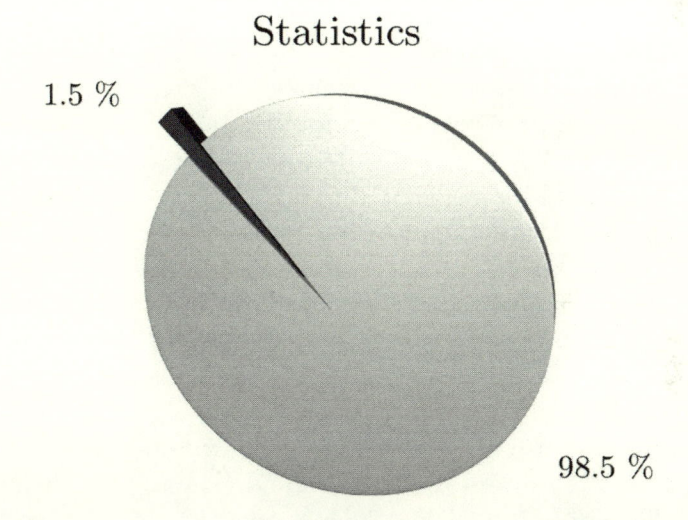

Statistics

1.5 %

98.5 %

- Verbs/nouns denoting God's speech (1882 occurrences)
- Verbs/nouns denoting God's silence (29 occurrences)

The ancient Israelites certainly did not regard God's speaking and keeping silent equally important. This simple observation points

---

[111] Our translation. German original: Wiesel 1987, 119.

[112] We counted only explicit terms denoting divine speech and silence. Implicit instances will be dealt with in this study, but are omitted here because they are debatable. In the New Testament direct speech of God is rare.

1.6.2.1 Contemporary Christian Theologians

For Karl Barth God is silent in the sense that man cannot really know him. But as an act of grace God has talked to man in his Word, the Christian Bible. The preaching of the Word under the guidance of the Holy Spirit is the way in which God continues to talk to man. If God is silent in our days this should be attributed to the failure of man, more specifically to historical-critical biblical scholarship.

In our opinion Barth's dismissal of the historical background of the Bible was a fundamental error. The enormous increase in knowledge about the actual circumstances in biblical times has taught us that it is impossible to explain the Bible without having recourse to the facts uncovered by archaeology and biblical scholarship. Of course the interpretation of those facts is often controversial, but that is the case in many other fields of scholarly research. Israel shared many religious concepts with its neighbors. Rejecting religious traditions other than those of ancient Israel, Judaism and Christianity as 'paganism', is unrealistic and contraproductive. Just as believers stand in a concrete historical situation and are called to testify to their faith given that situation, so it was in ancient Israel, Judaism and early Christianity.[113] Denying the reality of the day, including the progress of science, leads to a pietistic, unworldly kind of faith.

In this connection an often quoted passage which Dietrich Bonhoeffer wrote in a Nazi prison is relevant,

> While I'm often reluctant to mention God by name to religious people ... to people with no religion I can on occasion mention him by name quite calmly and as a matter of course. Religious people speak of God when human knowledge (perhaps simply because they are too lazy to think) has come to an end, or when

---

[113] See the fully justified criticism of James Barr on Barth and his followers with regard to their attempts to ward off the spectre of natural theology (Barr 1993; 1999, esp. 468-496). Barr's criticism also affects the arguments of Oswalt 2009 and White 2010.

human resources fail – in fact it is always the *deus ex machina* that they bring on to the scene, either for the apparent solution of insoluble problems, or as strength in human failure – always, that is to say, exploiting human weakness or on human boundaries. Of necessity, that can go on only till people can by their own strength push these boundaries somewhat further out, so that God becomes superfluous as a *deus ex machina*. I've come to be doubtful of talking about any human boundaries (is even death, which people now hardly fear, and is sin, which they now hardly understand, still a genuine boundary today?). It always seems to me that we are trying anxiously in this way to reserve some space for God; I should like to speak of God not on the boundaries but at the center, not in weaknesses but in strength; and therefore not in death and guilt but in man's life and goodness. On the boundaries, it seems to me better to be silent and leave the insoluble unsolved. ... The church stands, not on the boundaries where human powers give out, but in the middle of the village.[114]

Bonhoeffer hoped to overcome 'the forces that separate the world from God, religion from reality, faith from life, the church from daily routine.'[115]

The massive rejection of the 'pagan' world and its religions is not our only objection to Barth's treatment of the subject of divine speech and silence. In Barth's theology the nothingness of human effort is underscored far too heavily. This may be in line with a certain type of Protestant theology, but it is not in accordance with the biblical testimony.[116]

Moreover, Barth and his followers defined the Bible as the Protestant Christian canon. Even Miskotte, who far more than Barth was convinced of the indispensability, even the surplus value of the 'Old' Testament, maintained the unity of Scripture

---

[114]Bonhoeffer 2001, 93-94. Original text: Bonhoeffer 1998, 407-408.

[115]Dramm 2007, 193; on Bonhoeffer's 'religion-less' Christianity see especially her Chapter 20 and the volume published by Neumann 1990. Of course Bonhoeffer was by no means the only Christian who advocated openness to the world, see for example Boehme 2007 on Madeleine Delbrêl. See also Dietrich & Link 2002, 14: 'Kein Bereich unserer Wirklichkeit muß und darf von Gott abgetrennt werden' (No area in the reality around us must and may be separated from God).

[116]See e.g. Brueggemann 1973. See further below Chapter 7.

as defined in the Protestant tradition. That there exist other canons, for example the Jewish canon, or that of Alexandria, partly adopted by Rome and the Eastern Orthodox churches, was not considered important enough to take into consideration. Recent discoveries in the deserts of Judah (Hebrew, Aramaic, Greek) and Egypt (Coptic and Greek) have demonstrated that historically spoken the fringes of the canon are so frayed that one should not create the impression that with the acceptance of one particular canon the debate is closed.

There is no harm in showing more openness towards adducing and comparing other religious and philosophical systems, as has been the case in biblical times as well. Neither Israel nor the early church lived in splendid isolation. Both Testaments recognized the existence of other religions. Despite fierce antagonism and mutual claims to exclusivity, the Jewish and Christian scribes of the biblical books adopted elements from other, nonbiblical sources as well. If this was the case then and there, modern believers should not be more apprehensive of modern science and culture, or the exchange of compatible ideas with other religious or philosophical systems.[117]

Modern theologians who profess the weakness or even death of God are usually Christians for whom the death of Jesus on the cross is the most sublime event in human history.[118] Even if one broadens this approach in a trinitarian sense, attributing equal roles to the Father, the Son and the Holy Spirit, as Jürgen Moltmann did (Moltmann 1974), the pivotal role of the Cross tends to detract from the importance of the other two persons of the Trinity. Suffering and death are not the most prominent aspects of the image of God as the Bible sketches it. In contrast to the relics of other cultures in the ancient world, the Bible stands out as the daring testimony to the *living* God.[119] The often invoked model of

---

[117] Even in evangelical circles this is increasingly realized nowadays. See e.g. Sparks 2008.

[118] Cf. Section 1.3.2.3 and below. This was definitely not in line with Barth's approach for whom the resurrection of Christ was the central salutary event. Cf. e.g. Marquardt 1968.

[119] Kreuzer 1983; Mettinger 1988, 62-91; De Moor 1997, 147, 361-362; Dekker 2008, 222-225; Janowski 2009. Because dying deities are by no means rare in

taking up one's cross in imitation of the suffering of Christ (Phil. 2) is no doubt appropriate in many circumstances, but should not be used to argue for a drastic reduction of the much richer biblical message about how to order life making use of one's own abilities. Accepting suffering and self-denial as inevitable would also deprive believers of the courage to remind God of his covenantal promises. The theology of the Cross has been used too often to mask uneasy feelings about the resurrection of Christ, so that the proclamation of the victory of the living God over death was muted. John Caputo has rightly pointed out that by overemphasizing the Cross one risks to minimize the importance of the Hebrew Bible, Judaism and the Jewishness of Jesus.[120]

If believers state that God speaks or is silent, or that he is present or absent, they do not mean to describe an empirical reality that can be verified experimentally. They are talking about their *experiences* with God, about positive or negative developments in their *relation* to God.[121] It is a *relational truth* for them. Thomas Schärtl expresses this in the lapidary thesis,

> ...that *God is certainly a singular, but by no means (semantic or epistemological) relationless entity.*[122]

However, this inevitably prompts the question how believers become convinced that certain of their experiences relate to *God*. In Protestant Christian theology this question is answered with a resolute affirmation of God's initiative culminating in the cross of Jesus Christ. To quote only one from many,

> To sum up: the presence and absence of God is, in a phenomenological sense, always a presence and absence *for us*; it is, in a theological sense, a presence and absence *of God* only if it is God and God alone who determines both his presence and his absence as a mode of his divine presence, i.e. his presence *as God*; and this God-defining determination takes place, in a Christian eschatological sense, in the cross and resurrection of Jesus Christ

---

the ancient Near East, it is mistaken to claim a genuine christian origin for the concept of the death of God.

[120] Caputo in: Robbins 2007, 77-82, 140-141.
[121] Jüngel 1978; 1983; Dalferth 2006; 2009; Dekker 2008.
[122] In Halbmayr & Hoff 2008, 56, English translation ours.

in that God there discloses himself *as God* in a definitive way by becoming present as absent (in the cross), and absent as present (in the resurrection).[123]

Our problem with this kind of dialectic reasoning is not merely its ambiguity and its exclusively christological thrust, but above all its balancing of absence and presence of God, as if both were *equal* characteristics of God. In our opinion Willem Maarten Dekker has proposed an important correction on this scheme by distinguishing between characteristic and uncharacteristic properties of God,

> God is himself as a God of human beings, a God of love and grace. Therein his essence expresses itself. At the same time this is not the only mode in which God exists. He exists also as the wrathful one, as the one who has the *right* (because of sin) and the *power* (as the Almighty) to destroy the world, as the one who deplores his creation. Therein his non-essence expresses itself. Also in this mode God is God. But he is not himself therein. In his grace God reveals that he does not *want* to be God without mankind. In his wrath he reveals that he *can* be God without mankind. Speaking *concretely* about the relation of God means: speaking about God's *grace*. Speaking *concretely* about the independence of God means: speaking about God's *wrath*. The absence of God as it is experienced especially in European modernity must be interpreted as God's revelation of God's non-essence: his wrath, his 'deploring that he made mankind' (Gen. 6:7).[124]

In faith it is not sufficient to observe that God can be both absent and present, silent and speaking, dead and alive. The believer must know that the dark side of God does not belong to his essence. If God destroys, it is his *opus alienum*, an act running counter to his true essence (Isa. 28:21-22).[125] God may be silent, but he is not free anymore to remain silent, as Barth seems to suppose (Section 1.3.2.1). According to the biblical testimony he has voluntary committed himself to mankind to answer those who are in need, even if they themselves are unable to invoke him anymore because their tongue is parched with thirst,

---

[123] Dalferth in: Dalferth 2009, 19.
[124] Our translation. Dutch original: Dekker 2008, 376.
[125] Cf. Dietrich & Link 2004, 121.

> The afflicted and poor
> > are searching for water but there is none;
> > > their tongue is parched with thirst.
> >
> I am the LORD, I will answer them,
> > the God of Israel, I will not forsake them.[126]

For their part human beings are free to disbelieve him if his reply reaches them – even though they may regret their stubbornness later, as in the case of Job,

> If I would call and he answered me,
> > I would not believe that he was listening to my voice.[127]

Apparently their is a need to reconsider the biblical notion of a silent God. Because silence was understood as the interruption of the spoken or written communication between God and man, it will also be necessary to investigate how this communication was expected to take place normally.

1.6.2.2 Does a Silent God Require Silent Devotion?

With regard to the best way for man to respond to the silence of God many authors advocate answers that lean to pietism or mysticism.[128] We have seen that according to several religious orders silence is the best way to communicate with a silent God. We want to state right away that we are convinced of the power of silence in spirituality. This conviction is supported by factual data,

> Current brain studies show that silence does indeed exist as processes of traditional and religious practice and belief, as well as intrapersonal aspects of spirituality, contemplation, and meditation. Such processes have been largely neglected or even negated in much of behavioral communication research as unimportant simply because silence seems elusive and measures are not apparent or are difficult. Silence will be shown in this entry to concern valid neurological processes, metaphorical narratives, and aesthetics. More importantly, silence concerns synchronous psychological temporalities, or various temporary psychological states

---

[126] Isa. 41:17. See also Isa. 58:9; 65:24; Jer. 29:12-14; 33:3; Zech. 13:9; Ps. 81:8[7]; 91:15; Lam. 3:33. For the New Testament, see Mt 7:7-8, 11; Jn 9:31.
[127] Job 9:16, cf. 39:37-38; 42:6.
[128] Cf. Section 1.3.1 above.

occurring together, and the nonlinear brain processes necessary for creating spiritual aspects of consciousness. To believe in deep silence, then, is to believe in spirituality.[129]

Günter Stachel, an advocate of silent mysticism, states that there is no language in which one can speak 'of God' because if God is absent words cannot bring him back (Stachel 1989, 21).

> Therefore mysticism is somehow 'experience of God' and is understood by the one as becoming empty and as nothing (Nirwana), by another as becoming one with the God of biblical revelation (who, however, for his part has withdrawn in the darkness of the impossibility to name him or to understand him).[130]

However, is not filling emptiness with emptiness a sophism,[131] a too easy escape from the hazardous business of professing faith in the modern tumultuous world? Have the advocates of silence when approaching the Silent One realized the dangers of silencing oneself? Or of allowing others to cover up crimes by silence?

As is more often the case, Karl Barth writes somewhat ambiguously on the subject of silence in faith,

> Faith means motionlessness, silence, worship – it means not-knowing. Faith renders inevitable a qualitative distinction between God and man; it renders necessary and unavoidable a perception of the contradiction between Him and the world of time and things and man; and it finds in death the only (the only!) parable of the Kingdom of Heaven.[132]

---

[129] Bruneau 2009, 281.

[130] Stachel 1989, 126, our translation. On the so-called 'negative theology' in its different articulations, see also e.g. Oelmüller 1999, 124-126; Bulhof & Ten Kate 2000; Sorace & Zimmerling 2007; Halbmayr & Hoff 2008.

[131] Ekman Tam describes the highest level of prayer life as 'no one speaks; no one listens; there is pure silence' (Tam 2002, 162).

[132] Barth 1968, 202, slightly adapted to the German text which runs, 'Glauben heißt Halt machen, Schweigen, Anbeten – Nicht-Wissen. Der qualitative Unterschied von Gott und Mensch wird unverkennbar, der Widerspruch Gottes zu der Welt der Zeit, der Dinge und des Menschen zur unausweichlich notwendigen Einsicht, der Tod zum einzigen (zum einzigen!) Gleichnis des Himmelreichs.' (Barth 1940, 96, see also 183: '... die Erkenntnis also, daß wir Gott gegenüber Nicht-Wissende sind, daß wir vor ihm nur Halt machen, schweigen und anbeten können.').

Elsewhere Barth states that a Christian should *not* keep silent about God,

> God's revelation in its subjective reality is the person and work of the Holy Spirit, i.e., the person and work of God Himself. This does not mean that we cannot say anything about it, that we have to be silent. How can it possibly mean that? In this matter we have to follow Holy Scripture, which testifies that the person and work of God are manifest. Silence about the person and work of God means only that we reject the witness of Holy Scripture, and ultimately that we deny God's revelation.[133]

And further on in *ChD* 1/2,

> It is quite understandable that both in earlier times and to-day it could be proposed and the attempt made to achieve pure doctrine quickly, by either silencing the human word entirely, or accompanying it with silence, or by destroying its verbal and so its rational character in an attempt to express it in the speech of primitive poetry. This kind of silence was interpreted as the completest way of letting God speak, and it was thought to be better than speech, and to be what was really meant and intended in speech. Where there is a desire to replace or crowd out preaching by the sacrament and liturgy, no small part is usually played by the theme that pure doctrine is the result of doing nothing, of abstention from human words, which fall under the suspicion of being so solid that they cannot have the transparency required to reveal the Word of God. But the matter is not so simple. That any sort of human words have the required transparency is certainly not the case. But silence is also a human action, as is everything that man does instead of preaching.[134]

If we talk about God or if we remain silent about him, it is not our own decision, but the work of the Holy Spirit which Barth repeatedly calls 'the subjective reality of revelation'.[135] In his comment on Rom. 8:2 Barth wrote already,

---

[133] Barth, *ChD*, vol. 1/2, 232-233. German original: Barth, *KD*, Bd. 1/2, 254.
[134] *ChD*, vol. 1/2, 778. German original: Barth, *KD*, Bd. 1/2, 870.
[135] E.g. Barth, *ChD*, vol. 1/1, 238-239, 242.

> WE SPEAK CONCERNING THE SPIRIT. But can men dare to undertake such conversation? For the description of other possibilities we possess a large vocabulary, but we have no single word which we can make use of to define the impossible possibility of our lives. Why, then, are we not silent concerning Him? We must also be silent; but none the less we must bear in mind that our silence compromises Him no less than our speech. We do the Spirit no greater service by our silence. The Spirit remains the Word whether we proclaim Him in silence or in speech. Whether being speechless we are compelled to speech, or speaking we are compelled to silence, confronted by the Spirit we are equally embarrassed and have no means of escape. Could we but take care that we should speak or be silent as He willeth, in order that we might at once recognize that, if we should do right, it is not that WE do so in the speech or in the silence of religion, but that the Spirit Himself has spoken with or without words![136]

Despite the dialectic ambiguousness of Barth's statements[137] on human silence as a response to the silence of God, it seems clear that in the end he is of the opinion that speaking the Word of God is preferable to radical silence. However, even if human beings do speak Barth evidently minimizes their role as far as possible. It is not *their* speech or silence, but that of the Spirit. 'That any sort of human words have the required transparency is certainly not the case.' This is in line with his dismissal of ordinary everyday language as inappropriate. But are not human beings God's covenantal partners? Are we mere automata obeying the Spirit?

If God's silence is interpreted as his patience that should be matched by silence on the part of the church, as Rachel Muers advocates, this raises the suspicion that actually she is thinking along lines not all that far removed from the ideas of a fundamentalist like Robert Anderson. Basically humankind deserves to be punished for its sins, but God in his grace grants us some respite. She writes about the 'imperfect past' of the church and the need of repentance,[138] 'human evil' that causes God's silence,[139] 'our

---

[136] Barth 1968, 273. German original: Barth 1940, 256.
[137] Cf. Sneller 2000.
[138] Muers 2001, 87.
[139] Muers 2001, 89.

failed words and our wrongly kept silences',[140]

> ... a whole community developing habits of distorted listening, that perpetually fails to attend either to its own speech's failures or to the voices it does not recognise, or that is insufficiently attentive to be able to recognise pervasive falsehoods.
> ... the Church itself is an object of God's patience. Its mishearings and its failed mediations of patience are themselves heard and tested. Its silence–liturgical, theological and in public discourse–acknowledges that it has heard and hears the one reliable word of God; at the same time, they acknowledge that its practices of listening and speaking require conversion and transformation.[141]

She acknowledges that the silence of the church is 'a way of dodging the issues', but thanks God for his patience with it.[142] In its silence the church is the image of the silent, patient God who is silent because he is listening.[143]

Can this acceptance of the concept of a silent God and a silent community of believers be reconciled with the biblical emphasis on the speaking of God and his exhortations to his congregation to bear witness, also in the form of hymns and prayers? Muers is aware of the possibility that this objection might be raised but her attempt to attribute equal importance to God's silence and his speech is unconvincing (Muers 2004, 13-15 *et passim*). Moreover, being a Quaker who is captivated by the work of Dietrich Bonhoeffer, she opts for an exclusively christological interpretation of God's silence. She rarely quotes from the Hebrew Scriptures.

We have seen that in Philip Gröning's film *Die grosse Stille* (Into Great Silence, 2006) the silence of the Carthusian monks was seen as a positive way of communicating with a silent God.[144] However, a less harmonious picture is drawn in another recent film about monastic life: *In memoria di me* (In Memory of Me, 2007) by Saverio Costanzo. It was shot in the Basilica di San Giorgio

---

[140] Muers 2001, 93.
[141] Muers 2001, 94-95.
[142] Muers 2001, 95.
[143] Muers 2001, 96; Muers 2004, 14-15.
[144] Section 1.3.1 above.

Maggiore on the Venetian island of San Giorgio, designed by 16th century architect Andrea Palladio. In this case the film centers on three novices. Their spiritual crises are followed closely, and their emptiness and utter frustration are not concealed. When Andrea, the principal character, presents himself to the Father Superior of the Jesuit cloister, the latter says to him, 'Tomorrow you will enter into your personal silence. Silence which sharpens discernment.' ... 'We must envelop ourselves in silence and prayer. We are not accustomed to listening to the silence which speaks deep within us, where God dwells'.

Indeed silence reigns throughout the film. Conversation is limited to the absolute minimum. Early on in the film, one of the three novices, Fausto, revolts against the degrading discipline of the order. '... the silence of this church is empty. ... They need truth to be dead.' He leaves the cloister.

Zanna, another novice, tells Andrea that he has decided to leave too. They talk about faith and Andrea blurts out, 'I don't believe in anything. ... I'm coming with you. We're leaving tonight.' Later that night Andrea listens in on a brilliant defense by the Jesuit Superior who tries to convince Zanna to stay by invoking 'The terrifying mystery of a weak God.' But Zanna merely kisses the reluctant priest a farewell and leaves alone, without waiting for Andrea. The latter runs after him, outside the gate, but does not see him anymore and after long hesitation returns to the cloister. Merely by silent shots Costanzo suggests that he is afraid of the bustling outside world. Gradually Andrea becomes convinced that staying in the order is his duty. 'I was created to carry out a plan for which no one else was created.'

Certainly a deep thought, but any pious human being could have said it, and two out of three pious novices left. One realizes that it may be God's intention for Andrea to stay, but was it silent contemplation that brought about his decision?

For Bonhoeffer it was unthinkable that there might be a place where a Christian could withdraw from the world either outwardly or within the inner sphere.[145] Indeed, radical mystic si-

---

[145] See Section 1.6.2.1 above and Dramm 2007, 198.

lence is not a viable option anymore in modern society.[146] This is even admitted by a determined silence seeker like Sara Maitland,

> The reality is that it is impossible to live in complete silence for very long in the developed world in the 21st century without various and extensive negotiations, in part with oneself. And particularly if you need to earn a living.[147]

The reader of Maitland's report on her quest for silence soon realizes that her desire to exclude communication with the outside world results in a self-centered view of life. Even if one prays often, as she does, and if one reads as extensively as by a multitude of quotations she demonstrates to have done, it is a legitimate question whether this can really replace or even surpass direct social contacts. To her credit it must be acknowledged that she does attempt to deal with the dangerous effects of prolonged silence, voluntary or imposed. Silence can kill you, or drive you insane.[148] Characteristically, however, Maitland hardly ever considers the harm that a person's prolonged silence can do to others.

For this reason Ilse Bulhof cautions prudence,

> The possibility remains that the silence forced upon us by a radically transcendent God leads to complicity with the forces of evil ...,[149] which is a warning against an easy enthusiasm for silence and mysticism.[150]

We cannot hope to avoid collateral damage if we overemphasize our inability to describe the divine in familiar terms which at least hint at a knowable divine being.

1.6.2.3 A New Theism?

As we have seen, the Jewish philosopher Levinas juggles with the concept of an absent God who does not engage in dialogue

---

[146]Gebauer, in: Kamper & Wulf 1992, 27-37; Schorsch, in: Kamper & Wulf 1992, 52-64.
[147]Maitland 2009, 274.
[148]Maitland 2009, Chapter 3.
[149]Bulhof refers here to an essay on Mikhail Mikhailovich Bakhtin (1895-1975) by Simons 2000.
[150]Bulhof in: Bulhof & Ten Kate 2000, 387.

with man. Yet Levinas believes that technology as secularization is destructive of pagan gods,

> Through it, certain gods are now dead: those gods of astrology's conjunction of the planets, the gods of destiny [*fatum*], local gods, gods of place and countryside, all the gods inhabiting consciousness and reproducing, in anguish and terror, the gods of the skies. Technology teaches us that these gods are of the world, and therefore are things, and being things they are nothing much [*pas grand-chose*]. In this sense, secularizing technology figures in the progress of the human spirit. But it is not its end.[151]

Such a statement grossly misrepresents the concept of the divine in the so-called 'pagan' religions. The concept of divine transcendence was by no means foreign to ancient theologians in the world around Israel. Moreover, the statement conveniently skips the fact that on the one hand also the God of Israel is connected with certain localities on earth (e.g. Sinai, Horeb, Bashan, Zion) and, on the other hand, that universal, supra-territorial claims were also made by the worshippers of other ancient Near Eastern gods (e.g. the Mesopotamian deities Anu and Ninurta, Marduk, Assur, and the Egyptian god Amun-Re). It has rightly been observed that Levinas' view of non-monotheists, like his view on women, is dated, misunderstood and distorted.[152]

And isn't Yosl Rakover[153] himself an embodiment of the Law – an objective entity? Leon Wieseltier criticizes Lévinas in this respect,

> Levinas wants the courage of the atheist and the certainty of the theist. I do not see how he can have both, in his reflection on Yosl Rakover and in his other writings. The problem will not go away by declaring romantically that "God manifests Himself not by incarnation but by absence" and taking pleasure in the paradox. For this is not a paradox, it is a contradiction. The idea of a God who manifests Himself by not manifesting Himself is an idea in need of an explanation. Until then, it is only an intellectual's incredibility. Until then, an absent God is a God who has not

---

[151] Levinas 2000. 166. French original: Levinas 1993, 191.
[152] Perpich 2008, 177-198.
[153] See above, Section 1.3.2.5.

manifested Himself, and the rest is nothing more than desire, which is an engine of superstition.[154]

We encountered this kind of juggling with a concept of God who is totally absent as well as totally present also in the works of modern Christian theologians. But does it provide solid ground to stand on? In the end Tom Milazzo opts for Jesus as the ultimate example of a human being standing up against the silence of God. But only a believer may find the absurdity of the last sentence of his book *Protest and the Silence* acceptable,

And though God may slay us, yet shall we love God unto death.[155]

It has been objected to the use of expressions like 'the disappearance of God' or 'the death of God' that they imply that at a certain moment he *was* present or even *alive*. Gregory Erickson and others tried to get around this objection by using the word 'absence' instead (Erickson 2007, 3). As we have seen earlier, several philosophers preceded them in this respect. One look in a good dictionary reveals that 'absence' is an ambiguous term too. That is exactly why it is chosen. The word 'absence' can mean both physical non-presence and a lack of companionship, a failure to be present where one is needed or expected. In other words, it depends on the context in which the expression 'the absence of God' is used which meaning is intended.[156]

We have seen that a 'new theism' is emerging that is supported by many distinguished scientists.[157] To be sure, it is based not on revelation or tradition, but on fresh cosmological and biological insights which seem to favor the theory of intelligent design by a Superior Mind. Although honest atheists may find the reasoning behind the 'new theism' difficult to rebut, it should be observed

---

[154] Wieseltier, in: Kolitz 1999, 85.
[155] Milazzo 1992, 167.
[156] One example: when Pope Benedict XVI in an Angelus address on Mark 1:29-31 par. called the absence of God 'man's truest and deepest illness', he obviously meant agnosticism and atheism.
(http://www.vatican.va/holy_father/benedict_xvi/angelus/2009/documents/hf_ben-xvi_ang_20090208_en.html)
[157] Section 1.5.

that also the proponents of 'new theism' rely on a still unproven theory. There might exist other explanations and some have been proposed already. One of the disadvantages of the 'new theism' is that it too is deterministic. After the Big Bang God has remained inactive and silent. This comes close to the Deism of the 17th and 18th centuries. There is no possibility of feedback from the side of the living beings that ultimately sprang from an omnipresent and omniscient spirit. Small wonder that the 'new theist' Anthony Flew concludes his book *There Is a God* with the following statement,

> The discovery of phenomena like the laws of nature ... has led scientists, philosophers, and others to accept the existence of an infinitely intelligent Mind. Some claim to have made contact with this Mind. I have not – yet. But who knows what could happen next?
>
> Someday I might hear a Voice that says, "Can you hear me now?"[158]

For the 'new theists' God does exist, but he is still silent. But would not an omniscient Mind have deliberately provided human beings with intelligence and imagination so that they might converse with It? Why would It have remained silent if meaningful communication was its aim? Can some form of immaterial contact between the omniscient Mind and the human mind really be excluded? If the Mind cannot read our mind and cannot address it, the Mind would not be omniscient. So Flew was right to leave open the possibility that one day he might still be illuminated by the Mind.

1.6.2.4 Is Atheism the Solution?

Protests against the new, often aggressively propagated atheism abound. Atheists tend to underestimate the fact that there are religions, for example Buddhism, which do not recognize deities, but rest just as well on presuppositions that are not verifiable by empirical tests. Characteristic is Richard Dawkins' statement,

---

[158] Flew 2008, 158.

... I shall not be concerned at all with other religions such as Buddhism or Confucianism. Indeed, there is something to be said for treating these not as religions at all but as ethical systems or philosophies of life.[159]

Is the truth claimed by philosophies and ethical systems more reliable than Jewish, Christian or Muslim monotheism? If that were the case, there would be a lot less dissent in the world. In reality, however, social values are established on the basis of a consensus which is heavily influenced by religion. If for whatever reason this consensus is eroding, a society experiences this as a crisis which requires new spiritual leadership and the creative transformation of existing values.

Let it be clear: we do not prematurely take a position in this matter. But just like many Jewish, Christian and Muslim apologetics, the new atheists exhibit a certain zeal in trying to convince or even silence those who raise objections to their argument. And let it be granted, they have been successful in propagating their ideal of a secular society based on rationalistic reasoning. At the same time it should be admitted that this became to a large extent a value-less society. As Mark Taylor formulates it poignantly,

> The echoes of the death of God can be heard in the disappearance of the self, the end of history, and the closure of the book.[160]

In his hugely successful novel *Nachtzug nach Lissabon* (Night Train to Lisbon) Pascal Mercier, a Swiss professor of philosophy, makes a character called Amadeo Inácio de Almeida Prado, a brilliant seventeen year old Portuguese student, his advocate of atheism.

> I revere the word of God for I love its poetic force. I loathe the word of God for I hate its cruelty. ... The poetry of the divine word is so overwhelming that it silences everything and every protest becomes wretched yapping. That's why you can't just *put* away the Bible, but must *throw* it away when you have enough of its unreasonable demands and of the slavery it inflicts on us. It

---
[159]Dawkins 2007, 58-59.
[160]Taylor 1984, 7.

> is a joyless God far from life speaking out of it, a God who wants to constrict the enormous compass of a human life–the big circle that can be drawn when it is left free–to the single, shrunken point of obedience.[161]

However, later in life this 'godless priest' states,

> I live in myself as in a moving train. I didn't board voluntarily, didn't have a choice and don't know the name of the destination. ... I can't get off. I can't change the tracks or the destination.[162]

And after having had to sacrifice his friendship with his best friend in order to save the life of the girl Fátima whom he loves,

> Our life, those are fleeting formations of quicksand, formed by one gust of wind, destroyed by the next. Images of futility that blow away even before they have properly formed.[163]

However, even his love for Fátima is a mere matter of chance. When she asks him 'Do you also think we were destined for each other?' he observes skeptically,

> No one is destined for another. Not only because there is no Providence and no one else who could arrange it. No: because there is simply no inevitability between people beyond accidental needs and the powerful force of habit.[164]

Do human beings have to resign to a life governed by randomness? Are they doomed to live futile lives without destination? Mercier's novel illustrates vividly the truth of Taylor's thesis that an atheistic society runs the risk of becoming a valueless society.

Atheism is often presented as the logical consequence of the Enlightenment, the emancipation of modern man. But is it? There have always been people who stated, 'There is no God!' (Ps. 10:4; 14:1; 53:1). Job definitely has a point when he sees atheism as an attitude which is only possible if one is rich, safe and well-nourished (Job 21). He quotes those lucky fellows,

---

[161] Mercier 2008, 169. Similar passages 216, 236, 255, 273, 276, 340, 366. German original: Mercier 2006, 199-200).
[162] Mercier 2008, 369. German original: Mercier 2006, 423.
[163] Mercier 2008, 411. German original: Mercier 2006, 467.
[164] Mercier 2008, 426. German original: Mercier 2006, 483-484.

> And they say to God, 'Leave us alone!
>   we do not appreciate knowledge about your ways!
> What is the Almighty, that we should serve him?
>   And what would we gain by praying to him?[165]

If atheism is a luxury that only the prosperous can afford, the door to asocial exploitation of less lucky people is wide open. Of course also modern atheists advocate generosity and altruism, but merely as a form of self-interest because the law of survival of the fittest simply requires that they obey their selfish genes if the worst comes to the worst.

1.6.2.5 Conclusion

Believers will have recognized many of the above attempts to explain God's silence and some may have found several of these answers comforting and helpful in their own situation. Non-believers will have felt the need to riposte. Indeed, not all apologetic answers to God's refusal or inability to reply to man's prayers and laments are satisfactory. The idea that it is inadmissible to call a silent God to account in the context of a lament is questionable, not only because many biblical passages contradict this theological shift,[166] but because it is incompatible with the concept of man's free will and God's free decision to enter into a covenant with man.

To attribute God's silence to human sins, as Job's friends do, is unacceptable because it does not take the fierce denials of Job and the Psalmists seriously. It is also unacceptable in view of the cries of those who became the victims of genocide or natural disasters – we cannot make all of them sinners who would have deserved punishment (Berges 2003, 27-30).

A book such as that of Anderson 1897[167] tries to resolve the problem by denying that we can still expect spoken messages or miracles from God. This undermines the clear biblical message of God's continuing work of creation and revelation, as well as the faith in inspired persons which is acknowledged in both Judaism and Christianity. Anderson's emphasis on the absolute

---

[165] Job 21:14-15.
[166] As was demonstrated brilliantly by Berges 2003.
[167] Often reprinted, we used Anderson 1978.

sufficiency of the divine revelation in Christ often borders on anti-Semitism.[168] Critical biblical scholars are denounced as agnostics. Anderson's approach boils down to the most simplistic form of Christian fundamentalism.

The 'new theists' have not drawn the full consequences of their acceptance of an omniscient and almighty Spirit. Communication is a two-sided process, so why are they waiting for the Spirit's voice whereas they might just as well address It?

The concept of divine silence as found in modern literature and theology is evidently based on the biblical concept of a God who allegedly has spoken in biblical times, but is now forever silent. In this study we retrace the early history of the concept of divine speech and silence in the ancient world. In an epilogue we explore the question if use of this concept can still be continued or has to be abandoned.

---

[168] E.g. Anderson 1978, 78: 'The jews had crucified the Messiah'. And 85: 'And finally we have seen how the rejection of that testimony by the favoured nation led to the unfolding of the Divine purpose to deprive the jew of his vantage-ground of privilege and to usher in the Christian dispensation.' And pp. 86-87: 'What concerns us is the fact that Israel's fall was due to the national rejection of the Messiah, and that that fall was "the reconciling of the world" – a radical change in God's attitude toward men, such as the Old Testament Scriptures gave no indication of, and even the Gospels foreshadowed but vaguely.' See also p. 163.

CHAPTER TWO

PREREQUISITES FOR A FRESH INVESTIGATION

2.1 Defining the Scope of This Study

It is more difficult than it may seem to define what 'silence' is (Maitland 2009, 25-28). It may be the absence of sound or the absence of speech. Silence has to be *interpreted* to acquire meaning. Since this book will deal mainly with the concept of silence in the ancient Near East, and in particular with the silence of deities, we will try to establish what the Ancients meant when they assumed that under circumstances God remained silent. The truth about God is not objectively accessible to man. We do not really know who He is. What then is divine 'silence' as perceived by the Ancients?

Divine silence is related to, but not the same as divine absence. Obviously an absent deity does not speak because he is not there to enter into a dialogue with mankind,[1] whereas a silent deity can be attentively listening or may have reason to keep silent, but might speak again if he wants to. Joel Burnett ends his fine study on the absence of God in the Hebrew Bible as follows,

> Through the theme of divine absence, the Hebrew Bible portrays a God who freely chooses relationships with humankind, a God whom human beings are free to seek, a God who responds.[2]

The very last part of this statement is problematic. The God of the Hebrew Bible does not always respond. Nor did other deities of the ancient world. In this study we concentrate not on the absence of God, but on his silence although he is thought to be present.

If the Word of God is inextricably connected with the word of man, as has been emphasized by many theologians, including Karl Barth and the Second Vatican Council,[3] we need to know more about the religions of the world in which the Hebrew Bible

---

[1]Cf. Levinas, Sections 1.3.2.5 and 1.6.2.3.
[2]Burnett 2010, 178. See also pages vii, 2, 108 where he seems to equate divine absence and silence.
[3]With regard to the latter, see e.g. Rahner 2008; Hieke 2009, 96.

came into being, because that was the reality in which the biblical writers wrote down what they believed to be the word of their own God. As will appear later on in this study, recent discoveries in the Near East have revealed that there are far more points of contact and similarities between the religion of Israel and the religions of its neighbors than is commonly realized or admitted. This is also true of prophecy, the most prominent mode of communication between God and man in the Bible.[4] Of course these parallels render the differences all the more interesting, and of course these too will be discussed.

We limit our investigation to the silence of human and divine beings. For example, the silent hymn that the heavens sing to God according to Ps. 19:2-4 may once have been ascribed to deities personifying sun, moon and stars, but in its present form the Psalm does not concern animated beings anymore. The poet is merely using bold metaphorical language to indicate that the silent skies are singing a wordless ode to their Creator.

With regard to the demarcation of the ancient world we confine ourselves to written texts and will only rarely indulge in the interpretation of iconographic evidence because the interpretation of the latter is often hypothetical. In contrast to what has been the custom since the rise of Classicism we include early Greek texts in our inquiry. Intensive contacts between Greece and the Near East existed at least since the 12th century BCE and there is every reason to regard early Greece as part of the Near Eastern world.[5]

Every nation of the ancient world and every period in its long history had its own religious peculiarities, but that does not preclude the possibility to study similarities that need not be the result of direct contacts between religions, but reflect a similar reaction to what was experienced as silence on the part of the deity. Respected works like Pritchard's *Ancient Near Eastern Texts Relating to the Old Testament*, Kaiser's *Texte aus der*

---

[4] It is always risky to argue that certain biblical notions are 'unique'. New finds may invalidate such statements.

[5] See e.g. Davies & Schofield 1995; Kropp & Wagner 1999; Brown 1995-2001; Loretz 2002; Burkert 2003; Kaiser 2003; Alkier & Witte 2004; Görg 2005; Korpel 2006; Villing 2006; Dietrich 2007.

Umwelt des Alten Testament, Hallo's *The Context of Scripture* as well as countless monographs and collaborative volumes exploring similar phenomena in the world of the Bible demonstrate the usefulness of this approach.

Since we are primarily interested in the *phenomenon* of divine silence we will quote sources from Antiquity not always in strict chronological or geographic order, although we will mostly provide some information on date and origin. However, in many cases the age of a certain tradition cannot be established with certainty because the available fragments do not allow us to follow the history of a literary tradition in great detail. The Mesopotamian Gilgamesh traditions, for example, cover a history of transmission of about two millennia and the extant tablets show an extremely complicated genesis up to *c.* 1200 BCE, with many gaps.[6]

Some theologians may object to comparing other religions with the Holy Bible. Especially Karl Barth advocated the view that revelation inevitably means the end of religion.[7] Yet it may be asked if Barth did not place theology in a false dilemma between faith-talk and ordinary discourse where persons as subjects preside. It would seem that Barth's view implies an underestimation of the anthropological side of the process of revelation.[8] His view of the God of Israel as the God who acts, in contrast to the speculative thinking of myth,[9] influenced Old Testament scholars like Gerhard von Rad and George Wright, but has been shown to be based on a no longer tenable view of ancient Near Eastern religion.[10] Other deities in the ancient world too were supposed to act in human history (e.g. the Babylonian Marduk, the Egyptian Amun-Re, the Moabite Kemosh).

Since human beings cannot describe the divine adequately by means of the limited possibilities of human language a paragraph will be devoted to the human nature of religious language (Section 2.2).

---

[6]Tigay 1982; George 2003; Fleming & Milstein 2010.
[7]Barth, *KD*, Bd. 1/2, 304ff. Cf. Marquard 1968.
[8]Cf. High 1967, 188ff.; Pöhlmann 1990, 371. See also above, Section 1.6.2.1.
[9]Especially clear in *KD*, Bd. III/2, 536.
[10]See e.g. Albrektson 1967.

If the way in which people speak about God is patterned after human behavior, we must conclude that also the silence of God is patterned after the function of silence in human communication. Therefore, it is useful to first look at the function of silence on the latter level. Human communication always needs interpretation on the basis of the actual situation in which words are spoken. Silences are part of every human utterance and by their very nature require even more explanation (cf. Sections 2.3-5). Therefore exegesis of the texts involved is imperative (Hieke 2009), but for the purpose of this study it will not be necessary to delve deeply into form and redaction history of every individual passage. Our approach will be pragmatic, making use of existing translations of primary sources[11] and restricting technical discussion to the absolute minimum. Quotations are given in English translation. In this way we hope to make the book accessible also to non-specialists.

Since human utterances about the divine are inevitably patterned after ordinary human discourse, we first investigate what reasons people in Antiquity may have had to keep silent among themselves (Chapter 3).

In Chapter 4 we discuss how human beings did address the deity in Antiquity. Hymns, lamentations, prayers, letters to deities, magic rituals, requests for signs and acts were some of the more common ways of approaching the deities. Also silence was a way of asking the deity to pay attention to one's misery.

In Chapter 5 we relate how the deity did address man according to the sources available. Direct communication was restricted to certain privileged persons. Mostly intermediaries relayed the messages of the deities.

Chapter 6 is devoted to the silence of deities as recorded in the extant writings of the ancient world and in the Hebrew Bible.

To allow the reader a convenient overview of categories of silence in the ancient sources we discuss we group the reasons for silence under the following headings,

---

[11] Texts from the Bible will be provided with a translation of our own in order to avoid a choice between the often widely diverging existing translations which all too often have been influenced by theological or esthetic considerations.

1. Silence because of offenses
2. Silence because of awe or fear
3. Silence because of forbearance or prudence
4. Silence because of incapacity
5. Silence because of sleep

Whereas silence among humans could mostly be explained along these lines, the alterity of divine beings made it often difficult to fathom the reasons for silence on the part of the gods. So we devote an extra section to incomprehensible divine silence (Section 6.2.2).

We fully realize that there are other possibilities of categorizing[12] and that any such classification is imperfect because in reality categories overlap to some extent.

In an Epilogue (Chapter 7) we tentatively explore the consequences of what we have found, and try to establish in which way our findings may be relevant to those who experience God's silence as utterly frustrating. We realize that further philosophical, psychological, systematic and practical theological studies on this subject are indispensable, but we deemed it useful to start the investigation from the disciplines with which we are more or less familiar. But even this field of studies has grown so fast over the past century that we can only offer a modest selection from the material available and may well have overlooked some relevant evidence.

2.2 The Human Nature of Religious Language

If people state that God 'keeps silent' they presuppose that normal audible or written communication between God and human beings is possible. Mostly they assume that God has spoken in the past, for example directly addressing the biblical patriarchs, Moses and the prophets. It is important, however, to realize that the concept of a speaking God belongs to the domain of metaphorical religious language. To be more specific, phrases like these

---

[12] E.g. the 10 categories used by Brunner-Traut 1979, or the 12 categories enumerated by Pelsy 1995, 31-34, or the 14 categories distinguished by Barrado 1997. As a matter of fact, Muers 2004, 8-9, 12 shows how difficult it is to interpret silence without sufficient context.

originate from the common idea that God can be described analogous to a human being. Anthropomorphic concepts of God dominate all God-talk from ancient times until today, even though the inadequacy of this 'humanizing' of God is generally admitted.[13]

The metaphorical (or analogous) nature of the biblical and other oriental descriptions of the divine has long been recognized.[14] For the purpose of our study it is sufficient to briefly review the major philosophical and theological positions taken with regard to the metaphorical nature of religious language.

2.2.1   *Metaphor in the Philosophy of Language*

The term 'metaphor' derives from the Greek μεταφορά (*metafora*), composed of μετα 'trans-' and φέρειν 'to carry,' or transporting the meaning from one word to the other. The word was coined by Greek grammarians of the classical period (5th century BCE). In those days political strategy was a major subject of study. One of the qualities a politician needed was eloquence. The technique of eloquence could be learned in the schools of rhetoric. Here the study of language itself was fostered as a by-product because speech was a formidable weapon in a verbal duel. People could be influenced by the conscious use of language. One of the tricks of eloquence was the willful misunderstanding of an opponent's ambiguous use of words. Initially, this strategic weapon in political debates was called 'metaphor'.

---

[13] See e.g. Rahner 1994, 135-136; White 2010. However, see also a statement by Lenzi 2010, 309, n. 14: 'Humans generally think of deities as if they were people, despite the objections of theologians. The cognitive scientific branch of religious studies is empirically establishing the cognitive basis for this universal religious conception. It is, in a sense, therefore natural for people to look to their own social conventions for interacting with the gods.'

Modern empirical research demonstrates that concepts of God are mostly *relational*, i.e. that communication with God is seen as comparable to conversation between humans. Cf. Van der Lans 2001, 356; Schaap-Jonker 2008, 140-142.

[14] See *e.g.* Soskice 1987; Brettler 1989; Korpel 1990; Eidevall 1996; Seifert 1996; Jablónski *et al.* 1998; Aaron 2002; Van Hecke 2005; Basson 2006; Bergmann 2008; White 2010.

Next to the importance for rhetoric, metaphor played a major role in the science of poetics.[15] Here its function was totally different. The purpose of metaphor in poetics was not to persuade people, but to express as purely as possible what one experienced and could not express in literal terms. As a result, the original concept of metaphor was characterized by a certain duality.

So the word 'metaphor' had been in use for some time already when Aristotle (384-322 BCE) started to describe the phenomenon in a more systematic way.[16] His view became known as the so-called *substitution theory of metaphor* – mistakenly, because Aristotle was not as simplistic as thinking that metaphor works by substituting one word for another.[17]

From the 4th century BCE to the middle of the 19th century little was added to the theory of metaphor that went beyond what Aristotle had stated. Mostly, metaphor was regarded as a stylistic ornament that belonged to the domain of literature and aesthetics.

Some writers and poets, like Jean-Jacques Rousseau (1712-1778)[18] and Percy Bysshe Shelley (1792-1822),[19] however, dared to go further and advocated the primacy of figures of speech in the development of language. Friedrich Nietzsche (1844-1900) was one of those who embraced this concept, but he carried it to its extreme consequences. In denouncing not only metaphor itself, but all human language as nothing but faded, empty metaphor, Nietzsche paved the way for the modern research into this remarkable figure of speech. Is it true that language, and metaphor in particular, is unable to convey truth?

The first to take on that challenge was Ivor Richards. Although he had earlier defined metaphor along the lines of logical

---

[15] Aristotle 1926, 1406-1407 (366-369); Aristotle 1932, 1457b (78f.).

[16] For some particularly illuminating discussions of Aristotle's views on metaphor and analogy see Derrida 1974; Ricoeur 1978, 9-43; Kirby 1997; White 2010, 7-9, 27-72. The different types of metaphor Aristotle distinguishes are discussed in detail by Levin 1982.

[17] Korpel 1990, 36-37; Kirby 1997, 519-521, 538-539.

[18] Rousseau 1966, Ch.3.

[19] Shelley 1962, 301. Others followed suit, e.g., Paul 1804, 179; Biese 1893, 24; Runze 1889, 14.

positivism, denying it all cognitive value,[20] he made a complete *volte-face* in a later and far more influential study.[21] He criticizes rhetoric for its treatment of metaphor as a secondary element of language, as a mere ornament. On the contrary, metaphor is omnipresent, permeates all our discourse, is used in all sciences, and may rightly be called the constitutive form of language. Therefore it is extremely important to understand the way metaphor works. In the analysis of metaphors, two elements have to be distinguished, the *tenor* and the *vehicle*.[22] The tenor is the meaning of the metaphor or the underlying idea, the vehicle is the figure.[23] When we are using a metaphor, the two thoughts render their meaning by interaction, not by substitution. The effect of this is 'a meaning of more varied powers than can be ascribed to either', tenor or vehicle.[24] Therefore metaphor cannot be reduced to a literal paraphrase.

It took another twenty years before the new insight in metaphor provided by Richards was taken over and expanded by the philosopher Max Black. Black introduces some new terms for the analysis of metaphor. An example he uses is 'The chairman plowed through the discussion.' This sentence he calls a case of metaphor. 'With this we are implying that at least one word (here the word "plowed") is being used metaphorically in the sentence, and that at least one of the remaining words is being used literally.'[25] Black calls the word 'plowed' the *focus* of the metaphor, and the remainder of the sentence the *frame*.[26] Metaphor works like a filter. In the metaphorical expression 'man is a wolf,' there are *two* subjects. When in the metaphorical expression the word 'wolf' is linked to 'man' some of the commonplaces associated with 'wolf' will be pushed into the background because they cannot be related to man. 'If to call a man a wolf is to put him in a special

---

[20] See Ogden & Richards 1946, 149. Cf. Johnson 1981, 17-18; Kjärgaard 1986, 15-16.
[21] Richards 1936, 89-138.
[22] Richards 1936, 96.
[23] Richards 1936, 97.
[24] Richards 1936, 100.
[25] Black 1962, 28.
[26] Black 1962, 28.

light, we must not forget that the metaphor makes the wolf seem more human than he otherwise would.'[27]

An in many respects novel approach to the problem of metaphor was introduced by the linguist George Lakoff and the philosopher Mark Johnson (Lakoff & Johnson 1980). Their first, rather radical, though not innovative statement is that almost all language is metaphorical. They use the conceptual metaphor ARGUMENT IS WAR to illustrate their view. This metaphor is reflected in a wide variety of expressions used in everyday language, e.g. 'Your claims are *indefensible*' and 'He *attacked every weak point* in my argument'. It has to be understood that these expressions not only reflect a way of talking but also a way of acting. Arguments really can be won or lost, and the person we are arguing with is really seen as an opponent. In this way, Lakoff and Johnson want to emphasize that metaphor is more than just a matter of language. Metaphor also is a part of life. The principal idea of Lakoff and Johnson is that metaphors structure the ordinary conceptual system of our culture as reflected in everyday language.[28] The theory of Lakoff and Johnson became widely accepted and was elaborated by others.[29]

One of the subconscious root metaphors used in the medical profession, for example, is THE DOCTOR IS A DETECTIVE. Such a conceptual metaphor generates a host of related associations. The doctor has to 'find' the cause of the disease. The disease is a 'criminal' who has to be 'tracked down' and therefore the patient has to be 'interrogated' about his background and about the symptoms of the illness. On the basis of the interrogation the doctor may arrive at certain 'suspicions'. Even surgery can be explained in this frame as a kind of 'forensics', research to find out more about the disease. Also warlike imagery appears to be helpful. Thus, the outbreak of SARS in 2003 was described as a 'threat'. Illness was an 'enemy' that had to be 'traced'. There

---

[27] Black, 1962, 44. This is the so-called *interaction view of metaphor*, a term introduced by Black 1962, and based on the ideas on metaphor developed by Richards.

[28] See also Lakoff & Turner 1989, 51; Yu 2008; Basson 2006, 34-35.

[29] E.g. Fauconnier & Turner 2003 as well as Kövecses 2010, a book completely built on their conceptual system of metaphors.

even was a special 'incident command post' in the province of Ontario to monitor the development of the disease in the region (Villamil Touriño 2006).

For the understanding of metaphor in ancient religious language only a few aspects from the general discussion on metaphor are really important.

1. The creative power of metaphor, as it is used in religious language, to describe God whom no one has ever seen.

2. The culturally based associations connected to specific religious metaphors.

3. The existence of conceptual metaphors (root metaphors) generating a tree of related metaphors – the beginning of theology.

All further discussions on the mental processes active when people use metaphor or when they read metaphor in fact do not add much to the understanding and interpretation of culturally based religious language.

2.2.2   *Metaphor in Religious Language*

Conceptual metaphors create a fuzzy set of associations between related images and targeted meanings, resulting in overviews of conceptual correspondences, nowadays referred to as *mappings* (Kövecses 2010, 7-10). An example from the biblical world is GOD IS A SHEPHERD. This conceptual metaphor results in the flock as metaphor for the people, the rod and staff of the shepherd as his guidance and care (Ps. 23:4), sheep as metaphor for the elderly people and lambs as the youngsters (Isa. 40:10-11). The green pastures become a metaphor for the fruitful land of Israel (Jer. 23:3; Ezek. 34:14, 18), the wolves trying to get the sheep represent the nation's enemies (Ezek. 34:8).

In the same way concepts like divine speech, words, revelation, can be regarded as belonging to the same domain or mapping. There is no basic difference between religious and other metaphors.[30] However, religious metaphor is used in an especially creative way, for describing objects and ideas for which no literal terms exist.[31] To speak about the 'arm' of God is just as accurate, or inaccurate, as to speak about a 'black hole' in modern astronomy. In both cases the metaphor *hints* at a truth, based on analogy, that will gradually become more clearly defined as it is accepted and further explored by an ever growing circle of initiated. However, the theologian and the astronomer will be humble enough to concede that they will never arrive at a fully adequate description in any particular case. Because of its special capacity to hint at a truth that cannot be described adequately in terms of general human experience, metaphor is the ideal vehicle to talk about God whom 'no one has ever seen.'[32] It has been established that both in Israel and in the surrounding world people were using their metaphors and similes for the divine knowingly.[33]

Since human beings cannot adequately describe God and the divine world, they have to make do with terms borrowed from ordinary human discourse. It is their conviction that the words they use do hint at a reality, but since the approximation is admittedly inaccurate, their faith discourse is replete with metaphors and should for that reason always remain open to interpretation. This is even more true of silences which can have many different meanings in ordinary discourse (cf. Section 2.3 below).

Divine speech and silence are common elements in the Bible and its world. They form a subcategory of the major conceptual

---

[30]See e.g. Kövecses 2010, 26, who lists religion under his thirteen examples of target domains of metaphor.

[31]See e.g. Soskice 1987; Korpel 1990; Stiver 1996; Aaron 2002; Van Hecke 2005. Compare the advice of the 'Languedoc Strangler' in Schmitt's novel *Oscar and the Lady in Pink*, 'Every time you believe in him, he'll exist a bit more. If you keep at it, he'll exist completely', quoted in Section 1.5 above.

[32]John 1:18; cf. 5:37; 6:46; 14:8ff.; 1 Cor. 2:9; 13:12; 1 John 4:12. A philosopher who tried to explain divine speech in a more literal way, without equating it with revelation, is Nicholas Wolterstorff. In our opinion, however, he misses the special quality of metaphor to describe the divine when he demands 'what is *the fact of the matter* to which metaphor points?' (Wolterstorff 1995, 10). See also the critical review by Childs 2005 who rightly stresses that the role of the human biblical witnesses is neglected by Wolterstorff.

[33]Korpel 1990, 82-87.

metaphor or simile[34] GOD IS (LIKE) A HUMAN BEING, and more specifically his discourse belongs to the source domain of *intellectual capacities*, especially *mind and communication*.[35] Therefore divine speech and silence should be interpreted against the background of human discourse. However, time and again the Ancients make it abundantly clear that this is merely a way of speaking, because everything in the realm of the divine is greater or smaller than human beings can imagine, let alone understand. To illustrate this with an example, in many religions of Antiquity the voice of God is represented as thunder which, as a Ugaritic myth states, is not understood by mankind.[36] Yet it is also in the power of a deity to address a person through silence (e.g. 1 Kgs 19:11-13).

Black's interaction theory of metaphor applies here too. By making a mental comparison of God with human beings the latter somehow assumed theomorphic features.[37] Especially kings and

---

[34] On the difficulty to distinguish metaphor and simile see Korpel 1990, 54-58.

[35] On this conceptual group of metaphors see the Chapter on Intellectual Capacities in Korpel, 1990, 147-164.

[36] Cf. De Moor 1987, 10.

[37] *Pace* Lakoff & Turner 1989, 131-133, who erroneously conclude that the interaction view means that the metaphor can be reversed. The point is, that by combining source domain and target domain *associations* of both fields are also combined subconsciously, thus giving God, in the metaphor GOD IS A SHEPHERD, features of a shepherd, but *vice versa* the human shepherd receives divine features in the minds of people acquainted with this biblical metaphor. Consequently, this implicitly means that superhuman qualities were ascribed to shepherds which also applied if the metaphor was applied to other leaders, e.g. kings.

Or let us contemplate the example of 'man was created in the image of God' (Gen. 1:26). Because of this comparison believers must behave as more than just human beings, they are expected to behave as if they were remotely reflecting God's goodness, wisdom, etc. The idea of the philosopher Ludwig Feuerbach (1804-1872), adopted by Sigmund Freud (1856-1939) and later psychoanalytics, that the phrase could be just as easily be reversed ('man created God in his own human image') turns out to be wrong. The interaction view merely suggests the comparison of associations from both the source and the target field. Source and target of the metaphor, however, can *not* simply be exchanged. 'Man is a wolf' evokes the *evilness* of mankind, but hardly its *hairiness*. The conceptual spheres overlap only partially. Compare Davis 2009, 149: 'if we are similar to God *in some ways* then God is similar to us

queens often acquired divine status in the propagandistic court poetry of the ancient world and were sometimes deified after their death.[38] Later on this concept was democratized and all Israelites became favored children of God (Korpel 1996b). A remarkable feature in the priestly creation story of Gen. 1 is the theomorphousness not only of the king but of all mankind. According to this rather late account God created man and women 'in our image' and 'after our likeness'.[39] Because his human creatures are called 'very beautiful' this justifies the assumption that the physical appearance of man reflected the beauty of God himself. In the ancient Near East the ruling principle was that *royal* figures resembled the gods, an idea which was idealized in the reliefs and statues representing the royal family. In the creation story, however, the ruling power is not given to a king but to all humankind (Gen. 1:28). By mentioning this ruling power, the author of the creation story implicitly emphasizes the royal status of humankind, and therefore its beauty and appearance was assumed to resemble that of God. In a world where the divine and human nature were so closely interrelated it was not experienced as abnormal when human beings claimed to speak in the name of God, even if the word of God was mediated by someone else (e.g. Exod. 4:13-16). Or if their prayers remained unanswered, they sought for explanations they knew from the realm of interpersonal relations to explain God's silence.

2.2.3 Religious Language: Conclusion

Although some ignore or dispute the metaphorical character of religious language, the general view is that in fact human beings are unable to speak of God, because his essence is beyond all human imagination. All this means that whatever human beings say about deities, including the messages for which they claim a divine origin, are merely a bleak reflection of a totally different

---

in some ways' (italics ours). But a complete reversal is impossible: 'Wolf is a man' is immediately recognized as nonsense, however 'human' the wolf may seem in the tale of Little Red Riding Hood.

[38] Korpel 2011.

[39] Both words refer to physical appearance. Cf. De Moor 1998a, 115.

reality. This is the axiom of the so-called apophatic or negative theology: the totally different nature of the deity, the transcendence of God which renders any comparison with the human experience inadequate. We can only talk about God by way of negation.

It is sometimes surmised that this negative theology is a construct of modern times. Others seek the roots of the negative theology in the works of Plato (*c.* 428/7-348/7), the Jewish philosopher Philo of Alexandria (*c.* 20 BCE-50), the Neo-Platonist Plotinus (*c.* 205-270) or in some later Christian mystics (cf. Section 1.3). All these views are misconceptions. The total alterity of the divine being was realized much earlier by Egyptian theologians of the New Kingdom, long before the earliest strata of the Hebrew Bible were written.[40] The paradoxical nature of religious language was realized already more than 3000 years ago. The same Egyptian theologians who said that Amun-Re cannot be described in human language or art, who emphasized his total incomparability, hiddenness, unapproachability, nevertheless gave him descriptive names, sang hymns to him, ascribed to him many properties, among them speech, and worshipped him in anthropomorphic and theriomorphic shapes. This is the paradox of faith that inevitably crops up whenever people want to share their worship of a transcendental deity.

This paradox is also present in the Hebrew Bible, for example in Isa. 45,

> [15] However, you are a God who hides himself,
>   O Savior God of Israel!
> [16] They are ashamed and disgraced, all of them;
>   altogether they go in disgrace,
>   the craftsmen with their drawings.
> [17] But Israel is saved by the LORD,
>   a salvation of ages.
> They will not be ashamed and not be disgraced
>   to ages everlasting (Isa. 45:15-17).

Although Second Isaiah rejects the images worshipped by other

---

[40] Hornung 1971; Assmann 1979; 1983; De Moor 1997, 41-64. Cf. Section 6.1.1 below.

nations, this prophet believes that his hidden God manifests himself by delivering his people, just as He had done in the past, especially during the Exodus from Egypt. For this prophet it was not contradictory to believe that his hidden God would act again in a concrete, visible way. And he intones time and again, 'Thus says the LORD ...'. It has been pointed out that Isa. 45:19 ('I have not spoken in hiddenness') is relevant to the interpretation of v. 15: to Israel God has revealed himself in the spoken word (Fornara 2004, 85-87).

The negative theology[41] that denies any possibility of God-talk is often attributed to Friedrich Nietzsche (1844-1900). He preferred silence over natural language (Angier 2006, 121-122), yet he himself too was unable to free himself from inadequate, worn metaphors. Is it really so objectionable to talk about the divine in human language? Charles Wackenheim nicely sums up our predicament,

> In the end everything which human beings have ever said on the subject of or in the name of God – including analogical and metaphorical language – is expressed within the limits of human discourse. To say that 'only God can really talk about God' is a figure of style, because no word of God reaches us without the mediation of a human discourse or a human word.[42]

Early on it was realized that there is simply no other possibility. One of the earliest proponents of the so-called accommodation theory – God accommodates himself to what human beings can understand – was Ephrem the Syrian (*c.* 306-373). In a poem the refrain of which runs 'Blessed is He who has appeared to our human race under so many metaphors', he continues,

> We should realize that, had He not put on the names of such things, it would not have been possible for Him to speak with us humans. By means of what belongs to us did He draw close to us: He clothed Himself in our language, so that He might clothe us in His mode of life.[43]

---

[41] For some succinct criticism see Wackenheim 2002, 93-97.
[42] Our translation. Original French text: Wackenheim 2002, 29.
[43] Translation Brock & Kiraz 2006, 19.

We hope to demonstrate in this book that if we accept this line of thinking about divine speech, we will also be in a better position to understand divine silence. However, faith is not merely some highly personal experience. Faith must be shared to find confirmation in the community of faith. It is not one face that dimly reflects divinity, in the community of faith we discover that many more have seen similar glimpses of the Eternal. The Letter to the Hebrews defines faith as 'the assurance of things hoped for, the conviction of things not seen' (Heb. 11:1), but continues immediately with 'for therein the ancients received (God's) attestation' (Heb. 11:2, cf. 11:4, 5, 39). It is a long line of pious people, a 'cloud of witnesses' (Heb. 12:1), that gives the faithful the assurance that there is truth to be found in the imperfect images we perceive. As Pope Benedict XVI wrote in his Encyclical Letter *Spe Salvi*,

> Faith is not merely a personal reaching out towards things to come that are still totally absent: it gives us something. It gives us even now something of the reality we are waiting for, and this present reality constitutes for us a 'proof' of the things that are still unseen. Faith draws the future into the present, so that it is no longer simply a 'not yet'. The fact that this future exists changes the present; the present is touched by the future reality, and thus the things of the future spill over into those of the present and those of the present into those of the future.[44]

2.3 Silence Presupposes Speech

2.3.1 *Introduction*

Silence cannot exist without sound. But it would be too simple to describe silence merely negatively as 'the absence of sound'. If we talk about the calm before the storm we describe a natural

---

[44] *Spe Salvi*, § 7, authorized English translation. Original Latin text: 'Fides non est solum personalis inclinatio ad ea quae ventura sunt sed adhuc omnino absunt; ipsa nobis quiddam largitur. Nobis iam nunc tribuit aliquid realitatis exspectatae, et haec praesens realitas 'probationem' quandam nobis constituit rerum quae nondum conspiciuntur. Ipsa attrahit futurum intra tempus praesens, eo ut hoc extremum tempus non sit amplius solum illud 'nondum'. Existentia huius futuri mutat praesens; praesens futura realitate attingitur, et ita res futurae in praesentes vertuntur et praesentes in futuras.'

phenomenon which we know will be broken soon by a lot of noise. But this kind of silence is not a break of communication. Nobody is sending a signal. If all the birds in our garden suddenly fall silent we start looking for a raptor or cat. Yet this bird silence is more than the calm before the storm. It is a rupture of the normal multi-sided communication between birds that serves as a warning.

In human communication silence often means much more than the absence of sound.[45] Christoph Wulf describes the absence of speech as follows,

> Being silent forms the horizon before which all talk happens. It permeates and encloses the process of speaking. The melody of speech consists in words and pauses. Silence has its place and time in the pauses between words and phrases in which thoughts are formed. For the listener it is a necessary preliminary to the decoding of the semantic and metaphorical dimension of speech. Every speaker uses not only words, but also non-words, the pauses, the places and moments of being silent. Silence is a constituent of all interaction. A person speaking causes others to be silent, making them his audience and determining their silence by his speech. Their listening is part of the talking and therefore also of the understanding. The hearers help the speaker to create and develop his thoughts.[46]

It is evident, however, that an unnaturally long silence on the part of a speaker causes uneasiness among the hearers. Does he feel unwell? Has he lost the thread of his speech? Does it suddenly strike him that what he wanted to say is utter nonsense? Has he lost heart seeing the scowls on the faces of his audience?

Also the shortening or total lack of pauses can have an alienating effect.[47] When we hear a so-called 'rapper' delivering his text, the lack of natural pauses between words contributes to the feeling of uneasiness many of us will experience.

---

[45] Jaworski 1997, 3, proposes to view silence as a metaphor for communication, but this seems overextending the common understanding of the term.

[46] Our translation. Original German: Wulf 1992, 7. See also Barrado 1997, 7-8; Van Dijk 2006, 31-35.

[47] Cf. Dorfles 1992, 24.

So there are pauses which by our long training as listeners we interpret as 'normal' and silences which are experienced as abnormal and call for an urgent resumption of normal oral communication.

The use of silence in spoken language is an unspoken invitation to interpretation.[48] The hearer is forced to formulate a hypothesis about its meaning. There are many kinds of eloquent silence – silence expressing awe, sorrow, despair, ignorance, embarrassment, indignation, contentment.[49] It depends on the situation how we interpret such silences.

2.3.2 *Spaces Marking Rhetorical Silences*

Of course it might be objected that in the case of the Bible we are severely handicapped because we cannot hear Moses or any other person from biblical times speaking anymore. However, to some extent this also applies to modern written or printed texts. We use all kinds of graphical substitutes for emphasis or silence. We hardly realize it anymore, but layout is a mighty means to steer our interpretation of texts. Without underlining, boldface, italics and all kinds of punctuation it would be hard for us to understand what the writer intended. In written texts the blanks between words, blanks between lines, extra empty space at the end of verselines, indentation to mark off new paragraphs are substitutes for silence (Fierro Bardají 1992). Few people realize that many of these clever tricks were already used in some of the oldest alphabetic texts we have, for example the clay tablets of Ugarit[50] dating from around 1200 BCE.[51]

It has long been known that horizontal lines on Babylonian and Ugaritic clay tablets were used to demarcate logical sec-

---

[48] Cf. Muers 2001, 90: 'The keeping of silence is a communicative action the content of which is underdetermined.' (with references).

[49] For fuller lists of this kind and evaluation of their importance in cultural and interpersonal relations see Wulf 1992; Jaworski 1993; Jaworski 1997; Ephratt 2007.

[50] A Canaanite city on the coast of modern Syria.

[51] We thank Professor Wayne T. Pitard for his permission to check some Ugaritic passages in the InscriptiFact database.

tions in literary texts.[52] For us it is confusing that the ancient scribes used this kind of ruling for various purposes, e.g. to demarcate strophes *and* paragraphs.[53] Moreover, duplicate copies of the same text demonstrate that the scribes inserted these horizontal lines inconsistently, omitting them at will.[54] Where they employed them, however, it seems likely that they often wanted to mark a silence, for example when a priest had to establish if a sacrificial victim was without blemish. Because if it was not, there was no need to recite the rest of the text anymore.[55]

It is useful to observe that Ugaritic tablets divided into sections by rulings are also divided by empty spaces because the last line of each section is often left blank. It is our contention that in Ugaritic literary texts blanks at the end of lines often fulfill the function to mark a pause when the text was recited. A few examples may illustrate this statement.

When Kotharu[56] urges Ba'lu[57] to slay his opponent Yammu[58] and to reestablish his kingship, wide spaces after the crucial lines (KTU 1.2:IV.9-10) mark this exciting turn of the story. A moment of tension also occurs when it is narrated that Ba'lu is afraid of the god of death Môtu. Will he give in to the latter's demand to surrender? Indeed there is a blank at the beginning of Ba'lu's unintroduced reply just after KTU 1.5:II.7 where the narrator relates that Ba'lu was afraid of Môtu. Again there are blanks after line 9 and line 12 when Ba'lu actually announces his surrender in a message to Môtu: 'I am your slave, yes, yours for ever!'

Several times wider spacing seems to mark the introduction of direct speech. However, a line where it is evident that no switch of speaker is involved, but a rhetorical effect is intended is the blank at the end of KTU 1.5:I.25. Here the space indicates a dramatic silence. Môtu has just observed that Ba'lu was celebrating the completion of his new palace with all the other gods, happily

---

[52] Cf. Korpel 2000; 2005a; Mabie 2004.
[53] Korpel 2000, 40-3.
[54] Korpel 2005a, 148.
[55] Korpel 2005a, 146.
[56] The technician among the gods of Ugarit.
[57] Weather-god. His name is actually the same as that of the biblical Baal.
[58] Sea-god.

dining and wining, when he lets fall a meaningfull silence and continues, 'but I was forgotten, O Baʿlu!'.

The use of spaces to divide paragraphs is also attested in other Northwest Semitic inscriptions, as has been demonstrated by Ingo Kottsieper (Kottsieper 2003). In the Phoenician Karatepe inscriptions (c. 720 BCE), for example, sense units are clearly marked by spaces. Mostly this happens at the end of lines, as in Ugarit, but sometimes also in the middle of lines of writing, what in the Hebrew tradition would be called a Setumah (closed section). Also in the Aḥiqar papyri from Elephantine and in some Punic texts spaces are used to delimit paragraphs.

If we now look at the Hebrew evidence, it appears that several of the earliest manuscripts from the Judean Desert exhibit many more spaces than the later Masoretic manuscripts. Emanuel Tov and Eugene Ulrich have called such deviating spacing 'impressionistic'. Is it? Such a term seems to presuppose that there existed some kind of standard from which imaginative scribes deviated at will. It is true that the rabbis have strived after uniformity with regard to spacing, but in reality the use of spaces remained inconsistent up till the late Middle Ages.

In 2007 we described spacing in the Hebrew manuscript 80 of the French National Library (De Moor & Korpel 2007). This codex contains the Prophets and Writings. Unfortunately it is undated, but it is a rare and hitherto unnoticed example of a so-called Tibero-*Palestinian* manuscript. The spacing in the Paris codex deviates in many instances from the exemplary Tiberian manuscripts and we were able to establish that its division of the text often concurs with pre-Tiberian traditions. This counsels against dismissing such spacing too soon as 'impressionistic'.

In this book we will give many examples where blank spaces in the Hebrew tradition evidently mark rhetorical silences. Silences were not only described in words, they were also indicated by blank spaces in the text (cf. Index of Subjects: space).

2.4 The Silent God: The Biblical Roots

Because for most Jews and Christians the roots of the faith in a speaking or non-speaking God lay in the Bible, and consequently those who denounced their belief often referred to the same source, it is sensible to start with a re-examination of the biblical data on the silence of God. A relatively small number of scholarly studies deals with the concept of silence in the Bible and discusses a number of passages in which God is said to be silent.[59] However, none of these studies places the biblical data in the context of its own world. Was there a difference in the way other ancient Near Eastern peoples conceptualized divine speech or its absence? Moreover, only Barrado has treated the subject of the silence of God in connection with human silence, but his treatment was rather superficial and he did not draw the consequences of dealing with divine silence as an anthropomorphic concept.

It can be stated right away that it is understandable that the theme has not been discussed very often in the exegetical literature. In comparison with the thousands of places where the Bible describes divine speech the number of passages where it deals explicitly with divine silence is dwindling.[60] However, in view of its prominent place in modern drama and thought it is certainly worthwhile to reexamine the biblical data and confront them with the skepticism of our own era. Was it justified to accuse God of unwarranted silence in view of what people in biblical times thought about the reasons why their deities fell silent?

The problem we are dealing with concerns biblical theology[61] as a whole. It is for this reason that we will refer to the 'Old' Testament as the Hebrew Bible, even though we will occasionally also pay attention to the New Testament and some relevant Judaic sources.

2.5 The Silent God: The Biblical World

Since the Bible originated in the ancient Near Eastern world, it is useful to have a look at statements about human and divine

---

[59] Neher 1970; Barrado 1997; Dietrich 2004. For the Psalms, Gillmayr-Bucher 2003; Spieckermann 2004.

[60] See above, Section 1.6.2.

[61] We understand 'biblical theology' as comprising the main theological views expressed in the biblical canon which, however, cannot be understood without recourse to the world in which it originated, and so has a religion-historical aspect too.

silence in documents from Antiquity. So we start every chapter with a brief review of written material from the ancient Near East and occasionally Greece. We hope to demonstrate that also in the world around ancient Israel there was an acute awareness that in times of crisis, when the old paradigms did not work anymore, it was imperative to formulate fresh answers to the challenges of the moment (Lanczkowski 1955). Since trust in divine guidance was still quite normal in those days, it was felt as particularly grievous when the gods did not seem willing to speak or act anymore in such situations of distress.

We intend to refer to quite a number of passages in the literature of the Ancients where this silence on the part of deities occurs. The anthropomorphic nature of human utterances about the divine world[62] induced us to also study a number of situations in which human beings kept silent among themselves (Chapter 3). Since we want to study the phenomenon of divine silence, we first discuss how people tried to communicate with their deities (Chapter 4) and next how deities were supposed to communicate with man (Chapter 5). Finally, Chapter 6 will describe the situations in which deities were said to be silent. In an Epilogue (Chapter 7) we try to take stock of the consequences of our findings.

2.6 Why This Approach?

The prerequisites formulated above may seem to imply a rather laborious approach to our subject. Why do we deem this necessary? First of all because many readers will have an understandably limited knowledge about the ancient world and many of them will still cherish the idea that Israel was a unique people chosen by God and living in splendid isolation in the land that God had promised to Abraham. Some passages in the Bible itself certainly suggest this view (e.g. Gen. 12:1-9; Num. 23:9). To many believers who accept the biblical testimony all this is true and will be of lasting value.

However, as in modern times, many other nations of Antiquity regarded themselves as the unique and privileged favorites of their

---
[62] Cf. Section 2.2.

deities. Not only Israel, but also other nations regarded their territory as an inalienable inheritance from their gods. Not only the God of Israel revealed himself in spoken and written language, the same was said of other deities. Everywhere in the ancient world people expected their deities to speak or write words of salvation in reply to their prayers. Of course some freethinkers of the past few centuries have long suspected all this, but only fairly recently these new insights that have come to light as a result of the work of archaeologists and orientalists can be proved convincingly. The realization of this fact may help to put the modern discussion about the silence of God in proper perspective. We hope that our broad approach will clarify the relationship between the human and the divine factor in the transmission of speech and silence as recorded in ancient sources, including the Bible.

As we have seen, discussions about the silence of God tend to become heated as soon as the eternal validity of what the LORD has spoken in the distant past seems to have become obsolete in our age. What we hope to achieve with this book is to demonstrate that it is false to impose dogmatic absolutism on divine speech or silence that was described millennia ago by saintly people living in totally different circumstances. We are convinced that the inevitability of picking out what is still enormously valuable and the reinterpretation of what cannot be accepted unconditionally anymore in the light of the progress of science may prove to be extremely helpful to induce moderation in these discussions that are bound to go on as long as people take divine messages or silence seriously.

CHAPTER THREE

SILENCE BETWEEN HUMANS IN ANTIQUITY

3.1 Introduction

The metaphorical nature of descriptions of deities and the divine world implies that if people state, or have once stated, that God keeps silent, we have always to compare this with what they say about silence on the part of human beings.

In the past decennia several studies have been devoted to the subject of silence between human beings, the function of silence in human discourse or in literature.[1] Silence appears to be an indispensable, but often underestimated element in human communication. Silence can be an instrument to exercise power (Achino-Loeb 2006), but mostly it points to a certain aporia on the part of the speaker or the hearer. It depends on the context or situation how we interpret such silences. In written texts all kinds of graphical substitutes for silence are used, mostly blank spaces (Van Dijk 2006). It is little known that this use of blanks is already attested in clay tablets from the Canaanite city of Ugarit, dating from the beginning of the twelfth century BCE.[2] Layout is one of the earliest means to steer the interpretation of texts. In music rests are necessary to make a piece of music performable (Beeman 2006).

Since we want to study the phenomenon of divine silence in Antiquity it is warranted to concentrate on a few passages in ancient texts dealing with silence between human beings. What reasons for silence did people in the Bible and its world have?

3.2 Reasons for Silence between Humans

3.2.1 *Silence Because of Offenses*

Keeping silent about one's involvement in morally dubious activities is of all times. Often such silences are widely known ('the silent majority'), but nobody has the courage to break them (several contributions in Kamper & Wulf 1992).

---

[1] E.g. Kane 1984; Kamper & Wulf 1992; Jaworski 1993; 1997; Loevlie 2003; Muers 2004, 4-10; Ephratt 2007; Bruneau 2009.

[2] Cf. Sections 2.3.2 and 2.3.3.

3.2.1.1 Silence Because of Offenses in the Ancient Near East

As in our own times, there was always a natural inclination to conceal offenses in Antiquity. A Sumerian saying runs, 'He keeps silent like an ox fleeing from the threshing floor', meaning 'a slave who fled from work',[3] a serious offense at that time. Keeping silent about stealing is wrong according to several Babylonian sources.[4] A Hittite goldsmith asks a colleague to keep silent about a theft of gold.[5] Priests who have changed the ancient rites arbitrarily order their subjects to remain silent about the matter.[6] Adultery was considered a grave sin in all civilizations of the ancient Near East.[7] In view of the severe penalties the partners risked they tried to keep their affair secret.[8]

There were occasions when keeping one's mouth was considered morally wrong. In the Egyptian *Wisdom of Merikare* (*c.* 2000 BCE) the king is admonished 'He who is silent toward violence diminishes the offerings'.[9] A king should not let theft pass over in silence.[10] In the Demotic Papyrus Insinger it is stated, 'Do not let yourself be called "idiot" because of silence when it is time to speak.'[11]

In the Egyptian *Complaint of the Eloquent Peasant* a bureaucrat is accused of not being able to persuade a wronged humble man who hitherto has kept silent to speak up.[12]

A king should not remain silent when his country is in danger,[13] or when his subjects have lodged a well-grounded complaint.[14] A king's dilemma was that other speakers on behalf of

---

[3] Alster 1997, vol. 1, 62-63; vol. 2. 369.
[4] CAD (Š) 1, 490-491.
[5] Hofner, CoS, vol. 3, 58.
[6] Cole & Machinist 1998, No. 134, r. 16*.
[7] Cf. Marsman 2003, 168-175. For Greece see Wagner-Hasel 2010.
[8] E.g. Homer, Odyssey, XV.430; XXII.445.
[9] Cf. Lichtheim, CoS, vol. 1, 65. See also Kammerzell & Sternberg, TUAT, Bd. 2, 104.
[10] Parpola 1993, No. 107, r.e. 12-13.
[11] Lichtheim 1980, 187; Thissen, TUAT, Bd. 3, 283.
[12] Brunner 1988, 365, B I, 285-288. Cf. Lanczkowski 1955, 190.
[13] Cf. Kaplony-Heckel, TUAT, Bd. 1, 561; Lichtheim, CoS, vol. 2, 43.
[14] Lambert 1960, 112-113, line 16, as rendered by Von Soden, TUAT, Bd. 3, 172. See also Parpola 1987, No. 29, r. 14.

the gods might encourage him to remain silent because his god would no doubt deliver him.[15] Of course their subjects were not inclined to accept such a passive attitude. An officer who is holding the city of Babylon for the Assyrian king writes to his master,

> Now, as the prefect has left Bit-Dakuri, the whole of Babylon lives in fear, saying, 'We have been handed over to the dogs.' Why is my lord silent, while the whole of Babylon (pleadingly) raises its hands towards my lord?
>
> ...
>
> Why does my lord remain silent, while Babylon is being destroyed? Šamaš[16] and Marduk[17] have installed you for intercession in Assyria. Persuade the king to come here and to exempt Babylon for Marduk, and (make) your name everlasting in Esaggil and Ezida![18]

When rebellious enemies threaten to overthrow Egyptian civilization this state of anarchy is experienced as a return to primordial chaos[19] and under such circumstances it would be wrong to remain silent,[20] even though the one who speaks up may well be silenced quickly.[21]

According to the Ugaritic *Legend of Aqhatu* it was a son's duty to silence people who slandered his father.[22] As in modern usage, 'to silence' a person might be equivalent to killing him. The Ugaritic goddess ʿAnatu, for example, silences (destroys) various monsters as well as human beings.[23]

An Old Babylonian diviner assures his master king Zimrilim that he will not keep secret any oracular inquiry about an upcoming rebellion (Lenzi 2008, 43). A servant of the Hittite king

---

[15] Parpola 1997, No. 2, iii, 11'.

[16] Sun god.

[17] The most important god of Babylon.

[18] Dietrich 2003, No. 21, r. 2-6, 11-16. Esaggil and Ezida were temples in Babylon.

[19] Barta 1971, 37; Lichtheim 1973, 141; Foster 2001, 76-84. See also below Section 6.1.1.

[20] Barta 1971, 37; Lichtheim 1973, 140-141; Shupak, CoS, vol. 1, 106, with n.25; 108.

[21] Barta 1971, 42; Lichtheim 1973, 142; Shupak, CoS, vol. 1, 108.

[22] KTU 1.17:I.28-29 par., cf. Wyatt 1998, 257-258. For comparable usage in Akkadian, see CAD (S), 75.

[23] KTU 1.3.II.8, 44.

should not cloak himself in silence about anything that might endanger his master.[24] The Assyrian king Esarhaddon (681-669 BCE) forces his vassals to swear that they will not keep secret any inappropriate talk about or conspiracy against his successor Assurbanipal (Watanabe 1987, *passim*). In the Assyrian empire royal servants should not keep silent about offenses.[25]

3.2.1.2   Silence Because of Offenses in the Bible

Whereas most people, like Adam (cf. Gen. 3:8-10), are inclined to keep their offenses secret because they fear punishment or scorn from others, Job declares that he has nothing to hide (Job 31:33-34).[26]

According to Lev. 5:1 and Prov. 29:24 it was a sin to keep silent about an offense one had witnessed.[27] The narrator of Judg. 17–18 clearly disapproves of the behavior of a priest who agrees to keep quiet about the theft of cultic paraphernalia in order to get a better job (Judg. 18:19).[28] King Saul is not answered by his subjects because they disapprove of his rash vow (1 Sam. 14:39, cf. v. 24). Four lepers who found the camp of the Aramaeans deserted initially kept their discovery secret and started to loot. Eventually, however, they came to see the errors of their ways and decided to break their silence because they were afraid to be punished (2 Kgs 7:9).

Kings should not remain silent when parts of their country were occupied by enemies (1 Kgs 22:3). Modern translations often render the verbal form here as 'we do nothing', but in view of the Egyptian parallel referred to above it is better to maintain the literal interpretation.[29] Apparently the king of Israel implies that they should have called up their troops earlier. The same motif is present in 2 Sam. 2:26 where Abner asks David, 'How long will it

---

[24] Cf. Von Schuler, TUAT, Bd. 1, 125.

[25] Parpola 1987, No. 244, r. 13; Lanfranchi & Parpola 1990, No. 149, r. 5.

[26] Cf. Clines 2006, 1029-1030.

[27] See Milgrom 1991, 293-294 for further parallels.

[28] According to Judg. 18:20 the heart of the Levite gladdens at the request of the Danites to become their priest. Cf. Younger 2002, 342; Phillips 2004, 272.

[29] Cf. Cogan 2001, 489.

be before you say to the people to turn from the pursuit of their brethren?'

According to Deut. 3:23-28 Moses prays that he may be allowed to see the promised land at the other side of the river Jordan. God refuses because of sins of the people and orders Moses not to bring up the matter anymore (v. 26). This account differs in essential points from the presentation of the facts in Exod. 17:1-7 and Num. 20:2-13, the latter making Moses himself the culprit.

Just as elsewhere in the ancient world it was a king's task to speak up for the poor and oppressed who themselves lack the courage to speak (Prov. 31:8-9). The Khirbet Qeiyafa inscription seems to prove that this was a duty of a king already in the tenth century BCE.[30]

However, an offense like rape was considered an offense about which it was better to keep silent because the honor of the family was at stake. Apparently this was more important than the rights of the violated girl. When Jacob's daughter Dinah had been violated and Jacob heard about it, he said nothing until Dinah's brothers came back (Gen. 34:5). When Amnon overpowered his half-sister Tamar, her brother Absalom asks her to keep silent about what happened. The reason Absalom gives for this request is the circumstance that Amnon is Tamar's (half-)brother (2 Sam. 13:20). Also Absalom himself does not speak to Amnon anymore (2 Sam. 13:22). In both cases it must be assumed that the concealing of the crime was in the interest of the family until a brother or brothers had taken revenge.[31]

Although they correctly suspected that Jeremiah had told them a lie which had been dictated to him by king Zedekiah, the princes went away silently because they had no proof (Jer. 38:24-27).[32] Their silence is graphically expressed by a space (Petuchah) following v. 27.

---

[30] http://qeiyafa.huji.ac.il/ostracon2.asp; Puech 2010; Becking & Sanders 2010.

[31] Westermann 1981, 655. See further Marsman 2003, 68, 81, 248-252, 280, 460, 470, 714, 731, and on the relations between the two stories, De Hoop 1999, 518-519.

[32] Cf. Keown 1995, 225; McKane 1996, 966-967.

It was seen as wrong not to confess sins to the LORD. Initially the supplicant of Ps. 32 kept silent about his sins, but his conscience started to plague him (v. 3), even though nobody but the LORD seems to have known about his offense. Day and night God's hand was heavy upon him (v. 4a) and his tongue[33] became parched as by the heat of summer (v. 4b) so that eventually he might be unable to speak at all. After v. 4 a *Selah* follows, indicating a pause in reading, as if the supplicant hesitates whether or not to break his self-imposed silence. Then he continues,

> My sin I will make known to you,
>   and my transgression I do not cover up.
> I thought: 'I must confess my transgressions to the LORD!'
> And you forgave my sinful transgression (Ps. 32:5).

Perhaps the supplicant spoke his confession and received absolution from a priest or a prophet. But it is just as well possible that it was a silent exchange with his God during which the inner conviction grew in his heart that God had forgiven him.[34]

3.2.2 *Silence Because of Awe or Fear*

3.2.2.1 Silence Because of Awe or Fear in the Ancient Near East

A hunter who is faced with the wild, hairy appearance of Enkidu[35] grows silent for fear (Gilg. Ep. I.118).[36]

Silencing rebels and quelling turmoil was expected of kings.[37] Enemies of the Assyrian king Sargon II (722-705 BCE) are so impressed by his terror-inspiring eighth campaign that 'stillness spread over them, they became as the dead'.[38]

---

[33] For this reading cf. Craigie 1983, 264; Hossfeld & Zenger 1993, 202.

[34] See our treatment of Psalms 13 and 28, Section 6.2.2.2.

[35] Who grew up in the wild among the gazelles and later on became the friend of the Mesopotamian hero Gilgamesh.

[36] George 2003, vol. 1, 544-545. See also I.156, 546-547.

[37] Sumerian examples: Römer, TUAT, Bd. 2, 685; CAD (Š) 1, 491. Egyptian example, Foster 2001, 84.

[38] CAD (Š), I, 108a; see also Parpola 1987, No. 32, 14; Livingstone 1989, No. 2, 26-27; Dietrich 2003, No. 22, 17-18.

Rebellion might start already at a young age and earned the disobedient child a reprimand or even a beating.[39] Fear for corporal chastisement must induce a Sumerian schoolboy to keep silent.[40] That boys and girls were not always treated equally in this respect is suggested by a Sumerian proverb,

> A chattering girl is silenced by her mother.
> A chattering boy is not silenced by his mother.[41]

Another early example of silence because of fear is described in the tale of the Egyptian Sinuhe (20th century BCE) who upon his return home does not dare to speak to the Pharaoh for fear that he might yet be punished because of his desertion.[42] In *The Prophecy of Neferty*, from about the same period, people silently hand over their possessions to violent shouting barbarians (Foster 2001, 82).

The ancient Egyptians indicated silence iconographically by a hand or fist close to the mouth.[43] Covering the face with both hands as a gesture expressing horror is also attested in Egypt (Dominicus 1994, 68, 70). Because in this attitude speaking is difficult, we may assume that it is a graphical illustration of silence (cf. Brunner-Traut 1979, 201).

For fear that politically sensitive information might leak out kings swore their servants to secrecy. Shortly before the total collapse of the city of Ugarit a scribe warns another important officer at the court not to divulge the fact that the queen has left the country.[44] To prevent sacrilege scholars like scribes and diviners were obliged to keep their knowledge secret. Of course others tried to obtain that information by spying, bribing or stealing (Lenzi 2008).

---

[39] De Moor 2003.
[40] Römer, TUAT, Bd. 3, 71.
[41] Translation Alster 1997, vol. 1, 37 (1.185).
[42] Cf. Lichtheim 1975, 232; CoS, vol. 1, 81-82.
[43] Brunner-Traut 1977, 580. The gesture of putting a hand or a finger over the lips remained a universal symbol of silence up to our own days (Mancini 2008). See also Section 3.2.3.1 below.
[44] Pardee, CoS, vol. 3. 102-103; Bordreuil & Pardee 2010, 4-6.

3.2.2.2 Silence Because of Awe or Fear in the Bible

For fear of Joseph who had become vice-roy of Egypt his brothers did not dare to respond to his admission that he was indeed their brother (Gen. 45:3).

The fear of the Canaanites for the victorious Israelites was so great that no one dared to snarl[45] at them.

When prince Ishbosheth asks the general Abner why he has taken one of the wives of his father, Abner becomes very angry and gives a rude answer which does not satisfy Ishbosheth in the least. He, however, is so frightened by the general's brutal behavior that he does not dare to retort (2 Sam. 3:11). Again this silence is expressed graphically (Setumah).

After the battle in which the rebellious prince Absalom has been killed, the people requested the comeback of king David from the elders of Judah.[46] The latter, however, hesitated because they had anointed Absalom as their new king, even though David, the legitimate king, was still alive. Therefore they feared his wrath and kept silent (2 Sam. 19:11 [10]). A space (Setumah) expresses their silence graphically.

When both the prophets of Bethel and Gilgal independently ask the prophet Elisha whether he knows that Eliah will be taken away from him he hastily confirms that he knows and twice asks them to keep silent (2 Kgs 2:3-5). Normally his confirmation would have prompted howling and laments. Possibly Elisha wanted to prevent this. But it may also be that Elisha himself dreaded what was about to happen and did not want to talk about it.

Fearing the magic potential of the spoken word people often tried to silence prophets who announced doom (e.g. Isa. 30:10; Jer. 27–28; Mic. 2:6).

In Isa. 10:14 the Assyrian king is bragging that his awesome military exploits silenced all nations he subjected,

> there was none that moved a wing,
> or opened the mouth, or chirped.

---

[45] Lit. 'sharpen the tongue'.
[46] 2 Sam. 19:10[9]. Cf. 2 Sam. 19:12.

Kings will shut their mouths when they see the rehabilitation of the suffering Servant of the LORD (Isa. 52:15).

When Lady Zion[47] hears the noise of approaching armies her heart sinks and she cannot remain silent anymore (Jer. 4:19). Until then she had awaited her fate in anxious silence.

Silence because of fear could also be expressed not in words, but by blank spaces. In order to denounce David's adultery with Bathsheba the prophet Nathan tells David his well-known parable about a rich man who wrongfully took the only lamb of a poor man (2 Sam. 12:1-4). After vv. 5-6, with David's angry threat to execute this rich man, the venerable Aleppo Codex lets fall a first silence by means of a blank space to indicate that the audience realizes that David has just condemned himself. Then after Nathan's reply 'You are that man!' a second space underlines this dramatic turn in the story. These blanks are not merely the result of scribal caprice, because several other Hebrew and Greek witnesses support them.

Sometimes silence is expressed both in words and by a blank space. Initially Esther fears to address the Persian king because if she went to the king uninvited she risked to be killed (Est. 4:11-14). In Est. 7:4 she explains to the king that she would have kept silent if she and her people had been sold as slaves, thus indicating that it had taken her a lot to overcome her fear. There is a space (Setumah) after this verse, graphically expressing the tense silence that falls after her speech before the king answers.

3.2.3 *Silence Because of Forbearance or Prudence*

3.2.3.1 Silence Because of Forbearance or Prudence in the Ancient Near East

Silence on the part of the hearer may also signify respectful attention, so that the same Babylonian verb may also be rendered as 'to heed, listen'.[48] In Egypt putting the hand on the mouth was a gesture expressing the intention to maintain a respectful

---

[47]For the identity of the speaker see Korpel 2009b.
[48]CAD (Q), 73b-75b.

silence.[49] An Assyrian king is admonished to keep silent as a sign that he trusts his goddess.[50]

In many situations silence was deemed preferable to rash talking. Modern sayings like 'speech is silver, but silence is gold' and 'a still tongue makes a wise head' represent the kind of popular wisdom that is timeless and is also frequently found in ancient oriental wisdom literature.[51]

Raising your voice unnecessarily was seen as a lack of humility,

> I have trodden the square of my city unobtrusively,
> My voice was not raised, my speech was kept low.[52]

Apparently the choice between speaking up and remaining silent was often as difficult as it is now. The Neo-Babylonian version of a *Dialogue of Pessimism* suggests that one's choice does not really matter.[53] Eloquent silence under all circumstances is counseled in Old Egyptian wisdom literature,

> If you meet a disputant in action,
> A powerful man, superior to you,
> Fold your arms, bend your back,
> To flout him will not make him agree with you.
> Make little of the evil speech
> By not opposing him while he's in action;
> He will be called an ignoramus,
> Your self-control will match his pile (of words).
>
> If you meet a disputant in action
> Who is your equal, on your level,
> You will make your worth exceed his by silence,
> While he is speaking evilly,
> There will be much talk by the hearers,

---

[49] Couroyer 1960, 204-209; Dominicus 1994, 19-21. See also Section 3.2.2.1.
[50] Nissinen 2003, 115.
[51] Lanczkowski 1955; Brunner-Traut 1979; Hornung & Keel 1979, 173-216; Assmann 1984; Englund 1987; Brunner 1988, 222:8; 228:175; Assmann 1990, 259, 268-269; TUAT, Bd. 2, 873, 878, 883; Shlomit-Groll 1990; Shupak 1993, Ch. 4; Alster 1997, vol. 1, 23 (1.96); Frandsen 1998; Shirun-Grumach, TUAT, Bd. 3, 223-224, 226, 229-230, 234; Lichtheim, CoS, vol. 1, 117.
[52] *Babylonian Theodicy*, 291-292, translation Lambert 1960, 89.
[53] Lambert 1960, 146-147, lines 2'-6'.

Your name will be good in the mind of the magistrates.

> If you meet a disputant in action,
> A poor man, not your equal,
> Do not attack him because he is weak,
> Let him alone, he will confute himself.
> Do not answer him to relieve your heart,
> Do not vent yourself against your opponent,
> Wretched is he who injures a poor man,
> One will wish to do what you desire,
> You will beat him through the magistrates' reproof.[54]

In many situations the Egyptian sages counseled silence rather than speaking (Assmann 1984). Even when provoked by an older man, a younger one should not resort to violence, but should silently accept his scolding and beating,

> Let him beat you while your hand is on your chest,
> Let him revile you while you are silent;
> If next day you come before him,
> He will give you food in plenty.[55]

And from the Papyrus Insinger,

> He who is silent under wrong is one who escapes from harm.[56]

The powerless poor did not have any other option than to bear their lot in silence. 'The poor are the silent ones of the country' is a Sumerian proverb.[57] In the New Kingdom of Egypt it became fashionable for the upper classes to represent themselves as humble and poor, but pious people. Keeping your silence was seen as an expression of pious trust in the deity and in the ideals of a society based on solidarity and altruism (Assmann 1990, 259, 268-269).

Obviously such counsel could easily be misused to maintain the *status quo* in an authoritarian society. A righteous Babylonian sufferer laments about his opponents,

---

[54] *Instruction of Ptahhotep*, §§ 2-4, translation Lichtheim 1976, 63-64. See also §§ 9 and 24.
[55] Translation Lichtheim 1976, 161.
[56] Translation Lichtheim 1976, 161.
[57] Alster 1997, vol. 1, 51 [2.32].

>   My eloquent mouth they checked, as with reins,
>   My lips, which used to discourse, became those of a deaf man.
>   My resounding call struck dumb ...[58]

There could be still other reasons to keep quiet. According to the Ugaritic Legend of king Kirtu he and his army stayed quiet during the first seven days of their siege of the city where his bride dwelt, probably because it was deemed prudent not to frighten Kirtu's future father-in-law by the intimidating noises that normally accompanied an attack.[59]

Later on, when he is mortally ill, Kirtu commands his son not to weep for him and not yet to tell his sister of his grave condition lest she would burst into tears.[60]

3.2.3.2 Silence Because of Forbearance or Prudence in the Bible

According to Num. 30, probably a collection of late prescriptions, a wife's vow could be annulled by her husband and a daughter's vow by her father. However, if the man under whose authority the woman stood did not protest, but kept silent, her vow had to be honored.[61] Because failure to honor a vow provoked the anger of the deity and could have terrible consequences, the silence of the father or husband may be interpreted as an act of piety and prudence.

By definition spying is a secret business and for that reason many scholars want to delete the adverb 'secretly' in Josh. 2:1. However, it occurs more often that something circumstantial is added at the end of a Hebrew phrase, as a kind of afterthought. The secrecy has to do with the sending: 'Joshua son of Nun secretly sent two spies from Shittim' (JPS). Apparently he did not talk about the mission with others to prevent treason.

Prompted by his uncle to tell him about his visit to Samuel Saul relates the finding of his donkeys, but modestly keeps silent

---

[58] Translation Foster, CoS, vol. 1, 487. See also Von Soden, TUAT, Bd. 3, 118.
[59] KTU 1.14:III.10 (par.). Cf. De Moor 1987, 196; Wyatt 1998, 194, and for the noise e.g. Josh. 6:5, 16, 20; 7:19-22.
[60] KTU 1.16:I.25-35.
[61] Cf. Marsman 2003, 572-597.

about his anointing as king by Samuel (1 Sam. 10:16). A space (Petuchah) marks his reticence graphically.

When some fellows openly vent their contempt for the newly installed king Saul, the latter wisely keeps silent, apparently understanding their irritation (1 Sam. 10:27).[62] Tsumura writes that the verse 'prepares the audience for the next stage of this drama with expectation' (Tsumura 2007, 301). In the Masoretic tradition the chapter ends with a space (Petuchah) expressing Saul's silence graphically.

When Saul notices David's absence at a sacrificial banquet he keeps his mouth shut because he assumes that David could not come because he was ritually unclean (1 Sam. 20:26). David's servants consider it prudent not to tell David immediately that his child has died lest he might do himself harm (2 Sam. 12:18). When Abigail returns from her visit to David she finds her husband Nabal drunk and decides that it is better to tell him nothing immediately (1 Sam. 25:36).

If a prophet was preaching in the streets it was by no means necessary to raise his voice (Isa. 42:2), even though on other occasions this might be unavoidable (Isa. 52:8; 58:1). Also the expression 'to put the hand on the mouth' as a gesture of remaining silent occurs just as well in Hebrew.[63]

At the end of his career the prophet Micah[64] counsels his surroundings not to trust anybody and even to 'guard the doors of your mouth from her who lies in your embrace' (Mic. 7:5). Apparently it was wisdom[65] not to provoke the ruling class.

Of the servant of the LORD it is said twice in Isa. 53:7 that he did not open his mouth even though he was oppressed and afflicted. Like a young ram he was led to the slaughter, and like a ewe that is dumb before its shearers. Because the following verses state that he was taken away without restraint and without

---

[62]LXX and an interlinear gloss in 4QSam[a] read differently, but the Masoretic Hebrew text deserves confidence. Cf. Herbert 1997, 53; Fincke 2001, 78.

[63]Judg. 18:19; Mic. 7:16; Job 21:5; Prov. 30:32. See also Job 40:4 and Wisd. 8:11-12.

[64]On the authenticity of the passage see De Moor 2000c.

[65]Cf. Prov. 13:2; 21:23.

arbitration, and had done no violence and did not deceive, one can only conclude that the servant's silence was a sign of piety.[66]

Elihu introduces his speeches against Job[67] with the words,

> I am young in days, and you are aged;
> > therefore I hesitated and feared to show you my knowledge.
> I thought, 'Let the days speak,
> > and let a multitude of years make known wisdom.'
>
> (Job 32:6-7)

He has kept silent for so long[68] out of respect for old age, but is no longer able to restrain himself seeing that the friends have been unsuccessful in convincing Job that he must repent (32:12, 15-16).

Especially the book of Proverbs contains several sayings advocating the prudence of silence, e.g. Prov. 10:19,

> When words are many, transgression is not lacking,
> > but he who restrains his lips is prudent.

And Prov. 11:12-13,

> He who derides his friend is heartless,
> > but a man of understanding remains silent.
> He who overflows with slander uncovers social ties,
> > but a man of trustworthy spirit covers up things.

And Prov. 17:27-28,

> He who is sparing with words is a knowledgeable man,
> > he who has a cool spirit is an understanding man.
> Even a fool who keeps silent is deemed wise,
> > when he presses his lips shut (is deemed) understanding.[69]

---

[66] So we disagree with Barrado 1997, 18-19 who interprets the silence of the Servant as resignation and powerlessness.

[67] These speeches that cover Job 32:1–37:24 are a late addition to the Book of Job, see e.g Strauß 2000, 266-267.

[68] See also Job 32:11, 16, 19-20.

[69] For more examples and discussion, cf. Bühlmann 1976. For the impact on later rabbinic literature Stemberger 2003. In the Sentences of the Syriac Menander, 311-313, similar counsel is found, but borrowing seems unlikely.

And yet the wisdom teachers of Israel were well aware of the dilemma created by all these summons to keep quiet under pressure from the mighty. Prov. 31:8 states,

> Open your mouth for the dumb,[70]
> for the rights of all who are left destitute.
> Open your mouth, promote righteousness,
> and the case of the wretched and poor.

It is appropriate to continue here with Amos 5:13, a verse usually regarded as part of a later addition to the book (vv. 13-15).[71] This verse creates the impression that a learned reader quotes an existing wisdom saying of the kind we have quoted above. In view of the injustice described in the preceding verses a sensible man is advised to keep a low profile,

> Therefore he who is prudent will keep silent in such a time;
> for it is an evil time.

One might assume that this inserted quotation implies also a mild criticism of the prophet Amos himself who certainly did not mince his words. And indirectly the speaker seems to address God, asking if it was wise to send out prophets on such dangerous missions against the rich and powerful. In early Judaism people felt very sorry for the fate of the prophets of doom. According to a legend Amos would have been tortured and finally been killed by the priest Amaziah and his son.[72]

Job's friend Zophar denies Job's arguments against God any cogency,

> Should your babbling silence people?
> If you stammer, should nobody protest? (Job 11:3)

Apparently it was a ploy among 'philosophers' to attempt to silence their opponents by irrefutable reasoning,[73] as Elihu does in Job 33:31-33,

---

[70] The dumbness described here is not a literal, but a metaphorical one, because other physical problems are not mentioned (Murphy 1998, 241; Fox 2009, 888).

[71] E.g. Wolff 1985, 293-294; Van Leeuwen 1985, 204-205.

[72] *Vita prophetarum*, 7.1-2. Cf. Amos 7:10, 17.

[73] Cf. Hartley 1988, 194; Clines 1989, 259.

> Give heed, O Job, listen to me;
>   be silent, now I will speak.
> If you have anything to say, answer me;
>   speak, for I would like to justify you.
> If not, pray listen to me;
>   be silent, and I will teach you wisdom.

Job for his part keeps his end up too. He is only prepared to keep his mouth if his friends come up with cogent arguments (Job 6:24; 13:19). It is commonly assumed that in Job 13:5 he quotes a proverb like Prov. 17:28 to silence his friends whose words he regards as folly,

> O that you would keep totally silent,
>   that would be wisdom for you![74]

Job expects their silent attention when he himself speaks (Job 13:13, 17). Later on, he reminds his friends of previous times, when he still received respect from the community. In the past, when he spoke people were silently listening to him (Job 29:9-10, 21-22). It is quite clear that Job considered himself a wise king[75] whose argument could not be countered.[76]

What should be avoided above all is self-praise,

> Let another man praise you, not your own mouth,
>   a stranger, not your own lips (Prov. 27:2).[77]

The late book of the Wisdom of Ben Sira gives all kinds of reasons for silence between people, but stresses especially the wisdom of biding your time,

> If you know something, answer your neighbor,
>   if not, put your hand on your mouth (Sir. 5:12).

---

[74] Clines 1989, 307 aptly remarks, 'The *via negativa* of silence about God is preferable to cheap theologizing that ignores the dark side of God. Better, indeed, than any talk *about* God is dialogue *with* God, even if it must be painful and bitter disputation (v.6).'

[75] On Job's quasi-royal status see De Moor 1997, 154-157.

[76] Cf. v. 22; Judg. 3:19; Rowley 1970, 189; Hartley 1988, 394.

[77] Cf. Prov. 30:32.

According to the Wisdom of Solomon 8:12 other rulers will wait for the king to resume when he falls silent and will put their hands to their mouth when he speaks at length.

> When a rich man speaks all are silent.
>   they extol his wisdom to the clouds.
> When a poor man speaks, they say 'Who is that?'
>   if he stumbles they knock him down.[78]

> There is someone who is silent and is deemed wise,
>   and there is someone who is despised because of quarrelsome lips.
> There is someone who is silent because there is no answer,
>   and there is someone who is silent because he sees the right time (coming).
> The wise is silent till the right time (comes),
>   but a fool does not bide his time.[79]

Many commentators have noted the close resemblance between such sayings and the Egyptian wisdom literature,[80] but other Hebrew sources may have inspired the author too, e.g. Qoh. 3:7,

> [There is] a time to rend, and a time to sew,
>   a time to keep silent, and a time to speak.

Several scholars[81] relate the silence to mourning,[82] allegedly following rabbinic sources which, however, offer different explanations.[83] Mourners commonly expressed their sorrow by loud wailing, but silent mourning did occur too.[84] However, it seems better to explain the alternatives of silence and speech in Qoh. 3:7 in accordance with the broad wisdom tradition referred to above.

---

[78] Sir. 13:23.

[79] Sir. 20:5-7.

[80] E.g. Couroyer 1960; Scott 1965, 111; McKane 1970, 507; Shupak 1993, 158-182; Murphy 1998, 132.

[81] E.g. Gordis 1968, 230-231; Crenshaw 1987, 96; Murphy 1992, 34; Krüger 2000, 159. But Seow 1997, 162, expresses doubt.

[82] See on this Section 4.5.3.

[83] Cf. b. Zev. 115b; Qoh. R. 3:9; Targum Qoh. 3:7.

[84] See Sections 4.5.3 and 4.5.4.

Also in Israel silence in connection with military action is attested. Joshua orders the people to remain silent until he gives the order 'Shout!' whereupon the walls of Jericho will collapse (Josh. 6:10).[85] According to Judg. 16:2 the Gazites kept quiet all night to be absolutely sure that they would be able to overpower Samson in the light of the morning.

3.2.4 Silence Because of Incapacity

3.2.4.1 Silence Because of Incapacity in the Ancient Near East

Dumbness in otherwise healthy persons was not attributed to natural causes, but was seen as an abnormality that had to be attributed to the machinations of evil demons or witches. By magic one tried to undo this state.[86] The gruesome punishment of cutting out the tongue was another possibility to silence a person for ever.[87] The Assyrians applied it specifically against enemies who dared to utter blasphemy against their gods.[88] And finally, the Egyptian sage Ptahhotep (c. 2380-2342 BCE) appears to know full well that with old age the ability to speak may cease,

> Old age has come, the years weigh heavily,
>   misery my lot, and infant helplessness returns.
> Repose for such a one is sleeplessness each day;
>   the eyes are dim, the ears benumbed,
> Strength ebbs from the faltering heart,
>   the mouth is still and cannot speak ... [89]

---

[85] Obviously there is a certain tension in the present narrative which makes the priests blow the ram's horns whereas the people should keep silent. Probably this is the result of redactional combining of different traditions. Cf. e.g. Butler 1984, 66-68.

[86] See e.g. Šurpu V-VI.3-4, 15-16; VII.17-18, 33-34 (Reiner 1958, 30, 36-37); Maqlû VII.38 (Abusch 1987, 99-124; Abusch, in: Krüger 2008, 171), and the Aramaic text translated by Delsman, TUAT, Bd. 2, 433.

[87] CAD (L), 210-211; ANET, 288. The proverb 'He who has been stabbed in the back has (still) got a mouth to speak, but he who has been stabbed in the mouth, how can he speak?' (Parpola 1993, No. 294:12-13) may refer to a similar cruelty.

[88] CAD (Š) 2, 445.

[89] Translation Foster 2001, 187.

When the waters of the great Flood had ebbed away Utanapishti, the Babylonian counterpart of the biblical Noah, observes,

> I looked at the weather; silence reigned, For all mankind had returned to clay.[90]

According to Mesopotamian and Canaanite mythology mankind had been fashioned from clay, so what is described here is the total destruction of mankind but for the Flood hero and his family who were saved in their boat. The silence is caused by the incapacity of the dead to speak (cf. Section 3.2.5 below).

Silence might also be caused by embarrassment. Not knowing what to answer to the sarcasm of the king of Byblos, the Egyptian diplomat Wenamun (c. 1090 BCE) remains silent.[91] Similarly the steward Rensi in the Egyptian *Tale of the Eloquent Peasant*: 'The high steward Rensi, son of Meru, was silent; he did not reply to these magistrates; he did not reply to the peasant.'[92] If a Babylonian scholar did not know how the react to a problem, he should keep silent.[93]

When people expect solutions from their superiors but do not receive adequate help or reply, they feel abandoned and write desperate letters, reproaching their masters that they keep silent.[94]

Written texts are dumb. Until relatively recent times all written texts were meant to be read out aloud, or at least to be murmured. Silent reading did occur, but was uncommon.[95] This meant that people unable to read had to remain silent while others read texts to them aloud. Towards the end of his famous stele on which his laws were inscribed the Old Babylonian king Ḫammurapi (c. 1795-1750 BCE) writes,

> Let the oppressed man who has a cause go before my statue (called) 'King of Justice' and then have the inscription on my monument read out and hear my precious words.[96]

---

[90]We follow the rendering by Dalley 1991, 113.
[91]Lichtheim, CoS, vol. 1, 91.
[92]Translation Shupak, CoS, vol. 1, 100.
[93]CAD (Q), 72b.
[94]Fuchs & Parpola 2001, No. 288:4-8; CAD (Q), 72-73; (S), 75a.
[95]See e.g. Driver 1954, 70, 72, 228-229; Ben Zvi in: Ben Zvi & Floyd 2000, 22; Grayson 2000; Maitland 2009, 147-148.
[96]Translation Driver & Miles 1955, 97.

Even though this invitation will hardly ever have been followed up, the situation described proves that an ordinary person was unable to read but had to put his trust in someone who had mastered this skill, usually a scribe. It is only against this background of reading texts aloud that a phrase like the following is understandable, 'And let none of the words of this book be silent!'[97] The 'book' is an inscription in stone containing the text of a treaty between two Aramaic kings. It dates from *c.* 740 BCE. Apparently it too was intended to be read out aloud.

In the report of the Egyptian envoy Wenamun it is told that the prince of Byblos has the daybook of his forefathers brought in and has it read before him. Apparently the king himself was not able to read. The Egyptian envoy himself is not able to write a letter. He has a scribe called in to do that for him.[98]

In the Hebrew Bible 'to read' is actually the same verb as 'to call out, read aloud' and this usage is already attested in Lachish ostracon No. 3 (*c.* 586 BCE),

> And when my lord says, 'Don't you know how to read a letter?' As the LORD lives! I swear that no one has ever tried to read me a letter! On the contrary, I swear that I have read every letter that came to me!

This passage shows that normally one would ask a literate person to read out a letter aloud, but that this particular officer was proud to be able to do the reading himself. In such a world it was an unbearable insult if one scribe accused a colleague 'You are deaf to the scribal art, and silent in Sumerian!'[99]

Messengers carrying tablets had to deliver their message orally: the recipients *heard* the message.[100] The silent tablets merely served to confirm their words if doubt about their trustworthiness arose. According to Nah. 2:14[13] the bellowing voices of Assyrian emissaries will be silenced for good.[101]

---

[97] *KAI* No. 222B:8-9.
[98] Lichtheim, CoS, vol. 1, 91-92.
[99] Vanstiphout, CoS, vol. 1, 589.
[100] Cf. De Moor 1965, 5-7; Meier 1988; Greene 1989.
[101] On the textcritical problem involved see e.g. Barthélemy 1992, 814-815; Spronk 1997, 109-110.

3.2.4.2   Silence Because of Incapacity in the Bible

In the Hebrew Bible dumbness is seen as inability to speak clearly (Houtman 1993, 410). According to the Hebrew Bible it were not evil demons who made people dumb, but the LORD himself,

> Who provided man with a mouth?
>   Who will make dumb or deaf?
>   Or seeing or blind?
> Is it not I the LORD? (Exod. 4:11)

Although this is formulated as a general principle,[102] the context renders it likely that in this particular case it was at the same time a warning to Moses who had shown himself reluctant to speak in the name of God and had tried to justify himself by invoking that his mouth had difficulty with speaking (v. 10). God who gave mankind a mouth to speak can also take away that gift. Ezekiel and Daniel suffered from temporary bouts of dumbness[103] which illustrates that according to the biblical writers God did indeed control their power of speech. Therefore the self-curse of Ps. 137:6 'let my tongue cleave to the roof of my mouth, if I do not remember you [Jerusalem]', must be seen as an ultimate type of oath.

In Isa. 29:18 it is foretold that in a bright future the deaf will hear the words of a book. Similarly Isa. 32:3-4 and 35:5-6 foresee that the ears of the deaf will hear and the tongue of the dumb will sing and speak distinctly. Evidently this was seen as a miracle, just as the ability of the blind to see and of the lame to leap. Since these phenomena are connected with God's return to Zion (Isa. 35:2-4)[104] the undoing of these afflictions is a divine prerogative here too.

If one did not want to listen to malicious and treacherous talk it was possible to feign dumbness and deafness (Ps. 38:14-15 [13-14]).[105]

---

[102] God is also the agent in Ezek. 3:26; 24:27; 33:22; Ps. 94:9; Prov. 20:12; Dan. 10:15-19.
[103] Cf. Section 5.2.2.2.
[104] Perhaps also Isa. 29:17 if the 'Lebanon' is a designation of Zion there.
[105] Seybold suggests that the patient's enemies may have recommended him

If Benjamin Foreman is right, Jer. 18:18b testifies to a plot to silence the prophet Jeremiah by cutting out his tongue (Foreman 2009). As we have seen, such a cruelty was committed elsewhere too.

During the Assyrian king Sennacherib's siege of Jerusalem king Hezekiah's emissaries and the people standing on the city walls were unable to counter the Assyrian general's blasphemy. Normally blasphemers had to be put to death.[106] Apparently Hezekiah had foreseen such a situation and had instructed the people to keep quiet.[107] Inability to wail loudly or to deliver a prophecy was sometimes expressed by covering the mouth up to just below the nose.[108]

People might feel unable to count (aloud) because the number of items became to large (Gen. 41:49). Naomi stops speaking when she notices that her daughter-in-law Ruth is determined to accompany her (Ruth 1:18). The singer of Ps. 77 who has called to God in his distress (vv. 2-3[1-2]) feels unable to speak while he lays awake at night, thinking of God (vv. 3-5[2-4]).

When Job's friends acknowledge that they are unable to refute his argument, they fall silent (Job 32:3, 5, 12, 15-16). Job, however, does not give in until God himself answers him. God's long defense against Job's complaints ends with the following lines,

> [1]Then the LORD said to Job:
> [2]'Will he who contends with the Almighty correct him?
>   Let him who accuses God answer him!'
> [3]Then Job said to the LORD:
> [4]'Look, I am a nobody – what can I answer back?
>   I lay my hand on my mouth.
> [5]I have spoken once, but could not answer;
>   twice, but I will proceed no further.[109]

---

to renounce his God (cf. v. 16[15]) and resort to forbidden magic (Seybold 1996, 160).

[106]Lev. 24:15-16; Dan. 3:29. Cf. Exod. 22:27[28].

[107]2 Kgs 18:36. The subject 'the people' is missing both in the LXX and in the parallel text Isa. 36:21. For this reason some scholars delete the word 'people' here too. However, since exchanges of abuse were normal during a siege, Hezekiah may have given a general order beforehand.

[108]Lev. 13:45; Ezek. 24:17, 22; Mic. 3:7. Cf. Himbaza 1997.

Spaces (Petuchot) mark the rhetorical silences after vv. 2 and 5. Finally Job admits here at the end of the canonical book that he is unable to refute the arguments of the Creator of all. He underlines this with an expressive gesture (v. 4[39:34]) that was apparently known everywhere in the ancient world.[110] Neither this passage nor Job 42:6 implies that Job takes back his protest against God's silence. He merely acknowledges his inability to contend with the Almighty.[111] His position is still the same as in Job 9,[112] but as a true sage he deems it wiser to stop his defense.[113]

Silence caused by embarrassment is also attested in Neh. 5:8. Nehemiah accuses his fellow men that they force Jewish people to sell themselves and their children as slaves, because they were exacting high interest on loans. The accused people kept silence after this accusation, not knowing what to say. Apparently, they know in their hearts that Nehemiah is right, since he and others had sacrificed a lot to buy other enslaved Jews free (Neh. 5:7).[114] After Neh. 5:8 there is a physical marking of a long silence (Setumah).

Resigned silence in anticipation of being silenced forever is attested in Jer. 8:14 where the meaning of v. 14aB is determined by the parallel 'Why are we sitting still' in v. 14aA (cf. Lundbom 1999, 519, 524). Of course inability to speak or give any other sign of life was seen as an indication that a person had died (2 Kgs 4:31).

In Job 30 the sufferer complains that God does not reply to his laments (v. 20), he is surrounded by evil (v. 26), his bowels are in turmoil and refuse to keep silent (v. 27) which appears to be the opposite of a restful state.[115]

---

[109] Job 40:1-5[39:31-35].
[110] Cf. Section 3.2.2.1.
[111] Cf. De Moor 2000b, 340-342.
[112] See especially Job 9:3, 14-15, 21, 32.
[113] Cf. Strauß 2000, 375.
[114] Williamson 1985, 238: 'The loaning of money on pledge and the practice of debt-slavery were not illegal as such; cf. Exod. 21:2-11; 22:24-26[25-27]; Lev. 25; Deut. 15:1-18; 24:10-13.' So the embarrassment must have been caused by Nehemiah's example.
[115] Cf. Isa. 16:11; 63:15; Jer. 4:19.

According to Luke 1:18, 19, 63-64 an angel struck the priest Zechariah with temporary dumbness because he expressed doubt about the angel's annunciation of the birth of his son, John the Baptist. Elsewhere in the New Testament it are demons again who, in contrast to the Hebrew Bible, were held responsible for dumbness (Mt. 9:32-34; 12:22-24; Luke 11:14-15).

Silence by embarrassment because of not knowing what to answer is also attested in the New Testament where the Jewish leaders admit their inability to refute Jesus' arguments (Luke 14:4, 6; 20:26; cf. Mt. 22:46).

3.2.5 *Silence Because of Sleep*

3.2.5.1 Silence Because of Sleep in the Ancient Near East

By necessity most human beings are silent when they are asleep.[116] Of course the sleep of human beings is mentioned often in texts.[117] An Old Babylonian prayer to the gods of the night describes the silence as the stopping of all human noise,

> The noble ones are safely guarded(?),
>   doorbolts drawn, rings in place,[118]
> The noisy people are fallen silent,
>   the doors are barred that were open.
> Gods of the land, goddesses of the land,
>   Shamash, Sin, Adad, and Ishtar
>   are gone off to the lap of heaven.[119]
> They will give no judgment,
>   they will decide no cases:
> The veil is drawn for the night,
>   the palace is hushed,
>   the open land is deathly still.[120]

---

[116] Not only at night, but also during a siesta. The female demon Lamashtu enters preferably at noon, the most silent part of the day. Cf. Farbe, TUAT, Bd. 2, 257.

[117] E.g. Seux 1976, 247; Jacobsen 1987, 428-429; Guinan 2009.

[118] The translation is somewhat uncertain, cf. CAD (Š) 2, 326. Weippert 1997, 105-106 proposed 'sleeping-mats are put in place'.

[119] I.e., sun, moon, storm and evening-star have all gone to sleep. Probably a variant reading that has Ea, the god of wisdom, instead of Sin, the moon god, is to be preferred.

[120] Translation after Foster 2005, 207. See also Hecker, TUAT, Bd. 2, 719.

Apparently also gods needed sleep at night, even the peculiar Egyptian creator god Aten,

> When you set in western lightland,
> Earth is in darkness as if in death;
> One sleeps in chambers, heads covered,
> One eye does not see another.
> ...
> Darkness hovers, earth is silent,
> As their maker rests in lightland.[121]

What is striking in both texts is the explicit parallel drawn between human sleep and divine sleep, although the 'resting' of Aten might imply that he was thought to be awake. We will discuss other texts describing divine sleep later.[122]

The sleep of death was a metaphor in Egypt,[123] Mesopotamia,[124] and Ugarit.[125] The comparison between sleep and death is attested in Homer too,

> There she encountered Sleep, full brother of Death.
> She caught him by the hand and spoke, calling him by his name,
> 'O Sleep, ruler of all gods and all human beings ...[126]

3.2.5.2 Silence Because of Sleep in the Bible

Peaceful sleep is seen as a gift of God (Ps. 127:2).[127] Only in extreme distress a supplicant may forego the blessed silence of the night (Ps. 22:3[2]). In Ps. 4:5[4] a pious Israelite admonishes his powerful adversaries,

> Toss around, but do not sin;
> speak in your heart on your bed, but be silent.[128]

---

[121]Translation Lichtheim, CoS, vol. 1, 45; see also Assmann 1999, 218; TUAT, Bd. 2, 849.

[122]See Section 6.2.1.

[123]Zandee 1960, Ch. 1.

[124]CAD (Ṣ), 69; Spronk 1986, 98-99; Guinan 2009, 201-202.

[125]KTU 1.19:III.45, cf. De Moor 1987, 259.

[126]Iliad, XIV.231-233. See also XVI.454, 672, 682 and Stenger 2009.

[127]For an admirable overview of the problems connected with this verse see Zenger in: Hossfeld & Zenger 2008, 513-529. See also Prov. 3:24; 19:23; Jer. 31:26.

[128]A *Selah* marks the silence that falls after this verse.

Those in power devise evil plans against the poor on their beds (Mic. 2:1), tossing around restlessly, whereas the pious poor can sleep the undisturbed sleep of the just (Ps. 4:9[8]).

The incompetent leaders of Israel are compared to watchdogs that do not bark in time because they have fallen asleep,

> All its watchers are blind, they notice nothing,
>   all of them dumb dogs,
>   that cannot bark;
> sleeping visionaries[129] who love to slumber (Isa. 56:10)

Visionary leadership would have issued timely warnings that enemies were approaching.[130]

The metaphor of the sleep of death was also known in ancient Israel,

> Look! Answer me, O LORD, my God!
>   Enlighten my eyes, lest I sleep the sleep of death!
>   (Ps. 13:4[3])

Normally death silenced a person for ever. The poor woman at Gibeah was unable to answer her husband's summons anymore (Judg. 19:28). At the order of Elisha his servant Gehazi places the prophet's staff on the face of the dead boy of the Shunamite woman but this magic did not work, 'there was no sound and no response' (2 Kgs 4:29-31). Because Gehazi reports, 'The boy has not awakened' (v. 31) it may be assumed that he had hoped to rise the boy from the sleep of death.

Just like the neighboring nations Israel imagined the realm of death as a place of utter silence,

> For the Nether World does not praise you,
>   (nor) does Death jubilate for you,
>   those who descend into the Pit do not hope for your trust-
>   fulness (Isa. 38:18).

---

[129] We opt for the reading of the great Isaiah scroll from Qumran (1QIsa^a) that is supported by the Peshitta and the Vulgate. Also the parallelism favors this reading.

[130] Young 1972, 395; cf. Sections 3.2.1-2.

> For in death there is no remembrance of you;
>   in the Nether World who can give you praise? (Ps. 6:6[5])

> What profit is there in my blood if I go down into the abyss?
>   Dust – will it tell about my faithfulness? (Ps. 30:10[9])

At the end of the Psalm the singer proclaims his intention to sing hymns to the LORD forever because his prayer has been heard,

> So that my inner self will sing for you,
>   and will not be silent O LORD, my God,
>   I will praise you forever (Ps. 30:13[12]).

Other Psalms depicting the Nether World as a place of utter silence are,

> Do you work wonders for the dead?
>   Do the shades rise up to praise you?
> Is your faithfulness recounted in the grave,
>   your trustfulness in the place of perdition?
>   (Ps. 88:11-12[10-11])

> If the LORD had not been my help,
>   my soul would soon have dwelt in silence (Ps. 94:17).[131]

> The dead will not praise the LORD,
>   nor any of those who descend into silence (Ps. 115:17).

The theme is also found in the wisdom of Ben Sira,

> Who in the Nether World will glorify the Most High,
>   in place of the living who praise him?
> Since they are no more, there is no praise of the dead,
>   only those who are alive and well praise the Lord
>   (Sir. 17:27-28).

The absence of praise in the Nether World does not imply that God has no control over the silent multitudes of the dead. He is just as powerful there as in heaven (Amos 9:2; Ps. 139:8). Even the poet of Ps. 88 who states

---

[131] 'Silence' short for 'the land of silence', cf. e.g. Seybold 1996, 375.

>   Among the dead I am free[132]
>   like those killed in action who lie in the grave,
>   those whom you do not remember anymore,
>   since they have been cut off from your hand (Ps. 88:6[5]).

The singer knows that it is God who has put him there (Ps. 88:7[6]).

In Jer. 51:39, 57 the prophet anounces that the Babylonians will sleep a perpetual sleep. The same concept underlies 4 Ezra 7:32 and the unprovenanced song quoted in Eph. 5:14.

In 1 Kgs 19:4 Elijah asks God permission to die because queen Jezebel has sworn to kill him. Apparently convinced that his request will be granted he lies down and falls asleep, as if in anticipation of his eternal sleep. However, he is touched by an angel who summons him to rise and eat. Job too asks for eternal sleep (Job 3:13) because in the Nether World everybody is resting quietly, even the wicked (Job 3:17,18; see also Ps. 31:18[17]). To 'silence' a person is sometimes meant literally as 'to stop someone's mouth',[133] but can also be equivalent to killing someone.[134]

3.3 Conclusions on Silence between Humans

The reason for discussing silence among humans in the ancient Near East is the fact that all God-talk is based on the analogy of human talk.[135] Silence is a normal element in all human discourse.[136] Therefore we assumed that it would be worthwhile to establish what reasons for interpersonal silence can be derived from ancient Near Eastern sources and the Bible (Section 3.1).

In the first section (Section 3.2.1) we discussed silence because of offenses. It was shown that often silence was kept in case of morally dubious activities. Several texts mention silence in connection with theft, telling lies, adultery, abritrarily changing of religious

---

[132] An ironic designation of the state of the dead who are locked up forever in the Nether World.

[133] Ps. 63:12; 107:42; Job 5:16.

[134] 1 Sam. 2:9; Jer. 8:14; 25:37; 48:2; 49:26; 50:30. See also texts like Isa. 15:1; 47:5; Jer. 6:2; 47:5; 48:2.

[135] Cf. Section 2.2.

[136] Cf. Section 2.3.

rituals, acts of violence, neglect, for example when enemies endanger the country. In some cases people kept silent because the honor of the family was at stake.

However, it was not always easy to decide what was better, secrecy or openness. Several texts affirm that one should *not* keep silent about crimes, such as violence, threatening enemies, slandering, etc. In the Bible it is explicitly stated that people are not allowed to conceal sins from God. Also elsewhere in the ancient Near East sins had to be confessed to the gods. It is unclear if in such cases people actually confessed to a priest or soliloquized with their own conscience. Of kings it is said that they should not keep silent if the poor and weak were oppressed. Generally speaking, concealing offenses was seen as immoral.

Silence might also be caused by apprehension (Section 3.2.2). When facing wild animals or human enemies people kept silent for fear of being hurt or even killed. Furthermore, politically sensitive information had to be kept secret. Silence because of fear was depicted by a hand or finger to the mouth, or even by fully covering the face with both hands. Kings were supposed to silence any threat to their nations. Parents were expected to silence disobedient children. People tried to silence prophets who announced doom.

Silence because of forbearance or prudence was seen as a sign of wisdom (Section 3.2.3). Silence was kept out of respect before esteemed speakers, kings, elderly people, wise men and women. The still well-known saying 'speech is silver, but silence is gold' appeared to have ancient roots. Furthermore, keeping silence could be taken as an indication of piety. Especially in temples noise had to be avoided. Silent agreement with decisions of superiors was expected. Sometimes people temporarily kept silent about someone's death because of the grief this would cause to the nearest relatives, if it would be told immediately. Silence also could have its meaning in a military situation. Normally an attack on a city was accompanied with a lot of shouting, but sometimes silence was deemed wiser in order to take the enemy by surprise or to grant the defenders some respite to surrender without losses. As in case of silence because of fear, silence out of wisdom could be expressed by covering the mouth with the hand.

Obviously silence could also be caused by physical or psychological incapacity (Section 3.2.4), as in the case of permanent or temporary dumbness. A special case of dumbness is that of written texts. They 'spoke' by being read aloud by people able to read, like priests and scribes, but remained silent to those unable to read unless someone read it to them. Dumbness and deafness could be feigned if one did not want to listen to certain talk. Cutting out someone's tongue was a possibility to silence a person for ever, both in the ancient Near East and in the Bible. Another reason for silence could be embarrasment. In such cases people did not know what to say and in fact became unable to speak. Worst of all was the incapability to speak anymore because of death.

Of course people did not normally speak when asleep (Section 3.2.5). A widely used metaphor was the sleep of death. The realm of death was seen as a place of utter silence, both in the ancient Near East and the Bible. There, deities were no longer praised. Intriguing is the fact that in the ancient Near East the sleep of human beings and of deities was evidently seen as comparable and parallel. Also deities needed their sleep and did not reply to the prayers of worshippers when asleep.

The various types of silence between human beings we looked for appeared all to be present in Egypt, Mesopotamia and Israel. The circumstance that we did not find all types in Anatolia, Canaan and Greece should no doubt be attributed to our imperfect knowledge of the sources.

In several cases we observed that in the written text of the Hebrew Bible the silence of human beings was expressed not in words, but graphically by a blank space (cf. Section 2.3.2).

The results of this chapter can be summarized in the following table which will serve later as a model for comparison with various types of silence occurring when humans are addressing deities (Section 4.6) and with silence on the part of deities (Section 6.3).

Silence of Humans before Humans

Reasons	ANE	Bible
↓	Humans ↓ Humans	Humans ↓ Humans
Offenses	x	x
Awe / Fear	x	x
Forbearance / Prudence	x	x
Incapacity	x	x
Sleep	x	x

A cross (x) indicates that we found that particular reason to remain silent in the ancient sources at our disposal. With regard to interpersonal silence there appears to be little difference between the reasons found in ancient Near Eastern texts and the reasons found in the Bible.

CHAPTER FOUR

HOW DID MAN ADDRESS THE DEITY?

4.1 Introduction

In the ancient world personal piety is rarely expressed in written texts. The main speakers in the cult were the king and religious functionaries such as magicians, priests, singers, diviners and prophets. In Egypt space for personal prayers of ordinary people was created outside the Eastern Temple in Karnak. The creator god Amun was invoked there as 'Amun who listens to prayers' or 'Amun the listening ear'.[1] A similar place outside a temple for Ptah is called 'the great rampart, the place where prayers are heard'. The temple itself is called 'Ear of God'.[2] Epithets of various deities show that at least since the New Kingdom (c. 1570-1070 BCE) the Egyptians expected the gods to listen to their prayers. Their gratitude for being heard they expressed by dedicating so-called ear-stelae which expressed the conviction that the deity would continue to listen to the supplicant's prayers. Sometimes the image of a listening god was provided with as many as 777 pairs of ears. By speaking into the ears, people were certain that their words would be heard. At the same time the stelae encouraged the pious not to give up their invocations.[3]

These stelae testify to the fact that ordinary people did not dare to address the deity directly themselves. Next to 'buffers' like stelae or images, they made use of professional intermediaries, such as priests, prophets, astrologers, diviners, magicians, spiritualistic mediums, or learned scribes.[4] According to the Hebrew Bible the number of legitimate intermediaries between God and man was much smaller, though there is reason to suspect that in pre-exilic times more religious officials may have worked in Israelite sanctuaries too. In distress king David calls upon God and professes, 'From his temple[5] he heard my voice, and my cry came

---

[1] Altenmüller 2009, 32.
[2] Altenmüller 2009, 33.
[3] Schlichting 1977; 1982a; Morgan 2004; Martin 2005, 102-108.
[4] Cf. Section 5.2.
[5] In view of the following description of the theophany it is probably God's

to his ears' (2 Sam. 22:7 = Ps. 18:7[6]). How could the supplicant arrive at this certainty unless he really thought to 'hear' the voice of God in the temple? Either through a human intermediary or by a a sudden inner illumination?

Normally the people stood in the court of the temple (Jer. 19:14; 26:2; Ps. 135:2; 2 Chron. 20:5). Similarly it is said in 1 Kgs 8:35 'if they (the people) pray toward this place' which seems to imply that the people are not *in* the temple. According to 1 Kgs 8:39, 42 the supplicants had to stretch out their hands 'toward this house'. In 1 Kgs 8:44 this formula is broadened to praying toward the city (of Jerusalem) and to the house Solomon built there for the LORD. And if one is praying from captivity abroad even praying in the general direction of the land, the city and the house of God suffices (1 Kgs 8:49).

Asking God for illumination in difficult situations was quite normal (Madl 1977; Thelle 2002). Even in mundane cases like lost asses a visionary was consulted (1 Sam. 9). But also in matters of state nothing was decided without the advice of a priest or a prophet. King Hezekiah, for example, asks God to incline his ear and listen to Sennacherib's mockery (2 Kgs 19:16 = Isa. 37:17). The prophet Isaiah answers him, even though he was not present when Hezekiah was praying (2 Kgs 19:20-34).

Intercessory prayer was quite common. Abraham prays for Abimelech (Gen. 20:17), Moses prays for the Israelites (Num. 11:2; 21:7; Deut. 9:26), as do Samuel (1 Sam. 7:5; 8:6; 12:19), Solomon (1 Kgs 8) and Hezekiah (2 Kgs 19:14-19 ‖ Isa. 37:14-20). Jeroboam asks a 'man of God' (prophet) to pray for him (1 Kgs 13:6), as does king Zedekiah ask Jeremiah (Jer. 37:3) and as does the people (Jer. 42:2, 4). God instructs Jeremiah not to pray for his people (Jer. 7:16; 11:14) which suggests that normally this was expected from a prophet, especially if he had predicted disaster. Jeremiah even encourages the exiles to pray for the prosperity of the foreign city where they are living (Jer. 29:7).

---

heavenly temple that is meant here. Cf. Mic. 1:3-4. However, one of the pre-Solomonic sanctuaries is not excluded. Cf. 1 Sam. 7:5-11.

4.2 Songs and Prayers

4.2.1 *Songs and Prayers in the Ancient Near East*

Everywhere in the ancient Near East people addressed the gods in hymns, lamentations and prayers. Especially in Egypt prayers and lamentations are more rare than hymns, possibly because of the basically positive attitude of the ancient Egyptians towards the divine world and afterlife. The closest parallels to biblical lamentations and prayers are found in Sumerian and Hittite literature. But even there we have to be cautious in drawing parallels because genres may differ considerably.[6] In any case it is impossible and unnecessary to review the enormous number of possibly comparable texts here. A few examples must suffice.

The supplicants expected their gods to react to their prayers and laments. If no response came, they vented their disappointment. In a Sumerian incantation of the second millennium BCE a suppllicant prays to his god,

> How long shall you remain silent?
> What keeps you quiet?

Yet the same person is supposed to have extolled the virtues of his god in the very same composition,

> Lord, you are exalted. Who can compare to you?
> Asarluhi, you are superior to any god, whatever he be named.[7]

A similar prayer is found in a testimony of the so-called 'personal piety' of the Ramesside period in Egypt,

> Prayer to Pre︎ᶜ-Harakhty[8]
>
> Come to me, Preᶜ-Harakhty,
> that you may perform (your) will.
> You are the one who takes action,

---

[6] Lenzi 2010, especially 315: 'There is still a mountain of work to be done on the comparison of the prayers in the Hebrew Psalter with those from Mesopotamia'.
[7] Cohen 1988, vol. 1, 416.
[8] A Late Egyptian name of the sun god in his daytime form.

> there being none who takes action apart from you,
> ...
> Hear my prayers –
> my supplications by day,
> my hymns by night.
> For my petitions are constant in my mouth,
> They are heard throughout the day.
>
> O sole one, unique!
> O Pre‛-Harakhty,
> the likes of whom does not exist here.
> Protector of millions,
> who delivers hundreds of thousands,
> the helper of the one who cries to him,
> the lord of Heliopolis.
>
> Visit not my many offenses upon me,
> I am one ignorant of himself.
> I am a mindless man,
> who all day follows his mouth,
> like an ox after grass.[9]

Such prayers should be a warning to avoid two simplifications,

a) Seemingly 'monotheistic' or 'henotheistic' statements in the context of worship should not lead to premature conclusions about the singularity of a deity.

b) Presumed silence on the part of the deity is often nothing more than an argument to mollify that deity and urge him or her to answer.

In an Egyptian hymn to Amun-Re it is apparently assumed that the god will hear the prayer of a person in distress and will utter words effectuating his salvation.[10] Presumably an officiant or prophet answered in the name of the deity.[11] The fugitive Egyptian Sinuhe prays,

> Whichever god decreed this flight, have mercy, bring me home! Surely you will let me see the place in which my heart dwells! ... may he hearken to the prayer of one far away![12]

---

[9] Translation Fox, CoS, vol. 1, 47. See also Assmann 1999, 408.
[10] Ritner, CoS, vol. 1, 38-39.
[11] Cf. Section 5.3.3.1.
[12] Translation Lichtheim, CoS, vol. 1, 80.

In some skeptical Egyptian laments about the fate of the dead it is stated blandly that no deceased will ever come back to tell the living how it is in the hereafter,

> I have heard the words of Imhotep and Herdedef,
> Whose sayings are recited whole.
> What of their places?
> Their walls have crumbled,
> Their places are gone,
> As though they had never been!
> None comes from there,
> To tell of their state,
> To tell of their needs,
> To calm our hearts,
> Until we go where they have gone![13]

This was certainly not the prevailing belief in the ancient Near East. Most people assumed that the spirits of the dead did visit the living and did tell them about both their state as well as about the past and future.

Out of a feeling of awe, human beings often shrank back from addressing great deities directly. In many Mesopotamian incantations a minor or more approachable deity is asked to intercede with mightier colleagues.[14] The Hittite king prays the Sun-god to intercede on his behalf with an unknown angry god, 'Whether that deity is in heaven or whether he is in earth, you, O Sun-god, shall go to him. Go, speak to that deity and [tell(?)] him. Transmit the following words of the human: [follows a prayer pleading before the angry god]' (Singer 2002, 37). The Hittite queen Puduḫepa asks various deities to relay her prayer to the Sun-goddess of Arinna (Singer 2002, 104-105).

4.2.2 Songs and Prayers in the Bible

In the Bible too people often inquired a solution to their problems from God (Begg 1992). As one from many similar prayers we quote Ps. 55:2-3a[1-2a],

---

[13] Translation Lichtheim, CoS, vol. 1, 49.
[14] E.g. Mayer 1976, 230-239; Maul 1988, 116:28; Lambert 1989.

> Give ear to my prayer, O God;
>   and hide not yourself from my plea!
> Attend to me, and answer me!

It is our subjective impression that the Hebrew Psalmists resorted more often to supplication and lamentation[15] than other peoples of the ancient Near East. We have no ready explanation for this phenomenon, but factors that may have played a role are the stricter concentration on one God and the heightened feeling of collective guilt after the collapse of the Judean kingdom.

Of course intercession by other deities is absent from the canonical books of the Hebrew Bible, even though it may have occurred in pre-exilic Israel, especially in the form of consultation of deified ancestors.[16] In the Bible human intermediaries take the place of deities. When the Israelites felt threatened by the Philistines (1 Sam. 7:1, 7-14) they asked Samuel to intercede for them with the LORD (v. 8).[17] After various rites – libation of water (v. 6), burnt offering of a suckling lamb (v. 9a) – Samuel prayed to God who answered him (v. 9b). The content of the reply is not recorded, but when the Philistines attacked, God's thundering voice confused them so much (v. 10) that it was easy for Israel to defeat them.[18]

4.3 Letters to Deities

4.3.1 *Letters to Deities in the Ancient Near East*

Oscar[19] was by no means the first to write letters to God. One of the most ancient manners of sharing one's experiences with a god or goddess are the letters addressed to the deity. Sumerian

---

[15] Lately some scholars have criticized the use of the term 'lamentation' (Villanueva 2008, 253-254). However, since this designation is so well established in biblical scholarship we have decided to keep using it.

[16] Cf. Section 5.3.3.2.

[17] Barrado 1997, 12 rightly remarks that Samuel's silence seems to imply that he was reluctant to intercede for the people.

[18] Although it is difficult to peel off the various redactional layers in 1 Sam. 7 (see e.g. Caquot & De Robert 1994, 104-106) this seems an acceptable reconstruction.

[19] The mortally ill boy in Schmitt's short story, cf. Section 1.5.

examples are attested in Mesopotamia since the end of the neo-Sumerian period, at the end of the 3rd millennium BCE.[20] A few centuries later, Yašmaḫ-Addu, king of Mari, writes a long letter to the god Nergal because he fears that his dynasty will come to an end. The letter contains so many details about the political history of the royal family that it is hardly possible that Yašmaḫ-Addu would have composed it himself.[21] When Elamites invade his country, king Zimrilim of Mari writes letters to several gods asking for help and receives written answers from prophets speaking in the name of the deities, assuring him of their help (Durand 1988, 413-414). Also several Neo-Assyrian kings wrote letters to their gods.[22]

In Egypt prayers were written on ostraca since the early 14th century BCE. Most were intended for Amun-Re whose oracle was consulted when his image passed by during a procession.[23] Since letters to deities are also attested in the early Demotic period,[24] it seems likely that such practices have been fairly common.

4.3.2 Letters to God in the Bible

In the Hebrew Bible no letter to God has been preserved. But king Hezekiah goes to the temple and spreads the letter of the Assyrian king before the God, apparently assuming that he will be able to read it (2 Kgs 19:14). So it may be assumed that the practice of writing to God was not unknown in Israel either.

4.4 Magic and Sorcery

4.4.1 Magic and Sorcery in the Ancient Near East

Not only by words people tried to influence the deities. In all civilizations of the ancient Near East complicated magic to ward off evil demons, or to persuade 'good' deities to help, accompanied the incantations or prayers.[25] The goal of magic and sorcery was

---

[20] Hallo 1996, 231-235, with earlier literature.
[21] Durand 2000, 69-74.
[22] See e.g. Mayer 1984; Keller 1991; Leichty 1991.
[23] Altenmüller 2009, 35-37.
[24] Migahid 1986; Vittmann 1995; Migahid & Vittmann 2003.
[25] See e.g. Borghouts 1980; Cryer 1994, 42-123; Bottéro 1987-1990; Haas 1987-1990; Koenig 1994; Jeffers 1996; Abusch & Van der Toorn 1999; Mirecki

to ward off suffering from oneself or one's family and friends, or, conversely, to inflict suffering on one's enemies, whether human or divine. The performer of magic may be cast in the role of a messenger, healer, sorcerer or even a divine being himself, because he stands partly in the divine realm, partly in the human realm. Similarity between the two realms is often explained by myth, from which in some cases extensive quotations are given. In magic the word was more important than the act. What Joris Borghouts writes with regard to ancient Egyptian magic is true for the entire ancient world,

> Its mediating bridge is primarily the word (spell, as curse or conjuration) complemented by an act (both eventually abbreviated to a mere allusion or gesture) and often by an instrument or medicine whose power is endorsed (or even rationalized) by the spell.[26]

4.4.2 *Magic and Sorcery in the Bible*

In contrast to what is commonly thought, certain forms of magic were also deemed admissible in ancient Israel, even though magic and sorcery are expressly forbidden in texts like Exod. 22:17[18]; Lev. 19:26; 20:6; Deut. 18:9-13.[27] Moses and Aaron, for example, perform miracles with Aaron's staff which becomes a serpent (Exod. 7:9-10) and turns the Nile into blood (Exod. 7:19-20). The Egyptian magicians are able to imitate these acts.

In Qumran and early Christianity magic was apparently common practice.[28] In rabbinic Judaism the ban was upheld officially,[29] but the prohibition became never really effective.[30] The same ambiguous attitude is found in the New Testament. Jesus often casts out demons and does not even prevent a non-follower from casting out demons in his name (Mk 9:38-40), but Paul opposes magic and sorcery (e.g. Acts 13:6-12).

& Meyer 2002; Klutz 2003; Jean 2006; Schwemer 2007; Collins 2008.

[26] Borghouts 1980, 1137.

[27] Cf. Jeffers 1996; Klutz 2003; Schmitt 2004b; Römer 2009.

[28] See e.g. Kee 1986; Meyer & Smith 1999; Conner 2006; Labahn & Lietaert Peerbolte 2007.

[29] m. Sanh. VII.4; VII.11; j. Sanh. VII.19 [25d]; b. Sanh. 67a-68a.

[30] See e.g. Trachtenberg 1939; Naveh & Shaked 1985; 1993; Schäfer 1990; Schäfer & Shaked 1994; Schäfer *et al.* 1998; Klutz 2003; Bohak 2008.

4.5 Silence of Man before the Deity

4.5.1 *Silence Because of Offenses*

Many pious men and women have concluded that the best way to communicate with a silent God is stillness.[31] When was silence better than speaking according to texts from Antiquity?

4.5.1.1 Silence Because of Offenses in the Ancient Near East

We have found no cases of human beings keeping silent about offenses before their deities in the ancient Near Eastern sources. Probably this must be attributed to our imperfect knowledge of the available sources. Priests in the Assyrian empire who have arbitrarily changed the ancient rites instruct their subordinates to keep silent about the matter,[32] but this is not the same as hiding the offense from a deity. Perhaps people were reluctant to assume that it would be possible to conceal sins from the all-knowing gods.

4.5.1.2 Silence Because of Offenses in the Bible

When God calls his people to account through the message of his prophets they may remain silent because they do not believe he will help them (Isa. 50:2) or because they want to conceal to have participated in pagan worship (Isa. 66:3-4). The supplicant of Ps. 39 knows that he is suffering because he has sinned (Ps. 39:9[8], 12[11]). Therefore he decided to undergo his punishment in silence (Ps. 39:2-3[1-2], 10[9]). But after a while he could not restrain himself any longer and started to call on God (Ps. 39:3b-4[2b-3]), asking him to listen to his prayer and break the silence (Ps. 39:13[14]). Apparently, if God is silent, human beings need not remain silent too, even if they deserve God's silence.[33]

If an answer from the deity failed to come through, the frustration of the supplicants was growing rapidly. When the Babylonians had devastated the temple in Jerusalem and had deported many Judeans people lamented,

---

[31] Cf. Section 1.3.1.
[32] Cole & Machinist 1998, No. 134, r. 16.
[33] See further Section 4.5.3.2.

> Even when I call out or cry for help,
>   he shuts out my prayer (Lam. 3:8).

One possible reaction to God's refusal to listen was resignation,

> They sit on the ground, they keep silent,
>   the elders of the Daughter of Zion,
> they have sprinkled dust on their heads,
>   have put on sackcloth (Lam. 2:10).

Silent mourning was one of the means to express acceptance of the inevitable consequence of a decision on high to terminate a life.[34] This point of view is elaborated more fully in Lam. 3:26-29,

> He is good, one should wait quietly
>   for the LORD's salvation.
> ...
> One should sit down alone and be silent,
>   for He has imposed it on him.
> He should press his mouth to the dust,
>   perhaps there is still hope.[35]

When the LORD will forgive Lady Jerusalem her sins she will never open her mouth again because of shame (Ezek. 16:63).

However, when Second Isaiah had announced that Jerusalem had repaid her iniquity (Isa. 40:2) people did no longer accept that God remained silent. Third Isaiah intones,

> For Zion's sake I will not keep silent,
>   for Jerusalem's sake I will not keep quiet,
> till her righteousness comes forth as brightness,
>   and her salvation blazes like a torch (Isa. 62:1).

Scholars differ on the question whether it is God or the prophet who is speaking here in the first person,[36] but the latter option is preferable, if only because of vv. 4 and 12 (cf. Isa. 61:10).

---

[34] See Sections 4.5.3 and 4.5.4.2.
[35] Cf. Renkema 1998, 394-399.
[36] God according to e.g. Young 1972, 467; Whybray 1975, 246-247; Oswalt 1998, 578-579. The prophet according to e.g. Westermann 1986, 297; Childs 2001, 511-513; Blenkinsopp 2003, 233-234.

The verb we have translated with 'to keep quiet'[37] normally describes the trusting, peaceful attitude of the pious, whereas the refusal to keep quiet was seen as typical of hotheads and rebellious sinners.[38]

4.5.2 Silence Because of Awe or Fear

4.5.2.1 Silence Because of Awe or Fear in the Ancient Near East

For various reasons human beings might fall silent before deities. A bad dream renders both deity and man speechless.[39] The Sumerian god Ninurta commands the rebel lands to fall silent before his awesome exploits.[40] Of course also the silence in the sanctuary which we will discuss below (Section 4.5.3) implies a certain amount of awe or fear for the deity.

4.5.2.2 Silence Because of Awe or Fear in the Bible

At the sight of the mighty acts of the LORD when he led his people out of Egypt the nations writhe, shake, are terrified, struck down by fear and dread (Exod. 15:14-15). Finally they become dumb

---

[37] Hebrew שקט (šqṭ).

[38] Cf. Section 3.2.3.1. The verb 'to remain quiet' is a synonym of 'to control oneself' and the opposite of turmoil (Isa. 7:2) and fear in Isa. 7:4. In contrast to a hothead, a man able to restrain himself quiets strife (Prov. 15:18). Naomi's confident statement that Boaz will not tarry to conclude the matter of marrying Ruth (Ruth 3:18) is clearly a humorous understatement – on the contrary, he will act swiftly. Also 'to rest' and 'to sleep' are close in meaning (Isa. 14:7; 30:15; Job 3:13, 26), as are the nouns 'rest', 'peace' and 'quiet' in 1 Chron. 22:9. To dwell in peaceful quiet was everybody's ideal (Ezek. 38:11; Zech. 1:11). Trust characterizes the self-controlled behavior of the pious (Isa. 30:15) that contrasts sharply with the desire of the disobedient to plunge into the turmoil of battle (v. 17). Isaiah criticizes the wealthy ladies of Jerusalem who are at ease and trust that nothing will befall them (Isa. 32:9) in their bustling city (Isa. 32:14) whereas soon enough (Isa. 32:10) disaster will strike. True peace, trust and quiet are the result of righteous deeds (Isa. 32:17; cf. Ps. 94:12-15). The restlessness of the wicked is compared to the inability of the sea to remain quiet (Isa. 57:20; Jer. 49:23). After the return from the terrors of the exile, the LORD's pious 'servant Jacob' will have quiet and ease (Jer. 30:10; 46:27).

[39] Römer, TUAT, Bd. 2, 28, 34; Von Soden, TUAT, Bd. 3, 169.

[40] Black et al. 2004, 170.

as a stone when they see how the Israelites cross between walls of seawater (Exod. 15:16).

When God orders the nations to be silent in Isa. 41:1 the immediate context suggests an analogy to the common attempt to silence adversaries in a lawsuit.[41] However, this would imply the possibility that the other party might use the same strategy and summon God to be silent. This can hardly have been Second Isaiah's intention.[42] The following verses (Isa. 41:2-6) describe the terror that campaigns of Cyrus inspired among the nations. This and the parallels discussed above suggest that silence out of fear definitely plays a part too.

4.5.3 *Silence Because of Forbearance or Prudence*

4.5.3.1 Silence Because of Forbearance or Prudence in the Ancient Near East

From early times on virtuous silence was seen as an implicit appeal to the gods who were expected to reward such a pious attitude.[43]

In the Ugaritic Legend of Aqhatu, for example, king Dani'ilu[44] lies for seven consecutive days in silent supplication before the gods, merely clad in sackcloth and with his boots on – a sign of total self-neglect that expressed the grief of mourners (KTU 1.17:I.1-19). Dani'ilu does not explain why he is doing this, but probably it is because he realizes that silence is wiser than speech because the all-knowing gods might be offended if he were to assume that they were ignorant of his problem – the lack of a son and heir.

In wars the kings of the ancient Near East had to rely totally on the protection of their gods. The Assyrian king Esarhaddon (681-669 BCE), for example, is admonished to keep silent in a

---

[41] Cf. Beuken 1979, 59, 61; Berges 2008, 177.

[42] It is a way out to describe the nations as 'silent witnesses' (Blenkinsopp 2002, 196-197). They are invited to speak (v. 1b) and they do speak in v. 6.

[43] See e.g. Lanczkowski 1955, 196; Brunner-Traut 1979; Shupak 1993, 161-162.

[44] His name is identical to 'Daniel' in the Hebrew tradition. This Canaanite Daniel is mentioned as a righteous sufferer in the Bible, Ezek. 14:14, 20; 28:3. Cf. De Moor 1997, 149-150.

threatening situation,[45] even though this contrasts starkly with the behavior expected from a king according to other sources.[46]

Excessive noise had to be avoided in the sanctuary. So keeping your quiet was a virtue of the Babylonian pious.[47] Mesopotamian prayer was normally murmured (Grayson 2000, 306). In the fourth chapter of the Egyptian *Wisdom of Amenemope* the behavior of an excited man in the temple is contrasted with that of a 'truly silent man', someone who prefers harmony over conflict and clamor. The sage observes,

> But all the silent in the temple,
> They say: 'Re's blessing is great.'
> Cling to the silent, then you find life,
> Your being will prosper upon earth.[48]

> Indeed you do not know the plans of god,
> And should not weep for tomorrow;
> Settle in the arms of the god,
> Your silence will overthrow them.
> The crocodile that makes no sound,
> Dread of it is ancient.
> Do not empty your belly to everyone,
> And thus destroy respect of you;
> Broadcast not your words to others,
> Nor join with one who bares his heart.
> Better is one whose speech is in his belly
> Than he who tells it to cause harm.[49]

Also the Egyptian *Wisdom of Any* states that silence is the prudent attitude in the temple,

> Do not raise your voice in the house of god,
> He abhors shouting;
> Pray by yourself with a loving heart,
> Whose every word is hidden.
> He will grant your needs,

---

[45] Parpola 1997, 17, No. 2, iii.11'.
[46] See Section 3.2.1.1.
[47] CAD (Q), 75b.
[48] Translation Lichtheim 1976, 151.
[49] Translation Lichtheim 1976, 159; CoS, vol. 1, 120.

> He will hear your words,
> He will accept your offerings.[50]

Another wisdom text contains a similar passage,

> Beware of raising your voice in his house,
>   god appreciates silence.
> ...
> (Amun) loves the silent one more
>   than the one with a loud voice.[51]

Also the late Demotic Papyrus Insinger criticizes a person who is loud-mouthed in the temple.[52] Especially the priests who had access to the most holy room where the image of the deity stood affirm that they kept complete silence during their service (Brunner-Traut 1979, 199-201).

Also in Greece silence was deemed appropriate in sacral surroundings, as is illustrated by Socrates' remark, 'Now listen to me in silence, because the place is holy' (Plato, Phaedrus, 15). Silent prayer is also attested in Greek literature, e.g. in Homer, Iliad, VII.194-195. In Neoplatonic thought, prayer was seen as a way of becoming one with the deity, something that was attainable only in total silence (Damascius 1967, 64f.). This comes close to mysticism.

4.5.3.2 Silence Because of Forbearance or Prudence in the Bible

When God commands Abraham to sacrifice his only son Isaac, Abraham does not protest, but silently obeys (Gen. 22:2-3). He does not divulge the purpose of their journey to his son and he does not pray to God to rescind the cruel order. Abraham's silence has aptly been described as a terminal silence that bespeaks his piety (Muers 2004, 6).

---

[50] Any IV.1; translation Lichtheim 1976, 137. See also Brunner-Traut 1979, 199; Brunner 1988, 201; Shupak, CoS, vol. 1, 111.

[51] Papyrus Chester Beatty VI, verso 5, 1 and 5, 8. Cf. Brunner-Traut 1979, 199-200; Brunner 1988, 228.

[52] Cf. Lichtheim 1980, 211; Thissen, TUAT, Bd. 3, 317.

Another example of this pious attitude is found in Gen. 24. Standing by the well the servant of Abraham prays that his mission may succeed, asking for a specific sign that one of the maidens coming down to draw water will be the future wife whom God has destined for Isaac (Gen. 24:13-14). Then Rebekah arrives and does exactly as the servant had asked for in his prayer. At that moment he still keeps silent prudently (Gen. 24:21), because he wants to know for sure if God has answered his prayer so soon.[53] The reader of the book of Genesis already knows Rebekah's name and pedigree (Gen. 22:23; 24:10), but the servant does not.[54] Yet he has learnt enough to reward her kindness with golden jewels (Gen. 24:22, 30). Only when she has told him the name of her father and grandfather, and has offered him hospitality, the servant kneels down to thank God (Gen. 24:24-27).

When the Egyptians pursued the Israelites after their flight from Egypt, the Israelites cried in panic to God (Exod. 14:9-10) and reproached Moses to have brought them in this dangerous situation (Exod. 14:11-12). Moses reassures them that the LORD will deliver them,

> The LORD will fight for you,
>   and you must be still (Exod. 14:14).

Instead of protesting loudly (Exod. 14:10-12) the Israelites should show forbearance, putting their trust in God. An open space (Petuchah) after v. 14 underlines their silence graphically.[55]

When God has burnt Aaron's sons Nadab and Abihu to death because they had burnt incense although they did not have the

---

[53] Cf. Westermann 1981, 474.

[54] Cf. Wenham 1994, 144: 'the narrator lets us know much more about the girl than was apparent to the servant: her name, her family, and her marital status. Having already met her name in the genealogy in 22:23, we suspect at once that Rebekah is the appointed bride. If she passes the test, that will clinch the issue, but as yet the servant is totally in the dark.'

[55] In the present context v. 15 would support this interpretation if the singular 'you' is taken as addressing the collective body of all Israelites, including Moses who must have participated in the crying to the LORD (v. 10) then. However, the source critical analysis of the chapter indicates that the tension between Exod. 14:9-14 and Exod. 14:15 may be the result of the weaving together of three different sources. Cf. e.g. Propp 1999, 468, 478-479.

right to do so (Lev. 10:1-2), Moses justifies this severe punishment, but his brother Aaron remains silent (Lev. 10:3). Whether Aaron's silence meant that he resigned to Moses' judgment or that he felt it was too harsh cannot be decided with certainty. But the first option seems the most likely one (Levine 1989, 60; Maarsingh 1989, 84; Barrado 1997, 19). Aaron does not cry out as a mourning father would be expected to do (Milgrom 1991, 604) because he realizes that God's severe retribution was deserved. Similar wordless prudence occurs in Amos 5:13.

Moses and the priests command the people to be silent to listen attentively to the blessings and curses that are about to be pronounced by Moses (Deut. 27:9-10). After v. 10 the silence that falls is expressed by a space in the text (Setumah).

A good parallel to the Ugaritic king Dani'ilu is king Ahab. When Elijah has announced the terrible punishment that awaits Ahab for the murder of Naboth he does not say a word in reply but starts fasting, dons mourning garb, and walks cautiously (1 Kgs 21:27). A graphical space (Setumah) underlines his silent repentance. And as in the case of Dani'ilu his silent plea is (partially) successful (1 Kgs 21:28-29).

In the presence of the LORD clamor is unseemly. Excessive noise is a characteristic of the ungodly in the Hebrew Bible and is incompatible with proper service in the sanctuary.[56]

In Ps. 65:2[1] the poet says 'To you silence is praise, Oh God in Zion!' The translation of this colon is disputed. Most common English translations have 'Praise awaits you, O God, in Zion' or something similar, though there are also translations that have preserved the meaning of 'silence' in this verse.[57] In our opinion

---

[56] 1 Kgs 18:25-29; Isa. 5:14; 16:14 (loud-mouthed multitude); 17:12-14; 25:5; Jer. 3:23; 50:42; 51:55; Ezek. 5:7; 7:11-14; 23:42; 31:18; 32:16; 39:11; Amos 5:23; 6:5; Ps. 41:12; 46:7; 59:7, 15; 65:8; 74:23; 83:3; Prov. 7:11; 17:1.

[57] E.g. NASB: 'There will be silence before You, and praise in Zion, O God'; *The Message*: Silence is praise to you, Zion-dwelling God'; *Amplified Bible*: 'To you belongs silence and praise is due and fitting to You, O God, in Zion'; *God's Word Translation*: 'You are praised with silence in Zion, O God', etc. Also a French translation (French Nouvelle Version Segond Revisée, 1978) preserved the translation 'silence': 'Pour toi le silence est louange ô Dieu, dans Sion', as well as the German Luther Bible: 'Gott, man lobt dich in der Stille zu Zion' and the *Bibel in* gerechter *Sprache* (^{3}2007): 'Für dich ist Stille

the Hebrew text does not need emendation. The expression used here cannot be very different from that which is used in Ps. 83:2. The rendering 'To you silence is praise'[58] is simply the best. The idea is that God does not appreciate clamor because it is a characteristic of the ungodly. The silent praise of the humble supplicants is contrasted with 'the clamor of the nations' in Ps. 65:8[7]. Just as the silence of the pious is connected here with paying of vows (v. 2b[1b]), so Qoh. 5:1-6 recommends the prudent worshipper to pay his vows punctually and avoid a flood of words.

Of course there is the expectation that God will listen to these silent prayers (Ps. 65:3a[2a]), but no audible reaction is expected: 'You will answer us fairly through tremendous acts, Oh God of our salvation!' (v. 6a[5a]). And this is elaborated in the rest of the Psalm, especially in vv. 10-14a[9-13a] where abundant harvests and prosperity are awaited from the Creator of all. In this way the meadows and valleys will shout and sing the praise of the LORD (v. 14b[13b]) – silently, it may be presumed, like the heavenly bodies (Ps. 19:2-5a).

Whether or not according to the Priestly source (P) complete silence reigned in the inner priestly service in the temple on Mount Zion is a disputed issue.[59] In our opinion it is likely that just as in other sanctuaries of the ancient world a higher degree of silence was observed the closer one came to the place where the deity was thought to be residing.

In any case the call 'Silence!' seems to have preceded the theophany according to Hab. 2:20, Zeph. 1:7 and Zech. 2:17[13] (cf. Lux 2005). In all three cases a blank space in the Hebrew text marks this silence physically.[60] Later on when the Feast of Booths and the reading of the Law was resumed, 'The Levites were quieting the people, saying, "Hush, for the day is holy; do not be sad." ' (Neh. 8:11; cf. Deut. 27:9). If v. 11 is not seen as a (later) paren-

---

Lobgesang, Gottheit auf dem Zion!', and also the Dutch *Naardense Bijbel* (2005): 'U komt toe stilheid, een lofzang! O God op Sion' and older Dutch translations.

[58] So e.g. Delitzsch 1867, 407; *DCH*, vol. 2, 426.; Goldingay 2007, 272.
[59] Knohl 1995; 1996; Wick 1998.
[60] In the case of Zeph. 1:7 a space is missing in the Codex Leningradensis, but many other reliable and older manuscripts do have it.

thetical insertion (Williamson 1985, 293), this instruction seems to reflect the order not to mourn and weep in vv. 9-10. Normally mourning and weeping were rather loud affairs (cf. Sections 4.5.4.1-2).

A pious supplicant might feign deafness and dumbness to mollify God (Ps. 38:14-15[13-14]; 39:2-3, 10[1-2, 9]). It is unknown if such Psalms were meant as silent prayers. In any case there was no need to cry out aloud to God. When Hannah ardently prayed for a son the text says explicitly that 'only her lips moved, and her voice was not heard' (1 Sam. 1:13).[61] The truly pious put their trust in God and wait patiently for their salvation, even if it seems that the wicked are blessed with prosperity.[62] Truly pious people keep quiet (Ps. 35:20), pray with their head bowed down, i.e. silently (v. 13), even if the wicked open wide their mouths against them (Ps. 35:21). In accordance with this attitude it is stated in Isa. 30:15 that Israel should have kept quiet and silent awaiting God's delivery. Instead they put their trust in strong cavalry (Isa. 30:16).

However, just as elsewhere complete silence was unthinkable in a community of worshippers that felt the urge to praise the LORD (Ps. 30:13[12]; 40:10[9]). Even the Song of Moses – which accuses the Israelites of many sins in the past – should not be forgotten out of the mouths of their posterity (Deut. 31:21).

The supplicant in Ps. 39 suffers from a grave affliction which affects his outward appearance (vv. 11-12[10-11]). He fears that he will die shortly (vv. 5-7[4-6], 12b[11b], 14b[13b]), but since he realizes that his sorry state is the deserved punishment for sins (v. 12a[11a]), he feels that he has no right to call God to account and has tried to remain silent in order not to curse God in front of other sinners (vv. 2-3[1-2]). 'I kept quiet in silence' (v.3a[2a]), 'I shut up without goodness' (v. 3b[2b]), so even though he did not receive the good he expected from God, he kept his mouth shut. The word 'goodness' here has the meaning of 'prosperity',[63] the supplicant is living without prosperity, whereas the wicked

---

[61]There is no proof whatsoever that silent praying was uncommon, as Stoebe 1973, 91 asserts.

[62]Ps. 37:7; 62:2, 6[1, 5]; 131:2.

[63]Cf. similar use in Ps. 25:13, despite Craigie 1983, 309.

apparently prosper (v. 2[1]). He did not want to denounce God because of this. However, his pious attitude increased his pain so much that he could not keep his tongue in check any longer and starts to speak now (vv. 3-4[2-3]). He wants to know: will his all too short life end prematurely? (vv. 5-6[4-5]). The way in which the supplicant describes his pain resembles Job's complaints,[64] with this difference that Job persistently affirms his innocence. If the supplicant himself would try to answer the questions to this dilemma he would imply injustice on the part of God.[65]

The supplicant's only hope is a merciful God (v. 8[7]). Just as he has saved God from scorn from the side of the wicked (v. 2[1]), he hopes that God will spare him the scorn of fools by delivering him undeservedly from his transgressions (v. 9[8]). However, now he encounters a problem that imposes silence upon him again: he may have sinned but the same God whose deliverance he awaits has done it (v. 10[9]). In view of the goodness of v. 3[2], there can be hardly any doubt that the supplicant deliberately refrains from filling in the word 'evil'[66] because this would bring him too close to the blasphemy he attempts to avoid. The supplicant considers this argument strong enough to ask God to terminate the stubborn silence on his part before his worshipper is no more (vv. 13-14[12-13]). Ps. 39 is one of the many examples of a certain correspondence between human and divine silence.

According to Qohelet one should restrict speaking in the sanctuary to the absolute minimum,

> Guard your feet when you go to the house of God;[67]
>   to draw near to listen is better than the offering of sacrifices by fools,
>   for they do not know that they are doing wrong.
> Be not rash with your mouth,
>   and let your heart not hurriedly utter a word before God,

---

[64]On the connections with the wisdom literature, see Hossfeld & Zenger 1993, 249. See also Section 3.2.4.2 on the wisdom aspect of Job's decision to stop his defense against the Almighty.

[65]Cf. Craigie 1983, 308-309.

[66]'Goodness' and 'evil' are a standard word pair.

[67]Egyptian parallels show that this refers to avoiding unnecessary noise by walking hurriedly. Cf. Brunner-Traut 1979, 198.

for God is in heaven, and you are upon earth,
therefore your words should be few (Qoh. 4:17–5:1[5:1-2]).

This reductionist counsel of the skeptical sage is the consequence of his conviction that God will not answer prayer or lament. Surely there is still a messenger in the sanctuary (Qoh, 5:5[6]), but the sage shrinks back from calling him a 'messenger of God', because he does not expect any answer from heaven anymore, not even by a human intermediary. Qohelet's God remains silent (Kaiser 2008, 1-23; Spieckermann 2008). He has no need of a prophet anymore, because he is convinced that human beings cannot discover anything about the future (Qoh. 7:14; 9:1). What God does remains an unfathomable secret (Qoh. 8:17).[68]

4.5.4 Silence Because of Incapacity

4.5.4.1 Silence Because of Incapacity in the Ancient Near East

One of the most universal experiences of powerlessness is mourning the dead. This might be expressed by loud wailing, but sometimes also by paralyzed silence. Normally worshippers were not silent before their gods. Singing, praying, lamenting and recitation of holy texts filled the temples of the ancient Near East quasi-continuously with sound,[69] though irreverent clamor had to be avoided. Therefore it was a sign of utter sorrow on the part of man if total silence replaced this sign of active worship.

It is debatable if silence because of the loss of beloved ones should be assigned to the rubric 'Silence before the Deity because of Incapacity'. We might have grouped part of the following material under Section 3.2.4. However, in the ancient world the deities were ultimately held responsible for life and death, even if human beings were instrumental in the implementation of their will. For that reason we deal with these texts at this point.

When the Sumerian god of wisdom Enki and his wife Damgalnunna departed from their defiled sanctuary Apsû (groundwater)

---

[67] Egyptian parallels show that this refers to avoiding unnecessary noise by walking hurriedly. Cf. Brunner-Traut 1979, 198.

[68] Cf. Schoors 2003.

[69] See e.g. Kaplony-Heckel, TUAT, Bd. 1, 539.

in Eridu, silence reigned (Cohen 1988, vol. 1, 59). In the destroyed temples of Sumer one of the most horrible descriptions of abandonment by the gods is silence on the part of their worshippers.[70] Silent mourning is also attested in Egypt.[71] According to Isa. 23:2 the inhabitants of Phoenician colonies would have fallen silent because of the destruction of Tyre, but Isa. 23:1, 6 create the impression that silent mourning alternated with loud wailing.

It was often difficult to keep silent. People lamenting the loss of their dearest might refuse to be silenced. When Gilgamesh mourns the early death of his friend Enkidu he cries out, 'How could I stay silent? How could I stay quiet?'[72] When countless calamities strike Egypt even a normally quiet sage finds it hard to keep silent.[73] However, weeping over the impending death of one's father was not manly according to the Ugaritic legend of Kirtu,

> My son, do not weep for me,
>   do not mourn for me!
> Do not use up, my son, the fountain of your eyes,
>   the marrow of your head for tears.
> Call your sister Thatmanatu,
>   the daughter whose passion is strongest:
>   let her weep and mourn for me![74]

In many cultures of Antiquity weeping and wailing were considered a specialism of women.[75] In such lamentations human

---

[70] Cooper 1983, 185; Cohen 1988, 70, 140, 171, 218; Black *et al.* 2004, 130, 136; Römer 2004, 93, 96; idem, TUAT, Bd. 2, 706; Von Soden, TUAT, Bd. 3, 120, lines 100, 106; Hallo, CoS, vol. 1, 420; Tremper Longman III, CoS, vol. 1, 481; Foster, CoS, vol. 1, 488; Klein, CoS, vol. 1, 538. The theme was even transferred to other genres, cf. Vanstiphout 2003, 41.

[71] Dominicus 1994, 20-21.

[72] Gilg. Ep. X.67 par.; George 2003, vol. 1, 682-683.

[73] Cf. Shupak, CoS, vol. 1, 106. Cf. above, Section 2.4.2.4.

[74] KTU 1.16:I.25-30, translation De Moor 1987, 212-213.

[75] De Moor 1987, 261, n. 234. Some scholars, e.g. Gibson 1978, 114 and Wyatt 1998, 294, assume that in the Ugaritic legend KTU 1.19:I.34-35 a girl is stifling her sobs, while others, among them De Moor 1987, 250, translate differently, supposing that on the contrary she wept unrestrainedly when she noticed the ominous signs of disastrous drought and death at the court of her father.

beings accused the deities directly or indirectly of incomprehensible behavior, like the girl Thatmanatu when she hears the news of Kirtu's impending death,

> She raised her voice, shrieked,
>   she raised her cry,
> she wept and gnashed her teeth,
>   made her voice heard in weeping:
> 'In your life, o father, we rejoiced,
>   in your immortality we exulted.
> (Now), like dogs we prowl through your house,
>   like puppies – ah! – through your basement.
> Ah father! Should you die like mortal men?
>   Alas! Should weeping pass through your basement?
>   Dirges of father's wife on the heights?
>
> Alas! Do gods die?
> Does not a child of the Benevolent live?[76]

It is worth noting that the girl Thatmanatu does not accuse the gods directly, but her intention is clear: she challenges the existing royal theology which propagated the doctrine of the divine nature of kingship. Therefore she and her mother feel free to raise their voices.

Also in Greece mourning in silence, by foregoing the wailing that was customary, is attested (Iliad VII.427-428; VIII.28-29; IX.695).

4.5.4.2 Silence Because of Incapacity in the Bible

In Israel too loud wailing gave expression to the feelings of frustration accompanying the death of a beloved one.[77] Mostly God is not openly held responsible, but it is evident that the laments

---

[76] KTU 1.16:II.33-44, translation De Moor 1987, 215-216. 'Benevolent' is an epithet of the highest god, Ilu. Tropper & Hayajneh 2003 propose to render the epithet as 'scharfsinnig' (sagacious). In both cases the irony is obvious. In the royal cult prayers were sent up to wish the king immortality, like the gods whose 'son' he presumably was. Traces of this ideology are still found in the Hebrew Bible, cf. 1 Kgs 1:31; Ps. 2:7; 45:7[6]; 89:27-28[26-27].

[77] E.g. Isa. 15:2-3, 8; 16:7; Jer. 4:8; 25:34; Mk 5:39 par. Also if killing was awaited only, cf. Est. 4:1.

are directed to the Lord of life and death. In Israel too it was in the first place a task of women to moan over the death of beloved ones and sometimes it is stated explicitly that they were not able to restrain themselves.[78]

But silent mourning is attested as well. Those who bury or burn the bodies of deceased sinners have to execute their task in silence, not invoking the name of God (Amos 6:10).[79] Wailing over the dead and the temple has to stop when punishment is deserved (Amos 8:3). Job's friends rend their clothes and strew ash on their heads when they see his sorry state. They sit with him for seven days and seven nights in complete silence.[80] Possibly they feel too embarrassed to address Job unless he himself starts speaking. Or had they already decided that his punishment was no doubt deserved?

After the destruction of Zion its elders sit dumbfounded on the ground, sprinkle dust on their heads and put on mourning attire (Lam. 2:10).[81] In Lam. 3:28 the intention is somewhat more positive, implying also humble resignation of those waiting for the LORD's salvation (cf. v. 26), though the associations with mourning are still present.

As in the world around Israel the destruction of the temple caused the silencing of music and songs according to Amos 8:3 and 4 Ezra 10:22.

The silence in destroyed cities or countries is implied in Isa. 15:1; 47:5; Jer. 6:2; 25:37; 47:5; 48:2. Also shame over defeat and destruction of cities might be a reason to suppress loud wailing. The prophet Micah laments about the destruction of Samaria and the subsequent fall of Jerusalem he expects (Mic. 1:8-9), but warns his compatriots not to weep in front of their enemies, the Philistines (Mic. 1:10).

---

[78] E.g. 'Rachel' in Jer. 31:15; Lady Zion in Jer. 4:8, cf. Korpel 2009b; Lam. 1:16.

[79] Cf. Stuart 1987, 364; Lux 2005.

[80] Job 2:12-13. Normally a period of mourning lasted seven days. Cf. De Moor 1987, 261, n. 240. Lohfink 1962 assumes the existence of a cultic period of silence, but the evidence for anything like that is too meager.

[81] Cf. Renkema 1998, 264: 'The intention behind the action, therefore, would appear to be a desire to share in the silence of the dead, made real by their own silence and paralysis.'

Elsewhere we will discuss Ezekiel's inability to speak anything else but the word of God.[82] But here we want to discuss Ezra 9:4-5. Having heard the news that many Jewish men have married foreigners (Ezra 9:1-2), Ezra rends his clothes, performs what are evidently further rites of mourning and sits down in silence, appalled by such behavior (Ezra 9:4-5). Evidently he does this because he is sure that the same God who allowed Moses to take a foreigner as a wife did not allow later generations that freedom anymore (Ezra 9:6-15).

A reason to remain silent could be that people accepted that they were confronted with a decision of God which made it impossible for them to pronounce judgment (Gen. 24:50). When God finally answers Job's tormented questions, after so many chapters of deep silence on God's side, by invoking his awesome power as the Creator and sustainer of the world (Job 38–39), Job realizes his human limitations and is unable to refute God's argument. He lays his hand on his mouth to indicate that henceforth he will remain silent (Job 40:4-5[39:37-38]).[83]

4.5.5 *Silence Because of Sleep*

What is rather surprising is that the ancient sources mention human and divine sleep at night several times side by side. Apparently because it was seen as quite normal that deities needed sleep just like human beings. This point illustrates well our thesis that the Ancients were fully aware of the anthropomorphic nature of their god-talk.

4.5.5.1 Silence Because of Sleep in the Ancient Near East

In all cultures of the ancient Near East people went to sleep in the temple deliberately because they awaited an oracle from the deity in the form of dreams, visions or direct spoken revelation.[84] They expected salvation in the morning (Janowksi 1989). If the deities addressed did not react it seemed logical to suppose that

---

[82] Cf. Section 5.2.2.2.
[83] See for this gesture Sections 3.2.3.1-2.
[84] Cf. Section 5.3 above, especially the passage about the silent supplication of the Ugaritic hero Dani'lu.

they too were asleep. With regard to the sleep of death and the lack of praise in the Nether World see Section 6.2.1.5a.

4.5.5.2 Silence Because of Sleep in the Bible

Israel is no exception with regard to the belief in the revelatory nature of dreams and visions received while sleeping (cf. Section 5.3.1.2). Possibly the Psalms which speak of salvation in the morning[85] reflect a time when incubation was also practiced in Israel.[86] With regard to the sleep of death and the lack of praise in the Nether World see Section 6.2.1.5b.

4.6 Conclusions on Man Addressing the Deity

In normal communication between humans silence presupposes speech (Section 2.3). Therefore we explored the modes in which human beings addressed their gods in this Chapter 4.

Usually ordinary people did not dare to approach the deity directly. They made use of 'buffers': stelae, images or professional intermediaries such as priests, prophets, singers, scribes. Even praying in the general direction of the sanctuary was deemed sufficient to be heard by the deity (Section 4.1).

The gods were invoked in more or less standardized hymns, lamentations and prayers. The deity was mollified with exuberant praise of his or her unique qualities. Several of these texts betray frustration because the supplicant did not receive the answer he or she expected, but there is reason to suspect that this too was merely an attempt to put pressure on the god or goddess. Instead of the most powerful gods people often addressed minor divine beings asking them to convey their request to the right deity (Section 4.2.1).

It is our subjective impression that in the Hebrew Bible more supplication and lamentation is preserved than in the surrounding cultures. The closest but still remote parallels are found in Sumerian and Hittite texts. Factors that may have played a role are the stricter concentration on one God and the heightened feeling of collective guilt after the collapse of the Judean kingdom. Intercession by other deities is absent from the canonical

---

[85] Ps. 30:6[5]; 46:6[5]; 90:14; 92:3[2] 143:8.
[86] Cf. Ps. 3:6[5]; 4:9[8].

books of the Hebrew Bible, even though it may have occurred in preexilic Israel, especially in the form of consultation of deified ancestors. In the Bible human intermediaries take the place of divine intercessors (Section 4.2.2).

In contrast to other kings in the ancient Near East the kings of Israel and Judah do not seem to have written letters to God, even though he is evidently supposed to be able to read a letter written by a human being (Section 4.3).

In all civilizations of the ancient Near East complicated magic and sorcery were accompanying incantations to ward off suffering from oneself or one's family and friends, or, conversely, to inflict suffering on one's enemies, whether human or divine. Even though such practices are expressly forbidden in the Bible there is reason to suspect that people continued to believe in their effectiveness (Section 4.4).

In Chapter 3 we explored the reasons for interpersonal silence in Antiquity. Did the same reasons apply in communication with deities? This was the question we have tried to answer in Section 4.5. Silence because of offenses committed did occur, but more often virtuous silence was a way to incite the deity to show pity. Also terrifying exploits of deities might cause human beings to keep silent. Sometimes the gods themselves urged their protégés to remain silent while they were busy punishing their adversaries. Excessive noise had to be avoided in the temple, but complete silence was impossible and undesirable. In general wordless prudence was seen as a sign of piety. Silent mourning might alternate with loud wailing. Incubation in the temple in the hope to receive dreams or visions promising divine intervention was common, possibly also in Israel.

If we now compare the results summarized in Section 3.3 with those of Section 4.5 it appears that the reasons human beings may have had for keeping silent before their deities are practically the same:

Silence of Humans before Humans and God(s)

Reasons ↓	ANE Humans ↓ Humans	Bible Humans ↓ Humans	ANE Humans ↓ Gods	Bible Humans ↓ God
Offenses	x	x	∅?	x
Awe / Fear	x	x	x	x
Forbearance / Prudence	x	x	x	x
Incapacity	x	x	x	x
Sleep	x	x	x	x

CHAPTER FIVE

HOW DID THE DEITY ADDRESS MAN?

Now that we have discussed the way in which man addressed God (Chapter 4) we need to deal with the other side of the communication between deities and human beings. How did people in the ancient world describe their experiences with a speaking or writing deity? Or a deity reacting to their prayers or anxious questions by acting, for example by delivering the supplicants or by giving them an unmistakable sign or token? Or by addressing them?

We confine ourselves in this introductory section to some Hebrew examples – some collateral evidence from other ancient Near Eastern civilizations will follow later. It is evident that according to existing literary tradition the deity expected that human beings were attentively listening to any message from above.[1] If humans neglected this apparently self-evident obligation punishment had to be expected.[2] So people promised to listen attentively to the word of God (e.g. Exod. 24:7; Josh. 24:24) and were sure that he would answer (e.g. Ps. 86:7).

From his side God promised to answer swiftly to the prayers of the pious,

> Before they call I will answer,
>   while they are yet speaking I will hear (Isa. 65:24).

> For I know the plans I am planning for you, declares the LORD,
>   plans for prosperity and not for evil,
>   to give you future and hope.
> Then you will call me and I will certainly come,
>   and you will pray to me and I will hear you.
> You will seek me and will certainly find me
>   when you search for me with all your heart (Jer. 29:11-13).

But the worshippers soon forgot to do so, triggering a certain reciprocity – if people did not listen to God, he refused to listen

---

[1] For the Hebrew Bible, see e.g. Gen. 22:18; 26:5; Exod. 15:26; Deut. 15:5; 26:17; 27:9-10, etc.

[2] Lev. 26:14, 18, 21, 27; Deut. 28; 30; Isa. 1:18-19, etc.

to them.[3] If they do not listen (Jer. 6:10), his prophet may try to keep the word of God down (Jer. 6:11). God may even make the sinners deaf to the admonitions of the prophets, Isa. 6:9-10, etc. Similarly Lady Wisdom will refuse to answer those who have neglected her wise counsel (Prov. 1:28, cf. 1:24-25 and Prov. 21:13).

5.1 Direct Communication between Deity and Man

5.1.1 *Direct Communication in the Ancient Near East*

Directly hearing the voice of the gods was a privilege of divinely elected people like kings.[4] An interesting example is the recently published fragmentary dialogue between one Išme-Dagan[5] and the then highest god Enlil who for political reasons is identified with Assur in this and other contemporary documents. The ruler is informed that Enlil wants to talk to him. The text continues,

> Išme-Dagan addressed his Lord as follows:
> '[...], O our Lord, why are you angry? [Whereas his servant (?)] walks constantly behind him? Listen [to his prayers (?)!]'
> He (the god) opened his mouth with him:
> '[...] I am furious at my city, my temple, my house. There I am furious at Nippur, here at Baltil,[6] my cult center, because a descendant of a foreigner has stopped the big sacrifices and (because) the exalted sanctuary of my two cult centers[7] has been destroyed.
> Išme-Dagan replied with these words:
> 'Speak to us and we will restore the regular cult and the plans of your two cult centers.'
> [Thereupon the god] spoke as follows:

---

[3] E.g. Deut. 1:43-45; 3:26; Isa. 1:14, 19-20; 65:12 ↔ 65:24; Jer. 7:16 (according to the Septuagint and 4QJer^a) ↔ Jer. 7:23-28; Jer. 11:11, 14 ↔ 11:7-10; Zech. 7:7 ↔ 7:13.

[4] E.g. the Old Babylonian kings Ibalpiel II (DeJong Ellis 1987; Lenzi 2008, 58-62) and Samsu-Iluna (Sollberger & Kupper 1971, 223ff.; Van Dijk 2000).

[5] Probably Išme-Dagan II, son of Šamši-Adad who appointed him viceroy of Ekallatum and Assur. Išme-Dagan II ruled, with mixed success, in the early 18th century BCE. Cf. Frahm 2009, 148-149.

[6] Another name of the city of Assur.

[7] In the cities of Nippur and Assur.

'Go in the early morning, enter the Ekur temple. On the spot where you see a white raven [shall my sanctuary be rebuild (?)].'[8]

The white raven is an omen by which the god will indicate where his sanctuary should be rebuild. In the subsequent badly damaged lines the god promises Išme-Dagan that if he rebuilds the sanctuaries in Assur and Nippur, and resumes the lavish contributions to the temples, his dynasty will be successful and will never come to an end.

A similar divine speech is directed to Ibalpiel II of the city of Eshnunna who reigned *c.* 1779-1765 BCE,

> O king Ibalpiel, thus says Kititum:[9] The secrets of the gods are placed before me. Because you constantly pronounce my name with your mouth, I constantly disclose the secrets of the gods to you.
>
> On the advice of the gods and by the command of Anu,[10] the country is given you to rule. You will ransom the upper and lower country, you will amass the riches of the upper and lower country. Your commerce will not diminish; there will be a perm[anent] food of peace [for] any country that your hands keep hold of.
>
> I, Kititum, will strengthen the foundations of your throne; I have established a protective spirit for you. May your [e]ar be attentive to me![11]

Scholars agree on the divinatory, prophetic nature of such dynastic oracles.[12] The standard phrases in which they are couched justify the assumption that we are dealing here with *literary* creations which to a considerable extent should be attributed to the scribes who wrote the oracles down. This is also the case if other persons, like prophets, priests or servants of the king, acted as additional intermediaries between the deity and the king since quite similar dynastic oracles are found in this indirect form. The

---

[8] Our translation after Frahm 2009, 146-147, omitting line numbers and other epigraphic details.

[9] Goddess.

[10] High god.

[11] Translation Nissinen 2003, 94, omitting line numbers and notes. See also Pientka-Hinz, in: Krüger 2008, 57.

[12] E.g. Nissinen 2003, 93; Lenzi 2008, 61.

direct addressing of the king is therefore a literary ploy and one might treat such texts in which the impression is created that a deity addresses the king directly also under the Section 5.2.2.

A Babylonian legend relates how Shamash (sun god) and Adad (storm god) once invited the Sumerian king Enmeduranki, legendary ruler of Sippar, to the divine assembly. They taught him how to observe oil on water (a type of omen) and gave him 'the tablet of the gods, the liver', the main source of information in hepatoscopy.[13] Upon returning on earth Enmeduranki taught the priests of the cities of Nippur, Sippar and Babylon the secret techniques of the diviners. Every priest is bound by an oath before Shamash and Adad to guard his secret knowledge which included the ability to use tablet and stylus (Lambert 1967, 132). Enmeduranki presumably reigned before *c.* 2900 BCE but the Babylonian version of this legend is much later (*c.* 1100 BCE) and serves to make Enmeduranki the ancestor of all divination priests.

Even if the impression is created that a deity writes a letter directly to a king it must be assumed that it was dictated to a scribe by a human messenger of the god.[14] When a man sees in a dream that an oracle for the Assyrian king Assurbanipal (668-627 BCE) is written on a pedestal of the moon god Sin, this person assumes that the inscription was written by Sin himself.[15] But according to a variant version of this dream Nabû, the god of the scribal art, read the text to the dreamer which suggests that it was a human hand that wrote the oracle.[16] Other Babylonian tablets refer to religious texts which were presumably written by deities themselves but were no doubt the work of human scholars.[17]

Deities might also address officers of the king directly. In what is possibly a precursor of the later Harpers' Songs, an Egyptian singer of the 20th century BCE prays to the goddess Hathor,

> Pray hear my supplication, your Majesty, Golden One!
> Turn your heart toward me.[18]

---

[13] See Section 5.3.3.1.
[14] Cf. Pongratz-Leisten 1999, 202-265; Durand 2008, 487-490.
[15] 'I put my trust in the words of Sin'.
[16] Van der Toorn 2007, 180-181.
[17] Van der Toorn 2007, 209.
[18] Cf. Altenmüller 2009, 29.

Apparently he expected a direct reply from the goddess. Similarly the Egyptian administrator Paheri (15th century BCE) prays to his favorite god Osiris,

> May you (Osiris) hear my calling,
> May you fulfill what I have said.[19]
> For I am one of those who worship you.[20]

A high officer of the Egyptian New Kingdom praises the goddess Hathor in the hope she will commend him to Horakhty and other deities. Her reply is couched in the form of a direct reply, 'Words spoken by Hathor, mistress of Thebes' (Frood 2007, 91-94).

In many letters from the Old Babylonian kingdom of Mari (18th century BCE) servants of the king report that a deity directly addressed them, usually with a message intended for their master. Because in other cases it is a prophet or prophetess who speaks on behalf of the deity, it may be that the officers omitted the medium sometimes to make themselves more important.

Kings believed in the possibility of direct conversation with their patron-god. A Hittite king prays,

> O Sun-god! A human, your servant, herewith speaks a word to you and listens to your word.[21]

The apparently angry god must tell him in a dream, or by a seeress, or a diviner able to interpret a liver omen, what the king's sins are (Singer 2002, 32, 38). The Hittite king Muwatalli prays,

> Divine lords, lend me your ear, and listen to these my pleas! And the words which I will make into a plea to the divine lords, these words, divine lords, accept and listen to them![22]

In a Hittite expiation ritual a session of a court of Nether World deities is simulated. The sun goddess of the earth (Allani) takes

---

[19] His preceding wishes for a happy afterlife.
[20] Cf. Altenmüller 2009, 31-32.
[21] Singer 2002, 37.
[22] Singer 2002, 87. See also Singer 2002, 91: 'The words of prayer which I will present to the gods, let them not turn them back to me!'

the stand as a witness and speaks out either a favorable or unfavorable oracle for the royal family. It must be assumed that in the ritual her text was spoken by an officiant or a prophet (Taracha 2000, 51, 183-184).

According to the Ugaritic legends of Kirtu and Aqhatu kings had access to the divine council in which the gods directly addressed them.[23]

Often deities address human beings directly in a dream (cf. Section 3.2.3). An Egyptian dream book enumerates all kinds of dreams and interprets them as either good or bad omina. At the end of the session in which a man has his dream explained the following dialogue between him and the goddess Isis is recorded,

> [DREAMER:]
> 'Come to me, come to me, my mother Isis! Behold, I am seeing what is far from me in my city.'
> [ISIS:]
> 'Behold me, my son Horus,[24] as one come forth bearing away what you have seen, so that your deafness be ended as your dream recedes, and fire go forth against him who frightens you. Behold, I have come so that I might see you, that I might drive off your ills, and that I might eradicate all terror.'
> [DREAMER:]
> 'Hail, good dream seen (by) night and by day. Drive off every evil terror that Seth,[25] son of Nut,[26] has made. As Re[27] is victorious against his enemies, so I am victorious against my enemies.'[28]

Here a standard prayer is answered by a standard oracle of salvation in the name of a goddess. Yet the illusion is created that a genuine direct dialogue takes place between the goddess and the dreamer.

According to an Assyrian dreambook a dreamer may repeatedly hear speaking voices from heaven but the identity of the

---

[23] For Kirtu, cf. KTU 1.15:II-III. For Dani'ilu in the Legend of Aqhatu, cf. KTU 1.20–1.22.

[24] The identification with the god Horus might mean that originally this dream book was intended for the benefit of the king.

[25] Evil god.

[26] Goddess of the (night)sky.

[27] Sun god who dispels the terrors of the night.

[28] Translation Ritner in: CoS, vol. 1, 54.

speakers is not disclosed.[29] A voice from heaven – probably the voice of the sun god Shamash – instructs Enkidu to prevent his friend Gilgamesh from entering the forest.[30] The Ugaritic sun goddess Shapshu calls 'from above' to put an end to a fight between gods.[31] In Mesopotamia thunder was interpreted as the heavenly voice of the storm god Adad.[32]

In his prayer to Amun at the battle of Kadesh (c. 1285 BCE), the Egyptian king Ramesses II claims to have heard the god answer him from behind his back,

> But then I found Amun mighty for me
>   above a million soldiers, a hundred thousand charioteers,
> More than ten thousand men, comrades and children,
>   united in singleness of heart.
> No, not the work of multitudes of people –
>   Amun is mightier than they!
> I learned these things from your own mouth, O Amun;
>   and I did not exceed your counsel.
>
> So, I prayed at the far end of the world,
>   and my voice echoed through Thebes;
> And I found that Amun would come
>   once I cried out to him.
> He put his hand in mine
>   and I was happy.
> And he called as if behind me,
>   'Go forward! I am with you!
>   I am your Father, my hand is in yours!
>   I am stronger than hundreds of thousands of men!
>   I am the Lord of Battle, Lover of Victory!'[33]

The Pharaoh claims to have heard the voice of Amun speaking directly to him, encouraging him to attack and promising him victory. Modern readers may grow somewhat suspicious of the

---

[29] CAD (T), 457.

[30] Gilg. Ep. IV.194-195; VII.132-133. Cf. George 2003, vol. 1, 599, 641; vol. 2, 820, 848.

[31] KTU 1.6:VI.23. See also 1.82:6

[32] CAD (R), 322-333.

[33] Translation Foster 2001, 98-99. See also Gardiner 1960, 10, and for parallels De Moor 1997, 52.

fact that the god's voice came from behind the king, but that is not the point here.[34] For the Egyptians god and man are partners (Hornung 1977). A god dwells inside every human being (Grieshammer 1977) and so it is by no means strange to hear an inner divine voice addressing you (Brunner 1977b, 1162). Man is free to follow this divine guidance or to reject it, but exactly this liberty entails that the choice often remains difficult, especially when the heart remains silent in situations where it should provide divine inspiration (Brunner 1977b, 1162-1163).

In the Ugaritic Legend of Aqhatu, the god of rain and fertility Ba'lu[35] addresses king Dani'ilu[36] directly when for seven consecutive nights Dani'ilu has laid in silent supplication before the gods (KTU 1.17:I.1-19). In this case the wish for a son is at issue. The high priest Attanu who dictated the epic to his scribe Ilimilku relates a heavenly discussion between Ba'lu and Ilu, ending with Ilu blessing Dani'ilu with a son. It is probably Ba'lu himself who passes the good news on to Dani'ilu (KTU 1.17:II).

The thundering voice of Ba'lu was heard especially in spring and autumn.[37] In the Ugaritic myth KTU 1.4:V.6-9 his mother-in-law, Athiratu, observes,

> Also it is the prime time for his rains,
> Ba'lu should appoint the time of the barques on the waves
> and of the giving forth of his voice in the clouds,
> of his letting loose the lightnings to the earth.[38]

And sure enough, somewhat later Ba'lu gives forth his thundering voice,

> Ba'lu gave forth his holy voice,
> Ba'lu repeated the u[tterance of his li]ps.
> His holy voice made the earth [qu]ake,
> [the utterance of] his [lips] the mountains:

---

[34] See the rather close Hebrew parallel below, Section 5.1.2.
[35] 'Baal' in the Hebrew tradition.
[36] Cf. Section 5.5.3.
[37] De Moor 1971; De Moor 1988b.
[38] New translation by De Moor. For other opinions see Smith & Pitard 2009, 537.

"I want to invade the inaccessible [   ]
    [   ] the ancient [mountains]!"[39]

Evidently the direct speech that follows the description of Ba'lu's thundering is the *interpretation* of the thunder. Who provided this explanation? Probably the diviner and high priest Attanu whose recitation of the myth was recorded by his scribe Ilimilku.[40] In many cultures of Antiquity brontoscopy (the interpretation of thunder and lightning) was among the divinatory techniques, it seems likely that this has been the case here too.[41]

In the Ugaritic tablet KTU 1.3 Ba'lu announces to his partner 'Anatu,

> For I have a word, which I want to speak to you,
>   a message which I want to communicate to you,
> a word of trees and a whisper of stones,
>   a groaning of the heavens to the earth,
>   of the Flood to the stars:
> I understand the lightning which the heavens do not know,
>   a matter that mankind does not know,
>   and the multitudes of the earth do not understand![42]

Apparently trees and stones which were animated beings to the Ugaritians were supposed to inform Ba'lu about the secrets of the lightning which announced the arrival of the rains that were so vitally important to the semi-arid region of Ugarit. Here too it must be assumed that it was the diviner and high priest Attanu who was able to 'make' rain[43] who was the man revealing some of his secrets here – the little signs he observed in nature that announced to him the coming of thunderstorms: the creaking of

---

[39]KTU 1.4:VII.29-34, Translation De Moor 1987, 63, with comments. Differently e.g. Smith & Pitard 2009, 557-558.

[40]De Moor 2009.

[41]In Homer, Odyssey, XX.98-121 Zeus answers the hero's prayer through thunder which, however, has to be interpreted for him by a slave woman. According to Cicero, *De divinatione*, I.72 (33) the Etruscans used books to interpret thunder and lightning.

[42]KTU 1.3:III.20-28 (par.). Translation De Moor 1987, 9-10, with comments. Similarly Smith & Pitard 2009, 202-203.

[43]De Moor 2009; 2010b.

wood, the rattling of stones, the mysterious groaning of the whole cosmos.[44]

In inscriptions of Mesha, king of Moab (9th century BCE), his national god Kemosh speaks directly to him, 'Go! Take Nebo from Israel!' and 'Go down, fight against Horonain'.[45] In another Moabite document, the so-called Marzeaḥ Papyrus of the 7th century BCE, the gods speak directly to a certain Gera.[46]

Most of the examples hitherto discussed concern important people like kings and their officers. However, it was to be expected that written documentation from the ancient world concerned them in the first place. It must be assumed that personal piety was not restricted to these circles, but was simply not recorded. An Egyptian prayer states in a very general way about the deity, '(He) who listens to the prayer of him who loves to invoke him' (Brunner 1977a, 456-457).

The Greek philosopher Socrates saw himself as a diviner who sometimes heard a voice instructing him to make the right decisions in religious matters.[47]

5.1.2 Direct Communication in the Bible

Direct communication between God and certain privileged people is confined mainly to descriptions of the early history of Israel. God addresses the first human beings directly in the Garden of Eden. He visits the patriarchs of Israel and engages in conversations with them. The LORD used to speak face to face to Moses, conversing with him as with a friend (Exod. 33:11; Num. 12:8).[48] After such meetings the face of Moses was radiating (Exod. 34:29, 30, 35). Some similarity has been noted between the revelation to the Sumerian king Enmeduranki and the Hebrew descriptions of the way in which Moses received the Torah.[49]

---

[44] Cf. Hos. 2:23-24; Hab. 3:10; Ps. 19:2[1]; 42:8[7]; 96:12; Rom. 8:19, 22.

[45] See e.g. Smelik, CoS, vol. 2, 137-138; Aḥituv 2008, 389-418.

[46] For this text see Section 5.2.1.1.

[47] Plato, *Phaedrus*, 20. The Codex Bodleianus B adapts the text to Plato, *Apology*, 31.

[48] Miriam is punished when she and Aaron claim that God has spoken through them too (Num. 12:1-15).

[49] Lambert 1967, 127; Van der Toorn 2007, Chapter 8.

Whereas the idols of other deities are unable to speak and hear (Deut. 4:28), the people of Israel was privileged to hear God himself speaking from fire on the mountain according to Deuteronomy, though they were not allowed to see their interlocutor (Deut. 4:12, 15, 33, 36; 5:4-5, 22-23). However, Deut. 5:4 states that the LORD spoke from face to face to the people. According to the older, Elohistic account in Exod. 20:18-21 the people did witness the thunderclaps,[50] lightning, and smoke, but did not hear understandable speech and asked Moses to act as their intermediary. According to Deut. 4:36 and 5:23-27, however, the people would have asked Moses to act as intermediary only *after* having heard the Ten Commandments directly from the mouth of God himself. Yet Deut. 5:5 creates the impression that already during the pronouncement of the Commandments Moses stood between God and the people as an intermediary,

> I myself stood between the LORD and you at that time
> to tell you the word of the LORD
> because you were afraid of the fire
> and did not go up into the mountain.

Confusing as these different accounts may be,[51] all ultimately agree that the thundering voice of the deity had to be interpreted by an exceptionally gifted human intermediary – Moses.

Also other texts interpret thunder as the heavenly voice of God.[52] According to Ps. 81:8[7] God answers prayers in the mysterious language of thunder which no human being can understand (cf. v. 6[7]) but which subsequently is 'translated' into a long, but understandable oracle of salvation (vv. 7-17[6-16]). Ezekiel hears the thundering voice of God from above the firmament 'as on a rainy day' (Ezek. 1:24-25, 28). Such texts gave rise to the concept of the voice from heaven in the apocalyptic literature.[53] Its divine origin is intimated, but not stated explicitly.

---

[50]The Hebrew text has 'voices'.

[51]Cf. e.g. Weinfeld 1991, 240-241; Tigay 1996, 61.

[52]1 Sam. 7:10; 2 Sam. 22:14; Ps. 18:14[13]; 29:3-9; Isa. 30:30; Job 37:2-5; 40:9. In Ezek. 43:2 the voice of God is compared to the sound of many waters, but the circumstance that the earth lights up at the same time suggests that a rainstorm with thunder is intended (Zimmerli 1969, 1077).

[53]Ruf 2010, 89, n. 353 refers to Dan. 4:31 LXX; Rev. 10:4, 8; 11:12; 14:13;

God even addresses the non-Israelite seer Balaam directly (Num. 22–24). Direct addressing continued for some time in the post-Mosaic period,

> In the earlier parts of the Deuteronomic History, God often speaks directly to individuals, such as Joshua and Samuel. In the later books, for the most part, the divine locutions are put into the mouths of prophets. These prophetic oracles function as an ongoing commentary on the narrative and are an elaboration of the divine promise of continued prophetic guidance found in Deuteronomy 18.15-19 (Coogan 2006, 193).

It is noteworthy that in its present form the Deuteronomistic history does not attribute the privilege of direct conversation with God to the early Israelite kings. King Saul is acting like a prophet (1 Sam. 10:6, 10-12; 18:10; 19:22-24), but does not seem to have received any spoken revelation. King David is usually addressed indirectly (2 Sam. 7; Ps. 89:20[19]), though 2 Sam. 23:2-3 creates the impression that the Spirit of God spoke in his heart. With king Solomon God talks in a dream (1 Kgs 3:5-15).

Pious kings were thought to have access to the divine council,[54] but later on prophets became the normal intermediaries between God and kings in Israel. Prophets were sometimes privileged to witness the proceedings in the divine council and hear God speaking.[55] When God calls young Samuel (1 Sam. 3) the latter thinks initially that it is Eli who calls him. Only after the third time it is Eli who tells him that it must be the LORD calling him (1 Sam. 3:8-9). Apparently to Samuel the voice of God sounded not much different from that of his master. Later on God continued to appear to Samuel in Shiloh and 'he let none of his words fall to the ground' (1 Sam. 3:19-21).[56] The similarity between the reception of the word of God by Moses and Samuel

---

1 Enoch 13:8; 65:4; 2 Bar. 13:1; 22:1.

[54] Cf. De Moor 1997, 156; 1998b; 2010a.

[55] Examples are found in 1 Kgs 22; Isa. 6; Jer. 23:18, 22; Ezek. 1–2; Amos 3:7; Zech. 3 (cf. Gordon 2007).

[56] Since the words of Samuel are apparently the words of God himself, it is a moot question whose words are meant here. However, in the Deuteronomistic corpus the expression most likely refers to the implementation of a divine promise. Cf. Josh. 21:45; 23:14; 1 Kgs 8:56; 2 Kgs 10:10.

is striking and the tradition made them both prophets, recipients of the word of God. However, after Deut. 34:10[57] it was obviously impossible to stress the parallelism.[58]

In the Hebrew Bible God himself is said to have written the commandments, or even the complete text of the covenant treaty, on natural stone or on clay tablets (Exod. 24:12; 31:18; 32:15-16; 34:1; Deut. 4:13; 5:22; 9:10; 10:1-5. Cf. Korpel 1990, 471-474). If so, God would also have communicated with his people in written form. However, already within the tradition process of the Bible itself it was supposed that Moses broke the original tablets on Mt. Sinai and that Moses had to rewrite the commandments himself.[59] Obviously the concept of God himself writing a document destined for human eyes was regarded as too anthropomorphic by later generations.

In Daniel 5 a hand writes 'MENE, MENE, TEKEL and PARSIN' on the plaster of a wall of Belshazzar's palace,

> At that moment fingers of a man's hand appeared and wrote on the plaster of the wall of the king's palace, opposite the lampstand; and the king saw the hand as it wrote (Dan. 5:5).

The emphasis that is put on the fact that it was not the hand of God or an angel that wrote,[60] but a man's hand 'opposite the lampstand' suggests that the writer suspected a human mediator behind the miraculous writing. In any case it is important that the king's wise counselors are unable to read the text until Daniel, 'a man in whom is the spirit of the holy gods' who had become 'chief of the magicians, enchanters, Chaldeans, and astrologers' (v. 11), finally explained the riddle. So, also in this case the mediator was a presumably inspired expert.

An angel calls from heaven to Hagar in Gen. 21:17. However, the passage is probably adaptation of an earlier description in which the messenger of the LORD encountered Hagar on earth,

---

[57] Cf. Section 5.2.2.2.
[58] Originally the text of 1 Sam. 3:21–4:1a might have run 'Like the word of the LORD was the word of Samuel to all Israel'. Cf. 1 Kgs 8:56.
[59] Exod. 34:27-28, presupposing the breaking of the original tablets (Exod. 32:19). But see also Exod. 24:4; 34:1.
[60] Dan. 5:24 states that it was God who *sent* the hand.

as in Gen. 16:7.[61] So it is questionable if one can use this as an example of direct communication.

An unidentified voice from heaven addresses Nebuchadnezzar according to Dan. 4:28[31] but it is unlikely that it was the voice of God. The Aramaic text uses a neutral participle plural for the speakers in v. 28 and in v. 29 'the Most High' occurs in the third person.

The New Testament too avoids direct identification of the occasionally speaking voice from heaven or the clouds with the voice of God himself.[62] The voice from heaven in Jn 12:28 is explained by some bystanders as thunder or the voice of an angel in Jn 12:29. The heavenly voice of Jesus occurs in Acts 9:3-6 and is heard by all companions of Paul. Since Paul is blinded by the light accompanying the voice one might think of thunder here too. However, according to Acts 22:9 the bystanders did see the light, but did not hear the voice. Of the various explanations for this phenomenon that of Jerome is still the best: variants in the sources Luke used. In any case the compiler of Acts did not deem the difference important.

Also according to the Hebrew Bible God may communicate with human beings through an inner voice, commonly designated as his Spirit.[63] According to rabbinic Judaism every Jew has to learn the Law by heart and no new revelation is possible after Moses, whereas at the same time the *interpretation* of the Word of God (by legal scholars, not by anybody) is left more or less free (Tigay 1996, 286-287). The latter can hardly be what is meant in Deut. 30:14. Even Deut. 31:12 argues against this interpretation, 'Assemble the people, men, women, and little ones, and the sojourner within your towns, that they may hear and learn to fear the LORD your God, and be careful to do all the words of this law'. To un-

---

[61] Westermann 1981, 418-419.

[62] Mt. 3:17; 17:5; Mk 1:11; 9:7; Lk. 9:35; Jn 12:28; 2 Pet. 1:17-18. For an overview of the New Testament texts and their parallels in the Greek Old Testament see Ruf 2010, 88-100.

[63] It is often difficult to distinguish between 'a' spirit as messenger of God (cf. Section 5.2.1) and 'the' Spirit of God as the breath of life and immanent guide of human beings.

derstand how to do the Word of God always presupposes some kind of interpretation and therefore interpretation cannot be the privilege of scholars alone. This is definitely not how Mosaic tradition is seen in Jer. 31:31-34.[64] The decisive factor is whether the Spirit of God is working through a human being.[65]

However, the Spirit did not provide guidance on command. Jeremiah for example once had to wait ten days before God spoke to him (Jer. 42:7) and the message was not what those urging him to intercede on their behalf had hoped for.

Psalm 51 is enlightening if it comes to describing the interactivity of the divine Spirit and the human spirit.

> 12[10] Create a clean heart for me, O God,
>   and renew a steadfast spirit[66] within me;
> 13[11] Do not cast me away from before you,
>   and do not take away your holy Spirit from me.
> 14[12] Do return to me the joy of your deliverance,
>   and may a willing spirit support me.

The Spirit of God and the spirit of man are inextricably interwoven here and it is not at all certain that only in v. 13[11] we have to write 'Spirit' with a capital letter.[67] Most versions translate v. 14[12] 'uphold me *with* a willing spirit', but the 'with' is lacking in the Hebrew text. Since the Hebrew word for 'spirit' is used in the feminine gender here,[68] the rendering we prefer is just as well possible.[69] The Hebrew word for 'willing' always indicates

---

[64] See Becking 2004, 244-63.

[65] Num. 11:25-29; 1 Sam. 10:6, 10-12; 19:20, 23:20-21; Isa. 48:16; Ezek. 11:5, 24; 37:1, etc. (cf. Section 5.2.2.2). A prophet could be designated as a 'man of the Spirit', Hos. 9:7.

We read Num. 11:25b as 'and they did not stop', cf. Deut. 5:22; Est. 9:28, or with the Samaritan Pentateuch and some other witnesses, 'and they were not brought in', cf. Num. 11:30. The present Masoretic text is vouchsafing the unique position of Moses, but stands in stark contrast to v. 29.

[66] The parallelism argues against the proposal of Dalgish 1962, 154 and others to render 'the spirit of a steadfast man'.

[67] After all it is a Spirit of God that dwells in man (Gen. 6:3; cf. Scheepers 1960, 315). It is his gift to every human individual until death (Qoh. 12:7). However, because of man's sins his spirit might be corrupted and had to be renewed (v. 12[10]; cf. Ezek. 11:19; 36:26).

[68] Cf. Scheepers 1960, 86.

[69] Cf. *DCH*, vol. 6, 168.

free will, so both the free will of God and the free will of man might have been meant (note the parallel '*your* deliverance').[70]

The reason that we have chosen to write 'spirit' in v. 14[12] is v. 19[17]. There it becomes clear that it is the 'broken' spirit of the supplicant that needs repair. As John Goldingay writes,

> The fact that the spirit is broken, the heart crushed, actually clears the way for renewing. Only something that is broken can be made new. Being broken is not a sufficient condition for being renewed, but it is a necessary one.[71]

Only a heart that is willing to clean up can receive the Holy Spirit to be made whole again. Although the Spirit of God and the spirit of man do cooperate, it is the spirit of man that is in need of steadfastness and support, not the other way around. Only if God restores man's spirit (v. 12[10]) and opens his lips (v. 17[15]), the latter finds the courage to tell the sinful world about God's greatness (v. 15[13]).[72]

Of particular interest is Isa. 30:19-21, a passage that is part of a late addition[73] to the book of Isaiah.

> [19]Truly, you people who dwell on Zion, in Jerusalem,
>   you will definitely weep no more.
> He will definitely be gracious to you
>   at the sound of your cry for help,
>   as soon as he hears (you), he will answer you.
> [20]Though the LORD has given you bread of distress,

---

[70] Because spirits are sometimes acting as messengers of God (Judg. 9:23; 1 Kgs 22:21-23), one might also think of a guardian angel. But this does not make a big difference, because God would be the one who acts.

[71] Goldingay 2007, 133. See also Levison 2009, 30-31.

[72] In a similar vein Paul writes in Romans 8:14, 'The Spirit himself testifies with our spirit that we are God's children.' The Greek verb used here describes the close interaction between the divine Spirit that works in the heart of children of God (Rom. 8:9, 11) and the human spirit that in itself does not find the strength to bear witness: 'the Spirit comes to help us in our weakness, for, when we do not know how to pray properly, then the Spirit personally makes our petitions for us in groans that cannot be put into words' (Rom. 8:26).

[73] Cf. Beuken 2010, 165-166.

> and water of oppression,[74]
> your teacher will not hide himself anymore,
>   and your eyes will be seeing your teacher.
> [21] And your ears will hear a word,
>   saying from behind you,
> 'This is the way, walk in it,
>   whether you turn to the right or to the left.'

From early times on there has been dissent with regard to the correct reading and interpretation of v. 20. Grammatically the Hebrew text allows both interpretation as a singular and as a plural. The great Isaiah scroll from Qumran, one of the earliest manuscripts of the Bible, opted for a plural: 'your teachers will not hide themselves anymore, and your eyes will see your teachers.' This reading might be geared to the situation of the sect of Qumran itself which had to hide from its persecutors in the Desert of Judah. Also the Old Greek version (LXX) and the Syriac version (Peshiṭta) rendered in the plural, but interpreted vv. 20-21 in a negative way as 'those who lead you astray' which in view of the context is a very unlikely choice. The Targum, a Jewish Aramaic translation, opts for the singular, clearly interpreting the 'Teacher' as the Presence of the LORD. Also the Latin Vulgate prefers the singular. As a result, up to our own days translations and commentaries offer different renderings and interpretations, some opting for the singular, others for the plural.

In our opinion the phraseology of Isa. 30:20-21 reflects Deuteronomic theology,[75] especially Deut. 5:32-33[29-30],

> So you shall be careful to do as the LORD your God has commanded you; you shall not turn aside to the right or to the left. In all the way which the LORD your God has commanded you to walk, that you may live, and that it may go well with you, and that you may live long in the land which you shall inherit.

This means that the way from which the people should not stray to the left or the right is the Law of God as mediated by Moses.

---

[74] There is no need to emend the text at this point. The expression refers to the frugal meal of prisoners, as in 1 Kgs 22:27.

[75] Deut. 5:32-33; 17:20; 28:14; Josh. 1:7; 23:6; 2 Kgs 22:2.

This argues in favor of a singular.[76] However, after Moses the teaching of the Law was delegated to others, priests and magistrates according to Deut. 17:8-13, esp. 17:11.[77] This passage probably reflects a secondary combination of offices.[78] It may safely be assumed that also a prophet was regarded as a divinely inspired teacher,[79] like Moses himself (Deut. 34:10). So the 'teacher' is an individual, but someone with special spiritual gifts.

There has been a lot of discussion about the identity of this teacher. Is he a prophet? A scholar? Why was he hidden at first? Why does he speak from *behind* the people? No doubt the best solution is to see God himself as the teacher, as is the opinion of the Targum, Rashi and several contemporary scholars.[80] According to the immediate context, the path from which the Israelites had strayed away is the path of God (Isa. 30:11; see also 63:17). The teaching (*tôrāh*) keeping Israel on the right track is the teaching of the LORD, even in the mouth of false teachers (Jer. 8:8; Mic. 3:11). Also elsewhere God is called a teacher (Job 36:22; see also Isa. 2:3 [Mic. 4:2]). The promise that those rescued will enjoy the privilege of seeing God with their own eyes is in line with Isa. 17:7; 33:17; 52:8. Especially significant is the parallel in Isa. 48:17, 'I am the LORD your God, who teaches you to profit, who leads you in the way you should go'. The Egyptian parallel cited above[81] lends strong support to the thesis that it is the voice of God that speaks from behind the back of his stricken people. However, in the Bible it is the voice of God mediated by human beings: Moses, priests, magistrates, prophets.

The underlying imagery in Isaiah is that of God (or his spokesman) as the shepherd who urges on his flock (the rescued of his people), walking behind them as oriental shepherds normally did

---

[76] The argument derived from Isa. 10:10-11 (Beuken 2010, 182) is not conclusive in this respect.

[77] See also Deut. 24:8; 2 Kgs 12:3; 17:27-28; Ezek. 44:23; Mic. 3:11; 2 Chron. 15:3. Ultimately all this derives from Exod. 18:17-26; Num. 11:17, 25-29 (the elders).

[78] Cf. Weinfeld 1972, 235.

[79] Cf. e.g. Isa. 8:16, 20; 9:15; 28:9. See also Section 5.2.2.2 on prophetic schools.

[80] E.g. Watts 1985, 400-401; Oswalt 1986, 560; Childs 2001, 228.

[81] Under Section 5.1.1.

when guiding their flock to different grazing grounds.[82] The deep frustration after the destruction of the temple in Jerusalem and the ensuing exile was that God remained hidden (Ps. 89:47[46]) and silent to the laments of his oppressed people.[83] This disaster was caused by a leadership lacking the guidance of God's Holy Spirit (Isa. 63:10-11; cf. Jer. 13:1-3). Early on in Israel this was seen as an absolute prerequisite for good leadership.[84]

Also Ps. 139:7 'Where shall I go from your Spirit? Or where shall I flee from your presence?' and the parallelism between 'the angel of his presence' in Isa. 63:9 and 'his holy Spirit' in Isa. 63:10 suggest that the Holy Spirit guided his people from *behind*. The word here translated as 'presence' – in conformity with existing custom – is actually the Hebrew word for 'face'. Isa. 63:14 proves beyond any doubt that it was the *Spirit* who guided the herd. Similarly Ps. 51:13[11]: 'Cast me not away from before your face' in parallelism with 'and do not take your Holy Spirit from me' points to the concept of God guiding the king through his Spirit from behind, as a good shepherd did.[85]

Therefore it is significant that after the destruction of the temple in Jerusalem and the end of the monarchy the promise of the gift of the Spirit became so enormously important and was no longer reserved for special people. A certain 'democratization' of the concept took place.[86] This gift of the Spirit was at the same time seen as the end of the period in which God had hidden himself from Israel (Isa. 45:15; Ezek. 39:19).

---

[82] Cf. Isa. 40:10-11; 62:11-12; 63:9, 11, 14; cf. Beuken 1997, 379-380; 2010, 183; De Moor 2010a. Of course it is no problem that Isa. 30:20 states that they will *see* their/teacher. Many illustrations from the Near East show that shepherds needed not to remain behind their flock when they were not on the move. Also Isa. 30:26b is in line with the imagery of the shepherd, cf. Ezek. 34:4, 16; Ps. 147:2-3.

[83] E.g. Isa. 64:11[12]. Cf. Section 6.2.1.1b.

[84] Scheepers 1960, 131-175; Fee 1994, 907-908. With regard to the prophets see Ezek. 2:2; 3:12-14, 24; 8:3; 11:1, 5, 24; 37:1; 43:5; Hos. 9:7; Mic. 2:7; 3:8; Zech. 7:12. With regard to artisans see Exod. 28:3; 31:3; 35:31.

[85] For the relationship between Isa. 63:11 and Ps. 51:13[11] as well as the imagery of the shepherd see Goldenstein 2001, 65-85.

[86] Isa. 32:15; 42:1, 5; 44:3; 48:16; 57:15-16; 59:21; 61:1 (contrast 61:3); Ezek. 11:19; 36:26-27; 37:5-6, 9-10, 14; Joel 3:1-2 [2:28-29]; Hag. 2:5 [6]; Zech. 4:6; 12:10.

So the voice from 'behind' of Isa. 30:19-21 is the voice of the Spirit of God as mediated by Israel's spiritual leadership.[87] It comes from the Shepherd keeping an eye on his flock and it does *not* exclude human freedom of choice. Those hearing the voice may go to the right or to the left, just as they wish,[88] but the Spirit will let them know whether they are on the right track or not.

John Oswalt wrote about Isa. 30:21,

> ...here is a person whose teacher is just at his shoulder and little more than a word of guidance from time to time is necessary for him to stay on the right path. This is the ideal of the Spirit-filled life, where contact between us and him is so intimate that only a whisper is sufficient to move us in his way (Gal. 5:16-25).[89]

In Gal. 5:13 Paul expressly states that Christians are called to freedom but that this should never be an excuse for selfish love. 'If we live by the Spirit, let us walk by the Spirit' (Gal. 5:25).

According to the Book of Revelation the apostle was seized by the Spirit on the island of Patmos and heard a voice speaking to him from behind, instructing him to write down what was revealed to him (Rev. 1:10, 12).

5.2 Communication through Intermediaries

The awe of deities was so great in the ancient Near East that most people did not dare to communicate directly with the most powerful gods. But even if they prayed to lesser deities as intermediaries, the answer usually came through human representatives of the gods, such as priests, prophets, astrologers, diviners, magicians, spiritistic mediums, scribes. Most of these specialists had gone through a long professional training and claimed to

---

[87] Beuken 1997, 380-381; 2010, 183-184, argues in favor of the Angel of God on the basis of Exod. 14:19. However, this too is a form of mediation which does not differ fundamentally from our view because of the 'name' (presence) of the LORD in his messenger (Exod. 23:20-21), whether an angel or a human being (cf. Propp 2006, 287).

[88] The Hebrew text is rendered correctly in the RSV and most other modern translations: '*when* you turn to the right or *when* you turn to the left'.

[89] Oswalt 1986, 560. See also Rom. 8:16 for this close interaction.

have access to secret knowledge of the divine world.[90] Sometimes these specialists wore anthropomorphic or theriomorphic masks to identify themselves with a deity in whose name they were speaking.[91] In many cases they combined offices, for example that of a priest and a diviner, prophet or exorcist. All of them claimed divine illumination and the privilege to make use of arcane knowledge of the deities.

In Deut. 18 all these forms of mediation are forbidden, except prophecy. But even in this case severe sanctions were necessary to prevent people from pretending to speak the word of God. As we shall see, it must be assumed that Deut. 18 is a relatively late text whereas in reality mantic practices, including the consultation of spirits, did take place in ancient Israel (cf. Römer 2009).

5.2.1 Divine Intermediaries

5.2.1.1 Lower Divine Intermediaries in the Ancient Near East

In Mesopotamia the seven antediluvian sages formed the scribal connection between the divine world and scholars (Lenzi 2008, 106-120). This lent a supernatural aura to the work of master scribes who were frequently consulted in difficult matters of state and religion. They guarded the written sources they consulted jealously, describing them as 'secret'.[92]

Babylonians and Egyptians often invoked guardian angels to mediate for them with the great gods. These lower inhabitants of the divine world are mostly represented as composite creatures, with beaks, wings and claws like birds, or partly anthropomorphic but with a body resembling ferocious animals. A well-known example is the great sphinx at Gizeh. Divine beings, also lower deities, were thought to be able to change their shapes effortless.

---

[90]See e.g. Kees 1953-1958; Sauneron 1988 [2000]; Koenig 1994; Van der Toorn 2007; Lenzi 2008.

[91]See e.g. Rittig 1989; Smith 1990, 134; Duquesne 2001. It should be remembered that deities had the power of metamorphosis, i.e. they were supposed to take on different shapes, among them the shapes of animals.

[92]Van der Toorn 2007, 208-211; Lenzi 2008, 140-215. Also a high priest in Ugarit, see De Moor 2009.

Also in such a non-anthropomorphic state they were able to speak like human beings. In the Egyptian *Tale of the Shipwrecked Sailor* a huge serpent is able to foretell the future.[93] In the *Tale of the Two Brothers* it is a speaking cow who warns the younger brother that his elder brother is about to kill him.[94] Later on the younger brother takes on the shape of a bull and speaks to his former wife.[95] When the Ugaritic goddess ʿAnatu has transformed herself in a cow she is still able to announce the birth of their calf to her husband Baʿlu (De Moor 1987, 115-116).

In all cultures of the ancient Near East and in Greece the concept of messenger deities existed.[96] These messengers could take on incorporeal shapes, like wind or shadows. But they could also transform themselves to more tangible forms, like statues or standing stones representing famous ancestors, or important functionaries, both iconic and aniconic. These too served as intermediaries between the great gods and humans.[97] It is certain that people directed their prayers to them in the expectation that they would convey them to the more powerful gods who were too high to be approached directly by ordinary people.[98]

A recently discovered relief stele from Zinçirli, at the Anatolian-Syrian border, confirms that the man who erected the slab for himself in a mortuary chapel assumed that after his death his soul would live on in the stone and that he would participate in yearly banquets provided by his posterity together with the great gods Hadad, Shamash and Kubaba.[99] A singular Egyptian text relates how the murdered king Amenemhet I rises from the Nether World to speak to his son (and later generations) in a revelation.[100] A Ugaritic official reports to his king,

---

[93] Lichtheim, CoS, vol. 1, 84. Cf. Shupak 1989-1990, 7.

[94] Lichtheim, CoS, vol. 1, 86.

[95] Lichtheim, CoS, vol 1, 88.

[96] See e.g. Handy 1994, 149-167; Reiterer *et al.* 2007.

[97] See e.g. Andrae 1913; Mettinger 1995; De Moor 1997, 350-356; De Moor 1998; Altenmüller 2009, 33-35, 37-44.

[98] This would also seem to be indicated by the Hazor stele on which two open hands are lifted to heaven.

[99] Schloen *et al.* 2009; Pardee 2009.

[100] Lichtheim, CoS, vol. 1, 66-68.

And when I was very ill, I was only a finger removed from death. Now I have recovered from my illness. For (the god) Apšukka of (the city of) Irḫanta came up and demanded of me that (I entered) into his alliance. But whoever makes the offerings of alliance to that god has to bring many presents.[101]

The expression 'he came up' suggests that in this case too the spirit rose from the Nether World to address the living.

Usually it was a priest who acted as a medium to conjure up the spirits who were supposed to listen to prayers and intercede on behalf of the supplicants.[102] Kings often consulted such spirits, mostly the spirits of their deified ancestors, in spiritualistic sessions.

The same word designates 'wind' and 'spirit' in Akkadian, Ugaritic and Punic.[103] These 'spirits' acted as messengers between high gods and lower gods or human beings. Probably their manifestation in the form of wind is merely a form of metamorphosis of the divine messengers who are elsewhere described as anthropomorphic or theriomorphic beings.

In the Moabite so-called Marzeaḥ Papyrus of the 7th century BCE we read:

> Thus say the gods to Gera: To you belong the Marzeaḥ and the two spirits[104] and the house. And Yisha should be far removed from them. And Malka is the trustee.[105]

The *mrzḥ* was a kind of religious society in which men gathered to inebriate themselves in order to communicate with the spirits

---

[101] Cf. De Moor 1997, 367-368.

[102] For Egypt, Wente in: Simpson 1972, 137-141; Von Beckenrath 1992; Posener 1960; Lichtheim, CoS, vol. 1, 134-136; for Sumer, Alster 1991; for Ugarit, e.g. De Moor 1987, 100, 164, n. 54; 165-168; De Moor 1997, 156, 336-361; 2010; Wyatt 1998, 420-441; Pardee 2000, 816-825.

[103] CAD (Š) 2, 135; De Moor 1987, 76, 79; Hoftijzer & Jongeling 1995, vol. 2, 1066.

[104] Most scholars translate *wrḥyn* as 'the millstones'. We regard it as a dual of *r(w)ḥ*, 'spirit', because a handmill in this context makes little sense. For other epigraphic attestations of *r(w)ḥ*, 'spirit', see Hoftijzer & Jongeling 1995, 1066.

[105] For the text see Aḥituv 2008, 427, who offers a partially different translation and duly notes that the authenticity of the unprovenanced papyrus is disputed. KTU 3.9 is a similar Ugaritic text.

of their dead.[106] These were rather raucous parties in which only 'virgins' were sometimes admitted, no married women. Much tact was required from the president of such a semi-religious club. Apparently a conflict had arisen between Yisha and Gera. The deities pronounced verdict and declared Gera the rightful leader and owner of the house where the club used to assemble.[107] According to our interpretation of the papyrus, Gera became also the 'owner' of two spirits who were regularly present at the spiritualistic meetings, just as the two spirits Yaraggib and Tharrumannu were under the control of the high priest Attanu of Ugarit (KTU 1.6:VI.58; cf. 1 Sam. 28:7). Also in Sumerian and Egyptian literature such meetings with dead ancestors who were interrogated in direct speech are recorded.[108] Malka as a third party had to supervise the correct execution of the divine verdict.

In Book XI of Homer's Odyssey the hero recounts in great detail his dialogue with the spirits of his dead comrades. He first digs a pit in which he pours a drink-offering of milk, honey and wine to the dead. Finally he cuts the throats of sheep, pouring their blood in the pit. At that moment the spirits (ψυχαί [psuchai], Odyssey, XI.37) rise from the Nether World and Odysseus converses with them. In Book XXIV the spirits (ψυχὰς, Odyssey, XXIV.1, 15, 35, etc.) of the wooers are called forth by Hermes and in this case too Odysseus is able to talk to them.

5.2.1.2 Lower Divine Intermediaries in the Bible

It has long been recognized that even though the Bible does not tolerate lower deities next to God, the existence of lower personnel in the divine world is accepted in both Testaments. We are accustomed to call such beings 'angels', 'cherubs', or, if they exercise a nefarious influence, 'ghosts' or 'demons'. Of course this is only a matter of naming. They are able to achieve things a human being is not capable of, for example, perform miracles like flying in the air or traveling underground. So the angels, cher-

---

[106] See on this institution e.g. Spronk 1986, 196-197; Lewis 1989, 80-81; King 1989; Loretz 1993; Loretz 1995; Hoftijzer & Jongeling 1995, 691-692; Klingbeil 2006; Miralles Maciá 2007; Janowski 2009.

[107] For the ancestral spirits as judges, see Loretz 2003, 211-336.

[108] Alster 1991; Posener 1960; Wente, in: Simpson 1972, 137-141.

ubs, seraphs and demons of the Bible are simply the successors of the lower deities of the ancient Near East.[109] They often function as intermediaries relaying the word of God to man, in fact acting just like the messenger-deities of the ancient Near East.[110] Just as these human messengers often required the services of a local interpreter, so angelic languages were not readily understandable to everybody and often required expert explanation (Poirier 2010).

In Job 4:12–5:1 the apparition of a spirit speaking to the Temanite Eliphaz is described,

> Then stealthily a word came to me
>   and my ear received a whisper of it.
> Among terrifying things from visions at night
>   when heavy sleep falls on men,
> dread came upon me, and shuddering,
>   which filled all my bones with dread.
> A spirit[111] glided past my face,
>   the hair of my flesh stood up.
> He stood still, but I did not recognize his appearance,
>   (his) shape was before my eyes.
> There was silence, and then I heard a voice:
> 'Can a man be righteous before God?
>   Can a fellow be pure before his Maker?
> Even in his (own) servants he puts no trust,
>   and in his angels he inspires terror.[112]
> ...
> Call now! Is there anyone who will answer you?
>   To which of the Holy Ones will you turn?'

Apparently Eliphaz supposes that a spirit might relay an answer from God to Job's angry questions, but that none of the Holy

---

[109] Freedman & Willoughby 1984, 895-904; Rosenberg 1986; De Moor 1988a; Mach 1992; Handy 1994; Noll 1996; Ahn & Dietrich 1997; Smith 2001, 27-53; Frey-Anthes 2007; 2008; Reiterer *et al* 2007; Wood 2008.

[110] E.g. Gen. 16:7-14; 19:15; 21:17; 22:11; 31:11; Judg. 2:1; 6:12; 13:3-23; 1 Kgs 19:5, 7; 2 Kgs 1:3; 19:7 (Isa. 37:7); Zech. 1:9, 14; 4:1, 4; 5:5. In several of these passages the angel is equated with God himself.

[111] Many translate 'wind' here (e.g. Clines 1989, 111), but Scheepers 1960, 111-112, argues convincingly for 'spirit' referring to 1 Kgs 22:21 and Job 4:17-18. Also the parallels collected above support this rendering.

[112] On the basis of the Arab. root *ḥwl* with its noun *taḥwīl* 'terror'.

Ones[113] will dare to reply in the name of God because Eliphaz considers Job guilty.

In other cases the Bible distinguishes more clearly between the human and supernatural emissaries of God. Flatterers *compared* king David to an 'angel of God' when he had to make a difficult decision (2 Sam. 14:17, 20; 19:28[27]). The simile suggests that the speakers denied David a divine status even though they wished him divine wisdom. Solomon asks God for the same gift (1 Kgs 3). In 2 Sam. 24 the demon Deber who brought pestilence over Israel at the orders of God, is called an 'angel/messenger'. It is the hand of this demon that threatens to destroy Jerusalem (v. 16), but David prays God to transfer *his* hand from his people to himself and his family, even though he had *seen* the demon (v. 17). His prayer is answered not by the demon-messenger, but by the prophet Gad (v. 18). Such passages testify to attempts to demythologize the concept of angelic messengers of God – attempts that were never completely successful. In the late parallel to 2 Sam. 24 adopted by the Chronist what David had seen is described as follows,

> And David lifted his eyes and saw the angel of the LORD standing between earth and heaven, and in his hand a drawn sword stretched out over Jerusalem (1 Chron. 21:16).

At first sight this description looks like a remnant of an older, more mythological tradition. However, it is rather in line with the later apocalyptic interest in giant angels. It is a pastiche from several other passages in Scripture (Japhet 1993, 384) and in this way it became an admissible elaboration.

Sometimes it seems that later redactors reworked older traditions in which God appeared in anthropomorphic shape to talk to human beings but deliberately left a few passages untouched, so that the reader would realize that it does not make a big difference if it was God himself who spoke or his messenger.[114]

In early Judaism speculation about the supernatural angels and celestial spirits increased enormously, but this too was ulti-

---

[113]The Holy Ones are spirits allowed to participate in meetings of the heavenly council, cf. De Moor 2010b.

[114]See e.g. Gen. 16:13; 22:12-18; Num. 22:22; Judg. 2:1-5; 6:14-18, 23; 13:22.

mately rooted in concepts inherited from the ancient Near East. Also in ancient Israel consultation of the spirits of the dead took place (e.g. 1 Sam. 28) although the practice was gradually phased out (Janowski 2009). As in other parts of the ancient Near East divine messengers often take the form of wind or spirit.[115] It is often difficult to distinguish the working in the heart of a recipient of the (Holy) Spirit and appearance of a messenger spirit.

Such spirits were subordinate to God, but still had a semi-divine status.[116] Whereas in the community of Qumran and in early Christianity the Holy Spirit of God continued to guide pious human beings, mainstream rabbinic Judaism became convinced that revelation through the Holy Spirit had stopped after the death of the last prophets,

> From the time when the last prophets Haggai, Zechariah and Malachi had died, the Holy Spirit was cut off from Israel. However, they caused them to listen to the Bath Qol.[117]

Immanence of the Holy Spirit is not impossible, but lies almost at the end of the road to sainthood.[118] The Bath Qol is a voice from an invisible being in heaven, either God himself or an angel. Literally 'Bath Qol' means 'daughter of a voice', but the origin of this designation is unclear.[119] A voice from heaven is mentioned in Gen. 21:17 and Dan. 4:28[31] as well as in the New Testament.[120] The Bath Qol is a concept that was clearly forged to avoid the idea that God spoke directly to sinful human beings after the closure of the Hebrew canon. Perhaps also apologetics against the Christian trinitarian doctrine may have played a role.

---

[115] Judg. 9:23; Ps. 104:30; 1 Kgs 22:21ff.; Isa. 6:8; Ezek. 37:9-10. Very frequently in early Judaic literature and the New Testament.

[116] This follows from the parallelism between 'god' and 'spirit' in Isa. 31:3. The spirit of Samuel is called a 'god' in 1 Sam. 28:13. Spirits had access to the divine council and worked in the hearts of prophets (1 Kgs 22:19-24).

[117] t. Soṭa XIII.4. For more parallels see Kuhn 1989, 16-17.

[118] m. Soṭa IX.15.

[119] On the basis of Exod. R. XXIX.9 it is sometimes assumed to be an echo, but this does not suit all places where the expression occurs.

[120] Mt. 3:17; 17:5; Mk 1:11; 9:7; Lk. 9:35; Acts 9:3-6. See further Section 5.1.2.

However, next to the mainstream opinion other voices in the rabbinic literature kept the possibility that the Holy Spirit might continue to guide certain particularly holy persons open.[121]

Although it would seem clear that the concept of the Holy Spirit evolved from the ancient oriental parallels discussed above, we had to take a decision here and treated the immanent role of the Holy Spirit under Section 5.1.2 (direct communication).

5.2.2 Human Intermediaries

If the deities of the ancient Near East wanted to address human beings they rarely made use of a lower deity as a messenger. Samuel Meier writes,

> It is typical for gods in the ancient Near East to have at their disposal specific, lower-ranking deities who do their bidding in running errands and relaying messages. These messenger deities function primarily as links between gods and not between gods and humans; when a major god wishes to communicate with a human, he or she can be expected to make a personal appearance.[122]

However, the latter statement applies only to special privileged people, like kings or queens, who stood close to divinity according to the prevailing ideology of those days.[123] Normally a deity would make use of a human-like emissary to communicate with people on earth. Mostly messengers of God, commonly designated as 'angels' in Bible translations, look exactly like ordinary human beings: they walk, speak, eat like normal men.[124] In the story about Elijah on Mt. Horeb nothing suggests that the 'messenger of God' is a supernatural being until the invigorating effect of the food he brings becomes apparent (1 Kgs 19:5-8) – though human prophets performed similar miracles. Only by miraculous deeds or announcements that come true the messengers of God

---

[121] See e.g. Kadushin 1952, 251; Schäfer 1972, esp. 147-162; Urbach 1975, 577; Levison 2009.

[122] Meier 1999b, 53.

[123] This is not only true of great civilizations like those of Mesopotamia and Egypt, but also of the much smaller Canaanite states, including Israel. Cf. Korpel 2007, 396.

[124] E.g. Gen. 16:7-14; 18–19; Judg. 6:11-24; 13:3-21.

may reveal their supernatural nature, but this is apparently not a prerequisite for their being a 'messenger' of God. The Hebrew and Greek words for 'messenger' designate both natural and supernatural beings[125] and the dividing line between the two was sometimes vague.[126] Especially human beings who were supposed to speak the word of the LORD could be designated as 'messenger of the LORD'. The prophet Haggai (Hag. 1:13) and a faithful Levitic priest (Mal. 2:7) bore the very same title attributed to 'angels'.

For fear of God people preferred to hear his word via an intermediary instead of hearing him speak directly.[127] But this did not make a big difference, since also if human intermediaries or angels in human shape were speaking in the name of God it was a sin to ignore their words.[128]

5.2.2.1 Prophets and Seers in the Ancient Near East

The best-known human intermediaries in the Hebrew Bible are the prophets[129] and seers – there is no functional difference between the two designations. Usually 'diviners' are seen as a separate category of specialists because they work with material objects like lots, entrails of sacrificial animals and/or handbooks explaining all kinds of celestial and terrestrial omens.[130] Here we shall deal first with the prophets and seers, postponing treatment of various forms of divination to Section 5.3.

For a long time it was thought that prophecy was a special feature of the religion of ancient Israel, even though the Bible itself mentions several non-Israelite prophets and seers (e.g. Num. 22–24; 1 Kgs 18). Nowadays we know that similar phenomena oc-

---

[125] Meier 1999a and b; Van Henten 1999.
[126] Cf. Sections 5.2.1-2.
[127] Cf. Exod. 20:19 ↔ Exod. 19:9; Deut. 5:23-31; 18:15-20.
[128] Cf. Exod. 4:8, 9; 5:2; 6:9, 12; 7:4, 13, 16, 22; 8:15, 19; 9:12; 11:9; 16:20; 23:20-23 (it is uncertain whether the Hebrew word designates an angel here or a human messenger speaking on behalf of God. Cf. Propp 2006, 287); Deut. 3:26; 8:20; 9:23; 11:26-28; 18:19; Josh. 1:17-18; 5:6; Judg. 2:17; 13:3-23; 1 Sam. 15, etc.
[129] On the difficulty of defining this concept see Nissinen 2004.
[130] On the difficulty of distinguishing the three groups see Nissinen 2004.

curred in Sumeria in the 3rd millennium BCE, in Old Babylonian Mari and Eshnunna in the 18th century BCE, in Assyria in the 7th century BCE, in the Levant (12th-7th century BCE), as well as in Egypt. It has become clear that human messengers of the gods are attested in many other civilizations of the ancient Near East.[131] These prophecies resemble the biblical prophetic literature in many respects. They often start with the introduction 'Thus speaks DN (divine name)', are delivered orally, usually in the temple, in front of witnesses, are mostly transmitted in writing by others, are often couched in a poetic style. They may start without introduction and jump unexpectedly from one person to another[132] – formal elements that have given rise to much speculation in scholarly literature of the past.

In the Old Babylonian kingdoms of Mari and Eshnunna (c. 1780 BCE) both male and female prophets were active. They are designated by various names, one of which is 'raving one'. Mostly their oracles were addressed to the king and in some cases can be understood as replies to prayers recited by, or on behalf of, the king. However, oracles against foreign nations are also attested (e.g. Nissinen 2003, 44).

We must confine ourselves to a few representative examples of such prophecies. It is reported in a letter from a certain Nur-Sin, representative of king Zimri-Lim of Mari in the city of Aleppo,

> Through oracles, Adad, Lord of Kallassu,[133] [spoke] to me as follows: 'Am I not [Ad]ad, Lord of Kallassu, who reared him (the king) between my loins and restored him to the throne of his father's house? After I restored him to the throne of his father's house, I have again given him a residence. Now, since I restored

---

[131] It is impossible here to review the enormous number of publications these discoveries generated. We confine ourselves to the following references: Ellermeier 1968; Barta 1972; Noort 1977; Wächter 1984; Durand 1988; 2002; 2008; DeJong Ellis 1989; Chappaz 1990; Heintz 1997; Parpola 1997; Malamat 1998, 59-162; Nissinen 1998; 2000a; 2000b; 2003; Starbuck 1999; Van der Toorn and Nissinen, in: Ben Zvi & Floyd 2000, 219-234, 235-271; Weippert 2001; 2002b; Charpin 2002; Köckert & Nissinen 2003; Hilber 2005; Szpakowska 2006; De Jong 2007; Blum 2008; Lenzi 2008.

[132] See e.g. Korpel & De Moor 1998, 18, n. 5; 71, n.6; 73, n. 10; 123, n. 16; 206, n. 7; 207, n. 8; 211, n. 36; 363, n. 8; 491, nn. 4, 6; Hilber 2005, 206-207.

[133] Local manifestation of the Babylonian weather god.

him to the throne of his father's house, I will take from him an estate. Should he not give (the estate), am I not master of throne, territory and city? What I have given, I shall take away.

If (he does) otherwise, and satisfies my desire, I shall give him throne upon throne, house upon house, territory upon territory, city upon city. And I shall give him the land from the rising (of the sun) to its setting.'[134]

Further on in the same letter another prophet of Adad of Kallassu admonishes king Zimrilim to judge the case of a wronged man or woman and to heed the word of Adad – the same kind of social standard that the 'good' prophets in Israel advocated. As Malamat and others have recognized, these oracles resemble the so-called dynastic prophecy of Nathan in 2 Sam. 7 in many respects.[135] We note that these Mari prophecies are conditional, like many Hebrew prophecies, and that the message is delivered indirectly through a royal steward who probably had heard it from prophets in his entourage. The elevated style, however, points to an educated person who edited this divine speech. Thus far there is little evidence that the prophets themselves were literate.

Sometimes Mari prophets received their messages in the form of dreams, as in the following report of one Malik-Dagan,

In my dream I was going, together with a companion, from the district of Saggarātum, through the upper district, to Mari. Before I got to my destination, I entered Terqa. As soon as I came into Terqa, I visited the temple of Dagan, and did obeisance to Dagan.[136] As I did obeisance, Dagan opened his mouth and spoke to me in these terms: Have the Yaminite rulers[137] and their armies made peace with Zimrilim's army that has come up? I said: They did not make peace. Just before I left he spoke to me: Why is it that Zimrilim's messengers are not steadily present before me? And why doesn't he put a complete report before me? Had he done so, I would have delivered the Yaminites into Zimrilim's

---

[134]Translation Malamat 1998, 107-108. See also Durand 2000, 130-133; Nissinen 2003, 17-21.
[135]See also Durand 2002 and 1 Kgs 1:47-48; Job 1:21.
[136]Dagan was the national god of the kingdom of Mari.
[137]The Yaminites were semi-nomadic tribes who often rebelled against their overlord in Mari.

hand a long time ago. Go now, I send you. You shall say to Zimrilim: Send me your messengers and put a complete report before me. Then I will make the Yaminites crawl in a fisherman's box and put them at your disposal.[138]

Among the interesting points in this report are the disobedience of king Zimrilim for which he is rebuked, the manifest political interest of the deity, the conditional promise of eventual victory and the circumstance that the prophet is addressed as the god's messenger. Parallels to what we find in the Bible come readily to mind.

Even if the Old Babylonian prophets from Mari were said to have *written* letters to the king[139] it must be assumed that in reality they made use of the services of scribes who will have felt free to modify the wording according to their own literary taste.[140]

It is also noteworthy that the Mari prophets sometimes performed symbolic acts to underline their messages. A prophet of the god Dagan, for example, devours a lamb raw in front of the elders sitting at the city gate. After having delivered his message – which is clearly related to his symbolic act[141] – he requests to be clothed in a garment, so that it must be assumed that he was naked while carrying out his divinely inspired mission.

Also in the kingdom of Emar on the upper Euphrates prophets and prophetesses appear to have worked *c.* 1200 BCE. Their professional designations are closely related to the Hebrew words for 'prophet' and 'prophetess' (Pentiuc 2001, 112-113).

The Egyptian Report of Wenamun (*c.* 1090-1080 BCE) relates how in the Canaanite city of Byblos an ecstatic prophet arose while the king of Byblos was sacrificing,

> Now while he was offering to his gods, the god took hold of a young man [of] his young men and put him in a trance. He said

---

[138] Translation Van der Toorn, in: Ben Zvi & Floyd 2000, 222 (explanatory notes added by us).

[139] Durand 1988, t. 1, Nos. 192-194; t. 2, No. 414:29-35. Cf. Charpin 2002, 8-9.

[140] Cf. Van der Toorn, in: Ben Zvi & Floyd 2000, 229-233; similarly Charpin 2002, 14.

[141] He says, 'A devouring will take place!' (Nissinen 2003, 38).

to him:[142] 'Bring [the] god up![143] Bring the envoy who is carrying him! ... It is Amun who sent him. It is he who made him come!'[144]

Several points are worth noting,

1. The spontaneous nature of the seizure by a god. The impression is created that the medium was selected at random ('a young man [of] his young men').

2. The cultic context in which the event took place.

3. The revelatory content of the divine message. The report indicates that the envoy Wenamun had kept the presence of an image of the Egyptian national god Amun-Re with him a secret. As he had not divulged that it was Amun-Re who had instructed him to undertake this voyage it had remained a complete secret. He had even hidden the god's image in a tent on the shore. Of course the 'prophet' may have had special intelligence enabling him to reveal these facts to his king, but this is irrelevant since both the king of Byblos and the Egyptian envoy believed that he spoke the words of a deity.

4. The message is clearly a warning, not a good tiding.

Next to these reports of prophetic activity more or less literary prophecies have been found in Babylonia, like the *Marduk Prophecy* (Foster 2005, 388-391), the *Shulgi Prophecy* (Foster 2005, 357-359) and the *Uruk Prophecy* (CoS, vol. 1, 481-482; Foster 2005, 1026-1027). All these compositions predict disasters and the ultimate delivery by a righteous king. It is clear that the events described have taken place already and so we are dealing with *vaticinia ex eventu*, texts in which the future tense is chosen to extol the virtues of victorious kings living much later. Perhaps it is better to regard them as apocalyptic literature.[145] In

---

[142] I.e. the man in trance says to the king of Byblos.
[143] I.e. the cult image of the Egyptian god Amun(-Re).
[144] Translation Lichtheim in: CoS, vol. 1, 90.
[145] See e.g. Hallo 1966; Grayson 1975; Lambert 1978; Ringgren 1983; Goldstein 1988; De Jong 2007, all with earlier literature.

most cases the author is unknown, but obviously it is the work of learned scribes. In the Marduk and Shulgi prophecies they make the deity speak in the first person singular, but also in the other cases a divine origin may have been assumed for such 'arcane' knowledge.

In Egypt too this type of apocalyptic literature existed. In the exceptional Coffin Texts Spell 1130 the creator god Atum predicts that after 'millions of years' he will join Osiris, the god of the Nether World and all created order will be overturned,

> I will come to sit with him in one place,
> and mounds will become towns, and towns mounds:
> one enclosure will destroy the other.[146]

Also in the *Book of the Dead*, 175, the total destruction of the created world is envisaged,

> Then I [Atum] shall destroy all that I have made. This land will return into the Abyss, into the flood as in its former state.[147]

In these cases too the deities speak in the first person singular. However, this is embedded in theological speculation about a process of rise and fall of deities that stretches over millions of years.

A similar compilation of apocalyptic predictions is the Egyptian *Prophecy of Neferty*, written during the reign of Amenemhet I (c. 1976-1947 BCE), but antedated under the reign of Snefru (c. 2614-2579 BCE).[148] Neferty is a lector priest, but also a skilled scribe.[149] He predicts a time of utter chaos resembling the state of the world before creation. Only when a savior, i.e. Amenemhet I, comes from the South order will be restored. Also in Egyptian literary compositions like the *Admonitions of Ipuwer*[150] and the

---

[146] Allen, CoS, vol. 1, 27.

[147] Allen, CoS, vol. 1, 28.

[148] Translations e.g. Simpson 1972, 234-240; Foster 2001, 76-84.

[149] Blumenthal 1982, 14-15, stresses the fact that he is a sage rather than a prophet in the Israelite sense. It is questionable, however, whether in the ancient world somebody able to predict the future in so much detail would not automatically be regarded as a messenger of the gods.

[150] Translation e.g. Shupak, in: CoS, vol. 1, 93-98. The prophetic nature of this text is disputed however, cf. Enmarch 2008, 41.

very late (2nd century BCE?) Greek-Egyptian *Potter's Oracle*[151] calamities of apocalyptic dimensions are announced, but here too a royal redeemer will eventually rehabilitate the country. Most scholars are convinced that all these works should be regarded as propagandistic *vaticinia ex eventu*, but this does not imply that they were not intended and understood as genuine prophecy.[152] Also in this case it has been defended that this genre of Egyptian literature stood at the basis of Jewish apocalyptic literature.[153] However, any direct link between the two is unlikely. Since the genre is also attested in Mesopotamia, and possibly in the Transjordanian Balaam text, there is reason to suspect that it was a generally accepted way to hold up a mirror to one's contemporaries.

Combinations of prophecy or oracles with hymns or prayers which were most likely recited in a cultic context are only rarely attested in the literature of the ancient Near East. But this may well be accidental. Several examples are known of endangered kings who pray to their deities for help and in answer to their prayers receive a good omen or an oracle of salvation.[154] A very clear example is found in the well-known inscription of Zakkur, king of Hamath (8th century BCE):

> Then Bar-Hadad, son of Hazael, king of Aram, united against me s[even]teen kings ... All these kings laid siege to Hazrach. They raised a wall higher than the wall of Hazrach, they dug a ditch deeper than [its] ditch. Now I raised my hands to Baʿlshamayn and Baʿlshamayn answered me. Baʿlshamayn [spoke] to me through seers and diviners, Baʿlshamayn said to me, 'Do not be afraid! Since I have made [you king, I will stand] beside you. I will save you from all [these kings who] have besieged you.'[155]

Here at least one gets the impression that a prayer was followed

---

[151] Translation e.g. Jördens, in: Krüger 2008, 420-426.
[152] Cf. Blumenthal 1982, esp. 13; Schlichting 1982b.
[153] References Blumenthal 1982, 17, n. 122; Schlichting 1982b, 1125, n. 20.
[154] See e.g. Dietrich 1990, 33-4; Fales 1991, 83-4; Parpola 1997, LXXIII.
[155] Translation Millard, CoS, vol. 2, 155. Instead of 'diviners' the rendering 'messengers' might be preferable, cf. Ugaritic ʿdd 'herald, messenger', with Becking 1987; Del Olmo Lete & Sanmartín 2003, vol. 1, 149.

174   CHAPTER FIVE

shortly by an oracle of salvation not unlike some Israelite prophecies[156] and it was mediated by acknowledged experts.

A similar combination of prayer and promise of salvation is found in the Ugaritic ritual RS 24.266 (KTU 1.119):26'-36':

> When a strong one attacks your gate,
>   a warrior your walls,
> You shall lift your eyes to Baʿlu and say:
>
> Oh Baʿlu, please drive the strong one from our gate,
>   the warrior from our walls,
> a bull, Oh Baʿlu, we shall sanctify,
>   the vows, Oh Baʿlu, we shall fulfill;
> the firstlings, Oh Baʿlu, we shall consecrate,
>   a ḥitpu-sacrifice, Oh Baʿlu, we shall fulfill,
>   the tithe, Oh Baʿlu, we shall pay,
> to the sanctuary, Oh Baʿlu, we shall ascend,
>   the path of the House, Oh Baʿlu, we shall walk.
> And Baʿ[lu will h]ear [your] prayer:
> He will drive the strong one from your gate,
>   [the warrior] from yo[ur] walls.[157]

Again it makes no sense to suppose that a long time elapsed between the prayer and the fulfillment of the promise. It is certainly noteworthy that both have been formulated in poetic form[158] and that the whole passage was inserted into a cultic text.

At the end of another Ugaritic ritual which describes a sacrificial banquet for the shades of the dead ancestors of the royal dynasty, it is intoned,

> Peace, peace on ʿAmmurapi![159]
>   And peace on his house!
> Peace on Tharyelly![160]
>   Peace on her house!

---

[156] See the parallels given by Millard, CoS, vol. 2, 155, notes n-p.

[157] Translations do not differ much, cf. for example, De Moor 1987, 173-174; Pardee 2002, 53, 149-50.

[158] Note the sevenfold promise of thanksgiving.

[159] Last king of Ugarit.

[160] Queen of Ugarit.

> Peace on Ugarit!
> Peace on its gates![161]

This looks strongly like a blessing for the ruling king, his family and his kingdom. Who is pronouncing it? Just like the preceding promise of deliverance the direct speech is not introduced. Moreover a blessing like this does not differ much from an oracle of salvation. The strong connection of both passages with the cult suggest that it was pronounced by a priest or a cultic prophet. The prophetic criticism of Israelite oracles promising peace seems to support this hypothesis.[162]

As indicated earlier, hymns and prayers in a prophetic context are rare outside Israel. But they are not completely absent. An example is a lament quoted in a favorable prophecy for Esarhaddon, king of Assyria (681-669 BCE):

> I am the Lady of Arbela.
> To the king's mother:
> Because you implored me, saying:
> 'You have placed the ones at the (king's) right and left side in your lap,
> but made my own offspring roam the steppe' –
> Now fear not, *my* king!
> The kingdom is yours, yours is the power!
>
> ―――――――――――――――――――――
>
> By the mouth of the woman Aḫat-abiša of Arbela.[163]

It may be noted that both the complaint and the divine reply are couched in the form of poetic verses with nicely balancing parallelism. It would be absurd to suspect a later insertion here. The lament is part and parcel of the prophecy.

The authority of persons claiming to speak in the name of deities was not accepted automatically. A Sumerian sage mocks humorously about verification of prophecy,

---

[161] KTU 1.161:31-34.

[162] Jer. 6:13-14; 8:10-11; Ezek. 13:10, 16; Mic. 3:5. Cf. 1 Chron. 12:18.

[163] Translation Parpola 1997, 9. The Lady of Arbela was the goddess Ishtar worshipped in the city of Arbela in northern Iraq.

> An ecstatic[164] positioned himself at Inanna's[165] gate.
> His woman spoke among the people,
> 'My mother's word(?) is verily true,' she said.[166]

The salient point in this little narrative gem is the change of gender. Rather than testifying to the truth of the message of her husband the prophet, she advises the audience to listen to the comments of her mother, possibly meaning Inanna.

In a Sumerian lament the disastrous effects of the word of the high god Enlil – apparently a prophecy of doom – are described as follows,

> Let me bring his word to the diviner
>   and that diviner will lie,
> Let me bring his word to the interpreter
>   and that interpreter will lie.
> His word afflicts a man with woe.
>   That man moans.
> His word afflicts a young woman with woe.
>   That young woman moans.
> As his word proceeds lightly, it destroys the land.
>   As his word proceeds grandly, it destroys habitations.
> His word is a covered fermentation vat.
>   Who may know what is inside it?
> His word, whose interior is unknown,
>   its exterior tramples down (everything).
> His word, whose exterior is unknown,
>   its interior tramples down (everything).[167]

The word of the highest god is unfathomable and its menacing contents may be such that diviners and interpreters prefer to lie about it instead of revealing the terrible truth. Also in Assyria the possibility of false prophecy was acknowledged.[168]

---

[164] A designation of a raving prophet.

[165] Goddess of love.

[166] Translation Alster 1997, vol. 1, 213 (13.42).

[167] Cohen 1988, vol. 1, 137.

[168] Nissinen 1998, 166-167. According to Durand 2008, 480-481, the sincerity of the Old Babylonian Mari prophets was never put in doubt, but the king remained free to ignore prophetic advice. However, there are also cases where the trustworthiness of a prophecy was tested by consulting another prophet or by performing hepatoscopy (Charpin 2002, 20-26).

An Assyrian officer complains,

> [I turned to] a prophet (but) did not find [any hop]e,
> he was adverse and did not see much.[169]

Apparently also private persons sometimes consulted prophets and might be disappointed by the outcome of their inquiries.

A Late Babylonian Chronographic text (dated in the month of Tishri, 133 BCE) relates how an ordinary person called 'Boatman' went into a frenzy and started to announce the arrival of several deities in various Babylonian cities on certain dates. These messages were received with much enthusiasm by the citizens. However, the temple council did not believe the prophet and urged his followers to go back to their cities,

> '[I am] a mes[senger] of Nanaya! I have been sent on behalf of the strong, hitting god, your God'. The council of that temple responded to [that] Boatman [and to the people with him], saying: 'Retreat back, return to your cities! Do not deliver up the city to loot and plunder! Do not let the gods like the city be carried off as spoils!' [... *Boatman*] responded to them, saying: 'I am a [mes]senger of Nanaya; I will not deliver up the city to loot and plunder! As the hand of the strong, hitting God [... s] to Ezida [...]'
> The council of that temple responded to the people who were wi[th] that [Boatman]: 'Do not listen to the words of that fanatic!'[170]

In Ancient Egypt the existence of prophecy that is comparable to that of ancient Israel is disputed. Nili Shupak has reviewed the relevant texts and concludes that there is indeed a remarkable resemblance, but the Egyptian admonitions are closer to the wisdom literature.[171]

Among the Hittites too the idea existed that ordinary people could become messengers of the deities.

---

[169] Parpola 1993, No. 294:32.

[170] Translation Nissinen 2003, 197-198, omitting line numbers and footnotes. See also Pientka-Hinze, in: Krüger 2008, 59-60.

[171] Shupak 1989-1990; CoS, vol. 1, 93-110.

> O gods, whatever sin you perceive, either let a man of god come [and declare it], or let the old women, [the diviners, or the augurs establish it], or let ordinary persons see it in a dream.[172]

The title 'man of god' resembles the title sometimes attributed to Israelite prophets and probably refers to a similar institution in Hatti (Prechel 2008). A scribe was instructed to daily read out a tablet inscribed with a prayer in the name of the king and queen (Singer 2002, 54, 56). Apparently a prophet or prophetess was among those who might deliver the deity's reply.

One of the most convincing testimonies of prophetic activity of seers in Transjordan is the famous, 8th century Balaam text discovered on the wall of a sanctuary in Tell Deir 'Alla', biblical Succoth, in Transjordan.[173] There is no doubt that this Balaam is the same man as the biblical Balaam, son of Beor.[174] In the text he is called 'a seer of the gods' to whom the gods reveal future disasters which the seer had to pass on to his people. His message is called a 'burden-oracle of El (God)'. The same term often heads prophecies of doom in the Bible (see especially Jer. 23:33-34, 36).

Earlier we discussed the Moabite Marzeaḥ Papyrus of the 7th century BCE which testifies to consultation of spirits.[175] For our investigation it is important to note here that even though the gods address Gera directly ('you'), the verdict is apparently relayed to him through another person. The messenger formula 'Thus say the gods' strongly resembles the introduction of prophetic speech in Mari, Eshnunna, Assyria and the Bible: 'Thus says (the deity)'.[176] Therefore it seems likely that this formula was uttered by a Moabite prophet, or a scribe posing as a prophet.

Also in Greece the phenomenon of prophecy was known. The μάντις (*mantis*, originally probably meaning 'raving one') was a prophet or prophetess who was consulted in difficult matters.

---

[172] Singer 2002, 52, 58; see also 60.

[173] See e.g. Levine, CoS, vol. 2, 140-145; Seow, in: Nissinen 2003, 207-212; Aḥituv 2008, 432-465.

[174] Num. 22–24; 31:8, 16; Deut. 23:4-5; Josh. 13:22; 24:9-10; Mic. 6:5; Neh. 13:2.

[175] See Section 5.2.1.1.

[176] Cf. Westermann 1960, 70ff.

Generals of armies made important military decisions on the basis of their advice which was based presumably on divine revelation, but certainly also on intelligent guesswork. One of the most famous prophets was the blind Teiresias from Thebes who even as a spirit was still consulted by Odysseus (Odyssey X.490-495; XI.90-151).

The Greek prophet/seer too did not always announce good news. A well-known example is the prophecy of doom which the seer Calchas, 'wisest of augurs, who knew things past, present and to come' (Iliad I.69-70), pronounced against Agamemnon (Iliad I.92-100) and which elicits the following angry retort from the latter,

> Seer of evil, you never yet prophesied smooth things concerning me, but have ever loved to foretell that which was evil.

This demonstrates that people expected positive messages from prophets and that bad news was exceptional. Mistrust of prophecy is also expressed by the chorus in Aeschylus' *Agamemnon*, 1130-1135,

> I cannot boast that I am a keen judge of prophecies; but these, I think, spell some evil. But from prophecies what word of good ever comes to mortals? Through terms of evil their wordy arts bring men to know fear chanted in prophetic strains.

False prophecy too appears to have been known among the Greeks, as is demonstrated by Cassandra's scornful remark, 'Or am I a prophet of lies, a door-to-door babbler?'[177] In her case too only the course of history could prove her prophecies to be right or wrong, 'What is to come, will come. And soon you, yourself present here, shall with pity pronounce me all too true a prophetess.'[178] In Lucian's sarcastic *Dialogues of the Dead*, 9 (28), Menippus ends his talk with the blind prophet Teiresias with the words, 'Ah, you love a lie still, Teiresias. But there, it is your trade. You prophets! There is no truth in you.'

---

[177] Aeschylus, *Agamemnon*, 1197. Cassandra herself was an ecstatic prophetess who was overwhelmed by the god Apollo, cf. Lindblom 1963, 27-28.

[178] Aeschylus, *Agamemnon*, 1240-1241.

One of the most famous prophetesses was the Pythia of the oracle of Apollo Pythius at Delphi. According to Plutarch she came from a simple peasant family and spoke incoherently in a hoarse voice, but on other grounds it must be assumed that normally her responses were clear and coherent, even formulated in verse (for which literacy was not a requirement). The historian Thucydides relates extensively how the false interpretation of a lunar eclipse by prophets became the undoing of the Athenians in their 415 BCE expedition against Sicily. Thucydides calls the Greek commander too superstitious, but of course this was easy criticism in hindsight.[179]

5.2.2.2 Prophets and Seers in the Bible

On a small hieratic ostracon from Ashkelon (late second millennium BCE) an officer reports 'There are no prophets' (Wimmer 2008). Apparently his superior had expected to find prophets in the Philistine Shephelah. This in itself is important information because it proves that at that time already prophecy was an established institution in the region.

At this time we still have no unequivocal extra-biblical evidence that prophecy was also an established institution in ancient Israel. But it does seem more than likely now. A Lachish letter dating from the time when Nebuchadnezzar's army was besieging Jerusalem and razing the cities of Judah (c. 587 BCE) proves independently from the Bible that in Israel too prophets worked in the service of the king and his officers. One of the officers in the Judahite army reports to his superior, 'And as for the letter of Tobijah, the servant of the king, which came to Shallum, the son of Jaddua, from the prophet, saying, "Be on guard!", your ser[vant] is sending it to my lord.'[180] It is unclear if the prophet himself wrote the letter received by Shallum or that Shallum recorded an orally delivered message of the prophet. Another very fragmentary letter from Lachish also refers to 'the prophet' which means at least that the man's office was well-known.[181] Meagre

---

[179] See on all this Flower 2008; Köckert 2009; Scherf 2009.

[180] Cf. Aḥituv 2008, 62-69 who points to the similar warning of the man of God in 2 Kgs 6:9.

[181] Seow on Lachish ostracon No. 16 in: Nissinen 2003, 217-218.

though this extrabiblical evidence is, it demonstrates that in the pre-exilic period prophecy did exist in Israel and its immediate surroundings.

The parallels discussed in the preceding section indicate that Israelite prophecy can no longer be seen as an isolated phenomenon. Just like their colleagues elsewhere, the Israelite prophets could work within the framework of the cult, but were not obliged to do so.[182] They often openly criticized the official cult, including the hymns and prayers that were sung in the temple (Isa. 1:15; Amos 5:23; Mic. 3:11.) Like their colleagues elsewhere, Israelite prophets performed symbolic acts, for example walking naked (1 Sam. 19:24; Isa. 20; Mic. 1:8), to draw public attention.[183] Like their Mesopotamian colleagues the Israelite prophets introduced their oracles as speech of the deity himself: 'Thus says the LORD'. In Jer. 38:20 the voice of God is explicitly identified with what the prophet is going to say. The spontaneous nature of prophecy did not preclude prophets to train for their job. There is sufficient reason to suppose that in ancient Israel schools for prophets existed. Those learning the skills of a prophet were designated as 'sons of the prophets'[184] or 'students'.[185] However, in Israel too ordinary people might be called to speak the word of God and in this way became prophets.[186] The word of God does not require some far-fetched, esoteric insight (Deut. 30:13-14).[187] In principle, no special intellectual capacities or education are required. Every Israelite can know the word of God and can act according to it (Deut. 30:14). The obvious meaning of this statement is that for every Israelite the Law of Moses ('this law', v. 10; 'this commandment', v. 11) should be the guiding principle.

Of course there were differences between Israel and its neighbors. Whereas the 'classical' prophets in the Hebrew Bible usually

---

[182]See e.g. Mowinckel 1923 [1962], vol. 2, 53-63; Johnson 1962; Booij 1978; Hilber 2005.

[183]Viberg 2007. Friebel 1999, 11-79 and Becking 2009, 35-36 prefer 'sign-acts' instead of 'symbolic acts'.

[184]1 Kgs 20:35; 2 Kgs 2:3, 5, 7, 15; 4:1, 38, etc.

[185]Isa. 8:16; 50:4; 54:13; 1 Chron. 25:8. Cf. Lemaire 1981, 57-61, 70-71.

[186]E.g. Exod. 7:1; 15:20; Num. 11:25-29; 1 Sam. 3:20; 19:20; Joel 3:1-2[2:28-29], etc.

[187]Cf. Weinfeld 1972, 258-259, 264.

pronounce oracles of doom in the name of the deity, the majority of the hitherto found prophetic oracles from elsewhere are promises of salvation on behalf of deities. However, we have to consider a number of factors that call for prudence in drawing conclusions. Critical admonitions to the king and oracles of doom, especially directed to foreign nations, may be rare outside Israel, but are certainly not absent from the prophecies found in the surrounding cultures. On the other hand also Israelite prophets of the pre-exilic period did pronounce oracles of salvation, not only the so-called 'false' prophets, but also 'genuine' prophets like Nathan, Isaiah, Micah. Moreover, Israelite prophecy has come to us only through a long chain of *literary* transmission and theologically motivated redaction. And finally, both the documentation about prophecy in the ancient Near East and the *selection* of prophecies we have from Israel are so incomplete that it is hazardous to overemphasize either the differences or the similarities.

This is also true of the presumed contrast between oral and written prophecy. It has often been pointed out that the prophetic messages of prophets outside Israel were mostly delivered orally whereas the main characteristic of Israelite prophecy would have been its scribal character. This is a biased representation of the facts. Of many Israelite prophets no written books have come to us (e.g. Elijah, Elisha, Gad, Nathan, Huldah, Uriah). The prophetic 'books' that acquired canonical status are the product of centuries of literary and theological reshaping. A text like the Balaam inscription from Deir 'Alla' is without any doubt a highly literary prophetic composition that was deemed important enough to be recorded on the wall of the sanctuary. As far as the fragmentary state of the text allows a judgment, it was directed not to a king, but to Balaam's compatriots (Blum 2008). It is fairly certain that at least some Israelite prophets have been able to read and write. Samuel first explains the legal consequences of kingship orally to the people and subsequently writes them in a 'book' which he deposits in the sanctuary at Shiloh (1 Sam. 10:25). It is uncertain if this rests on reliable historical tradition, but it might be if the 'book' was an inscription on a tablet or durable stone.[188]

---

[188] In Ugaritic *spr* may designate a clay tablet and in Phoenician and Old

The prophet Isaiah writes a short message on a polished bronze mirror,

> Then the LORD said to me, 'Take a big mirror[189] and write upon it with a normal stylus, "For Soon-spoil, Quickly-loot" ' (Isa. 8:1).

'Soon-spoil, Quickly-loot' was to be the symbolical name of Isaiah's unborn son (Isa. 8:3-4). The reason why Isaiah had to write this ominous name on a large reflecting surface was obviously to warn passers-by who saw their own reflection in the mirror that they themselves would soon become spoil of war. It is noteworthy that God also appoints two *oral* witnesses to testify to Isaiah's act (Isa. 8:2).[190]

Later on Isaiah has the scroll with his oracles bound up and sealed, to be kept among his students until his prophecies have come true (Isa. 8:16-18, possibly referred to in Isa. 29:11). It is not stated explicitly that Isaiah had written that scroll himself, but it cannot be excluded either (Dekker 2009). According to Isa. 30:8 the same prophet has to write a prophecy of doom on a kind of billboard.[191]

Aramaic an inscription in a durable kind of stone like basalt. Obviously this recalls the 'tablets of stone', given to Moses according to Exod. 24:12 (cf. Korpel 1990, 471-473). For Isa. 30:8 see the main text above and for writing the law on stones, Deut. 4:13; 5:22; 27:8; Josh. 8:30-32.

[189] Against all other proposals we see this is the best rendering of the Hebrew word which occurs also in Isa. 3:23, as will be demonstrated in a forthcoming publication.

[190] There is some discussion about the text to be preferred. One manuscript of Qumran and some ancient versions read an imperative: 'and appoint as witnesses'. However, this seems to be an adaptation to the context. Another manuscript from Qumran and the Vulgate support the Masoretic text which on the basis of Hebrew syntax most likely means 'and I will appoint as witnesses' (cf. Joüon & Muraoka 2006, §116b). Of course Isaiah will have to act as the instrument through which this will be realized (De Waard 1997, 34).

[191] It is possible that this passage is a later addition to the Book of Isaiah, but this does not diminish the worth of this testimony. The basic meaning of the Hebrew word used is 'board, plank'. The parallel word 'book' is commonly understood to mean that Isaiah would have written the *book* all by himself. However, the same word can also designate a tablet or a board (*pace* Beuken 2010, 172) and the Hebrew text definitely suggests here too a text that was inscribed in a hard surface to serve as a durable witness. Cf. De Moor 1997, 158.

According to Jer. 29 the prophet Jeremiah wrote two letters to the exiles in Babylonia. The letters are not preserved in their original form, but large portions are quoted from them. It seems likely that the chapter was heavily edited, according to many scholars by Baruch, Jeremiah's scribe,[192] but few scholars doubt the historicity of the fact that Jeremiah wrote letters to the exiles, even though he may have made use of the services of his secretary. It was not unusual for senders of letters to omit such information. The same observation is valid for the contract which Jeremiah wrote according to Jer. 32:10. Actually a scribe may have written it, even though the prophet asserts that he did so himself. With contracts too it was customary to have them verified by *oral* witnesses whose names were recorded at the end of the document (Jer. 32:10, 25, 44).

The prophet Habakkuk has to write a vision on publicly exposed tablets so that passers-by who read the text may decide to flee (Hab. 2:2). It is not entirely clear which vision the prophet meant, but since several tablets were needed one has to assume that it was a fairly long text. In any case it seems likely that also in Israel at least some prophets may have been able to check if their scribes had recorded their oracles correctly and in still fewer cases may have been able to write down their prophecies themselves.

Both outside and inside Israel the style of the prophecies is highly developed, often even poetic. This raises the suspicion that the scribes who were responsible for the recording of the words of a prophetess or prophet may well have adapted their basic, oral message to their own literary taste. This must have been all the more so the case when the prophet was in a state of frenzy when he gave his oracle so that it was impossible to refute a scribe's interpretation of the incoherent sounds.

However, with regard to ancient Israel it must be assumed that we certainly do not know the whole truth. For many centuries prophets were accustomed to pronounce oracles of salvation for the king and the nation, just as elsewhere prophets fulfilled this function. Some of the royal Psalms of Israel still contain

---

[192] Cf. McKane 1996, 726-748, as well as Section 5.2.2.4.

such oracles (Hilber 2005). Small wonder that later on, after the destruction of the Solomonic temple, many reproached God for having deluded them.[193] Often it is assumed that such oracles of salvation were the prophetic answer to prayers by or on behalf of the king, mostly in his function as the representative of the people. However, Frederico Villanueva has pointed out that the certainty of a hearing did not always follow a lament and that after praise there could follow lamentation again (Villanueva 2008). Later on[194] we will defend that in many cases not a prophetic message, but a growing inner conviction that God had heard the prayer stood at the basis of praise.

Witnessing the disastrous effects of the misdemeanor of their kings, some Israelite and Judean prophets started to emphasize the impending disaster. When both North Israel and Judah had fallen prey to destruction by foreign armies (Samaria in 622, Jerusalem in 587 BCE), this seemed to confirm the message of the prophets of doom. This must have caused a massive redactional censure of existing written prophetic literature. The message of doom had won and was heavily underlined with prophecies that were clearly *vaticinia ex eventu*, as was the accepted practice in the ancient Near East.[195] We must grow accustomed to the fact that redactional adaptation of prophetic texts to new situations was not uncommon. It is attested in the Neo-Assyrian period (Nissinen 2000b, 263-268) and there is good reason to suppose that it also did happen in ancient Israel. Recently discovered cryptograms in Ezekiel 19 even enable us to reconstruct such a redactional adaptation process fairly accurately (Korpel 2009a), but this is an exceptional case. Despite the development of ever more sophisticated methods to distinguish redactional layers in ancient sources, the results are hardly ever universally accepted. Authorship is blurred by tradition. Authenticity is a modern concept that was foreign to the ancient world.

> The *ipsissima verba*, that is, the actual spoken words of individual prophets, are as impossible to find in ancient Near Eastern

---

[193] See e.g. Renkema 1983, 90-145.
[194] Section 6.2.2.2.
[195] See above, Section 5.2.2.1.

186   CHAPTER FIVE

sources as in the Bible. A written prophecy is always scribal work, and it is ultimately beyond our knowledge to determine to what extent the scribe would, or could, transmit the exact wording of the prophecy.[196]

If a person claims to be relaying the word of God this creates the problem how hearers can be certain that somebody looking like an ordinary human being is truly speaking the word of God. Often prophets confronted each other with diametrically opposed messages, both invoking divine authority (e.g. 1 Kgs 22; Jer. 14:13-16; 23; 27–28; Ezek. 12–13). This made it very difficult to distinguish true from false prophecy.

Deuteronomy tries to solve this tricky problem by requiring consistency with earlier commandments of the LORD[197] or the fulfillment of his words.[198] Especially the latter criterion is puzzling,[199] because it works only afterwards. The application of this rule in the deuteronomistic corpus further complicates the matter. In 1 Kgs 13 the Judean prophet's message of doom against Jeroboam comes true, but he has to die because he does not recognize the prophecy of a colleague as false. In 1 Kgs 22 a faithful prophet first utters a false prophecy (v. 15) and the false prophecy of his opponents is attributed to a spirit executing God's command (vv. 19-23). There are many more examples of prophecies that remained unfulfilled or proved to be false even though they were spoken by 'true' prophets. In these cases too it was a human being's free choice to decide whether the use of the formula 'thus says the LORD' was justified or not.[200] Believing another

---

[196] Nissinen 2004, 29. See also Lindblom 1963, 159, 178-179.

[197] Deut. 13:2-6[1-5]. Christensen 2001, 273 applies this text as follows, 'Keeping close to our own sacred duty will keep us out of harm's way; for God never leaves us until we first leave him.'

[198] Deut. 18:21-22.

[199] Cf. Tigay 1996, 177-178; Christensen 2001, 410-413. It does not help much to observe that Deut. 18:21-22 may have been directed against a prophet who utters a false prophecy of *doom* ('you need not be *afraid* of him', v. 22, cf. Labuschagne 1990, 142; Kwakkel 2003, 24) because the same is said about a prophet who utters an oracle of salvation, Jer. 28:9, 15-17.

[200] Cf. e.g. Fabian 2000; Freedman & Frey 2004; Sweeney 2005, 78-93. When Amos announced in the name of God that the house of Jeroboam would be eradicated with the sword (Amos 7:9) the priest Amaziah of Bethel pointedly

person's claim to divine authority was and will always be a risky enterprise. We will return to this difficult matter at the end of the book (Chapter 7).

It is too simple to boldly assert that the prophets claimed divine authority for their messages to lend extra weight to what they themselves wanted to say. A deeper psychological experience must have been involved. Even if they themselves did not want to speak out, they were unable to hold back the word of God. The prophet Amos exclaims,

> Surely the Lord GOD does nothing,
>   unless he has revealed his counsel
>   to his servants the prophets.
> The lion has roared; who will not fear?
>   The Lord GOD has spoken;
>   who can but prophesy? (Amos 3:7-8).

Jeremiah[201] describes his thankless task as a messenger of doom in the name of God,

> And (when) I thought, I will not mention him,
>   and I will no longer speak in his name,
> then it became like a burning fire in my heart,
>   shut up in my bones,
> and I became weary of holding it in,
>   and I could not prevail (Jer. 20:9).[202]

God warns the prophet Ezekiel[203] not to keep an oracle of doom from the sinners he has to address,

> If I say to the wicked, 'You will certainly die!' and you do not warn him, and do not speak to warn the wicked to turn from his wicked way so that he may live, that wicked man will die for his iniquity, but I will require his blood from your hand (Ezek. 3:18).

---

relayed this prophecy as a word of Amos himself (Amos 7:10).

[201] It is irrelevant in this connection whether the speaker was Jeremiah himself (so e.g. Lundbom 1999) or a redactor allegedly speaking in his name (so e.g. Carroll 2006, vol. 1, 401).

[202] See also Jer. 6:11.

[203] It is likely that Ezek. 3:17-21 is a secondary elaboration of Ezek. 33:1-6, but for our argument that is not really important.

The prophet known as Second Isaiah states explicitly that he does not resist when God instructs him to speak his word,

> The Lord GOD gives me a tongue of disciples
> to know how to make witnesses those too tired for words.
> Morning by morning he wakens,
> he wakens my ear
> to hear like disciples do.
>
> The Lord GOD opens my ear,
> and I do not resist,
> I do not move backwards (Isa. 50:4-5).[204]

The prophet sees himself as an attentive student of the divine Teacher. He passes on the message to his compatriots who are too tired to speak up. He can only find the courage to become an unobtrusive teacher to the nations himself when God has put his Spirit on him (Isa. 42:1-4).

Remaining silent when God entrusted a prophet with his word was an option only if the life of the prophet himself became endangered. Contrary to an earlier oath to spare Jeremiah's life (Jer. 38:16), king Zedekiah threatens to kill the prophet if he does not keep secret a prophecy of doom he should have delivered in public (Jer. 38:24-27).

Normally, however, a prophet could not refuse to divulge the word of God. Jeremiah promises his compatriots that he will not keep back even one word from what God will reveal to him (Jer. 42:4). In Ezek. 2:9; 3:1, 2, 3 God presents a scroll with lamentations written on the outside and the inside – an exceptional procedure – to the prophet with the command to eat it. Its taste proved to be like sweet honey (Ezek. 3:3),[205] but caused bitterness in the end (Ezek. 3:14). Later on a spirit (the Spirit?)[206] enters him (Ezek. 3:24) who summons the prophet to let himself be locked up in his house. The spirit announces that his tongue will stick to his mouth and that he will become dumb. It seems likely

---

[204] For this translation see Korpel & De Moor 1998, 448.

[205] Jeremiah 'ate' and enjoyed the words of the law-book found in the temple by Hilkiah (Jer. 15:16, cf. 2 Kgs 22:13).

[206] Cf. Block 1997, 153-154.

that the eating of the scroll should be compared with Ezekiel's dumbness which made it impossible for him to speak anything else than the true word of God (Ezek. 3:26-27). He is not even allowed to vent his personal grief when his wife dies (Ezek. 24:15-27) and in this restricted sense he has to keep 'silent' throughout his career as a prophet (Ezek. 33:22). Only when he hears the voice of God speaking to him a spirit[207] enters him so that he is able to hear what God is saying (Ezek. 1:28–2:2). It is his task to relay the words of God to his compatriots, regardless 'whether they hear or refuse to hear' (Ezek. 2:5, 7; 3:7, 11). Later on he feels lifted up by a spirit[208] and the whole experience disturbed the prophet's spirit very much (3:14). Again we note a close interaction between the human spirit and spirits sent by God. The result is that Ezekiel no longer can act as a mediator (Ezek. 3:26) for the people, and he is unable to speak a word of his own.[209] It might be that Ezekiel suffered short moments of literal aphasy,[210] but this does not diminish the fact that Ezekiel from 3:24-27 on is able to speak only words of God.

A similar experience is related about Daniel. He is touched by an unknown hand; apparently it is a messenger of the LORD who does so (Dan. 10:10). Subsequently the unknown person is described as someone looking like a human being (10:16). When he speaks to Daniel, the latter seems to be frightened. He turns his face to the ground and immediately becomes dumb (10:15). Only after the messenger has touched his lips Daniel's mouth is opened again and he is able to speak words and to answer him. Nevertheless, Daniel does not feel strong enough, and complains that no strength is left in him, as well as no breath (Dan. 10:17). The messenger who looks like a human being touches him again and Daniel feels strong enough to answer. The chapter clearly recalls the prophet Ezekiel who was also struck by dumbness (Plöger 1965, 149).

Those who felt that they had to speak the word of God were fully aware of their own inadequacy: Moses (Exod. 3:11; 4:10-16),

---

[207]The article 'the' is missing in the Hebrew text.
[208]Ezek. 3:12-14; see also 8:3; 11:1, 24; 43:5.
[209]Dijkstra 1986, 54; Block 1997, 156; Friebel 1999, 184; Duguid 1999, 80.
[210]Dijkstra 1986, 54; Dijkstra 1989, 22.

Isaiah (Isa. 6:5-7), Jeremiah (Jer. 1:6-10), Daniel (Dan. 10:15-19). They knew that an 'unclean spirit' might lead a prophet astray (Zech. 13:2) and they had to resist that temptation. Only if Jeremiah repents from having uttered a 'worthless' oracle, he may act as the 'mouth' of God again (Jer. 15:19. Cf. Jer. 1:9 and Lundbom 1999, 749-750).

According to Exod. 3–4 Moses sees an angel (messenger) of the LORD appearing in a flaming thorn bush.[211] Miraculously, however, the bush is not consumed by the fire. The circumstance that later on it is God who addresses Moses (Exod. 3:4ff.) can be explained plausibly by the ancient oriental concept of a spokesman or messenger as the visible and audible representation of his master (Propp 1999, 198-199).

Moses communicates with God as with a human being. He first says that he is listening (v. 4) and after God has called him to become the leader of his people (vv. 7-10) he puts forward several objections why he would not be the right man for this demanding assignment (Exod. 3:11; 4:1). Finally he states that he is not an eloquent speaker (lit. his mouth and tongue are heavy, Exod. 4:10). God counters this with a rhetorical question,

> Who provided man with a mouth?
>   Who will make dumb or deaf?
>   Or seeing or blind?
>   Is it not I the LORD? (Exod. 4:11)[212]

It is useless to speculate about the precise nature of Moses' handicap.[213] In any case he was not completely dumb. God continues, 'Now go; for I will be with your mouth and will teach you what to say.' So Moses will have to speak the words of God who will make use of Moses' mouth. This is confirmed by Jewish interpretations. Targum Onqelos states that God said 'and my word will be in

---

[211] We skip the complicated source-critical and redactional history of these chapters here.

[212] On dumbness as an affliction caused by God according to the Hebrew Bible, see Section 3.2.4.2.

[213] In Exod. 6:12, 30 Moses states that he is 'of uncircumcised lips' which might mean that he regarded his mouth as too unholy to speak the word of God. Cf. Isa. 6:5-7.

your mouth' and Targum Neofiti 'with my mouth I will be with the speaking of your mouth' (Houtman 1993, 412-413). Just as the 'angel' represented God, so Moses will represent God.

Moses recoils yet another time, 'Oh, my Lord, send, I pray, some other person!' (Exod. 4:13), whereupon God becomes angry and says,

> Is there not Aaron, your brother, the Levite?
>   I know that he can speak well;
> and also, behold, he is coming out to meet you,
>   and when he sees you he will be glad in his heart.
> And you shall speak to him
>   and put the words in his mouth;
> and I myself will be with your mouth and with his mouth,
>   and will teach you two what you shall do.
> He shall speak for you to the people;
>   and he shall be a mouth for you,
>   and you shall be to him as God (Exod. 4:14b-16).

Aaron becomes the spokesman of Moses, just as Moses in fact is the spokesman of God. The comparison of Moses to God and Aaron as his spokesman is based on the similarity with the relationship between God and a prophet.[214] This human comparison clearly shows the idea behind the speaking of God: human beings have to become his mouthpieces, his spokesmen, just as in the human world people can be the spokesmen of others.[215] Moses has to speak with divine authority before Pharaoh[216] and apparently the latter does not doubt that it is possible that human beings speak on behalf of deities – he only does not know the God of the Hebrews (Exod. 5:1-3).

The idea of Aaron as the spokesman of Moses is repeated by the Priestly Source in Exod. 7:1, 'And the LORD said to Moses, "See, I make you as God to Pharaoh; and Aaron your brother shall be your prophet. You shall speak all that I command you;

---

[214]Childs 1974, 79; Hyatt 1980, 101; Noth 1988, 33; Houtman 1993, 417; Propp 1999, 229-231.

[215]Wolterstorff 1995, 48 aptly compares the commissioner who is allowed to speak on behalf of a president or a government.

[216]Childs 1974, 118; Houtman 1993, 524.

and Aaron your brother shall tell Pharaoh to let the people of Israel go out of his land." ' In accordance with the priestly theology Aaron the priest now becomes the indirect mouthpiece (prophet) of God.[217] It has been observed that Aaron only seldom serves as the spokesman of Moses, generally it is Moses himself who speaks on behalf of God (Hyatt 1980, 84). However, it was common in the literature of the ancient world to minimize the role of intermediaries and to create the impression that it was the deity or king himself who spoke or acted.

Deuteronomy finally resolves the problem of the conflicting nature of prophecies by declaring that 'there has not arisen a prophet since in Israel like Moses, whom the LORD knew face to face' (Deut. 34:10), thus lending a higher authority to Moses than to any other prophet.[218] It must be assumed that the Spirit of God rested upon the prophet Moses.[219] Unquestionably the guidance of the Holy Spirit was indispensable to prophets,[220] also to an eminent spokesman of God like Moses. But the work of the Spirit had to be matched by a willing spirit in man. If this willingness was lacking, a further link in the line of transmission had to be inserted.

Like his contemporary Micah (Mic. 2:11), Isaiah reproaches the priests, seers and prophets with their excessive consumption of wine which befuddles their brains so that they do not hear the voice of the LORD.[221] Their professional wisdom has become a purely human affair, there is no divine inspiration in it (Isa. 29:13-16; cf. Mic. 3:5-8). Because of their irresponsible behavior

---

[217] This is the only time that the Priestly Source uses the word 'prophet'.

[218] On the role of Moses as an intermediary even in places where God seems to address the people directly see Section 5.1.2.

[219] Cf. Num. 11:29; 27:28; Deut. 34:9; Isa. 63:11.

[220] Looking back, (pseudo)-Nehemiah states that God has warned the people by his Spirit through the intermediary of the prophets (Neh. 9:30; cf. Zech. 7:12; 2 Chron. 24:19-20). Since the structure of the verse makes it impossible to leave out anything this indicates that by this time it was the prevailing opinion that the prophets had been divinely inspired, yet had been badly understood.

[221] Isa. 28:7-10; cf. 29:9-10. It is generally recognized that Isaiah 28–31 does contain material that goes back to the first Isaiah, but that much editorial elaboration is of a later date (see e.g. Wildberger 1982, 1041-1368, 1557).

God has blinded the seers and prophets so that they do not foresee the impending disaster (Isa. 29:10).[222] God does not answer them anymore when they call to him for help (Isa. 28:7-11; cf. Mic. 3:4, 6-7).

The prophets willing to speak the word of God met with a lot of hardship. Prophets had to undergo long training for their profession which required also learning at least the basics of reading and writing. Speaking up against those in power required courage. Prophets had to face devastating criticism of their contemporaries and many of them paid for their audacity with their lives. Therefore it is mistaken to state that there is no merit whatsoever in the prophets' contribution to the proclamation of word of God. It is simply an exaggeration that 'as sinful and weak men, they can only make shipwreck with their words' (Barth, *ChD*, vol. 2/1, 221). No, they were courageous men and women who sacrificed a lot for the LORD. It is simply bad dogmatics to minimize the participation of human beings in the work of God to the point where one can qualify it as shipwrecking.[223]

Having denounced the self-interest of prophets, seers and diviners, who fail to get answers from God,[224] the prophet Micah continues,

> I, however, am filled with power,
> [the Spirit of the LORD,]
>   and with justice and courage,
> to tell Jacob his rebellion,
>   and Israel its sin (Mic. 3:8).

According to the canonical version of his book, Micah feels that next to the indispensable guidance of the Spirit his sense of justice and a certain amount of courage is necessary for his mission. However, there are strong indications that the phrase 'the Spirit of the LORD' is a later explanatory gloss.[225] To be sure, this gloss

---

[222] The glosses in Isa. 29:10 interpret the text correctly, cf. Watts 1985, 384; Oswalt 1986, 529-530, n. 3; Oswalt 2003, 328, 333; Childs 2001, 218.
[223] See further Chapter 7.
[224] Mic. 3:5-7.
[225] See e.g. Renaud 1977, 135-137; Ben Zvi 2000, 72. Contrast Levison 2009, 36, 41-45.

is certainly an apt elucidation of what Micah will have meant,[226] but originally he spoke merely with wonder about his own power, justice and audacity. For him it will have been self-evident that his decision to speak up against those in power derived from his divine Sender. However, it seems unwarranted to scale down his human effort to insignificance.

In the same chapter Micah predicts the destruction of the Solomonic temple in Jerusalem (Mic. 3:12), one of the most convincing examples of a prophecy that came true. Yet Micah himself did not live to witness that event,[227] and at the end of his career seriously considered the possibility that this might have been because of sins he himself might have committed.[228] Here we meet the tragic fate of a man who served God but never knew for certain if what he pronounced were words of God that were bound to come true.

Also a wisdom teacher could be filled with the Spirit of God and might be unable to repress his argument. Elihu justifies his decision to participate in the dispute with Job by invoking his divine inspiration. It is not old age that makes a man wise,

> But it is the Spirit in mankind
>> and the breath of the Almighty
>>> that gives them understanding (Job 32:8)

> I too will have my share,
>> I too will show my knowledge.
> For I am full of words,
>> and the Spirit within me compels me.
> Look, inside I am like bottled-up wine,
>> like new wineskins ready to burst (Job 32:17-19).

Some authors insist on taking 'the spirit' in the sense of breath here.[229] No doubt the breath was seen as a gift of God.[230] However, in the context of Job 32 it would be strange to argue that

---

[226] Cf. Mic. 2:7, 11.
[227] Jer. 26:17-19.
[228] See on this interpretation De Moor 2000c.
[229] E.g. Scheepers 1960, 179; Habel 1985, 450; Clines 2006, 718.
[230] Gen. 2:7; 6:8; Ps. 104:30; Job 27:3; 32:8; 33:4; 34:14.

every breathing human being is a wisdom teacher. That is exactly what Elihu disputes. He is claiming *divine* illumination here,[231] even though it is difficult to separate the human from the divine spirit.[232] In the late wisdom literature to which the speeches of Elihu belong the sages started to take over the place of the prophets as mediators of revelation (Fohrer 1963, 451). Jer. 9:11 which is part of a late theological amplification of the Book of Jeremiah (McKane 1986, 205) may reflect the same development because here the sage is the man to whom God has spoken.

Also in the New Testament the human spirit and the divine Spirit that are at work in the believer's life are often indistinguishable (Fee 1994, 24-26). But here too the possibility of an 'unclean' spirit was recognized.[233] Like the Hebrew prophets, the apostle Paul sees no possibility to hold back the word of God. He feels compelled to preach the gospel,

> Yet when I preach the gospel, I cannot boast, for I am compelled to preach. Woe to me if I do not preach the gospel! (1 Cor. 9:16)

This was also the conviction of the author of 2 Pet. 1:21,

> Prophecy has never occurred by the will of man, but moved by the Holy Spirit[234] men spoke as[235] God.

According to this view, prophets did not 'invent' revelation themselves, but were seized by God and driven to speak on his behalf. Of course modern man may doubt that this was what really happened, but such a modern view is not based on scribal tradition from Antiquity. To the Ancients 'invented' prophecy was 'false' prophecy because it did not originate in God.

---

[231] Cf. Gordis 1978, 367; Hartley 1988, 424.
[232] In this sense we can understand Levison's insistence on writing 'spirit' (Levison 2009).
[233] Mt. 12:43-45; Mk 1:23-27; 3:11, 30; 5:2, 8, 13, etc.
[234] An article is lacking in the Greek. This does not preclude the rendering 'the Holy Spirit' (cf. Fee 1994, 15-24) which in the light of vv.19-20 is far more likely than 'a holy spirit'.
[235] Literally 'out of God'.

5.2.2.3 Scribes in the Ancient Near East

Scribes were the scholars of the ancient world. Most of their contemporaries were illiterate and had to rely on their memory.[236] Although the capacity to memorize important data was much better developed than in the present world that has put its trust in the written or digital word, the only people able to transmit knowledge over very long stretches of time were the scribes. This gave them an enormous power that was often enhanced by the fact that they claimed to have received their revelations directly from the deities themselves. In this respect they too were considered messengers of the gods, carriers of divine revelation. An Egyptian scribe praises his teacher,

> You are the father of the god in command of mysteries ... You are a noble priest in the House of Ptah, versed in all the mysteries in the House of the Prince.[237]

The more advanced Egyptian scribes were seen as the keepers of the powerful secret language of the deities (Hornung 1996; Fischer-Elfert 2007). In the closing section of the *Wisdom of Amenemope* scribes are extolled as the only human beings who achieve true immortality through their writings (Foster 2001, 226-228). When the offices of scribes are destroyed, their secret knowledge is endangered according to the Egyptian skeptic Ipuwer who may have lived in the 18th century BCE,

> O, yet the sacred forehall, its writings have been removed;
> the place of secrets and the sanctuary(?) have been stripped bare.
> O, yet magic is stripped bare;

---

[236] Some ancient oriental kings boast about their ability to read. See for Egypt, Redford, in: Ben Zvi & Floyd 2000, 164. In Mesopotamia Shulgi, Išme-Dagān and Assurbanipal are examples of kings who boasted to have mastered the scribal art (Waetzoldt 2009, 264; Hunger 2009, 273); for the Hittites, see Van den Hout 2009, 277. Mostly this kind of praise will have been cheap flattering by their scribes. Assurbanipal's scribes had to annotate the tablets the king wanted to read aloud to show off his proficiency with interlinear clarifying glosses. Also some officers in the service of the king may have mastered reading. See below an example from Judah.

[237] Translation Lichtheim 1976, 173-174.

omens(?) and predictions(?) are made dangerous
because of their being recalled by people.[238]

Apparently knowing the will of the gods required access to the secret scribal lore. It might rest on oral tradition, but could not be replaced by it because the mere fact of the mortality of its carriers made it unreliable. Also other people, like priests, magicians, officials and doctors, were regarded as keepers of secret knowledge in ancient Egypt, but it is highly unlikely that all of them were skilled scribes.[239]

In Mesopotamia too scribes were the keepers of arcane knowledge. Even though other scholars such as diviners and sorcerers were also supposed to have access to the secrets of the gods, their revelations were recorded by scribes who had the power to modify their words.[240] Tablets containing explanatory commentaries on rituals were provided with the warning, 'Let not the knowing show this to the unknowing' and especially the proceedings during the Babylonian New Year festival were partly kept secret (Zgoll 2007). In Ugarit the scribe Ilimilku praises his master Attanu who was a high priest as the one who had dictated Ugaritic religious texts to him and was himself an accomplished scribe of Babylonian. Ilimilku describes him as a keeper of 'the secrets of Baʻlu (Baal)' in an eulogy after Attanu's death,

> Who was like the Holy Man?
>   [Who was like Attanu?]
> [Thri]ce he has made dew,
>   four times [drizzle for] me.
> So, he understood the secrets of Baʻlu,[241]
>   [grasped (?) the wisdo]m of Baʻlu.
> The great Holy Man [fell (?)] into the river,
>   [into] the wadi of Astarte, into the Raḥbanu[242]
> [he died (?) in] Araru,[243]

---

[238] Ipuwer 6.6-7, translation Enmarch 2008, 227-228.
[239] Kees 1953-1958; Altenmüller 1977; Fischer-Elfert 2007. Cf. Exod. 7:22.
[240] Nissinen 2000b; Van der Toorn 2007; Lenzi 2008.
[241] At the moment of writing, the weather god Baal was the national god of Ugarit. Astarte, mentioned a few lines further on, was one of his wives.
[242] Ugaritic name of the river Nahr el-Kebir.
[243] District south of Ugarit.

> in the sea of Baal's hill.[244]
> [What about] the secrets of Ba'lu?
> [Woe! (?) What about the se]crets of Ba'lu?[245]

Apparently Ilimilku ascribed to his master secret knowledge which had enabled him a few times to manipulate the rainfall that was vitally important to the semi-arid region of Ugarit.[246] What is important to note is the distribution of tasks between the learned high priest who recited the religious texts of Ugarit and the scribe who recorded the words of his master.

Karel van der Toorn has argued forcefully that in a predominantly illiterate world everything we know about the religious traditions of Israel must have been transmitted through the hands of scribes, many of whom were working in the service of the temple (Van der Toorn 2007). In a sense, this conclusion is too facile. What else than written documents have survived up till our own era? Yet his emphasis on the role of scribes is justified to a considerable extent. He and others have demonstrated that the scribes of the ancient world were not merely copyists, but also creative authors. Certainly they often invoked written sources to show that they stood in a reliable chain of tradition, but more often than not such claims have been proved to be false. The sources quoted and/or the quotations were sometimes invented to lend authority to what actually were reformations or innovations (see also Stott 2008). As Van der Toorn demonstrated, the scribes often weaved various threads of tradition, also from oral tradition, into a new composition. This mode of composition agrees to a large extent with the modes of textual creation supposed by literary-critical biblical scholarship in the past. In our opinion the latter approach far too often neglected the cumulative nature of literary production in Antiquity. Old material was woven into new compositions and this circumstance counsels prudence with regard to dating individual passages.

---

[244] Probably Mt Ṣapānu = Jebel Akra, north of Ugarit. The very imprecise designation of the locale might indicate that the exact spot of Attanu's death was unknown.

[245] RS 92.2016. For a full commentary on this text, see De Moor 2009.

[246] Cf. 1 Kgs 18.

Moreover, the possibilities of manipulation of existing tradition were limited by several factors. First of all the scribes had to satisfy their employers, usually belonging to the ruling elite, both priests and kings.[247] The propagandistic nature of royal documents, for example, made it impossible for a scribe to record the often disappointing truth. It might seem easy for a scribe to dupe his master who nearly always will have been unable to check himself what the scribe had written, but it has been demonstrated that also officers in the service of the court were often able to read, or could even write (Charpin 2008). So kings could have the content of a scribe's work checked.

It should be remembered that normally texts were read aloud and could be confirmed or contradicted by oral witnesses. This also applies to priests and other religious leaders. Their power rested on commonly understood traditional religious lore. Therefore radical innovation was possible only in the aftermath of great crises that undermined faith in existing theology or ideology. In a mainly illiterate society important lore is often carefully fostered by oral tradition (see below). Therefore a scribe could not present a version of a text that differed radically from what had been engrained in the collective memory of a socially coherent group.

A third objection to attributing too much weight to the freedom of scribes is the circumstance that sometimes the person who delivered a religious text orally may well have been able to check what the scribe who wrote down his words had made of it, as was doubtlessly the case with Attanu and Ilimilku of Ugarit.

And finally, the formation of canonical written versions of important, authoritative documents limited the freedom of the scribes. It has been demonstrated that after canonization only relatively minor differences could be introduced by later scribes.[248]

In all matters of importance the written text served as the ultimate testimony. Everywhere in the ancient Near East contracts were drawn up in front of witnesses, but the written contract

---

[247] In view of the close ties between temple and palace in the ancient world we do not think it is helpful to distinguish sharply between scribes in the service of the cult and scribes in the service of the king.

[248] See e.g. De Moor 1978; Tigay 1982; Tertel 1994; Hallo 1996, 144-153; Korpel 1998; 2005a; George 2003, 1-70.

was decisive. Messages were delivered orally, but were confirmed by written documents. Generally scholarly works, at that time mostly religious texts, had to be in conformity to the ancient scribal tradition, both in Egypt and in Babylonia.[249] This gave the scribes an enormous power over all sectors of society.

Yet the influence of scribes should not be overestimated. Most of the dissemination of culture, also religious culture, took place via oral channels in the largely analphabetic societies of those days.[250] Modern parallels, like oral Arabian poetry, show that oral and written tradition of the same (narrative) poems can coexist, both in reasonably stable form, over extended periods of time, centuries even.[251] Both channels of tradition exhibit many characteristics that are also found in the written literature of the ancient world, especially tricks to assist the memory of the reciter, such as repetition of phrases or scenes, standard epithets functioning as stopgaps, parallelism (standard pairs of words), rhythmical structure to promote cadence, acrostics and rhyme.[252]

However, not only existing tradition was fostered in this manner. The oral tradition also provided a means to expand or contract a poem according to the mood of the moment.[253] Apparently oral tradition served to promulgate texts among a wider audience and occasionally helped to actualize the written tradition. After such a revision the oral tradition in its turn may have been adapted to the updated written text, for some time at least.

Even in Egypt where writing was so all-important for the royal administration and the cult, texts were disseminated as widely as possible by means of reciting them aloud and certain types of literature were apparently based on oral tradition.[254] A good example demonstrating that oral delivery was seen as more impor-

---

[249] For Egypt, see Redford, in: Ben Zvi & Floyd 2000, 165-167.

[250] See for a fine overview of the relation between orality and literacy in Antiquity, Niditch 1996, esp. 39-59.

[251] See e.g. Sowayan 1985, esp. 6-10; Bailey 1991; Kurpershoek 1994-2002, esp. vol. 2, 10-12; Lyons 1995, esp. vol.1. See also Widengren 1969, 565-573. For the relevance of this type of research for the interpretation of the Bible, see De Moor 2000a.

[252] Cf. Niditch 1996, 8-24.

[253] De Moor 1978; Korpel 1998.

[254] Redford, in: Ben Zvi & Floyd 2000, 159-163, 171-218.

tant than writing a text down is the Sumerian proverb 'A scribe whose hand can keep up with the mouth, he is indeed a scribe!' (Alster 1997, vol. 1, 53 [2.40]). Such a saying proves that not every orally delivered text was subjected to scribal embellishment, but that literal dictation took place too.

Van der Toorn's thesis that the scribes of the ancient Near East 'invented' religious texts, including the Bible, does not do justice to their own testimony. They believed that deities guided them in their work. Even verbal inspiration is attested. One Old Babylonian scribe is praised as a man whose stylus was guided by the gods Marduk and Nabû (Charpin 2009, 268). Many pious prayers on behalf of scribes testify to the fact that they did not see their work as 'inventing' but believed to do what the deities wanted (Hunger 2009, 270). The scribe of the Babylonian Epic of Creation,[255] for example, closes the final tablet of his enormous work with the words,

> An elder scholar[256] spoke the revelation before him[257]
> he wrote (it) down and fixed it
> so that future generations would hear it. [...]
> Let them read the song of Marduk aloud,
> (Marduk) who fettered Tiâmat[258] and took the kingship.[259]

Again we note the precedence of oral delivery of both the original revelation and its later recitation. Similarly, the Babylonian Epic of Erra,[260] states,

> Kabti-ilāni-Marduk the son of Dabibi (was) the composer of this tablet (= of this poem):
> (The deity) revealed it to him during the night,
> and in the morning, when he recited (it), he did not skip a single (line)

---

[255] Usually the date of the main part of this composition is given as *c.* 1120 BCE, but the last tablet may be somewhat younger.

[256] Cf. En. el. VII.145.

[257] Marduk, the creator god to whom the epic was devoted.

[258] The monstrous sea, cf. Section 6.2.1.2a.

[259] En. el. VII.157-158, 161-162, our translation. Different renderings are found with e.g. Bottéro & Kramer 1989, 653; Foster, CoS, vol. 1, 402; Talon 2005, 108.

[260] See Sections 6.2.1.1a and 6.2.1.5a..

> Not a single line (of his own) did he add to it.
> Erra heard and approved it.
> It (also) pleased Išum, his herald.
> All the gods expressed their praise together with him.[261]

Why should we mistrust such statements? On what grounds does Van der Toorn dismiss the notion that these scribes honestly believed that their gods had inspired them to write down what they wrote? Just like diviners, prophets and other mediators of that era believed to speak the words of their gods? There is no apparent reason to assume that they engaged in deliberate delusion. It may be true that they developed new theological paradigms in response to periods of economic or social crisis when old religious paradigms broke down. But why not accept the idea that these scribes thanked their gods for enlightening them? Whether *we* believe their statements is a totally different issue that should not be projected back on the scribes of Antiquity.

In the texts quoted above oral and written transmission are clearly parallel. Written texts were intended for reading them aloud to promote subsequent oral transmission.

Also in Greece oral and written tradition coexisted. Formerly it was thought that one can recognize oral transmission on the basis of style. To some extent this is certainly true. A creator of literary work did not necessarily belong to the guild of scribes. What he or she needed above all was a good memory and thorough training. The problem is that scribes could imitate the traditional style of oral poetry, accommodating themselves to the oral style their readers were accustomed to as hearers. This renders it extremely difficult to separate oral and scribal input.[262]

Yet modern anthropological research, such as that of Kurpershoek and others referred to above, demonstrates that memory based oral literature can be just as sophisticated as written literature. And can be transmitted reliably over many generations.

Indicative of the legitimate place of oral tradition next to written tradition is the circumstance that in the ancient world blind

---

[261] Erra V.42-47, Cagni 1977, 60. Other translations hardly differ. See e.g. Bottéro & Kramer 1989, 706-707; Dalley, CoS, vol. 1, 415.
[262] Thomas 1989; 1992.

persons were often employed as singers or prophets. In Egypt blind persons often earned their living as singers in temples or at banquets (Brunner 1972, 829). Also in Babylonia blind girls were employed as musicians/singers.[263] In the Bible one encounters the blind prophet Ahijah (1 Kgs 14:4). Above we already encountered the blind Greek prophet Teiresias from Thebes. Accounts describing the Greek poet Homer himself as blind probably rest on etymologizing, but Odyssey, VIII.43-47, 62-83, 261-369, 482-521 describe a highly regarded blind bard called Demodocus who performed at the court of the Phaeacians. He is sometimes seen as a pen-name of Homer himself. Demodocus too presented his songs as free improvisations, sometimes on request. In the Homeric Hymns, III.172 another famous blind singer dwelling on the rocky island of Chios is mentioned. Both are thought to have inspired the legend of Homer's blindness. However that may be, it seems certain that nobody saw anything strange in a blind bard who improvised – always making use of existing tradition and techniques – songs on the spur of the moment. And who was obviously *not* a scribe.

Many courts of the ancient Near East were entertained by singers who did not sing in the language of their hosts. The king of the Old Babylonian city of Mari used Amorite singers,[264] Ugaritic singers sang in Hurrian, the Hurrian king of Carchemish listened to Babylonian singers, the king of the Canaanite city of Byblos employed an Egyptian songstress, Canaanite singers were imported by the Pharaoh, Hezekiah of Judah sent Israelite singers to the court of the Assyrian king Sennacherib,[265] Babylonians forced Israelite captives to sing for them (Ps. 137:3). These people too did not read or write, they were the carriers of *oral* tradition.

All this does not alter the fact that for information about the concept of silence in Antiquity we are entirely dependent on the work of scribes. As we shall see later on, they often mention silences of deities and human beings in their texts. But from early times on they also made use of other means to indicate silences. It

---

[263] CAD (N) 1, 382; Durand 1997, 92-94.
[264] See Malamat 2003.
[265] See for all this De Moor 1978, 131.

has long been established that horizontal lines on Babylonian and Ugaritic clay tablets were used to demarcate logical sections in religious texts.[266] In Egyptian texts and in the Balaam text from Deir ʿAlla rubrics were headed in red to indicate separation of sense units in literary texts.[267] In hieratic texts also spaces were used to indicate the beginning of new paragraphs (De Halleux 1986). This custom was taken over by other civilizations: Ugarit, Phoenicia, Israel, Greece, and it survives up to our present days. It may be assumed that the reader paused for a moment at such clearly marked points of transition.

In the literary texts of Ugarit horizontal lines mostly serve to demarcate portions of text not intended for recitation. It is our contention that in addition to that device, a blank space at the end of lines often fulfills the function to mark a rhetorical silence when the text was recited. Longer pauses are indicated by blank lines and an even longer moment of silence is required when a large number of blank lines or even an entirely blank page precedes a fresh chapter. Lately many studies have been devoted to blank spaces in inscriptions and manuscripts from Antiquity.[268]

5.2.2.4 Scribes in the Bible

In the Hebrew Bible as it has been transmitted to us secrecy on the part of the mediators of divine speech is absent according to Lenzi,

> Unlike the protective treatment of secret knowledge in Mesopotamia, in Israel, at least as presented in the Hebrew Bible, knowledge from the divine realm was proclaimed quite openly, even publicly. I suggest that this difference in treatment is rooted in a specific religio-political understanding of Israel in relation to its deity that has generally, even if not entirely, permeated the biblical materials.[269]

---

[266] Cf. Korpel 2000; 2005; Mabie 2004. See also Section 2.3.3.
[267] See e.g. Černy 1952, 24; Assmann 1983; Aḥituv 2008, 433.
[268] E.g. Oesch 1979; Korpel & De Moor 1988; 1998; Olley 1998; Steck 1998; Kottsieper 2003; Ulrich 2003; Tov 2004, and many more publications in the series *Pericope*, cf. http://www.pericope.net/.
[269] Lenzi 2008, 221.

As 'the most obviously relevant text' in this respect Lenzi refers to Deut. 29:28[29],

> The secret things belong to the LORD our god, and the revealed things to us and to our children forever, in order to do all the words of his torah.[270]

The cogency of this argument is questionable. According to Jewish interpretations, summarized by Tigay 1996, 283, the 'concealed things' are sins only known to God, 'the overt things' the fulfillment of the commandments. If so, we are not dealing with general statements about revelation here. The wording of the passage is thoroughly Deuteronomic (Weinfeld 1972, 336) and in our opinion it can hardly be doubted that with 'the revealed things' the commandments of the book of Deuteronomy itself were meant, i.e. 'the words of this law'.[271] This also determines the meaning of 'the secret things' – they are the uncertain future events, whether obedience and blessing, or disobedience and punishment.[272] The Deuteronomic writer does not want to detract from God's foreknowledge – God knows what will happen, but at this moment Israel still has its future in its own hands.

Lenzi's second example, 'The best evidence for this characterization of revelation', comes from Judg. 3:12-30, the story of Ehud's murder of Eglon. Admittedly, Ehud cleverly suggests that his 'secret word' (v. 19) was a 'word of God' (v. 20), but this ruse implies at most that Ehud assumed that the Moabite king would be eager to listen to him in private if he claimed to have a secret message from the God of Israel. It does in no way prove that in Israel 'knowledge from the divine realm was proclaimed quite openly, even publicly'.

A text like Isa. 48:6-7 proves convincingly that in principle also Israelite prophets asserted that they had knowledge of hitherto secret information, as Lenzi himself admits (Lenzi 2008, 227-229).

---

[270]Lenzi 2008, 223-224, translation Lenzi's.
[271]Deut. 29:28[29]c, 'that we may do all the words of this law', cf. 29:19[20]-20[21].
[272]Deut. 29:17[18]-27[28].

In our opinion Lenzi is right with regard to the easy access of prophets to the king and the temple, but the same kind of spontaneous revelation occurred among Mesopotamian, Caanaanite and Egyptian prophets. So we believe it is mistaken to make a sharp distinction between secrecy outside Israel and openness in Israel. Even in a late book like Daniel the hero is presented as a 'prophet' possessing secret knowledge (Lenzi 2009).

However, as a rule prophecy was *spoken*, mostly in the name of a deity: 'Thus speaks the LORD ...'. The examples of prophecies in other parts of the ancient Near East suggest that in Israel too their messages must have been quite short and that prophets delivered these revelations orally (cf. Jer. 18:18). The scribes were the experts who not merely wrote down literally what they heard, but elaborated the word of God according to their scribal training, explaining things where this seemed necessary, molding the text according to acknowledged stylistic literary patterns. A well-known example from the Hebrew Bible is the scribe Baruch who wrote down the word of God from the mouth of Jeremiah,

> And Jeremiah recited to[273] Baruch the son of Neriah; and from the mouth of Jeremiah Baruch wrote in a book scroll all the words of the LORD which he had spoken to him (Jer. 36:4).

The maximum length of a book scroll was about 20 sheets of leather or papyrus which were joined with glue (papyrus) or threads (leather).[274] It is not unlikely that originally a collection of disconnected short prophecies of a well-known prophet were collected on such a book scroll. Evidently this made regrouping of the written material relatively easy and in this respect too the scribes enjoyed considerable freedom, as is demonstrated by the different order of passages in the books of Jeremiah, Samuel and Song of Songs (and other biblical books) in the Qumran manuscripts.

It is important to note that actually God had ordered Jeremiah himself to take a scroll and write down everything God had

---

[273] Literally 'called to', harmonizing the text with that of v. 18 and Jer. 45:1.
[274] Tov 2004, 36-43. The overall length of the great Isaiah scroll from Qumran (1QIsa^a), for example, is 7.34 meter, divided over 17 sheets of uneven width.

revealed to him (Jer. 36:2). Apparently it was quite normal that Jeremiah called in a scribe to do the job for him, even though he himself may have been able to do it (Jer. 32:10; 51:60). It is also Baruch who has to recite[275] the words written on the scroll in the temple, in the hearing of all the people (vv. 6, 8, 10, 13-14). Having recited the prophecies, Baruch is requested to come to the chamber of the scribes (v. 20) and to recite the words of Jeremiah again (vv. 14-19). Subsequently an officer called Jehudi recites the scroll before the king and the princes of Judah (v. 21). Apparently only Baruch and Jehudi were able to read aloud from the scroll, the rest was illiterate, including the king. Apparently the repeated reading of the scroll served to verify that also the person who read it out aloud did not alter or omit anything.

People knew that a scribe like Baruch might influence the words of the prophet whose mediator he was (Jer. 43:1-3). This raises the question who has had more influence on the word of God as it was mediated by inspired persons like the prophets, the speaker in the name of God or the scribe who recorded his words? The scribes had ample opportunity to manipulate existing religious tradition (Jer. 8:8: 'behold, the false pen of the scribes has made it into a lie').

We have seen how the Ugaritic high priest who was a learned scribe himself dictated religious texts to the scribe Ilimilku who wrote them down. Apparently the oral recitation of texts was seen as the more original, authoritative act. The equally learned scribe had the right to elaborate and embellish the words he heard, but his freedom to do this was limited by several factors, among them the authority of his master who in the case of the Ugaritic high priest Attanu must have been able to check the work of his scribe Ilimilku. Also in the case of Jeremiah and Baruch this is clearly the case. When at the end of writing down Jeremiah's prophecies of doom Baruch complained that the grief and suffering Jeremiah had annnounced became too much for him, Jeremiah corrects him (Jer. 45).[276]

---

[275] The verb is the same as that which is used with Jeremiah in v. 4.

[276] Although scholars are divided over the originality of v. 1, most accept that here a real tension between the prophet and his scribe has been recorded.

It is simply wrong to construct an artificial opposition between authoritative oral prophecy and learned scribal scholarship. As Ehud Ben Zvi states,

> It is worth noting that the present discussion clearly leads to an image of 'restricted, high literacy' and 'general orality' as two deeply interwoven social phenomena. Within the proposed historical matrix, one does not and cannot take over and replace the other; rather, they complement (and sustain) each other.[277]

Van der Toorn 2007 compares the literacy in Mesopotamia and Egypt to that of ancient Israel. However, the cuneiform and hieroglyphic/hieratic/demotic scripts of the former are far more difficult to master than the alphabetic script used in Canaan and Israel. Here even a rudimentary reading ability sufficed to check at least superficially what a scribe had written. According to Judg. 8:14 a young man caught by chance was able to write down the names of 77 elders of Succoth. In one of the Lachish letters a subordinate officer assures his commander that he does read the letters send to him (Aḥituv 2008, 62-69). Such evidence suggests that the alphabet made acquiring basic reading skills a lot easier than in Mesopotamia and Egypt.

Yet also in Israel writing literary compositions of some length must have required thorough scribal training. According to the biblical testimony heroes of faith like Moses and Joshua would have been able to write large portions of the present text of the Hebrew Bible themselves. However, modern research has cast grave doubt on these statements. Of course it is not impossible that some written traditions go back to Mosaic times,[278] but for the time being honesty requires that we admit the speculative nature of such theories.

So it is uncertain when serious literary production may have started in Israel. If the ʿIzbet Ṣartah ostracon is seen as the earliest example of Israelite writing (so Aḥituv 2008, 249), the circumstance that it contains an encoded message (Korpel 2009a) would seem to indicate that Israelite scribes achieved some level

---

[277] Ben Zvi, in: Ben Zvi & Floyd 2000, 23. In the same vein other scholars contributing to this volume, e.g. Culley and Floyd.
[278] See e.g. De Moor 1997.

of sophistication already in the 12th century BCE. If the ostracon from Khirbet Qeiyafa is indeed a Hebrew text it is further evidence of Israelite writing skills in the 10th century BCE.[279] In this case the content of the message shows that the scribe(s) had mastered a fairly advanced level of literacy. From at least the 9th century onwards Hebrew inscriptions show the hands of experienced scribes. These scribes must have been able to write larger documents on papyrus and leather which due to the unfavorable climate of Palestine have gone lost.

On the basis of 1 Kgs 22:28 which he dates *c.* 560 BCE and Jer. 26:17-19 dating from the year 609 BCE Karel van der Toorn supposes that by the early 6th century a written scroll of Micah oracles must have existed (Van der Toorn 2007, 173-174). However, this is more than the two quotations prove.[280] The short quotation from Mic. 1:2 in 1 Kgs 22:28 does not fit the context and looks suspiciously like a pseudo-learned gloss of someone who has confused Micah ben Imlah with Micah the Morashtite. In the time of the glossator 'Hear, all you peoples' may have been the first words of the Book of Micah the Morashtite. First words of written documents were often used as titles. Apparently the present superscription of Mic. 1:1 was still lacking at that time, but since we do not know when the glossator lived, the reference to Mic. 1:2 in 1 Kgs 22:28 may have been inserted much later than *c.* 560 BCE.

With regard to Jer. 26:17-19 it is hardly imaginable that the elders (v. 17) would have been able to read a Micah scroll. Elders were carriers of oral tradition. They simply quoted from memory. They remembered Mic. 3:12 as a famous example of an unfulfilled oracle of doom.

So we simply do not know for certain when the writing of the biblical books started, though it seems likely that the collecting

---

[279] Cf. http://qeiyafa.huji.ac.il/ostracon2.asp; Puech 2010; Becking & Sanders 2010.

[280] Further on Van der Toorn broadens his thesis in an inadmissable way to state that this proto-Micah scroll would have consisted of only the three first chapters of the Book of Micah, 'precisely the part that many critics regard as the original core' (Van der Toorn 2007, 177). Yet later on he includes Mic. 7:1-6 as authentic, cf. 192, with 338, n. 32.

of prophetic oracles may have started as early as the 8th century BCE.[281] It seems logical to suppose that the same scribes who wrote them down have tried their hands on other literary genres, such as laws, annals, proverbs, hymns and prayers. But we have their legacy only in the form of heavily edited later documents, not in the form of autographs or even copies of autographs.

Also in the case of the scribes who were responsible for the compilation of the Scriptures it is unwarranted to assume that they engaged in willful deception. It is an undeniable fact that only thanks to the work of scribes we know about the intellectual heritage of the past. However, exactly because of the complex process of interaction between oral and scribal tradition we just described we are reluctant to accept Van der Toorn's thesis that the scribes 'invented' revelation (Van der Toorn 2007, Chapter 8). In many cases the 'inventor' must have been a speaker or singer who honestly believed to merely pass on words which a deity had prompted her or him to speak. They understood themselves as messengers, servants of the gods.

That also the scribes of Israel understood themselves as mere servants of God is abundantly clear in Ben Sira's eulogy on the scribe (Sir. 38:24–39:11). A scribe occupies himself with the Law and the Prophets (Sir. 38:34; 39:1, 8), prays frequently (Sir. 39:5-6) and if it pleases the Lord Almighty 'he will be filled with the spirit of understanding' (Sir. 39:6).

5.3 Dreams, Visions, Oracles, Omina

Uncertainty about the future has always vexed human beings. The conviction that life on earth was determined in heaven led people to surmise that there must be means to establish what the gods had in store for them. This was achieved by divination (Cryer 1994; Krüger 2008). Even though the reliability of divination was occasionally doubted, the enormous expenditure in time, money and training of the diviners testifies to the high esteem they enjoyed in the ancient Near East. Astrological observations, cloud formations, flights of birds, terrestrial events like floods and earthquakes, rustling leaves, physical abnormalities in

---

[281] Section 3.2.2.1.

humans and animals, inspection of the entrails of sacrificial victims, patterns of oil on water, curling smoke – all were used in attempts to clarify the unknown. In Mesopotamia enormous collections of observable phenomena were collected and in the form of 'if – then' phrases connected with certain consequences. Theoretically such learned collections of written omina enabled trained scholars to predict future events.[282]

Yet it would be erroneous to make a sharp distinction between such 'technical' approaches to divination and the more spontaneous phenomena like prophecy (cf. Flower 2008, 90-91). Rather the 'learned' approach was seen as complementary to inspired speech. A distinction between divination as an ineffective technical skill and 'true' prophecy as the word of God is made in the Bible alone where soothsaying is derided and condemned. Probably this is a late theological construction. Originally also in Israel itself other, more technical means of acquiring knowledge about the will of God were available. Some of these, for example the interpretation of dreams and lot casting, were tolerated until the closure of the canon.

Dreams, oracles and omina were enormously important to the political wellfare of the king and the state. Timely warnings about impending disasters, wrath of the gods, advancing enemies, illness or even death were vital to the rulers of antiquity. In times of distress they resorted to all kinds of divination in order to obtain certainty about what was awaiting them. The Hittite king Mursili II complains time and again that the gods do not listen to his prayers in which he asked for help against the plague that was ravaging his country. He begs them to clarify the situation by visions in dreams, oracles, men of god (prophets), or incubation-dreams of priests (Singer 2002, 60).

It would be haughty to dismiss such attempts as outdated and rather naive. The complexity of many situations in real life still causes people to resort to the same kind of outward pseudo-decisive phenomena – horoscopes, soothsaying, spiritualistic sessions, throwing dices, etcetera. Only in 2008 it became known that several politicians and captains of industry of the Nether-

---

[282] Maul 2003-2005.

lands made use of astrologers to predict the future.[283] As a matter of fact this is hardly surprising if one believes that in the end all processes on earth are governed by randomness and unpredictable chaos.

5.3.1 Dreams

5.3.1.1 Dreams in the Ancient Near East

From early times on mankind must have wondered about the meaning of dreams. Because often certain connections were possible with experiences, thoughts and worries which had occupied the dreamer during the day, people assumed that in a dream the gods revealed things that were inaccessible or incomprehensible to normal human beings, including what might happen in the future. However, the patchy and fuzzy character of dream fragments remembered made subsequent interpretation imperative and therefore specialist help was invoked. If necessary, incantations and magic might be necessary to ward off impending disaster and this too required the help of a trained and authorized person like a priest or magician. Therefore most dreams were not understood as direct communication with the divine world,[284] but as information that had to be decrypted by knowledgeable people.

As early as the 23rd century BCE a dream oracle is attested on a cuneiform tablet from the Mesopotamian city of Ebla. A 'seer' interprets an incubation dream of a woman (Bonechi & Durand 1992). According to the Sumerian account of the rise to power of the Old Akkadian king Sargon I (also 23rd century BCE) he had a dream when he was still a cupbearer to king Urzababa of Kish. In this dream the goddess Inanna announced that she would drown Urzababa 'in a river of blood', thus clearing the road for Sargon's ascendency (Cooper 1985). Dreams of or about members of the royal house were seen as politically important. However, also dreams on mundane matters like a missing servant girl were dutifully reported to the king.

---

[283] Published in the Dutch newspaper *De Pers*, November 12, 2008.

[284] With the exception of dream theophanies in which a deity addressed a human being directly (cf. Section 5.1).

When he was still a prince, the later king Thutmose IV (*c.* 1413-1403 BCE), received an oracle in a dream during a siesta in the shadow of the great Sphinx which is designated as 'this great god'. The god speaks directly to the future king,

> Sleep took hold of him, slumbering at the time when the sun was at (its) peak. He found the majesty of this august god speaking with his own mouth, as a father speaks to his son, saying: "See me, look at me, my son, Thutmose! I am thy father, Harmakhis-Khepri-Re-Atum. I shall give thee my kingdom ... upon earth at the head of the living. Thou shalt wear the southern crown and the northern crown on the throne of Geb, the crown prince (of the gods). Thine is the land in its length and its breadth, that which the Eye of the All-Lord illumines. Provisions are thine from the midst of the Two Lands and the great tribute of every foreign country. ... I knew that thou art my son and my protector. *Approach* thou! Behold, I am with thee; I am thy guide.'[285]

Similar dreams are attested of the Hittite king Hattushilis (*c.* 1290-1250 BCE). Also in his case the evidently faked dream supposedly substantiating his claim to the throne by divine election cannot be taken seriously as evidence of divine intercession, although it is certainly possible that the prince himself was convinced of this and that the scribe believed him. We noted already the similar revelation to the Old Babylonian king Ibalpiel (Section 5.1). Apparently it was a well-known literary genre legitimating the ruling king by divine approbation.

Divination on the basis of dreams (oniromancy) remained one of the important means to learn the will of the deities in Egypt and Mesopotamia.[286] The interpretation of dreams was a task of special people. They could be gifted lay men or women, but could also be trained professionals who used manuals to arrive at a presumably reliable result. An Egyptian dream book, for example, describes all kinds of dreams a person might have and explains them as either good or bad signs.[287] Even very late Demotic

---

[285] Translation Wilson, *ANET*, 449.

[286] Oppenheim 1956; Leibovici 1959; Sauneron 1959; Vieyra 1959; Gnuse 1984, 11-55; Cooper 1985; Durand 1988, 453-482; Butler 1998; Husser 1999; Szpakowska 2001; 2006; Zgoll 2002; 2006; Noegel 2007; Pientka-Hinz, in: Krüger 2008, 47-49.

[287] Ritner 2001; Ritner, CoS, vol. 1, 52-54.

dream books contain standard interpretations of dreams.[288] Neo-Assyrian kings like Esarhaddon and Assurbanipal firmly believed in dream oracles.[289] In civilizations that were influenced by Mesopotamia, such as those of the Hittites[290] and the Ugaritians,[291] the mantic significance of dreams was also accepted. The Greeks too regarded dreams as a source of enlightenment about the intentions of the deities, provided they were properly interpreted by an expert (e.g. Homer, Iliad I.62-67; V.144-151). However, some schools, notably the Epicureans, rejected the use of dreams for mantic purposes (Walde 2009).

Even much earlier doubt about the reliability of dreams is already expressed in the Sumerian epic *Lugalbanda in the Wilderness*,

> Dream – a door cannot hold it back, nor can the pivot;
> To the liar it speaks lies, to the truthful the truth;
> It may make one happy or sad
> But it remains the closed table-basket of the gods.[292]

A tragic example of a human being who was misled by a dream-revelation is the Canaanite king Kirtu. In a Ugaritic legend written towards the end of the 13th century BCE, but probably based on a much older story, the hero receives a dream from the highest god Ilu describing in great detail how he can obtain a bride with whom he will sire the many sons he is longing for. However, Ilu deliberately omits to give Kirtu instructions for one small episode. So Kirtu has to act on his own initiative at that moment and ultimately this will cost him all his sons again and leave him with his youngest daughter as his only remaining legitimate heir.[293]

Because doubt about the reliability of dream reports was expected the sender sometimes affirmed that another person had had the same dream (Durand 2008, 465).

---

[288] Quack, in: Krüger 2008, 350-362.
[289] Parpola 1997, lxxiv; Nissinen 2003, 144-145.
[290] Cf. Kammenhuber 1976; Taracha 2000, 59, 63; Singer 2002, 32, 38, 60; Mouton 2007.
[291] Cf. Caquot 1959; Husser 1994, 27-62; Jeffers 1996, 125-143.
[292] Translation Vanstiphout 2003, 123.
[293] For a full discussion of this legend and its intriguing plot, see De Moor 1997, 91-95.

5.3.1.2 Dreams in the Bible

It has long been recognized that ancient Israel shared its belief that dreams might contain important important messages from the deity with its neighbors.[294] The mainly positive view of the Bible on the revelatory value of dreams is so well known that it is hardly necessary to document this extensively here: Abimelech, Jacob, Joseph – they and many others in the Bible are reported to have had dreams that were deemed significant. As Cooper 1985 noted, the dream of Joseph resembles Sargon's dream about his own rise to power. It is possible that a story about the origin of the royal house of Israel formed the inspiration for the Joseph cycle. Even Deuteronomy recognizes dreams as a legitimate mode of divine revelation (Deut. 13:2, 4, 6[1, 3, 5]).

However, dreams were not trusted (Gen. 37:8-10, 19-20). At least from Jeremiah on, the revelatory nature of dreams is called more and more into question,[295] but so is prophecy (Section 5.3.2.2) and since also positive judgments about dreams are attested in the post-exilic period,[296] we are confronted with divided opinions.

5.3.2 *Visions*

5.3.2.1 Visions in the Ancient Near East

Several examples of visions exist. A letter from the Old Babylonian city of Mari records a presumably witnessed discussion between deities about the question whether or not they will pay a visit to the city and its king (Durand 2000, 319-321). An unfortunately heavily damaged tablet from the Canaanite city of Ugarit seems to relate a vision of the post-mortem fate of a beloved high priest in the Nether World.[297] One of the most impressive visions from Mesopotamia is the Nether World vision of

---

[294] See e.g. Ehrlich 1953; Gnuse 1984; Husser 1994; Jeffers 1996; Husser 1999.
[295] Jer. 23:25-32; 27:9-10; 29:8-9; Zech. 10:2; Qoh. 5:6; Sir. 31:1-8; 40:5-7; Letter of Aristeas, 213-216. Cf. Ehrlich 1953, 156-170.
[296] Ehrlich 1953, 170; Husser 1994, 263.
[297] RS 92.2016, cf. De Moor 2009. In some other Ugaritic rituals it is stated that the king will 'see' various deities (KTU 1.90:1; 1.168:8). It is unlikely that this refers to expected visionary experiences. Rather the king will be allowed to contemplate the images of the deities.

an Assyrian crown prince (Foster 2005, 832-839). Balaam who is also known as a visionary in the Bible (Num. 23–24) is designated a 'seer' in the Transjordanian inscription recording his terrifying visions.[298]

5.3.2.2 Visions in the Bible

Visions are recorded throughout the Hebrew Bible, the New Testament and apocalyptic as well as pseudepigraphic literature. This fact is so well-known that there is no need to discuss it in full here.

According to 1 Sam. 9:9 a prophet was formerly called a 'seer'. The word used here differs from a more frequent term for 'seer'[299] and the verbs from which these words are derived are often used to designate the activity of prophets. Like prophecy, clairvoyance was not confined to professionals. Balaam describes himself as,

> The oracle of Balaam, the son of Beor,
>   yea, the oracle of the man whose eye is perfect,[300]
> the oracle of him who hears the words of God,
>   who sees the vision of the Almighty,
>   who falls down, yet has his eyes uncovered (Num. 24:3b-4).

The last words seem to suggest that a vision differed from a dream in that it was perceived with open eyes.[301] But it is more likely that it is a description of inner enlightenment (Milgrom 1990, 203), because other elements in Balaam's description fit better into a prophet's experience.[302]

The Bible attributes the capacity to receive visions also to non-Israelites like Balaam and emphasizes the impossibility for such a foreign seer to deliver an oracle that would differ from what God had revealed to him,

> God is not a man, that he should lie,
>   nor a son of man, that he should repent.

---

[298] See e.g. Aḥituv 2008, 432-465.

[299] 2 Sam. 24:11; 2 Kgs 17:13; Isa. 29:10; 30:10; Amos 7:12; Mic. 3:7.

[300] This interpretation is suggested by a similar expression in a Phoenician amulet from Arslan Tash: 'whose mouth is perfect'.

[301] An argument in favor of this interpretation might be derived from Zech. 4:1-2 where an angel wakes the prophet before showing him the vision. See also Zech. 1:18; 2:1; 5:1; 6:1.

[302] He 'hears the words of God' and 'falls down' (cf. 1 Sam. 19:24).

> Does he speak and then not act?
>   Does he talk and not fulfill?
> I was instructed[303] to bless;
>   he has blessed, and I cannot reverse it (Num. 23:18-19).

The impression is created that Balaam received the literal wording of his blessing and that it was impossible for him to give in to Balak's pressure to curse the Israelites instead of blessing them.

5.3.3 Oracles and Omina

5.3.3.1 Oracles and Omina in the Ancient Near East

A very common way to consult the deities was in the form of a question to which a 'yes' or 'no' was possible. Such binary oracles are attested for Egypt since the 18th dynasty (Kákosy 1982; De Moor 1997, 104, 260-261), for Babylonia in the form of questions directed to Shamash, the sun god, and Adad, the storm god (Lambert 2007), and for the Hittite empire (Singer 2002, 59; Beal 2002). In Egypt the verdict of the deity was inferred from movements of his cult image, for example interpreted as choosing one from two contradictory documents, or it was communicated by a priest speaking through a tube in the mouth of the image (Kákosy 1982, 600-601). In any case professional help was necessary to learn what the deity meant. The political power of the oracle priests was enormous. They acted, for example, as intermediaries for the election of kings by the deity (Barta 1980, 476-477).

Queries to the Sun-god in Sargonid Assyria invariably begin with the phrase, 'O Shamash, great lord, answer me with a firm "yes" to what I ask you' (Starr 1990, XVI). This type of phrases too suggests a binary oracle – yes or no – but in reality the answer of the deity will not always have been so straightforward, because it should be derived by oracular means, most often by extispicy of the liver of a ram, with accompanying rituals and prayers. Though the idea was that the deity invoked had 'written' a firm 'yes' in the entrails of the sacrificial lamb,[304] the correct interpretation of this 'writing' required an expert (*barû*, literally 'examiner') who

---

[303] Cf. Levine 2000, 182.
[304] CAD (Š) 2, 231b.

was trained with the help of clay models of such livers.[305] Yet the outcome of his extispicy was regarded as a genuine reply from the gods. The god 'answered' through the signs on the organ, the diviner transmitted the 'word' of the deity (Jeyes 1989, 17-19). Or, to put it plainly, the diviner's word was seen as the word of the deity.

The technical nature of such oracles should not be interpreted as an indication that the ancients thought they could force the deities to pronounce a favorable judgment. King Zimrilim of Mari (*c.* 1779-1757 BCE), for example, ordered one of his servants to detain a convoy of Qaṭna until the omens were good. However, after five days of trying, the lambs available for extispicy were exhausted and a different solution had to be found (Durand 2000, 102). On the other hand, human beings could decide to ignore a positive oracle. A new priestess of Dagan, for example, objects against the house that had been allotted to her by means of a firm 'yes' of the deity. Subsequently another omen is obtained about a different house and this time too the outcome is 'yes' which is accepted by the priestess (Durand 2000, 105-106).

In satellite states under the influence of Mesopotamia, such as the kingdoms of Hatti and Ugarit, this practice of 'reading' the will of the gods in livers and other organs was imitated.[306]

In Emar, a Mesopotamian satellite state also close to Canaan, an interesting text records,

> As the Hurrian troops surrounded the city wall of Emar, the divination of Mašruḫe, diviner of the king and the city, came true. Pilsu-Dagan, the king, therefore, has given him this field as a present.[307]

As Tsukimoto notes, in this case we are lucky enough to have another Emarite report on this matter,

> The king of the troops of the Hurrian land treated Pilsu-Dagan, son of Baʿlu-kabar, the king of Emar, badly. Then, Pilsu-Dagan

---

[305] Jeyes 1989; Starr 1990, XXXVI-LV; Koch-Westenholz 2000; Lambert 2007, 4-5; Pientka-Hinz, in: Krüger 2008, 16-28.

[306] Dietrich & Loretz 1990; Arnaud 2007, 47-54; Haas 1994, 689-91; Haas 2008.

[307] Translation Tsukimoto 1990, 190.

raised his eyes toward Baʿlu, and Baʿlu gave him the favourable auspices which he wished. So the soldiers guarding (the city's) inner part and siege wall, in accordance with his divination, defeated (the enemy) and saved the city of Emar.[308]

In this case the oracle was obtained by inspecting the entrails of a bird, but obviously it required a trained diviner to establish whether or not the results he found warranted a favorable interpretation.

In Mesopotamia enormous collections of omina were compiled, not only by means of livers and lungs, but also on the basis of oil patterns on water,[309] astrological observations,[310] abnormalities in foetuses (Leichty 1970) patterns in curling smoke or flour,[311] etcetera. Divination became a 'science' there. If a king died on a day when a black dog strayed into the temple, this was reason enough to record: 'If a black dog enters the temple, the king will die'. The scribes not only had to acquire the skill to copy these very extensive divination manuals, they also had to learn them by heart. Modern man should not depreciate their work as mere human effort. Several of these textbooks are explicitly ascribed to utterances of the god of wisdom Ea himself (Van der Toorn 2007, 58). Despite this huge amount of 'expertise' based on divine revelation, the gods might deliberately give an unreliable answer to a question put before them.[312]

Ugarit, fairly close to the later territory of ancient Israel, also made use of extispicy of livers and lungs, necromancy and astrology, apparently imitating the Babylonian practice.[313] Also in Late Bronze Age Hazor, in what later would become Israelite territory, liver models for extispicy were found.[314]

Also among the Greeks hepatoscopy was a common method to learn more about the will of the gods (Plato, Phaedrus, 244c).

---

[308] Translation Tsukimoto 1990, 192.
[309] Pettinato 1966; Maul 2003-2005, 46-50; Pientka-Hinz, in: Krüger 2008, 31-34.
[310] Hunger 1992; Koch-Westenholz 1995; Rochberg 2004.
[311] Pientka-Hinz, in: Krüger 2008, 29-31.
[312] CAD (A) 2, 162a; (T), 364b.
[313] Dietrich & Loretz 1990, with plates of clay models.
[314] Horowitz & Oshima 2006, 66-68.

The Etruscans too used models of livers, as the bronze liver of Piacenza demonstrates (Van der Meer 1987).

Especially in the Levant which formed the main corridor for the great bird migrations between Europe and Africa interpretation of the flight of birds by diviners was common. In Ugarit and Egypt it was thought that the spirits of the dead, like the great gods themselves, could take on the shape of birds. The more important the dead, the more impressive species of bird they became – falcons, black kites or eagles. Small wonder that people tried to obtain oracles from the way birds behaved.[315] Also the Greeks believed that the flight of birds could be predictive (e.g. Homer, Odyssey II.182; XV.160-181; Iliad I.69; VI.76).

Trees and stones were thought to murmur oracles in the Canaanite city of Ugarit.[316] Also in the Greek religion stones were thought to be able to speak.[317] The very famous diviner's oak of Dodona is mentioned by Homer.[318] A Demotic Egyptian handbook relates oracles obtained through interrogation of a stone.[319]

Israel's close neighbor Moab entertained a 'sign house', probably a house where oracles were obtained (Aḥituv 2008, 423-426).

5.3.3.2 Oracles and Omina in the Bible

It is sometimes thought that Num. 23:23 would imply that from an early date on even a non-Israelite diviner like Balaam would have testified that there was no augury or divination in ancient Israel. However, the translation of the passage is contested and even if such a rendering is accepted it is possibly a late addition to the Balaam oracles.

In Israel too oracles could be consulted to learn the will of God. The best-known is the priestly oracle Urim and Thummim.[320] Although the precise shape and working of this oracle

---

[315] Cf. Spronk 1986, 185; De Moor 1987, 65, 266, 269; 1988b, 66-67; Korpel 1996a.
[316] De Moor 1987, 180-181 (KTU 1.82:36-43).
[317] Nonnus, *Dionysiaca*, XIV.269-283.
[318] Homer, Iliad, XVI.233-235. For later testimonies, cf. Graf 2009.
[319] Quack, in: Krüger 2008, 362-367.
[320] See e.g. Horowitz & Hurowitz 1992; Jeffers 1996, 210-215; Van Dam 1997; Houtman 2000, 493-497.

are unknown,[321] its result was interpreted by a priest as a decision of God. Often its consultation resulted in a firm 'yes' or 'no' on the part of God, so that it may be compared to the binary oracles referred to above.[322] Sometimes more elaborate statements were derived from it, as was the case with the Egyptian and Babylonian binary oracles. Under Saul the authority attributed to the Urim oracle equalled prophecy according to 1 Sam. 28:6. Under the Davidic monarchy Urim and Thummim seem to have fallen in disuse, at least in Jerusalem, possibly because the oracle gave the priests too much power over the affairs of state.[323] Consulting a prophet became the most common way of learning the will of God, even in mundane matters. However, also prophecies could acquire the character of a binary oracle by offering a choice between two alternatives.[324]

Also other types of oracles remained in use. In Hos. 3:4 the prophet announces, 'the Israelites will have to spend a long time without king, without prince, without sacrifice, without standing stone, without ephod and teraphim'. Standing stones and teraphim fulfilled a role in the consultation of ancestors (De Moor 1997, 336-361). According to Isa. 19:19-20 a standing stone will be erected for the LORD at the border of Egypt which will be a sign and a witness to the LORD. When the Israelites cry to him because of oppressors he will send them a savior, and will defend and deliver them. This text seems to confirm that at the time of its composition (4th century BCE?) standing stones were still admissible in the cult and were supposed to be able to 'speak' oracles of salvation. Zech. 10:2 demonstrates that up till very late times the teraphim were used in divination by Israelite rulers. The mention of the ephod in Hos. 3:4 seems to imply that at

---

[321] The most plausible explanation is that of Horowitz & Hurowitz 1992, but even their Assyrian parallel is uncertain, as they themselves acknowledge. Cf. Van Dam 1997, 40-42 and Lambert 2007, 19, 100-101.

[322] This is especially clear when the oracle was used to exclude one of two possibilities, as in 1 Sam. 14:41 according to the Old Greek. However, Van Dam 1997, 197-203, rejects the Greek version.

[323] Cf. De Moor 1997, 308. According to Van Dam 1997, 247-255, the consultation of counselors and the unfaithfulness of priests would have played a role.

[324] Becking 2009, 39-40 points to Jer. 38:17-18.

least in Northern Israel the oracular use of Urim and Thummim continued for some time (Macintosh 1997, 106-107). Apparently the LORD chose not to communicate with his people by these means any longer. Probably as a result of such prophetic criticism the standing stones and teraphim were forbidden later on (Deut. 16:22; 2 Kgs 23:24; Zech. 10:2).

Also the casting of lots continued. The land was divided by means of this oracle. If Josh. 18 is considered too late to be taken as evidence, Ps. 16:5-6 and Amos 7:17 attest to the practice in earlier days. Mic. 2:5 indicates that a special official had to pull ropes over the land according to the outcome of the lot. That this was a *religious* ceremony is attested by the fact that it took place 'in the congregation of the LORD'. Similar ceremonies are attested elsewhere in the ancient Near East (De Moor 2002, 93-96).

A 'Diviners' Oak' near Shechem is mentioned in Judg. 9:37. Probably it is the same tree that later on was renamed into the less offensive 'Teacher's Terebinth' (Gen. 12:6).[325] Next to the standings stones the Hebrew Bible often mentions the Asherah's. In Mic. 5:12-14 the diviners, the standing stones and the Asherah's are condemned in the same breath.[326] Generally it is assumed that the Asherah's were poles of wood. Hosea reproaches his compatriots that they seek oracles from their 'tree' and 'branches' which the prophet denounces as following of 'a spirit of harlotry', apparently contrasting this practice to the Spirit of God on which the prophets relied.[327] It is likely that the criticism of consulting trees or wood for divine guidance started fairly early in Israel, initially perhaps because the experts in such practices rivalled with the prophets. Earlier, however, David had got the signal to attack the Philistines from the sound of footfalls in the tops of balsam trees (2 Sam. 5:24). So it seems likely that originally the Israelites, like their neighbors, also derived oracles from trees and other wooden objects.

In Israel too the flight of birds was observed intently (Jer. 8:7;

---

[325] Cf. De Moor 1976.

[326] The passage is a later addition to the Book of Micah.

[327] Hos. 4:12. Others translate 'wood' instead of 'tree' and 'staves' instead of 'branches', thinking of oracles obtained by means of rhabdomancy, cf. Macintosh 1997, 151-152.

Job 35:11; 39:26). According to Ezek. 13 certain prophetesses in Israel symbolically caught souls of the dead in the form of birds with self-made nets. They did this to practice divination with these birds (Korpel 1996a). Ezekiel criticizes these women severely, but since nobody else seems to have hindered them it is likely that earlier it was an acceptable form of divination, as in the Levant.

Other signs may have had an oracular function in the cult (Ps. 86:17) and these too might be withheld (Ps. 74:4).[328] Possibly these signs were events announced by or symbolic acts performed by prophets,[329] but the possibility that also in Israel hepatoscopy (examination of livers) has occurred cannot be excluded, although later on it will have fallen under the prohibition of Deut. 18:9-12, cf. Ezek. 21:26[21].[330]

After having waited silently and patiently[331] for a reaction from God the Psalmist of Ps. 62 suddenly exclaims,

> One thing God has said,
>   two things that I have heard![332]
> Surely,[333] to God belongs strength,
>   and to you, O Lord, belongs faithfulness.
> Surely you will reward
>   everyone according to what he has done.
>
> (Ps. 62:12-13[11-12])

All kinds of hypotheses are possible with regard to what God said, but the most satisfactory solution is that the first favorable divine

---

[328] Cf. Keller 1946, 46-47.

[329] 1 Sam. 2:34; 10:7, 9; 2 Kgs 20:8-9; Isa. 7:10-17; 8:18; 37:30; 38:7, etc. Viberg 2007.

[330] For discussion on the possibility of hepatoscopy in Israel, see Cryer 1994, 295-305; Jeffers 1996, 158-160.

[331] The sixfold repetition of the word 'nevertheless' (Hebr. 'ak) points to the effort this patience cost him (Tate 1990, 122).

[332] Sometimes the verse is rendered 'Once God has spoken; twice have I heard this'. The philological basis for this rendering is too shallow and most modern dictionaries of Biblical Hebrew do not support it anymore.

[333] The Hebrew text twice has the same particle. It should not be translated first 'that', then 'surely'. Moreover, the Psalmist does not doubt God's power, so it would hardly be what he was waiting for if we were to render, 'that God has strength'. In our opinion the Psalmist does not divulge what he has heard, but his hymnic praise lets it be known that he received a favorable oracle.

oracle was confirmed by a second one – a common procedure in the biblical world, as we have seen.

The overall picture is that just as in the world surrounding ancient Israel magical arts and divinatory techniques did exist in the pre-exilic period, but were gradually phased out when the biblical canon was formed and the holy Book became the only authoritative source of revelation.

5.4 Conclusions on the Deity Addressing Man

This chapter about speaking deities is by far the longest of the whole book – a book about the silence of God... Actually this is not surprising because the God of the Bible is described far more often as a *speaking* God than as a *silent* God.[334] Everywhere in the ancient Near East people expected their deities to react promptly to their prayers. According to the available evidence deities for their part promised to do so, on condition that their worshippers would provide their cult with everything they needed and would honor their commandments. In this respect there was little difference between Israel and its neighbors. However, although it was impossible for us to prove this because of the enormous quantity of relevant data that have been amassed in the past few decades we have the definite impression that the God of the Bible is much more often represented as a *speaking* God than any of the other deities of the ancient world. Of course this may be due to the fact that early Judaism and Christianity were much later religious movements than most religions of the ancient Near East we have reviewed. But it might be interesting to investigate if the presumed difference between biblical and other Near Eastern divine oracles might be ascribed to the more routinely given answers in the much more extensive centers of religious worship elsewhere. Nevertheless a more detailed comparison of what evidence we have would seem warranted.

Direct communication between the deity and human beings was restricted to divinely elected people like patriarchs and kings of the distant past. It may be surmised, however, that the record-

---

[334] Cf. Section 1.6.2.

ing of direct dialogues between the gods and these divinely elect was a literary ploy to heighten the prestige of the latter. In later times, both in Israel and in the surrounding cultures, specialists like prophets, priests, diviners and scribes were openly described as the intermediaries between the deity and mankind. In Israel, however, the concept of direct communication between an individual and God was 'democratized' soon after the destruction of the Solomonic temple in 587 BCE. Jews had been dispersed all over the ancient world and did not have much faith anymore in a deity residing in an exclusively fixed place on earth.

Voices from heaven are mentioned both in the Bible and in documents from the ancient Near East. In the latter the sun deity is the speaker sometimes, but more often thunder was seen as the voice of a deity, especially the storm god. Also in the Bible, even in the New Testament, thunder is seen as the voice of God. However, ordinary human beings could not understand the meaning of thunder and therefore specialists trained in the interpretation of thunderstorms had to act as intermediaries.

Both in ancient Egypt and in the Bible the notion existed that the gods could address man 'from behind'. Here the imagery of the good shepherd who walks behind his flock when they are on the move stood at the background. The warning voice of the deity, mediated by human leadership, kept the 'sheep' on the right track.

Because the Ancients were convinced that a divine spirit inhabited every human being they also listened to this inner voice for guidance. Especially in the Bible it is often impossible to distinguish sharply between the Spirit of God and the spirit of man. Man is free to choose differently from what the Spirit counsels, but mostly the effect of a self-willed decision is described as detrimental.

Deities were also supposed to communicate in written form with their followers, but in this case too later generations openly admitted that human scribes had to do the actual writing. In the Bible Moses, Joshua and several prophets are described as writing down the words of God.

Communication between high gods and human beings might take place via lower divine beings, for example deified founders of dynasties, ancestors or heroes of the past. Because metamorphosis was a characteristic quality of godhead, such speaking deities could take on a wide variety of shapes, e.g. animals, standing stones, trees. In the Bible 'angels' became the messengers between God and human beings. The dividing line between these semi-divine messengers and human messengers was vague.

Anthropomorphic or theriomorphic images served as foci of the divine in all cults of the ancient Near East, but physical representation of God is condemned in the Bible. It is generally assumed that this was a late development in Israel.

Incorporeal spirits were imagined as shadows, smoke or wind. They were called up in spiritistic sessions to consult them on difficult matters and traces of such practices still exist in the Bible. They were assumed to be able to speak and acted as messengers between high deities and human beings. The medium controlling such spirits was usually a priest or diviner, but also great heroes of the glorious past, like the Mesopotamian Gilgamesh, the Ugaritic Dani'ilu and the Greek Odysseus were thought to have possessed this ability. Also the Israelite king Saul is reputed to have consulted the spirit of his mentor Samuel, but in order to make contact he had to pay a visit to a specialist medium (1 Sam. 28).

In early Judaism and Christianity the Holy Spirit of God continued to inspire people, but in mainstream rabbinic Judaism the opinion took hold that the inner voice of the Holy Spirit stopped speaking after the last canonical prophet had died.

Usually the deity would make use of human emissaries to address man, for example a prophet or a priest. For a long time it was thought that prophecy was a typical Israelite phenomenon. Nowadays it has become clear that all over the ancient Near East deities addressed their worshippers through prophets who were not always trained specialists because also spontaneous prophetic seizure of ordinary people is attested. The literary and theological refining of written Hebrew prophecy during the centuries after their first delivery makes comparison with the often much shorter oracles from elsewhere difficult. However, the main characteristics justify the thesis that prophecy was an established institution by which the deity addressed mankind, also in response to prayers spoken in a cultic context.

If a human being was the carrier of the words of the deity, inevitably the question presented itself if this woman or man was trustworthy. In all civilizations of the ancient world people were wary of false prophecy.

Although we do not want to overemphasize the differences, at this moment it is true that in no culture of the ancient Near East a singular 'prophet' like Moses arose – or was framed. And nowhere so many prophecies of doom were recorded as in Israel – although this might be the result of hindsight after the collapse of the monarchy.

Some prophets may have been able to write, but most were not. This means that initially their messages from the deity were passed on through oral transmission. In modern discussions the written nature of religious documents from Antiquity tends to be overestimated. Probably oral transmission was just as important, if not more important. Ethnological research has demonstrated convincingly that oral tradition is able to preserve texts reliably over many centuries. Yet it must be assumed that it was easier to adapt the oral tradition to new challenging situations than to introduce completely different ideas in the hoary legacy of generations of scribes. Because prophecy relied first of all on a live audience, it was experienced as the *spoken* word of God that opened up new vistas in times of emergency. Eventually, however, also the written tradition must have been adapted to the new situation that had already been addressed orally. The redactional processes involved to remodel the written tradition afterwards can in some cases be followed pretty closely.

The guidance of the Holy Spirit was indispensable to prophets according to the biblical testimony. Admittedly they might be deluded by evil spirits, in some cases presumably sent by God himself. Therefore it required courage and the power of discernment to be certain of their mission and refuse to utter prophecies of salvation even if the ruling class and their followers required only favorable predictions – without sufficient justification.

Despite the importance of orality in the ancient world we must acknowledge the fact that only the scribal tradition of the word of God has endured the ravages of time and renders it possible for us to vaguely conjecture what the scribes meant when they wrote down, 'Thus says the LORD...' They had the freedom to reword the original message of a prophet, to embellish it according to the best of their literary skills, and to adapt it to the needs of the moment. There did not exist any copyright and plagiarism was not punishable. To state that a biblical book was written by the prophet Amos or Isaiah because the Bible says so is an anachronistic misjudgment. Some of it may go back to the original words of the prophet speaking in the name of God, but certainly not all of it. The divine inspiration of the scribes who undertook the rewording of the prophet's original message centuries later should not be denied. They themselves at least were honestly believing they were carrying out a task entrusted to them by the deity. Whether or not we as modern readers believe them is a wholly different question which should not anachronistically be projected back on their achievements.

Next to prophecy there existed other means of learning what the gods had in store for their worshippers. In the world around Israel various modes of divination stood in high esteem and were seen as complementary to inspired speech. A distinction between divination as an ineffective technical skill and 'true' prophecy as the word of God is made in the Bible alone where soothsaying is derided and condemned. Probably this is a late theological construction. Originally also in Israel itself other, more technical means of acquiring knowledge about the will of God were available. Some of these, for example the interpretation of dreams and lot casting, were tolerated until the closure of the canon.

Also in divination human intervention was indispensable. The confusing nature of dreams necessitated the help of experts, like Joseph and Daniel in the Bible. Outside Israel inspection of the entrails of a sacrificial victim, especially the liver, was considered to provide important information about the future which the gods had 'written' there beforehand. This method, however, produced results only at the hands of thoroughly trained specialists. Also astrology, observation of bird flights, consulting trees or stones representing ancestors, and other forms of augury were gradually phased out in Israel, probably because in all these cases the 'witnesses' themselves remained silent and those who interpreted the signs often contradicted each other. Judaism became the religion of the codified Word of God.

The main general conclusion of this chapter must be that the words deities addressed to man were mediated by other human beings, usually religious specialists. Even if the impression was created that the deity spoke directly to certain privileged people or had entrusted his words to angelic messengers, there are strong indications that in reality human intervention was necessary. This cannot be seen as deliberate delusion of the ignorant masses, because the intermediaries themselves understood their mission as inspired by the deity. Of course all this has long been suspected, but as far as we know it has never been demonstrated as conclusively on the basis of a broad textual basis.

CHAPTER SIX

THE SILENT GOD

6.1 The Silence of the Remote God

Silence was one of the ways in which human beings tried to communicate with their deities (Section 4.6). In Chapter 5 we have demonstrated that divine messages were usually mediated by human beings. What did it mean when deities were believed to remain silent, even if humans implored them to speak or act?

6.1.1 In the Ancient Near East

According to Egyptian theologians of the New Kingdom stillness reigned on the primordial earth before the Sun-god Amun-Re created everything that exists, including the first deities.[1] He did so by being the first to speak.[2] Without the word of the Creator of life, the earth was silent. An Amun-hymn from a Leiden papyrus states,

> He opened speech from within the stillness:
>   and he opened each eye, letting it see;
> He began sounds while the world was silent –
>   and his unchallenged victory-shout encircled the earth.[3]

According to the creation theology of the Egyptian city of Heliopolis, the god Shu stilled the sky, earth and other deities before revealing his self-creation, 'I shall speak. Become still, Ennead! Become silent, gods, and I will tell you my evolution myself.'[4]

So the Egyptians thought that silence reigned before it was broken by the speech of the creator.

Already in the *Wisdom of Merikare* (*c.* 2000 BCE) it is stated that the good creator god erected a chapel for himself among his human creatures; when they weep, he listens to them.[5]

---

[1] Assmann 1999, No. 32:15-20 (117); No. 136:20-25 (330); Allen, CoS, vol. 1, 24.
[2] Assmann 1999, No. 136:15-19, 21-22 (330); Allen, CoS, vol. 1, 24.
[3] Translation Foster 1995, 76.
[4] Allen, CoS, vol. 1, 8-9. See also Coffin Texts Spell 1130, Allen, CoS, vol. 1, 26.
[5] Lichtheim 1973, 106; Foster 2001, 203; Altenmüller 2009, 25.

232   CHAPTER SIX

Can humans really hear the voice of the creator god? In principle this is deemed impossible. The absolute transcendence of the creator god Amun is expressed as follows in a Theban eulogy,

> Amun is one, hiding himself from them.[6]
> He is concealed from the gods, and his aspect is unknown.
> He is farther than the sky, he is deeper than the Duat.[7]
> No god knows his true appearance,
> no processional image of his is unfolded through inscriptions,
> no one testifies to him accurately.
> He is too secret to uncover his awesomeness,
> he is too great to investigate, too powerful to know.[8]

From another hymn to Amun-Re,

> Whose Form is mysterious, there is no knowing him,
>   who conceals himself from all the gods;
> Who hides himself in the sundisk, there is no comprehending
>   him.
> who masks himself even from those who emerged from him.[9]

Communication with such a transcendent, remote deity seems impossible.[10] Yet the same text affirms that messages are sent by him from the sky and heard in the sanctuaries of Heliopolis, Memphis and Thebes.[11] Although Amun-Re is infinitely remote, he is at the same time very close to his worshippers. It is therefore understandable that he became the focus of the much discussed 'personal piety' which reached its culmination point under the Ramessides, probably as an answer to the chill of the monotheistic revolution in the Amarna period. Now it becomes possible to address Amun-Re directly and the supplicant may expect the god to listen to his prayer and deliver him from distress,

---

[6] The great gods who had been created by Amun just before.
[7] The Abyss.
[8] Translation Allen, CoS, vol. 1, 25.
[9] Translation Foster 1995, 67.
[10] The Egyptian pessimistic sage Ipuwer states about the high god Ptah, 'There is none who can reach him' (Ipuwer 5.9; translation Enmarch 2008, 227, with his comments 110).
[11] Allen, CoS, vol. 1, 26.

> Who hears the prayer of the one in distress,
>> is kind to whoever calls on him,
> Saves the fearful man from the hand of the insolent,
>> judges fairly between the wretched man and the affluent.[12]

A similar ambiguous attitude is found in the *Babylonian Theodicy* which dates from about the same era. On the one hand it is stated,

> The divine mind, like the centre of the heavens, is remote;
>> Knowledge of it is difficult; the masses do not know it.[13]

Yet at the end of his long diatribe the sufferer turns to his god,

> I, though humble, wise, and a suppliant,
>> Have not seen help and succour for one moment.
> ...
> May the god who has thrown me off give help,
>> May the goddess who has [abandoned me] show mercy.[14]

Also the classic Babylonian wisdom text *Ludlul bēl nēmeqi*, again dating from the end of the second millennium BCE, reflects this paradoxical attitude towards the deity,

> My god has forsaken me and disappeared,
>> My goddess has failed me and keeps a distance.
> The benevolent angel who (walked) beside [me] has departed,
>> My protecting spirit has taken to flight, and is seeking someone else.[15]

The god who has forsaken the sufferer is the supreme Lord, creator and sustainer of the world, and master of all other gods, angels and spirits.

6.1.2 *The Silence of the Remote God in the Bible*

Just as in Egypt, the pseudepigraphic book 4 Ezra (late 1st century CE) assumes that stillness reigned in the cosmos before God began his work of creation,

---

[12] Translation Foster 1995, 61. See for further discussion De Moor 1997, 41-58; Altenmüller 2009, esp. 27-28.
[13] *Babylonian Theodicy*, 256, translation Lambert 1960, 87.
[14] *Babylonian Theodicy*, 289-290, 295-296, translation Lambert 1960, 89.
[15] Ludlul, I.43-46, translation Lambert 1960, 33.

> And then the Spirit was hovering, and darkness and silence embraced everything; the sound of man's voice was not yet there (4 Ezra 6:39).
>
> And the world shall be turned back to primeval silence for seven days, as it was at the first beginnings (4 Ezra 7:30).

Also in other pseudepigraphic literature the primordial silence is mentioned a few times. It is contrasted with the greatness of the Creator God,

> Or how shall we speak again about your glorious deeds? Or to whom again will that which is in your Law be explained? Or will the universe return to its nature and the world go back to its original silence? (2 Bar. 3:6-7)[16]

It is possible that a similar concept is at the background of Isa. 41:26 where the prophet emphasizes the absolute solitude of the Creator who was the first to speak,[17]

> Who told us from the beginning so that we might know,
>   and beforehand, so that we might say: 'He is right!'?
> No, there was no one who was telling,
>   no, there was no one who let hear,
>   no, there was no one who heard your words.

However, in Pseudo-Philo (1st century BCE) the Creator God himself is replaced by silence,

> Darkness and silence were before the world was made,
> and silence spoke a word and the darkness became light
>   (Ps. Philo 60:2).

The remoteness of God was felt painfully by several Psalmists (Ps. 22:2[1], 12[11], 20[19]; 38:22[21]; 71:12).[18] Also Second Isaiah states, 'However, you are a God hiding himself, O Savior God of Israel' (Isa. 45:15). Lady Zion complains, 'The LORD has forsaken me, and the LORD has forgotten me (Isa. 49:15).

---

[16] 2 Baruch probably dates from the early 2nd century CE.
[17] Cf. Isa. 41:20 and Korpel & De Moor 1997, 74, n. 17.
[18] More examples with Lindström 2003, 263-271.

The beauty of the cosmos fills the singer of Ps. 8 with wonder. How is it possible that the Creator of heaven and earth cares for mankind?

> When I look at your heavens, the work of your fingers,
>   the moon and the stars which you have created,
> what is man that you remember him,
>   and mankind that you take notice of him?
>
> Yet you made him lack only a little from being God,
>   you crowned him with glory and honor,
> you gave him power to rule over the works of your hands,
>   everything you have put beneath his feet.[19]

Certainly a text of timeless beauty which despite its gross anthropomorphism expresses on the one hand the immeasurable distance between God and man, on the other the proud awareness of the greatness of the human race as God's caretaker on earth.

However, other Hebrew poets were less optimistic. Job refuses to keep silent about the Creator's[20] constant watch over him,

> What is man that you make so much of him,
>   that you have set your heart on him,
> that you take notice of him every morning,
>   and test him every minute?
> Why don't you look away from me,
>   don't let me alone even for an instant? (Job 7:17-19)

The life of man being as short as it is,[21] Job feels that the Almighty should give him more leeway. A similar thought is expressed in Ps. 114:3-4,

> O LORD, what is man that you want to know him,
>   mankind that you want to think of him?
> Man resembles a breath,
>   his days pass by like a shadow.

---

[19] Ps. 8:5-7.
[20] Cf. Job 7:11-12.
[21] Cf. Job 7:21.

Also the poet of Ps. 90 complains about the inequality between the Creator, for whom a thousand years are like one day, and man whose lifespan is limited. Yet in all three cases these poets pray to this totally different Being to deliver them. This is the perseverance of the faithful.

Job too is convinced of his innocence and vents his disappointment over the stony silence meeting his legitimate protests,

> Behold, I cry out, 'Violence!' but I am not answered;
>   I call aloud, but there is no justice (Job 19:7)
>
> I cry to you, but you do not answer me;
>   I stand up, but you do not pay attention to me (Job 30:20).

Elihu[22] reprimands Job,

> Why do you quarrel with him
>   because he answers none of man's words?
> Though God does speak in one way,
>   or in another, but man does not perceive it.
> In a dream, in a vision of the night,
>   when deep sleep falls on men,
>   by shapes when they are in bed,
> then he may open the ears of men,
>   and seal them with chastisement
> to turn mankind from wrongdoing,
>   and to suppress pride in man (Job 33:13-17).

Even another of Job's interlocutors wishes that God would answer Job (Job 11:5), but Elihu states that God is completely free to remain silent – man cannot call him to account for that (Job 34:29). Walter Dietrich concludes,

> God is free up to arbitrariness. It is pointless to ask for his motives or to want to correct him. He can act as he wants, he can also *not* act when his acting would have been imperative, he can wrap himself in unapproachability when people (like Job) want to see him urgently.[23]

---

[22] Generally the Elihu speeches are thought to be a later addition to the Book of Job.

[23] Our translation. German original: Dietrich 2004, 1001.

It is questionable if it is acceptable to promote the fatalistic theology of the non-Israelite Elihu to a general principle of biblical theology. Dietrich acknowledges that Elihu's 'argument' will not have appeased Job and many other voices in the Hebrew Bible.[24] When God finally answers Job in the storm he does not defend his right to act as he wants, but emphasizes his own greatness as the Creator of all. He does *not* reply directly to Job's complaint that the Almighty has treated him unjustly and arbitrarily.[25]

The strangeness of the Book of Job within the canon of the Old Testament is due at least in part to the fact that Job does not see any possibility for man to appeal to God's covenantal loyalty. God has made a covenant with the monstrous Leviathan (Job 40:28, tr. 41:4), but not with Job. If God feels some kind of loyalty towards man, he is hiding it carefully (Job 10:12-13). When Job implores God to grasp his hand as a sign that he accepts him as a covenantal partner (Job 17:3),[26] God does not react. In none of the longer books of the Old Testament the number of terms connected with the covenant is as low as in the poetic part of the Book of Job.[27]

6.2 Broken Communication between God and Man

The experience of the absence or hiddenness of the deity is and was painful. A host of studies reflects awareness of exegetes that this is a very old problem indeed.[28] According to the Egyptian skeptic Ipuwer a hot-tempered man blurts out, 'If I could perceive, and know where God is, then I would act for him'.[29] Human beings speculated about the reasons why their deities seemed to have abandoned them and did not reply to their prayers. However, they did realize that there was a limit to a human's ability to fathom the mind of a deity. So there remained instances of

---

[24] *Ibidem.*

[25] Cf. Hieke 2009, 96-97. Contrast Dietrich 2004, 1000.

[26] Cf. Viberg 1992, 42-43.

[27] De Moor 1997, 146.

[28] See e.g. Perlitt 1971; Terrien 1978; Balentine 1983; Gerstenberger 1992; Milazzo 1992; Kutsko 2000; Burnett 2005; Groenewald 2005; Schellenberg 2009.

[29] Translation Enmarch 2008, 105, 226. Cf. Shupak, CoS, vol. 1, 95.

divine silence that could not be explained. Therefore we distinguish between reasons that were more or less comprehensible to man and divine silence that from the viewpoint of man was incomprehensible because no parallel with human silences could be discerned.

6.2.1   *Comprehensible Divine Silence*

6.2.1.1   Divine Silence Because of Offenses

6.2.1.1a   In the Ancient Near East

People realized very well that the silence of their deities might be caused by their own behavior. The Hittite prayers and rituals, for example, betray an acute awareness of sins that explained divine stillness.[30] Also elsewhere in the ancient world people were inclined to attribute illness or hunger or defeat not to caprices of the deities, but held themselves fully responsible (e.g. Van der Toorn 1985; Maul 1988). Within the horizon of their own world this may have been a logical conclusion.

Soon after coming into existence, the bustling creation became full of noise. In the first tablet of the Babylonian Creation Epic *enūma eliš* the divine pair Apsû (groundwater, male) and Tiâmat (seawater, female) create the other gods by mixing their waters. The noise made by their children is deafening Apsû. At first he is incapable of making the clamor stop. Also Tiâmat 'fell silent before them' (En. el. I.26).[31] Apsû wants silence so that they can sleep again (En. el. I.40). Following the counsel of his messenger Mummu, Apsû decides to annihilate his own offspring.

Gods do not appreciate noise from man. Also in the Babylonian epic *Atra-ḫasīs* it is the deafening noise made by mankind that disturbs the gods so much that they decide to destroy them by the Flood.[32] In this case too it is Ea who devises a plan to save humanity from total extinction.

---

[30] Cf. Section 6.2.2.1 below.

[31] The text we used is Talon 2005. See also Lambert, TUAT, Bd. 3, 565-593; Foster, CoS, vol. 1, 390-402.

[32] Lambert & Millard 1969, *passim*. Indeed the noise in the cities of Antiquity may have been a nuisance sometimes, cf. Weippert 2002a; Choi 2004; Saiko 2008.

The destruction of the world's population by the Babylonian evil god Erra is also justified by the noise human beings make.[33] Erra silences their noise by destroying entire cities.[34] Apparently the gods of Mesopotamia regarded clamor as sinful behavior which merited punishment even to the point of silencing the noise-makers.[35]

Silence on the part of the deity may also forebode divine punishment. When the Babylonian storm god Adad was on the brink of unleashing the Deluge that would destroy the whole earth a menacing calm preceded his fierce raging and when after seven days and seven nights the gale relented, stillness reigned on earth because all living creatures except those in the ark had died.[36]

6.2.1.1b Divine Silence Because of Offenses in the Bible

In the Bible the destruction by the Flood is attributed not to excessive noise but to the evilness of mankind (Gen. 6). Yet the idea that silence of God might be his answer to sinful behavior is also attested in the Bible. In Deut. 1 Moses recounts the history of the Exodus. In v. 45 he states,

> Then you [the Israelites] returned and wept before the LORD;
> but the LORD did not listen to your voice,
>   and did not give ear to you.

On the basis of the preceding account it may be assumed that the refrain-like reference to Israel's frequent rebellion[37] was omitted here to avoid repetitiousness (cf. Num. 14:45; Ps. 95:6-11). So the LORD's refusal to reply to their lamentation was based on their refusal to listen to him – a clear case of a reciprocal refusal to listen.

According to 1 Sam. 8:18, Mic. 3:4-7, and Job 35:12 God may also refuse to answer to prayers because of sinful behavior. The circumstance that the people wanted a king despite the fact that

---

[33] Cagni 1977, 29-30, nn. 12, 20, 21. See also Dalley, CoS, vol. 1, No. 113.
[34] Cagni 1977, 54, IV.68.
[35] See also Section 4.5.3.
[36] Gilg. Ep. XI.106, 130-135, George 2003, vol. 1, 708-711.
[37] Deut. 1:26-27, 32, 43.

God was their real king was interpreted as sin long after the end of the Davidic dynasty. Therefore Samuel is made to say that a king will oppress them so that 'you will cry out because of your king, whom you have chosen for yourselves; but the LORD will not answer you in that day.' (1 Sam. 8:18). Apparently God's silence is the consequence of sins.

Mic. 3:4 and 7 belong to the message of Proto-Micah. Here too the silence of God when people cry to him for help is seen as the sanction imposed because of social injustice.[38] The circumstance that this scheme is already present in this 8th century prophetic tradition indicates that one cannot easily dismiss it as a late theological construct.

In Job 35:9-14 Elihu reprimands Job, suggesting that God does not answer because he is a sinner,

> [9]Because of the multitude of oppressions people cry out;
> they call for help because of the arm of the mighty.
> [10]But none says, 'Where is God my Maker,
> who gives songs in the night,
> [11]who teaches us more than the beasts of the earth,
> and makes us wiser than the birds of the air?'
> [12]There they cry out, but he does not answer,
> because of the pride of the wicked.
> [13]Surely God does not listen to an empty cry,
> nor does the Almighty see it.
> [14] How much less when you say that you do not see him,
> that the case is before him, and you are waiting for him!

Verse 11 clearly refers to oracles derived from the consultation of Nether World spirits and the observation of the flight of birds.[39] Like the soothsayers of Mic. 3 they are unable to fathom God's answer.

Finally a similar argument is found in Isa. 42. The Israelites had deserved punishment because they had not listened to God, i.e. to his messengers, the prophets (Isa. 42:18-21). As one of the consequences he mentions that nobody, i.e. neither God[40] nor

---

[38] Cf. Section 5.2.2.
[39] Cf. Section 5.3.3.2.
[40] Blenkinsopp 2002, 217

man, saw ground for protest against the subsequent plundering of the nation.[41]

Also those who opposed David, God's chosen king, could not count on an answer from God when they appealed to him (2 Sam. 22:42 = Ps. 18:42[41]). The Deuteronomistic History stresses the point that sinners invoke the help of God in vain several times. An example is found in 2 Kgs 6 where an unnamed king[42] of Northern Israel[43] is exclaiming during the siege of Samaria,

> This trouble is from the LORD!
> Why should I wait for the LORD any longer? (2 Kgs 6:33)

The narrative as it is preserved in the canonical Hebrew version does not indicate that the king had prayed or had asked Elisha for a word from the LORD, but it may be assumed that he did, as was the custom in such a situation. Apparently the king looses his patience and does not ask himself if his own sinful behavior might have been the cause of God's silence. His blasphemous question causes an apprehensive silence to fall which is marked by a space (Setumah).

It was usual to accompany fasting with loud weeping.[44] But insincere fasting implied no genuine wish to be heard on high (Isa. 58:4). God will only reply to the cries of those who show true remorse by caring for others (Isa. 58:5-12; Prov. 21:13).

When God has shown the prophet Ezekiel all the illegal forms of worship practiced in the temple he concludes,

> But now I – I will act in wrath;
>   my eye will not spare, nor will I have pity;
> and if they cry in my ears with a loud voice,
>   I will not listen to them (Ezek. 8:18).

The few times that God is the subject of the Hebrew verb *šqṭ* 'to

---

[41] Isa. 42:22. Some further examples: Isa. 1:15; 59:1-3.

[42] The Hebrew text, supported by ancient versions, has 'messenger' (or: 'angel'), but the emendation to 'king' is universally accepted. Cf. Barthélemy 1982, 388-389.

[43] Probably Joram, cf. e.g. Sweeney 2007, 312; Korpel 2009.

[44] Judg. 20:26; 2 Sam. 1:12; 12:21-22; Neh. 1:4.

be silent' it denotes total passivity on his part.[45] In Isa. 62:1 the prophet declares that he will no longer resign to such a passive attitude. Persisting in wordless mourning is a form of self-pity that is unseemly if higher issues are at stake. In vv. 6-7 the prophet continues his argument,

> [6]On your walls, O Jerusalem, I have posted watchmen;
>   every day and every night – never they will be silent.
> Oh, you who call on the LORD,
>   do not allow yourselves silence,
> [7]and do not allow him silence
> till he founds and till he makes Jerusalem
>   a hymn in the country (Isa. 62:6-7).

Is this unrealistic? At this moment of Jerusalem's history the walls of the city did not exist anymore. This is pure faith-talk. The prophet is talking about the city he dreams up. The watchmen he appoints are the prophets[46] who share his dream. It is important to observe that people need not meekly resign to their fate, but may rebel against the silence of God and refuse to give up their dreams: 'do not allow yourselves silence, and do not allow him silence'. After the latter, rather daring statement the tradition places a major colon divider (Atnach) indicating a short, tense silence.

The penitent supplicants of Isa. 64 describe the malaise in their country after the Babylonian occupation, culminating in the destruction of the temple in Jerusalem where their fathers used to pray. They then cry out,

> Will you, O LORD, after all this, will you keep yourself
>   inaccessible?
> Will you keep silent and punish us beyond measure?
>   (Isa. 64:11[12])

They acknowledge their sins and admit that punishment was deserved (Isa. 64:4[5], 6[7]) but are of the opinion that they have

---

[45]Isa. 18:4; Ezek. 16:42; Ps. 83:2[1]. Some scholars assume that the latter text is dependent on Isa. 62, cf. Tate 1990, 345. But in Isa. 62:1 the speaker is the prophet, not God. Cf. Section 4.5.1.2.

[46]Jer. 6:17; Ezek. 3:17; 33:2, 6-7. Cf. Isa. 21:6, 8; 52:8; 56:10; Ezek. 33:7; Hos. 9:8; Mic. 7:4, 7; Hab. 2:1.

suffered enough now and that God should not remain angry beyond measure (Isa. 64:8[9], 11[12]). God's silence was the understandable consequence of their sinful behavior in the past, but it should end now.

After a silence indicated by a space (Setumah) God defends himself by pointing out that sinful practices still continue and that he will not keep silent[47] about these offenses until they have been repaid in full (Isa. 65:6).

The singer of Ps. 66 acknowledges that sinful behavior and the expectation that God will hear his prayer do not go together,

> Come, hear and let me tell you,
>   all you who fear God,
>   what he did to me personally.
> To him I cried with my mouth,
>   his praise was under my tongue.
> Iniquity – if my heart would have cherished that,
>   the Lord would not have listened.
> However, God did listen
>   and paid attention to my loud prayer.[48] (Ps. 66:16-19)

The singer does not indicate how he received the certainty that his prayer had been heard, but he awaited it – the hymn of praise was on the tip of his tongue.

Earlier[49] we discussed Job 4:12–5:1 where Eliphaz hears a ghost say,

> Call now! Is there anyone who will answer you?
>   To which of the holy ones will you turn?

The clear implication was that Job, being a sinner because he refused to accept undeserved suffering, had no right to expect an answer from God, not even by intermediaries like angels.

If God was displeased with the behavior of his people, prophecy and other means to learn the will of God became scarce, or even totally absent.[50]

---

[47]This reading is suggested by many Hebrew manuscripts as well as most ancient versions.

[48]See for similar reasoning Job 35:13-16.

[49]Section 5.2.1.2

[50]1 Sam. 3:1; 28:6; Ezek. 7:26; Amos 8:12; Mic. 3:6-7; Ps. 74:9; Lam. 2:9.

Even if Israel was lamenting about God's incomprehensible refusal to speak through signs and prophets when his people was in distress and even if he allowed its enemies to put up their own signs in the place where his congregation used to gather (Ps. 74:4, 9), there is a conviction that this must be a temporal decision. The very late Psalm 74 does not question the fact that God's anger may have been deserved, but it should not go on for ever (Ps. 74:1).

God's silence in the Hebrew version of the book of Esther may have to do with the fact that Mordecai and Esther act on their own initiative and seem to have partially lost faith in God.[51] Similarly, God is missing in the grisly chapters Jer. 40:7–41:18 where nationalists brutally murder Gedaliah and many of his supporters, acting on their own, without consulting God through the prophet Jeremiah who was available with Gedaliah in Mizpah.[52] The absence of God in the rape scenes of the Hebrew Bible[53] is another indication that at least some narrators shrank back from relating God to brutal violence.

The eschatological silence in heaven mentioned in Rev. 8:1 precedes the execution of the divine wrath.[54]

Already in Qumran the 'voice of a thin silence' of 1 Kgs 19:12 is applied to the heavenly beings before the throne of God.[55] In view of the impressive evidence collected by Richard Bauckham and Philip Alexander it is likely that according to Jewish tradition the angels interrupted their songs of praise during this silence to act as mediators bringing the prayers of those who had suffered on earth before God.[56]

---

[51] Korpel 2003; 2008. Attempts to explain the absence of God in the Hebrew Book of Esther positively as silent working in the background (e.g. Chalupa 2003) are mistaken.

[52] Jer. 40:6; cf. Stulman 2004, 311-318. The relationship with the much less detailed account in 2 Kgs 25:22-26 is a matter of discussion, cf. Becking 2007, 147-173.

[53] Dietrich 2004, 1006-1009; Schulte & Schneider 2009.

[54] We checked several manuscripts but none marks this silence with an open space, but just after the beginning of a chapter this was not to be expected.

[55] 4Q405, Frags. 20, 21, 22; 11Q17:VII.

[56] Rev. 8:3-4. Cf. Bauckham 1993, 70-83. See also Muers 2001, 90.

6.2.1.2   Divine Silence Because of Awe or Fear

6.2.1.2a   In the Ancient Near East

When the Sumerian creator god Enki and the birth-goddess Ninmaḫ have fashioned the first human being, 'a great silence fell' among the gods.[57] It is unclear whether the deities were stunned with admiration or with horror.[58] Similarly, all the gods bow down in stunned silence before the mighty creator god Marduk.[59]

But also the reversal of creation is met with stupefied silence. When in the Babylonian Epic of Creation (c. end 12th century BCE)[60] Apsû's[61] decision to annihilate his own offspring is communicated to the gods they are deeply disturbed and sit down in silence (En. el. I.58). The god of wisdom Ea, however, succeeds in baffling Apsû's plan and kills him. Subsequently Ea engenders Marduk to lead the battle against Tiâmat[62] under the pretext that she remained silent when her husband Apsû was killed (En. el. I.114). Tiâmat musters all her forces to battle Marduk and his allies. When Ea hears this, he falls silent at first (En. el. II.6), but then devises a plan. When this too fails, all the gods sit mutely together (En. el. II.122-126). But Ea counsels Marduk to go to Anšar, the father of the gods, to urge him to break his silence and allow him, Marduk, to go to defeat Tiâmat (En. el. II.139-142; III.1). Marduk conquers her and creates heaven and earth from her body. Later on Marduk is praised because he broke the stunned silence that had paralyzed the other gods (En.el. VII.42). In the Assyrian cultic calendar the 18th and 19th of the month of Shebat are called 'Silence' because Marduk was supposed to have killed his opponents on those dates.[63]

In accordance with this praise the Assyrian king Assurbanipal (668-627 BCE) honors Marduk in a hymn,

> He summoned the Igigi and the Anunnaki, they kneel before him, and the gods who begot him repose in silence at [his] f[eet]. To

---

[57]Klein, CoS, vol. 1, 518.
[58]Later on we will defend the latter option, cf. Section 6.2.1.4a.
[59]See also Hecker, TUAT, Bd. 2, 766.
[60]We use the edition by Talon 2005.
[61]Apsû is the god of the sweet ground water.
[62]Monstrous goddess of the salty waters.
[63]Livingstone 1989, No. 40, 3, 5.

take advice, to consult in lordly consultation, [their] at[tention] is directed towards Marduk alone.[64]

Even the deities of the Nether World fall silent when a human being risks his life by entering their realm.[65]

In a visionary experience an Assyrian crown prince is approaching the throne of the god Namtar, co-ruler of the Nether World. Because no man can go unpunished if he comes close to this redoubtable god all inhabitants of the Nether World fall silent, 'The nether world was full of terror; a mighty silence lay before the crown prince'.[66]

A deceased Egyptian may gain control over the dangerous deities of the Nether World by identifying himself with Heka, the eldest son of the creator. In this capacity he commands them, 'Be silent for me; Bow down to me!'[67]

In the Babylonian Epic of the evil god Erra (c. 8th century BCE) it is his herald Ishum who first sits in silent horror because of the magnitude of the slaughtering envisaged by Erra and his warriors (I.95), but towards the end of the story he succeeds in convincing Erra to stop the massacre. According to another text the gods of the Nether World fall silent at the terrifying cry of the warrior-god Nergal.[68]

According to Iliad I.511-512 Zeus, king of the gods, sits in silence, not knowing what to answer to the prayer of Thetis, because he fears the wrath of his wife Hera (Iliad I.518-519), just as she herself keeps silent when Zeus threatens her (Iliad I.568-569).

6.2.1.2b Divine Silence Because of Awe or Fear in the Bible

As we have just seen, silence out of fear or awe was not unknown among the deities of the ancient cultures surrounding Israel. It is no doubt significant that such feelings are rarely, if ever, attributed to God in the canonical books of the Bible.[69] Whereas other

---

[64] Translation Livingstone 1989, No. 2:26-27.
[65] Livingstone 1989, No. 32, r. 13.
[66] Livingstone 1989, No. 32, r. 13.
[67] Ritner, CoS, vol. 2, 58.
[68] CAD (Š) 3, 332.
[69] Korpel 1990, 178; Sanders 1996, 403-405.

negative emotions (e.g. wrath, sorrow, jealousy) are freely attributed to God in the Hebrew Bible, fear is not, probably because it would imply an infringement of the monotheistic principle. God's description of the Leviathan in Job 40:25–41:26[41:1-34] definitely betrays a certain awe for this redoubtable sea-monster which according to Canaanite myth the deities Baʻlu and ʻAnatu had only barely been able to defeat[70] so that Job 41:17[25] aptly states that 'deities' are afraid of him. But far from falling silent for this 'creature without fear' (Job 41:25[33]) the God of the Book of Job does not want to keep silent about its fearsome qualities (Job 41:4[12]).

6.2.1.3 Divine Silence Because of Forbearance or Prudence
6.2.1.3a In the Ancient Near East

According to the Babylonian myth *Adapa and the South Wind* the human being Adapa has broken the wing of the South Wind which enrages the highest god Anu. Adapa is summoned to ascend to heaven to give account for his crime. Adapa's explanation satisfies the god because he realizes that in fact another god, Ea, was responsible: 'His heart calmed, he became silent' (Izre'el 2001, 19, 62, 97).

In polytheism, one god may try to silence the other in order to draw his attention, e.g. 'Be silent, and listen to my speech',[71] as quarreling human disputants do (Section 3.2.3.2).

Earlier we have given some examples of silences on the part of deities that were marked not by words, but by blank spaces or horizontal dividing lines with a rhetorical function. In the Babylonian Gilgamesh Epic Gilgamesh responds rudely to the proposal of marriage by the goddess of love Ishtar (Gilg. Ep. VI.22-79). Two tablets mark the end of his speech by a horizontal line before the narrator starts to describe the goddess Ishtar's rage (George 2003, 622 and Plates 79 and 90). The reader expects immediate divine retaliation, but the goddess has to remain silent because she first has to obtain her father's permission to punish her reviler. Apparently the horizontal line marks a tense silence here.

---

[70]Cf. De Moor 1987, 69-70 (KTU 1.5:I.1-8).
[71]Dalley, CoS, vol. 1, 406, 415.

6.2.1.3b Divine Silence Because of Forbearance or Prudence in the Bible

There are several occasions when God might have spoken but has kept silent out of forbearance (2 Sam. 7:7; Jer. 7:22). Isa. 42:13-14 describes how God breaks a long silence,

> The LORD goes out like a hero,
>   like a warrior he wakes up fury,
> he shouts, even yells,
>   he shows himself a hero to his enemies.
> I have been quiet for a long time.
>   Shall I remain silent, restrain myself?[72]
> Like a woman in labor I will groan!
>   I will gasp and pant together!

The contrast between Isa. 42:13 where the LORD is depicted as a shouting warrior and Isa. 42:14 where he is compared to a pregnant woman who has been silent for a long time, but now has to cry out because of the pangs of childbirth, has given rise to various hypotheses about the redactional history of these verses (cf. Berges 2008, 253). However, there is little reason to neglect the careful composition of the final literary product (Korpel & De Moor 1998, 157-158). The contrast between vv. 13 and 14 may have been created deliberately. Had God manifested himself as a valiant warrior? No, he admits in v. 14, he was keeping a grip on himself for a long time until he could no longer remain silent anymore, like a woman in labor who cannot suppress her shrieks when her time has come. A space (Setumah) expresses God's long silence graphically. The reason for his silence is revealed in vv. 18-19 and 23-25: the Israelites failed to listen to the word of God as mediated by his servants.

A psalm closely related to the ideas of Second Isaiah is Psalm 50.[73] Also the theme of God's breaking the silence after a long

---

[72] An unintroduced rhetorical question, cf. Joüon & Muraoka 2006, § 161a.

[73] Although recently parallels with Neo-Assyrian cultic prophecy have been used as an argument in favor of a pre-exilic date of this Psalm (Hilber 2005, 162-166), the allusions to passages in the Pentateuch (vv. 5 , 16-20) and the close relations with the message of Second Isaiah make an exilic or post-exilic

period during which He restrained himself (Ps. 50:3, 21) was derived from the same source (Isa. 42:14; 48:9). The reason for God's silence were the sins of his people that are described in great detail in vv. 16-22 and this silence is contrasted with his decision to speak up now in favor of those who obey him and serve him with immaterial sacrifices (vv. 1, 4, 7-23).[74]

One might consider Isa. 42:14 and Ps. 50:3, 21 therefore as cases of silence because of offenses (cf. Section 6.2.1.1b). However, Isa. 57:11 emboldens us to interpret these instances as silences because of forbearance. God denounces the apostate sinners of pre-exilic Israel here,

> Who was it you dreaded, and feared, that you should lie,
>   whereas you did not recall me
>   and did not give (me) a thought?
> Was I not silent, for a long time even?
>   So you cannot have feared me.

This idea of divine forbearance is attested in several other passages, e.g. Neh. 9:30-31,

> You bore with them for many years, testified against them by your Spirit through your prophets, but they would not give ear, so you delivered them into the power of the peoples of countries. But, in your great compassion you did not destroy them completely and did not abandon them, for you are a gracious and compassionate God.[75]

---

date more likely. Later redactional reworking of the Psalm is not excluded (cf. Seybold 1996, 203-209). The theophany described in v. 3 has parallels in Isa. 40:10 and 42:13-15. The low esteem for bloody sacrifices in vv. 8-13 may be compared with Isa. 40:16 and 43:23-24. In Second Isaiah's new Zion there is no mention of sacrifices anymore, but only of singing hymns of thanksgiving (cf. Ps. 50:14). Also the universalism ('from the rising of the sun to its setting', Ps. 50:1, cf. Isa. 45:6) and the idea of a case pleaded in the divine court (Ps. 50:4-6) are typical of Second Isaiah (Isa. 41:1, 21-29; 43:9-21, etc.). Even the heavens testify to God's righteousness (Ps. 50:6), as in Isa. 45:8. Also the emphasis on the incomparability of God in v. 21 is characteristic of Second Isaiah (Isa. 40:18, 25; 43:10-11; 44:7-8; 45:21-22; 46:5, 9, etc.).

[74]Dietrich 2004, 998 creates an inaccurate contrast between the silent gods of Israel's neighbors and the LORD who would *not* be silent. Note the similarity with the ideas of Kornelis Miskotte, Section 1.3.2.2.

[75]See also Zech. 7:12; 2 Chron. 24:19-20.

Possibly also Zeph. 3:17 refers to the divine patience with sinful Israel if the text states indeed that God will be silent in his love, as Rashi has proposed (cf. Vlaardingerbroek 1999, 214). Although other interpretations and readings have been considered, the Masoretic text, already attested in Antiquity, is the best option (Barthélemy 1992, 913-915).

Sometimes God's restrained silence is not indicated by words, but by spaces marking rhetorical silences, for example after Moses' bitter complaints in Exod. 33:12-16, Num. 11:15 and 11:22. And after Joshua's complaint in Josh. 7:9. And after Elijah's complaints in 1 Kgs 19. The first time Elijah laments in this way God answers him not in the form of impressive natural phenomena like storm, earthquake or fire, but in the form of a 'sound of thin silence' (v. 12).[76] When Elijah stubbornly repeats his complaint[77] there falls an even deeper silence, again marked by a blank space (Setumah). In all these cases a rhetorical silence falls before the LORD answers. One expects a rebuke, a thunderclap even. But a prolonged anxious silence falls, as if the LORD has some difficulty to restrain himself.

6.2.1.4   Divine Silence Because of Incapacity

6.2.1.4a   In the Ancient Near East

Closely related to the preceding motif is inability of deities to deal with a menacing situation. According to the Old Babylonian version of the Myth of Anzû, the gods were dumbstruck when this terrible bird stole the supreme power of the pantheon – 'Silence reigned' (Anzû OBV II.2-3).[78] One after the other the deities

---

[76] See for an admirable overview of the interpretation of this 'thin silence' Thiel 2009, 268-272. We agree with Thiel, 268, that the proposal of Lust 1976 encounters insurmountable difficulties. Lust's appeal to Ugaritic rests on antiquated insights.

[77] Dietrich 2004, 1009 reads too much dialectic theology in this text: God would be a God of silence as well as a God of dialogue.

We see also insufficient support for Becking's idea that vv. 11-14 should be read as a *'nachholende Erzählung'* (Becking 2007, 23-34). The participles of v. 11 can hardly be interpreted as pluperfects.

[78] We follow the rendering of Dalley 1991, 222. See also Foster 2005, 556-558 and 564-566 for the later version, and Vogelzang, CoS, vol. 3, 328-329, 332. Exactly the same phrase describes the silence after the Deluge, cf. Section

called upon to destroy the bird back away, so that the divine assembly sits down in silent despair (Anzû OBV II.23).[79]

Fear or confusion is not the only reason why deities may remain silent. When the Sumerian fertility god Dumuzi has made love fifty times to his beloved Inanna and is exhaustedly waiting for her, 'she trembled underneath him, dumbly silent for him'.[80] Despite human fantasies about the potency of deities, there was apparently also an end to divine lust.

In the Sumerian myth of Enki and Ninmaḫ the deities are complaining about the toil Enki, the Sumerian god of wisdom, who was their creator, had imposed upon them on the primordial earth. Initially Enki refuses to arise from his sleep, until his mother convinces him to do something about it. The mother-goddess Ninmaḫ is appointed as Enki's helper. She boasts that she can create human beings good or bad. However, her first six attempts to make men from clay are all crippled failures. After the sixth attempt,

> Ninmah threw the pinch of clay in her hand on the ground, and a great silence fell.[81]

Apparently the gods are silent because the workers who would free them from their toil did not materialize. It is up to Enki himself to fashion the first sound human being, as the seventh in succession.

According to a late Assyrian text the gods lie down in silent exhaustion from toiling on earth before the creation of mankind that was destined to take over their labor.[82]

A Late Egyptian text relates how the gods laid their arms on their heads and became silent when they saw the cruelties of the evil god Seth (Dominicus 1994, 70).

In literary texts from the Canaanite city of Ugarit there are several passages where the gods sit silently together, apparently at a loss how to deal with a terrifying situation. When king Kirtu

---

3.2.4.1.
[79] Dalley 1991, 223.
[80] ETCSL translation, A balbale to Inana (Dumuzid-Inana D), c.4.08.04.
[81] Translation Klein, CoS, vol. 1, 518.
[82] Livingstone, CoS, vol. 1, 476-477.

lies dying, the head of the pantheon Ilu asks the assembly of the gods seven times, "Who among the gods is able to cast out the disease, to expel the illness?" and seven times the narrator has to observe, 'None of the gods answered him.' Finally Ilu sighs,

> Return, my children, to your dwellings,
>   to your exalted thrones.
> I myself shall perform magic and shall create,
>   I shall create a female being able to cast out the disease,
>   to expel the illness![83]

According to a passage in the Ugaritic Myth of Baʿlu the gods lower their heads on to their knees when they notice the arrival of frightening messengers of the Sea-god who have come to demand the extradition of Baʿlu. Apparently they feel unable to speak. Baʿlu offers to answer the messengers himself, but the head of the pantheon Ilu simply ignores him.[84]

Just like human beings, the deities of Ugarit were thought to mourn occasionally in silence. When Baʿlu has disappeared in the realm of death for seven or eight years,

> Surely [his] brothers were clothed in mourning dress,
>   in a mourning coat his kinsmen.[85]

The word translated as 'mourning' denotes *silent* mourning, instead of the loud wailing that was customary shortly after a death. Indeed, seven years of loud wailing might be too much even for the gods.

As in modern usage, 'to silence' was the equivalent of 'killing' someone.[86] In Ugaritic mythology, for example, major deities 'silence' their opponents.[87] To some extent even human beings were thought to be able to silence (lower) deities by magic. An exorcist calls upon a goddess of the Nether World to ignore the invocations of witches,

---

[83] KTU 1.15:V.10-28, translation De Moor 1987, 219.
[84] KTU 1.2:I.3-38, De Moor 1987, 32-33.
[85] KTU 1.12:II.46-47, translation De Moor 1987, 133, with comments.
[86] Cf. Section 3.2.5.2.
[87] Cf. De Moor 1971, 89. Contrast Del Olmo Lete & Sanmartín 2003, 786-787.

> If they call upon you, do not answer them,
>   if they speak to you, do not listen to them!
> If I call upon you, answer me,
>   if I speak to you, speak to me, me (alone)![88]

In 2 Kgs 18:34 (cf. Isa. 36:19) an Assyrian general poses the rhetorical question, 'Where are the gods of Hamath and Arpad? Where are the gods of Sepharvaim, Hena, and Ivvah?' clearly implying that they were nowhere to be found when their worshippers cried to them for help and asserting that Hezekiah too will call to his God in vain.

6.2.1.4b   Divine Silence Because of Incapacity in the Bible

Israel itself taunted the gods of other nations because of their incapacity to answer the prayers of their worshippers. When Elijah challenged the prophets of Baal to pray to their god to kindle the wood of the sacrifice on Mount Carmel the narrator observes sarcastically 'there was no voice; no one answered' (1 Kgs 18:26, 29).[89] It is appropriate to continue with 2 Kgs 19 here. There Hezekiah puts on sackcloth – a sign of mourning – and goes to the temple, apparently to pray in silence.[90] He sends his officers to the prophet Isaiah from whom he awaits God's reply (2 Kgs 19:1-5) and this reply comes immediately: a prophecy of salvation of the kind also attested in the world around ancient Israel,[91]

> Isaiah said to them,
>   'Thus you shall say to your master,
> "Thus says the LORD:
> Do not be afraid because of the words that you have heard,
>   with which the servants of the king of Assyria have reviled me.
> Behold, I will put a spirit in him,
>   so that he shall hear a rumor and return to his own land;
>   and I will cause him to fall by the sword in his own land." '
>   (2 Kgs 19:6-7)

---

[88] Maqlû I.56-59, cf. Meier 1937, 9; Abusch, in: Krüger 2008, 137.

[89] For a fine analysis of 1 Kgs 18–19 with regard to the silence motif see Spronk 2010. Similarly, Moab's prayers remain unheard (Isa. 16:12).

[90] Compare the silent supplication of Dani'ilu in the Ugaritic legend, see Section 4.5.3.1 above.

[91] See, for example, the promise of deliverance when a strong enemy attacks the city of Ugarit (KTU 1.119), Section 5.2.2 above.

And so it happens according to the biblical account.[92] According to Sennacherib's own annals he would have lifted the siege of Jerusalem voluntarily and would have been content to accept a large tribute only afterwards, when he had returned to Assyria. It is unlikely that the mighty Assyrian king would have permitted a rebellious vassal to escape so easily. Something, perhaps an urgent message from Assyria, must have compelled him to end the siege prematurely.[93] However that may be, the story reads as an explicit denial that the God of Israel would have remained silent because He, like the gods of other nations, would have been incapable of reacting adequately.

In post-exilic times Israel loved to mock at the dumbness of idols out of apprehension that the exiles might pray to images representing foreign deities. Deut. 4:28 is part of a passage that reflects the exile,[94]

> And the LORD will scatter you among the peoples, and you will be left few in number among the nations where the LORD will drive you. And there you will serve gods of wood and stone, the work of men's hands, that neither see, nor hear, nor eat, nor smell.

If somebody cries out for help to them, they are unable to answer and save (Isa. 46:7). They are more dumb than their makers.[95] It is difficult to say if Second Isaiah himself was the first to use this argument. Most scholars are inclined to attribute the passage 46:1-7 and other diatribes against the cult images of other nations in Second Isaiah to a later redactor, but this is by no means certain.[96] In Jer. 10 the theme is further elaborated. The speaking of the LORD in v. 1, with a voice like thunder (v. 13), is contrasted with the inability of the idols to speak (v. 5), because they have no breath/spirit (v. 14). According to the Book of Habakkuk stone and wood may speak to expose injustice (Hab. 2:11), but graven

---

[92] Which may have been expanded and embellished later on, 2 Kgs 19:8-37 (Isa. 37:8-37).
[93] Cf. Becking 2007, 141.
[94] Cf. Weinfeld 1991, 207, 209.
[95] Isa. 44:11, with Korpel & De Moor 1998, 207, note 11.
[96] Spykerboer 1976; Holter 1995; Blenkinsopp 2002, 263-270.

images of wood and stone are dumb – whoever thinks to hear them say something is deluding himself with lies (Hab. 2:18-19). Manmade idols do have a mouth, but they are unable to speak, no sound comes from their throat (Isa. 41:28; Jer. 10:5; Ps. 115:5, 7; 135:15-17).

In view of this fierce polemic against the representation of deities by other nations it is understandable that there remained little room for the concept of divine silence because of incapacity in the Hebrew Bible. Yet the circumstance that God sometimes seems to suffer when he must keep silent (cf. Section 7.8) indicates that the motif is not entirely absent in the Hebrew tradition.

6.2.1.5 Divine Silence Because of Sleep
6.2.1.5a In the Ancient Near East

In the Sumerian composition *Lugalbanda in the Wilderness*, probably dating from the third millennium BCE, it is seen as quite normal that the sun god Utu goes to bed just like mankind,

> Utu, shepherd of the land, father of the black-headed,[97] when you go to sleep, the people go to sleep with you; youth Utu, when you rise, the people rise with you.[98]

Apparently gods needed sleep just like human beings.[99] As we have seen earlier, the Ancients sometimes drew explicit parallels between human and divine sleep.[100] In the Sumerian myth of Enki and Ninmah it is the wise creator god Enki who is unwilling to rise from his bed when all other deities rebel against him because he has obliged them to toil for their own sustenance. Only when his mother Nammu suggests that he create mankind to take over their toil he does rise reluctantly from his sleep.[101] A similar reluctance to abandon sleep is attested in a later Babylonian epic about the redoubtable god Erra (Erra I.15-20).

---

[97] Inhabitants of Sumer.
[98] Translation Black *et al.* 2004, 17.
[99] With regard to Mesopotamia, see Guinan 2009, 196, 201.
[100] Sections 3.2.5.1 and 4.5.5.
[101] Cf. Klein, CoS, vol. 1, 516-517. See also Batto 1987; Mrozek & Votto 1999.

According to several Mesopotamian myths the gods could not sleep because of the noise other creatures made.[102] The goddess Ishtar could not sleep because of the destruction of her city.[103]

In early Greek mythology remarkably similar ideas are found. It is often told that also the Greek deities were sleeping just like human beings (e.g. Iliad XXIV.677-678).

In a metaphorical sense the sleep of death silences even divine visitors of the Nether World. Stillness is a characteristic of the world of the dead.[104] Even the goddess Inanna has to obey to the law of silence of the Nether World. After having shouted aggressively at the entrance of the realm of the dead, she is admonished, 'Be silent, Inanna, a divine power of the Nether World has been fulfilled. Inanna, you must not open your mouth against the rules of the Nether World.'[105] Also according to the Egyptians silence reigned in the Nether World, the realm of Osiris, 'the Lord of Silence'.[106] The *Book of the Dead* 125, 175 calls the Nether World 'the Land of Silence'.[107] When the Canaanite god Baʻlu is instructed to descend into the Nether World he is forewarned 'and you will experience dumbness/weakness as in the state of death'.[108]

Also the gods of Canaan needed their sleep.[109] According to a Canaanite myth preserved in an Egyptian version the goddess

---

[102] Cf. Section 6.2.1.1a.

[103] CAD (Ṣ) 67b.

[104] Cf. Gilg. Ep. VII.192 (Gilgamesh, Enkidu and the Nether World, A.184; George 2003, vol. 1, 644-5); KAR 1:8 (Borger 1979, 96, Ass. Vs. 8).

[105] Cf. Seux 1976, 243; Römer, TUAT, Bd. 3, 470-471.

[106] Brunner-Traut 1979, 198-199; Frandsen 1998; Shupak, 1993, 159; Shupak, CoS, vol. 1, 100.

[107] Ritner, CoS, vol. 1, 28; vol. 2, 62. See also the Great Cairo Hymn of Praise to Amun-Re, Ritner, CoS, vol. 1, 39. And in a Harper Song, cf. Foster 1995, 160; Assmann, TUAT, Bd. 2, 907; Ritner, CoS, vol. 2, 65. Also the dead who are identified with Osiris are sometimes called 'Lords of Silence', Shupak, CoS, vol. 1, 105.

[108] KTU 1.5:V.16-17. The translation 'dumbness' rests on the reading *ʼilm* which cannot be rendered 'the gods' here because *mtt* can hardly be the 2 sg. masc. perfect of *mwt* which would require *mt* = *mattā. However, the tablet is damaged at this point and the reading *ʼill* 'weakness' is equally possible.

[109] Cf. Korpel 1990, 208-211.

ʿAthtartu once was said to be asleep.[110] During a banquet the old creator god Ilu falls asleep as a result of excessive drinking. Although it is not expressly stated that he is sleeping, the circumstance that he is said to awake would seem to imply that he was either unconscious or asleep (KTU 1.114:28). Elijah mocks the prophets of Baal because their god might not answer them because he is asleep (1 Kgs 18:27).

That the Ugaritic deities could dream may be seen as a further indication that they were supposed to sleep at certain times. The god Ilu gets a dream in which he sees the heavens raining oil and the wadis running with honey (KTU 1.6:III.10f.) Another indication that the gods needed their rest is the circumstance that they possessed beds. The goddess Pidrayu was provided with a bed made with the sheets of the king (KTU 1.132:25-26).

From the viewpoint of human beings the sleep of deities was menacing. Without mentioning him directly, the Egyptian pessimist Ipuwer assumes that the creator god might be asleep instead of faithfully herding his people,

> One says: 'He is the shepherd of everyone.
> There is no evil in his heart'.
> (But) his herd is lacking, even though he has spent the day caring for them ...
> There is no pilot on duty.
> Where is he today?
> Is he perhaps asleep? Look, the wrath thereof cannot be seen!
> When we have been saddened, I could not find you;
> No one can call on you ...[111]

The full impact of this criticism becomes clear if we know that Amun-Re was praised as the good Shepherd who is constantly

---

[110] Ritner, CoS, vol. 1, 35.

[111] Ipuwer 12.1-5, translation Enmarch 2008, 235. The sole surviving manuscript of *The Admonitions of Ipuwer* dates from the 12th century BCE, but it is generally supposed that the original composition goes back to the Second Intermediate Period (c. 1850-1600), a time of upheaval and decline in ancient Egypt.

It does not make a big difference if the creator god is some manifestation of (Amun)-Re or the king in his role as the creator's mediator on earth. Cf. Enmarch 2008, 30-31.

looking after the herd of the living, the untiring watcher who never sleeps.[112]

However, the sleep of deities might be deceptive. Gods could pretend to be asleep, just like human beings (Guinan 2009, 200-201). Of the Babylonian god Nergal it is said, 'he is awake even when he seems asleep',[113] and the Egyptian supreme god Amun-Re is said to sleep never,

> Sole-one awake – for you detest slumber –
> everyone sleeps, yet your eyes are alert...[114]

However, yet another hymn to the same god states, 'Day itself passes and you go to rest'.[115] In Pyramid Text 573 the king prays,

> Awake in peace, O Rê, pure one, in peace.
> Awake in peace, O Eastern Horus, in peace.
> Awake in peace, O Soul of the East, in peace.
> Awake in peace, O Horus of the Horizon, in peace.
> Sleep in the Night Bark,
> wake in the Day Bark,
> For you are the one who watches over the gods,
> and there is no god to watch over you.[116]

Such texts seem to indicate that people realized that talking about the sleep of deities was inadequate because divine sleep did not preclude simultaneous awareness.

6.2.1.5b Divine Silence Because of Sleep in the Bible

A few times the Hebrew Bible seems to suggest that the God of Israel too needed sleep.[117] This is the case implicitly in Ps. 35:23 where God is implored to awake to vindicate the supplicant[118] and explicitly in Ps. 44:24[23], where God is asked why

---

[112] References De Moor 1997, 49-50.
[113] CAD (S), 68a.
[114] Translation Foster 1995, 71.
[115] Translation Foster 1995, 56. See also pp. 41, 46.
[116] Translation Foster 1995, 31.
[117] See Batto 1987; McAlpine 1987; Emmendörffer 1998, 118-119; Mrozek & Votto 1999.
[118] See also Ps. 7:7; 59:6; 78:65.

he is sleeping while his people is suffering. The poet accuses God of rejecting his people (v. 10[9]), handing them over to the enemies (v.12[11]), and even selling them for a ridiculous price (v. 13[12]). This evokes phrases from other biblical texts using the same metaphor of God as a seller of his people.[119] However, in all those cases he 'sold' his people because of their sins, whereas according to the poet of Psalm 44 they are innocent and pious (vv. 18-22[17-21]).

In Isa. 51:9 God, or more specifically his strong arm, is prayed to wake up (cf. Ps. 44:24[23]) as in the days of old (cf. Ps. 44:2[1]), and the speaker reminds God of his deliverance of his people Israel in Egypt, when he made a road in the depths of the sea so that they were able to cross over, and he asks for a repetition of these wondrous acts of the past. The same argument is used in Ps. 44:2-4[1-3]. In Ps. 44:25[24] the Psalmist complains that God hides his face. In Isa. 40:27 the prophet seems to quote this complaint, asking his audience why they say that God has hidden himself for them. In Isa. 54:8 God admits that for a moment he hid his face from his people, but that with everlasting kindness (cf. Ps. 44:27) he will have compassion for them.

However, the poet's reproach that God is asleep (Ps. 44:24[23]) is merely provocative language of the supplicant. The context indicates that he expects God to be wide awake, hearing his prayer loud and clear.[120]

Actually the Israelite knows that his vigilant Keeper will neither slumber nor sleep. The supplicant of Ps. 121 lifts his eyes up to the mountains and asks, 'where does my help come from?' (Ps. 121:1). Several scholars take the mountains as a menace, he would become afraid when looking at them,[121] but it is far more likely that 'the mountains' are a designation of the places from where he expects God's help to come,[122] as is suggested by his own answer in v. 2 with which v. 1 forms a strophe structurally. In his view

---

[119] Deut. 32:20; Judg. 10:7; 1 Sam. 12:9; Isa. 50:1; 52:3; Est. 7:4.

[120] McAlpine 1987, 196-197 points out that the net effect of this contextual evidence is to shift the language from a literal to a metaphorical level.

[121] E.g. Kraus 1978, 1013; Terrien 2003, 811; Becking 2008, 47. Seybold 1996, 478, even thinks of an accident in the mountains.

[122] Goldingay 2008, 456-457; Hossfeld & Zenger 2008, 436.

the mountains belong to God's work of creation and do not have to be feared by man. This in contrast to the view of surrounding nations who deified mountains.[123] Whereas the mountains seem asleep, Israel's Protector never sleeps.[124] If it takes some time before he intervenes, it is not because he is really asleep, but because it seems as if he is sleeping.

In Ps. 78:65 the poet uses daring similes,[125] 'Then the Lord awoke like a sleeper, like a hero brawling because of wine'. But this is nothing more than a simile which the poet uses to bring home his message that God could no longer bear the dumbfounded silence of young girls and widows whose dearest and priests he himself had allowed to be silenced for ever (cf. Ps. 78:63-64).

Yet in this case too it may be surmised that the difference between Israel and its neighbors was less pronounced than it may seem, on the one hand because outside Israel too there was an awareness of the incomparability of divine and human sleep, on the other hand because the Hebrew Bible does not shrink back from the idea that God might need what human beings call 'rest' or 'sleep'. After six days of creation work God rests on the seventh day (Exod. 20:11). In Gen. 2:2-3 the very anthropomorphic verb 'rest' is replaced by the less offensive 'to stop working'. It is noteworthy that the first verb is a general term which occurs frequently with human beings as its subject, but also with insects.[126] In Exod. 31:17 'to stop' is elucidated by a verb implying that God took a break to feel refreshed. That this anthropomorphism[127] was left intact is doubtlessly caused by the desire to preserve the symmetry between the resting of God and man (Exod. 31:15; cf. 23:12).

---

[123] Korpel 1990, 578-579; Haas 1994, 461-464. Becking 2008, 49, and others, reject the idea that vv. 3-4 form a deliberate contrast to pagan deities who rise and die with the seasons, because of the fact that the verbs used here are not the same as those in the texts describing the rising and dying of gods.

[124] Ps. 121:3-4. When it is suggested here that eventually he might sleep, it means that 'he gives the impression of being asleep' because he remains inattentive to the prayers of his people (Dahood 1965, 268).

[125] In this case too some scholars suppose a relation with the concept of the sleeping deity in the texts of Ugarit, cf. Kraus 1978, 711; Tate 1990, 294.

[126] Cf. Exod. 23:14; Deut. 5:14 (man); Exod. 10:14 (locusts).

[127] Cf. 2 Sam. 16:14.

The correspondence between divine silence and human silence because of sleep has as a consequence that it is not sufficient for Zion to urge the LORD to wake up (Isa. 51:9, cf. 52:10), Lady Zion herself must awake too, shake off her chains and restore her own strength (Isa. 51:17; 52:1-2).[128]

6.2.2 Incomprehensible Divine Silence

6.2.2.1 In the Ancient Near East

People were not always able to fathom a reason for the silence of their gods. In such cases they find silence on the part of the deity particularly difficult to accept because they cannot undertake measures to placate the gods. Given the unpredictable way the gods are wielding their awesome power, their silence may even forebode the total destruction of the human race.

Above we quoted some lines from the Egyptian *Admonitions of Ipuwer* expressing concern about unanswered prayers,

> When we have been saddened, I could not find you;
> No one can call on you ...

Ipuwer is wondering if the god might be asleep, but he realizes that this is no more than a hypothesis.

Fear of silence from the side of the deities is also at the background of Mesopotamian prayers. Praying without receiving an answer is experienced as utterly vexing. In a Sumerian incantation of the second millennium BCE a supplicant prays,

> How long shall you remain silent?
> What keeps you quiet?[129]

A Babylonian supplicant complains,

> Speaking, but not being heard, has kept me awake,
> calling out, but not being answered, has vexed me,

---

[128] See also Isa. 52:7-9 and 40:9, with the remarks by Korpel & De Moor 1998, 542-543.
[129] Cohen 1988, vol. 1, 416.

has drained my strength (?) from my heart,
has bowed me down like an old man.[130]

Another supplicant prays,

Bring about speaking and granting of [my prayer].[131]

Apparently these supplicants expected a spoken answer from the deities or their representatives. Such an answer is spoken by a prophet to reassure the Assyrian king Esarhaddon who reigned from 681-669 BCE,

> Fear not, Esarhaddon! I am Bel,[132] I speak to you! I watch over the supporting beams of your heart. When your mother gave birth to you, sixty Great Gods stood there with me, protecting you. Sîn[133] stood at your right side, Šamaš[134] at your left. Sixty Great Gods are still standing around you; they have girded your loins.
>
> Do not trust in humans! Lift up your eyes and focus on me! I am Ištar of Arbela.[135] I have reconciled Aššur to you. I protected you when you were a baby. Fear not; praise me!
>
> Is there an enemy that has attacked you, while I have kept silent? The future shall be like the past! I am Nabû, the Lord of the Stylus.[136] Praise me!

By the mouth of the woman Bayâ, a man from Arbela.[137]

---

[130] Ebeling 1953, 72-73; Seux 1976, 169-170 (English translation ours). For similar passages see Ebeling 1953, 114-115; Seux 1976, 313; CAD (Š) 2, 149a.

[131] Ebeling 1953, 84-85, cf. CAD (M) 2, 38-39. See also Ebeling 1953, 106-107.

[132] Bel means 'Lord' and is a title of the Babylonian creator god Marduk which was taken over by the national god of Assyria Assur.

[133] Moon god.

[134] Sun god.

[135] Ishtar was the goddess of love and war who was the patroness of prophets in Arbela, an important Assyrian city. Her gender was androgynous (she is Bel but at the same time Ishtar), as seems to have been the case with the female/male prophetess who speaks in her name.

[136] As the epithet indicates, Nabû was the patron of scribes. It was he who wrote the tablets of fate and thus determined the future.

[137] Translation Nissinen 2003, 105, explanatory notes ours.

The text clearly suggests that the goddess (who is identified with other great gods) will not remain silent when the king is attacked. She reassures him by invoking the salutary acts of the gods in the past, from Esarhaddon's birth on. The future will not be different.[138]

It was seen as a terrible curse to ask the gods not to listen to someone's prayers. On a Babylonian boundary stone the owner tried to prevent people to remove it by praying,

> May Shamash[139] and Marduk[140] not listen to him when he invokes them.[141]

The evil god Erra asks Marduk not to answer the prayers of the inhabitants of Mesopotamia when he starts devastating the country.[142]

Gilgamesh bewails the loss of his friend Enkidu before mighty gods like Enlil, Sin and Nergal, but they do not answer him at all.[143] However, the story also indicates that persistent prayer may be successful, because when Gilgamesh repeats his lament before the wise god Ea, the latter relents and grants him his wish to meet the spirit of his dead friend once more, if only to describe the horrors of the Nether World to him.[144]

Spurning of their prayers by the deities is also the complaint of Babylonian righteous sufferers. In *Ludlul bēl nēmeqi*, a poem composed at the end of the second millennium BCE, the protagonist wails,

> I called to my god, but he did not show his face,
> I prayed to my goddess, but she did not raise her head.[145]

The sufferer continues with a long list of all his pious acts and affirms emphatically,

---

[138] For a similar prophecy see Nissinen 2003, 110-111.
[139] Sun-god.
[140] Creator and head of the pantheon.
[141] King 1912, No. V, iii.42-44 (p. 29). See also Maqlû I.56-60.
[142] Erra II, Fragment C, 23 (Cagni 1972, 40).
[143] Gilg. Ep. XII.55-71, George 2003, vol. 1, 730-733.
[144] Gilg. Ep. XII.73-153, George 2003, vol. 1, 732-735.
[145] Ludlul II.4-5, translation Lambert 1960, 39.

> For myself, I gave attention to supplication and prayer:
> To me prayer was discretion, sacrifice my rule.[146]

So he contrasts the behavior of the deities with his own piety and concludes that divine reasoning is beyond human comprehension,

> What is proper to oneself is an offence to one's god.
>   What in one's own heart seems despicable
>   is proper to one's god.
> Who knows the will of the gods in heaven?
>   Who understands the plans of the underworld gods?
>   Where have mortals learnt the way of a god?[147]

Earlier this pessimistic sage has stated that in his case all specialists (diviner, dream priest, spirit, incantation priest) failed to obtain an answer to his complaints from the gods (Ludlul II.6-9). Later on, however, Marduk sends him several dreams promising him deliverance from his afflictions, sometimes addressing him personally.[148]

Also in the famous *Babylonian Theodicy*, possibly dating from c. 1100 BCE,[149] the sufferer expresses total incomprehension,

> Those who neglect the god
>   go the way of prosperity,
> While those who pray to the goddess
>   are impoverished and dispossessed.
> In my youth I sought the will of my god;
>   With prostration and prayer I followed my goddess.
> But I was bearing a profitless corvée as a yoke.
>   My god decreed instead of wealth destitution.[150]

Evidently this man has given up on his god, 'I will ignore my god's regulations and trample on his rites.'[151]

---

[146] Ludlul II.23-24, translation Lambert 1960, 39.

[147] Ludlul II.34-38, translation Lambert 1960, 41. See also the proverb quoted by Lambert 1960, 266.

[148] Ludlul III, Lambert 1960, 47-52.

[149] Van der Toorn 2003, 65-69.

[150] *Babylonian Theodicy*, 70-75, translation Lambert 1960, 75-77.

[151] *Babylonian Theodicy*, 135, translation Lambert 1960, 79.

In the moving Plague Prayers of the Hittite king Mursili II silence on the part of the deities is not mentioned explicitly, but is clearly supposed. 'O gods, my lords, you have turned your back on mankind' (Singer 2002, 65; Sanders 2007, 198). 'That deity has turned aside his eyes elsewhere and does not permit the human to act' (Singer 2002, 37). 'My father repeatedly inquired through the oracles, but he did not find you, O gods, my lords, through the oracles. I have also repeatedly inquired of you through oracle, but I have not found you, O gods, my lords, through oracle.' (Singer 2002, 65).

6.2.2.2 Incomprehensible Divine Silence in the Bible

Jacob wrestles a whole night with an unknown man. Neither man says a word. Until day breaks and the stranger asks Jacob to let him go. Meanwhile Jacob has realized that his attacker must have been God. He refuses to let him go unless he receives a blessing (Gen. 32:22-32).[152] Wrestling with God in the night and refusing to give up can end in a blessing.

In Ps. 91:15, a prophetic oracle of salvation for the king,[153] God promises to answer the ruler when he calls to him,

> When he calls me, I will answer him;
> I am with him in distress,
> I will deliver him and bring him honor.

Despite the affirmative tone of this oracle, a divine answer was not an automatism. It did occur that a king tried to learn the will of God, but was refused an answer. This is the case for example in 1 Sam. 14:37, 'Saul inquired of God, "Shall I go down after the Philistines? Will you give them into the hand of Israel?" But he did not answer him that day.' Apparently Saul waited a whole day for an answer, but finally concluded that there was no reply because someone, perhaps even his own son Jonathan, had committed a sin against the LORD. But even though all people knew that Jonathan unwittingly had violated his father's oath (1 Sam.

---

[152] For a Ugaritic parallel of a human being detaining deities until they bless him see KTU 1.15:II.13-16, with De Moor 1997, 92-93.
[153] Hilber 2005, 203-208.

14:24-30, 38-39), nobody dared to reply to Saul's outburst (1 Sam. 14:39). Indeed, who was the guilty party? Saul who pronounced a rash vow, or Jonathan who was a victim of ignorance? Eventually the divine oracle pronounces Jonathan guilty, but the people indignantly refuse to have him executed (1 Sam. 14:40-45).

This short story raises several questions. Why did God refuse to answer Saul first, but soon afterwards does instruct his oracle to convict the innocent Jonathan? The reader experiences this as blatant injustice and feels relieved when the people did not accept God's decision and Saul's acceptance of their disobedience. Apparently it is not always the best way to meekly accept God's decision. God does not rebuke the people for this, but leaves room for the sometimes rebellious free will of human beings.

A somewhat similar episode occurs in 1 Sam. 28:6.[154] In v. 3 the narrator has related that the prophet Samuel had died and that Saul had removed the mediums and wizards out of the land.[155] So when God did not answer Saul's request whether or not he should do battle with the redoubtable Philistines, Saul had to decide for himself what he should do. Through an 'illegal' medium in the town of Endor he consults the spirit of Samuel, repeating that God refused to answer him, either by prophets or by dreams (v. 15). Referring to an earlier prophecy (1 Sam. 15:28-29; cf. 16:1), Samuel points out that God had rejected Saul as king and that for that reason the latter should have known better than asking him, Samuel, for an oracle (1 Sam. 28:16-19). Even Saul's atonement and Samuel's acceptance of his repentance in 1 Sam. 15:30-31 had not altered God's negative judgment.

This story seems to imply that there is also a possibility to misuse human freedom. One may well ask if God would not have relented if Saul had remained true to his initial decision not to allow consultation of a medium. Perhaps Saul should have shown more patience and trust.

In many Hebrew laments the supplicant expresses his incomprehension by the interrogative 'why?'[156] A classical example is

---

[154]The narrative similarity was discussed by Craig 1994.

[155]There is insufficient reason to regard the verse as a later editorial addition, cf. Stoebe 1973, 489.

[156]See for example Jer. 14:8-9; 20:18; Joel 2:17; Ps. 10:1; 42:10[9]; 43:2;

Ps. 22:2-3[1-2],

> My God, my God, why did you abandon me?
>   far removed from my salvation, the words of my outcry?
> My God, I am crying by day, but you do not answer,
>   and by night, when I do not allow myself silence.[157]

The singer deplores that God has abandoned him, keeping his distance in order not to be obliged to come to the rescue of the supplicant who is crying out by day, but does not receive an answer (v. 3a[2a]). Even by night he does not allow himself to become silent (v. 3b[2b]). If God refuses to answer, the supplicant sacrifices his rest to implore him even at night (Ps. 22:1-3[0-2]). If God remains silent, the supplicant will not allow himself to keep silent too, even though his tongue is glued to his palate (v. 16[15]).

There had been happier days, when God saved previous generations who cried to him (vv. 5-6[4-5]), so that they had reason to praise him (v. 4[3]). Therefore he asks God not to remain distant (vv. 12[11], 20[19]). The supplicant's determination not to keep silent but continue his prayer for deliverance seems to be rewarded. The prayer ends with the joyful, but rather abrupt exclamation: 'You have answered me!' (v. 22aB), followed by abundant thanksgiving.[158] It seems logical to suppose that in the silence that fell after the lament a priest or cultic prophet spoke an oracle of salvation. Others see 'You have answered me!' as a later addition meant to explain the sudden transition from prayer to hymn. Still others regard the entire hymnic part of the Psalm (vv. 23-32[22-31]) as a later addition, perhaps by the Psalmist himself.

All this is possible, yet none of these solutions is entirely satisfactory. The Psalm is a well-composed whole (Van der Lugt 2006, 239-249) which renders the supposition of a later addition

---

44:23-24; Lam. 5:20.

[157] According to Mt. 27:46; Mk 15:34 Jesus quoted this verse on the cross.

[158] The text is not entirely certain. The Septuagint has a different reading which is favored by Villanueva 2008, 81-89. However, as Ridderbos 1972, 191, has seen, the inclusion between v. 3 'you do not answer' and v. 22 'you have answered me!' argues strongly in favor of maintaining the Hebrew text.

less likely. Despite his disappointment in his God the supplicant continues to put his trust in him: 'from my mother's womb on you are my God' (v. 10[9]). Therefore it cannot be excluded that a sudden inner conviction broke through that God had answered him. Just as he declares later on that God 'has done it' (v. 32[31]), although a promise of deliverance is not the same as its fulfillment. We have to reckon with the possibility of a proleptic, anticipatory use of the perfect in the Psalms.

People lament about the incomprehensibility of God's refusal to speak through signs and prophets when his people is in utter distress. He even allows its enemies to put up their own signs in the place where his congregation used to gather (Ps. 74:4, 9). In this Psalm there is no trace of any awareness of guilt on the part of the people, as Michael Emmendörffer observes,

> Between shepherd and sheep there exists a relationship of protection and trust. YHWH has revoked this. However, Psalm 74 does not provide information about the reason for this decision. Guilt and sin on the part of the congregation or their fathers do not come under consideration, seem to be excluded. The acting of the enemies can only be understood as expression of divine wrath. But the ground for the wrath remains elusive.[159]

The supplicant does not resign to God's silence and adamantly refuses to keep silent himself. This is a recurrent pattern of reciprocity. The poet of Ps. 35 describes himself as one of the 'quiet ones in the country' (v. 20). He is treated badly by his enemies (vv. 1-21) who rejoice about his downfall (v. 24). He anticipates God's help, promising that he will thank and praise God in the congregation (vv. 9-10, 18, 28). So, just as in other Psalms, God is prayed to rescue the supplicant who promises to praise God afterwards. The poet suggests a so-called win-win situation, both God and the supplicant will benefit from God's active intervention. This is a very frequent type of argument in ancient oriental supplications.

In spite of his sympathizers the poet feels himself alone, since God does not answer his prayers (Ps. 35:13). God keeps silent

---

[159] Our translation. German original: Emmendörffer 1998, 85.

and seems remote (v. 22), or is even sleeping (v. 23), although the poet is convinced that God has seen (v. 22) how he is treated by his enemies. In the supplicant's opinion God sees, but does not act, so he assumes that God knowingly remains inactive. Out of compassion with his enemies the supplicant himself has worn sackcloth, has fasted, has prayed with his head bowed on his bosom, i.e. silently (v. 13). Just as a man laments over a friend, a brother or a mother, so he prayed (v. 14). Thus he adopted the well-known attitude of a mourner expressing hope for mercy on the part of God.[160] What this supplicant wishes is that God will break the silence (v. 22) and will say to him, 'I am your salvation' (Ps. 35:3b).

As in this Psalm, supplicants often beg God to reply to their prayer.[161] They cannot endure his silence,

> O God, do not keep silence;
>   do not remain quiet
>   and do not be still, O God! (Ps. 83:2[1])

> Be not silent, O God of my praise! (Ps. 109:1)

The latter Psalmist contrasts God's silence with the hateful words of his opponents (vv. 2-3, 20, 25) and quotes their false accusations at length (vv. 6-19).[162] He represents himself as the personification of pious prayer (v. 4) and promises to praise God abundantly if he vindicates him (v. 30).

Another example of the inability of supplicants to resign to God's silence is found in Ps. 28,

> To you, O LORD, I call,
>   my Rock, do not remain silent,
> lest, if you keep silent to me,
>   I become like those who go down into the Pit (Ps. 28:1).

The argument is very clever. By using God's honorary epithet 'Rock'[163] the Psalmist evokes the equally frequent denunciation

---

[160] Cf. 2 Sam. 12:16, 21, 22; Joel 2:12-16; Jonah 3:5, 9, contrast Est. 4:3, 16.
[161] E.g. Ps. 39:13[12]; 55:2[1] (cf. Section 4.5.1.2).
[162] Cf. e.g. Seybold 1996, 434-435; Goldingay 2008, 279-280.
[163] A well-known biblical metaphor, cf. Korpel 1990, 579, 584-585; Ryken *et al.* 1998, 732-733.

of idols of stone that cannot speak (cf. Section 6.2.1.4b). And by hinting at the possibility that he will die he reminds God of the fact that the inhabitants of the Nether World remain eternally silent and do not praise him anymore (cf. Section 3.2.5.2). The Psalmist meets God's silence with persistent loud supplication (v. 2) and pleads his innocence in contrast to the wicked (vv. 3-5). In the hymnic thanksgiving (v. 6) he refers back explicitly to his loud supplication and affirms that he has been successful: God has heard him.

In this and other cases an oracle of salvation might have been pronounced by a priest or a prophet[164] promising concrete help in the name of God. If Ps. 28 is a royal Psalm (cf. v. 8) and v. 9 is part of it, a rather general wording of such oracles may be supposed.[165] In other cases it is evident that a spoken answer is not what is asked for, but rather a delivering act of God (Ps. 55:3, 10-24).

It has often been maintained that in Ps. 28:5 a different person pronounces an oracle that would be the answer to the preceding laments. However, Van der Lugt's careful structural analysis of the Psalm has revealed that vv. 4-5 cannot be separated from each other.[166]

This renders a break after v. 4 very unlikely. It is the same person who asks God to repay the godless their evil acts in vv. 4-5a and who announces their downfall in v. 5b.[167] 'Rock' is a characteristic divine epithet in Psalms that were ascribed to David.[168] Since Ps. 28 too is a 'Davidic' Psalm (v. 1) it is possible that in using this divine epithet the late[169] author may have wanted to

---

[164] Cf. Section 5.2.2.1-2.

[165] A fairly convincing example of this type of oracle is found in Ps. 60:7-10[6-9] = 108:7-10[6-9], cf. Hilber 2005, 192-202. However, others regard Ps. 28:8-9 as a later appendage. Cf. Hossfeld & Zenger 1993, 176.

[166] Van der Lugt 2006, 288-293; similarly Seybold 2003, 116-117.

[167] Note especially the impressive parallelism between 'their deeds' (v. 4aA), 'the work of their hands' (v. 4aC) and 'the LORD's deeds' (v. 5aA), 'the work of his hands' (v. 5aB).

[168] Ps. 18:3, 32, 47 (= 2 Sam. 22:3, 32, 47); 19:15; 31:3; 62:3, 7-8; 71:3; 89:27; 144:1.

[169] V. 5b strongly recalls Jeremiah's frequent parallel use of 'to tear down' and 'to build up'.

hint at David's last words in 2 Sam. 23:2-3, 'The Spirit of the LORD speaks by me, his word is upon my tongue. The God of Israel has spoken, the Rock of Israel has said to me ...'.[170]

So there is no need for a priest or a prophet as an intermediary. According to these Psalmists God spoke directly to David (cf. e.g. 2 Sam. 7) and his successors[171] and so the Davidic king they envisaged was endowed with the gift to hear the word of God[172] and was entitled to pass God's message on to his subjects (cf. Ps. 40:7-11). In a sense this endowed 'David' with the gift of 'prophecy', just as his predecessor Saul was thought to be among the divinely inspired prophets (1 Sam. 10:11-12; 18:10; 19:24).

Does this make the singer of Psalm 28 a prophet then? Certainly not, otherwise he would have passed on the oracle of salvation he heard and would not have ended his Psalm with a further request (v. 9). For our present investigation it is important to note that while the supplicant is still praying, the conviction grows in his heart that he 'hears' the voice of the 'silent' God promising him that He will punish his wicked opponents. This is the reason for his praise in v. 6, because he is convinced now that God did not remain silent, but did indeed listen to his passionate prayer. This certainty is reached not through hearing an external voice, but through an internal process that takes place while the supplicant is praying. Samuel Terrien aptly observes with regard to God's answering in v. 6 that 'deliverance has not yet taken place, but the certitude of its coming is so complete that the future itself is absorbed within the present' (Terrien 2003, 272). This is in accordance with what John Day writes about such sudden changes of mood in individual lament Psalms,

---

[170] Just as in Ps. 28:8, 'anointed' is used in 2 Sam. 23:1. See also Ps. 18:51; 89:39, 52.

[171] It was a common element in ancient oriental royal ideology that occasionally deities communicated directly with their chosen kings. See Section 5.1.

[172] Also in other 'Davidic' Psalms the expectation is that God will certainly not fail to answer him or has already done so, cf. Ps. 3:5; 6:9-10; 13:4, cf. 6; 17:6; 20:2, 7, 10; 22:3, 22; 27:7; 34:5; 38:16; 55:3; 60:7; 65:6; 69:14, 17-18; 86:1, 7; 108:7; 138:3; 143:1, 7. Note also the use of 'oracle of the LORD', in Ps. 110:1 which renders this Psalm a prophetic oracle, cf. Hilber 2005, 76-88.

It is more likely that the change of mood is to be explained by some inner psychological process in which the psalmist was able to look forward, anticipating the desired deliverance. This explanation gains support from the fact observed by students of prayer that it is not uncommon for those who pray to find that feelings of doubt and despair eventually give rise to feelings of confidence and assurance.[173]

A similar case is Ps. 13. The supplicant is afraid that God will forget him forever and will hide his face from him (v. 2[1]). 'Hiding the face from someone' was an expression of disgust, mostly because of offenses. It comes close to remaining silent (Job 34:29). That is presupposed here too, because the Psalmist asks God to look at him again and answer him (v. 4aA[3aA]). In v. 4aB[3aB] he explicitly asks God to lighten his eyes, otherwise he will fall into the sleep of death. This renders it very likely that the confident statement that God has been good to him (v. 6) was based on an inner conviction, not on an oracle of salvation.[174]

God might also choose to reply to a personal complaint of a prophet. An example of this is found in the book of Habakkuk. In Chapter 1 the prophet has complained about the injustice of the wicked because of which the righteous have to suffer distress (Hab. 1:4, 13a). He cannot understand why God remains silent (1:13b) when the righteous have to suffer under the doom and destruction that he as God's messenger has to announce because of the behavior of the wicked (1:5-11). Since the LORD is reliable, it cannot be the case that the righteous will die in the judgment destined for the wicked (1:12). Chapter 1 ends in a tormented question from the side of the prophet who had been obliged to announce this merciless warfare and destruction by the Babylonian king: 'Will he continue slaying nations for ever?'

This question remains unanswered and the tradition has marked this silence by wide spaces. Chapter 2 then starts with a monologue of the prophet which is answered by a further instruction of the LORD,

---

[173] Day 2003, 32. He refers to Heiler 1997, 259-260.

[174] Cf. Craigie 1983, 143, 'the knowledge that deliverance was coming created an anticipatory calm and sense of confidence' and Alter 2007, 39: 'Perhaps the prayer itself served as a vehicle of transformation from acute distress to trust'; similarly Dahood 1965, 76; Janowski 2001; Terrien 2003, 160.

¹ Let me stand at my watch,
   and station myself on the ramparts,
I will look out to see what he will say to me,
   and what I must answer[175] to my complaint.
² Then the LORD replied, saying:
Write down the vision, make it clear on boards,
   so that the one who reads it may hurry away.
³ For the vision still awaits the appointed time,
   but it pushes forward to the end, and does not lie.
If it seems to linger, wait for it,
   for it will certainly come, and will not delay.
⁴ Look, he is puffed up, (he) whose soul within him is not right,
   but a righteous man will live by his faith.

Apparently the prophet does not acquiesce in the silence that follows his anguished question of 1:17. He awaits a vision in which God will answer him so that he will know how to deal with his own complaint. As in Ps. 38:15[14] and Job 23:4, the Hebrew word which we translate here as 'complaint' is a forensic term, indicating the plea of an innocent man before the judge. In all three cases the speaker awaits an adequate answer. Since Hab. 2:4 forms a structural unit with 2:1-3,[176] the puffed-up must be the temporarily successful wicked, whereas the righteous who will not die are the faithful servants of the LORD, among them the prophet himself.

For our investigation it is important to note that here we are allowed a glimpse into the psychological process involved in the contact between a prophet and his God. When there was no divine answer to his question the prophet positioned himself in an ostensible attitude of waiting,[177] silently demanding a reply.

---

[175] Several ancient versions, modern translations and commentators betray uneasiness with the first person singular, and many feel that they should alter the text so that it reads 'what he (God) will answer'. Often the Peshitta is referred to as a witness supporting this emendation, but this version too is merely removing the difficulty. The Septuagint and Theodotion clearly support the first person singular and from viewpoint of textual criticism there is insufficient reason to reject this more difficult reading and proceed to a theologically more acceptable conjecture (cf. Haak 1992, 54).

[176] This solution is favored by the Habakkuk pesher from Qumran and several medieval Masoretic codices. Cf. Prinsloo 2009.

[177] Cf. Ps. 130:5-6 where the supplicant waits tensely for a word of God.

Which did come, apparently in the form of an inner enlightenment – a narrow escape is still possible for the faithful.

6.3 Conclusions on Divine Silence

The chapter bearing the same title as this book itself inevitably became relatively short because the evidence from the ancient Near East for silence on the part of deities appeared to be as meagre as it was in the case of the Bible (cf. Section 1.6.2). This indicates once again that divine taciturnity was not a major issue in the world of the Bible. The topical interest in the theme is a product of modernity. Yet our broad approach has elucidated many aspects of the involvement of man in the mediation of both divine speech and silence. Remarkable differences between the Bible and the literature of the nations surrounding ancient Israel came to light in this chapter.

According to both ancient Near Eastern sources and the Bible only the almighty Creator was able to break the primordial silence. Before he spoke, stillness reigned everywhere according to Egyptian theologians of the New Kingdom, Neo-Babylonian wisdom texts and much later Hebrew sages.

Even though they were deeply convinced of the Creator's absolute transcendence, they all assumed that he did listen to human complaints and would respond to their prayers. So they vented their deep disappointment if the remote deity remained silent. This attitude owed them reprimands from those who were of the opinion that God was completely free to ignore supplication. It is questionable, however, if this fatalistic view was shared by Israel as a whole. Neither Job, nor many Psalmists and prophets resign to God's silence because in the covenant God had willingly committed himself to answer the complaints of the righteous (Section 6.1).

We have divided the reasons for silence on the part of deities in two categories: comprehensible and incomprehensible silence. In the first category (Section 6.2.1) we found exactly the same reasons that were adduced for silence on the part of human beings before each other (Section 3.2) and before their gods (Section 4.5).

These silences were often expressed not in words, but by blank spaces (cf. Section 2.3).

Silence because of offenses like making too much noise so that the gods could not sleep is attested several times in Mesopotamian sources.

In Israel God refused to reply to prayers if the Israelites had sinned against himself or against his representatives on earth. In the post-exilic book of Third Isaiah the prophet admits that God has had every right to react to Israel's sins by remaining silent when they begged him to respond to their lamentations. However, they themselves refused to remain silent and in this way hoped to break God's silence.

It is noteworthy that God is left out from passages in the canonical version of the Hebrew Bible where grisly crimes are committed by human beings acting on their own. His silence should be seen as disapproval, not as 'working silently in the background'.

The eschatological silence in heaven mentioned in Rev. 8:1 precedes the execution of the divine wrath. It may be compared to the menacing calm that preceded the unleashing of the Deluge according to Babylonian myth.

Divine silence because of awe, fear or incapacity occurs fairly often in documents from the ancient Near East. It is certainly remarkable that this kind of silence is never attributed to God in the Hebrew Bible. In polytheism the rise and fall of other deities was a normal phenomenon which merely meant a (temporary) shift in power from one deity to another. So fear, weakness and even death, mostly temporary, did occur in the divine world, though 'temporary' might add up to millions of years, because divine time differed radically from human time. Apparently silence because of fear and weakness on the part of God has been avoided in the Hebrew Bible as we have it now. On the contrary, Israel taunted the gods and idols of other nations because of their incapacity to answer the prayers of their worshippers.

Conversely, silence of the deity because of forbearance or prudence seems to occur more often in the Bible than in the surrounding world. Possibly this has to do with the concept of divine grace that came more to the fore after the collapse of the monarchy and the realization that this grave sanction on their sins had been deserved and could not easily be undone. Sometimes this kind of silence is not expressed in words, but by blank spaces marking a rhetorical silence (cf. Section 2.3).

All deities from the ancient Near East, including the God of Israel, were thought to be asleep sometimes. During such periods they were not reacting to human prayers. However, here too it must be realized that divine sleep is not the same as human sleep. It is merely a human metaphor. While sleeping a deity might at the same time be fully awake. The common metaphor of the sleep of death, however, is never applied to the living God of Israel (cf. Section 1.6.2.1).

From the viewpoint of man the alterity of the deity implied that one could not always fathom the reasons why a divine answer remained forthcoming. Cases of divine silence which vexed the supplicant because he considered himself innocent were discussed in Section 6.2.1. Both in and outside Israel the conviction existed that persistent prayer of the righteous could break the silence of the deity. The answer might eventually be mediated by an oracle pronounced by a priest, prophet or diviner, but could also be the result of a growing inner conviction that the deity agreed to what the supplicant awaited so eagerly. In both cases the human and the divine side of the revelatory process appear to be indivisible.

At the end of this chapter we may conclude that both in the Bible and in its surrounding world people professed the incomparability of God and man even though they spoke about the divine in human metaphorical language. The consequence of the acceptance of the alterity of divine beings had as a consequence that humans did not always understand why their gods did not react. The remoteness of the Creator implied that he had been the first to speak and could chose to remain silent even if his creatures were in grave danger. The transcendence of God meant that the composers of the canon of the Hebrew Bible had to exclude certain typical human reasons for keeping silent, especially awe or fear, because such feelings might suggest that there existed other redoutable divine powers. Also some other reasons for silence, like incapacity or sleep, do not seem to have been not really applicable to the God of Israel (in the following table indicated by: x?).

Silence of Deities Compared to Human Silence

Reasons	ANE Humans ↓ Humans	Bible Humans ↓ Humans	ANE Humans ↓ Gods	Bible Humans ↓ God	ANE Gods ↓ All	Bible God ↓ All
Offenses	x	x	∅?	x	x	x
Awe / Fear	x	x	x	x	x	∅
Forbearance / Prudence	x	x	x	x	x	x
Incapacity	x	x	x	x	x	x?
Sleep	x	x	x	x	x?	x?
Incomprehensible					x	x

CHAPTER SEVEN

EPILOGUE

7.1 Faith Talk

On one of the first pages of his bestseller *Yosl Rakover Talks to God* Zvi Kolitz quotes the following lines,

> I believe in the sun, even when it doesn't shine.
> I believe in love, even when I don't feel it.
> I believe in God, even when He is silent.[1]

Allegedly these words were found on the wall of a cellar in Cologne where some Jews had remained hidden during World War II. The authenticity of the quote is disputed. A quick search on the Internet reveals that others state that it is an Irish saying. Since the whole book on Yosl Rakover rests on fiction, as Kolitz himself admitted,[2] it is possible that he picked it up from an Irishman while serving in the British army during the war. However, a text need not be authentic to contain truth. This is also true of many texts from Antiquity, including the Bible. We permit ourselves a few comments on it because it helps to understand the nature of the problem dealt with in this study.

The first statement is far from cogent. The presence of the sun can be established objectively by other means than visual observation. In a strict sense, no belief is required. Yet the phrase conveys an optimistic mood we all know. The weather may be gloomy now, but sooner or later the sun is bound to break through the clouds. This is a rational expectation based on common experience.

Belief in love is more difficult. Love can only partially be established in an objective sense. Even if there are observable outward signs of love, for example certain gestures, words, or the presence of certain hormones, the *meaning* of such indicators has been established by existing tradition and acquired knowledge. Unfortunately, love can be feigned. Most people will admit that

---

[1] Yiddish text and German transliteration: Kolitz 2008, 7. English translation: Carol Brown Janeway in: Kolitz 1999, v.

[2] Cf. Paul Badde in: Kolitz 2008, 105-169.

'love' does not depend on sexual arousal alone, so a hormone test would fail. And finally, 'love' is a fuzzy concept. Is 'feeling' it a physical sensation? Some psychological event? An innate social response? What do we mean when we say that we believe in love? Yet, despite this lack of precision, 'love' is a phenomenon that to some extent can be verified empirically, for example by the fact that many people have experienced it in their own lives.[3] But to a far greater extent love has to be *believed* to be true.

According to most people in our age this is not the case with God. He cannot be described adequately in human language. He is not verifiable by experiments.[4] Which God we mean has to be established by context. Is he the God of the Hebrew Bible, the Christian Bible, the Koran? Or the new theists' Superior Mind who designed the entire cosmos?

In this book a host of other deities from Antiquity has come under review and many similarities with the God of Israel came to the fore. Do we have to believe in all of them? On what rational grounds does a person expect an answer from the deity to whom she or he turns? God cannot be 'silent' if he does not 'speak'. He cannot 'speak' if He does not 'exist'. Belief in a 'silent' God presupposes at least the belief that he has spoken in the past and might speak again. For those who coined the saying

---

[3] Compare this statement: 'Negative theology affirms that a direct insight into *mystery*–for example, the mystery of love–is possible. This is a *knowledge derived from experience* that is usually called 'mysticism', a knowledge that cannot be logically proven, but only personally experienced.' (Bulhof & Ten Cate 2000, 6.) See also Marion 2010, 119-142.

[4] Soares 2006 reports: 'The three-year Study of the Therapeutic Effects of Intercessory Prayer (STEP), published in the April 4 *American Heart Journal*, was the largest-ever attempt to apply scientific methods to measure the influence of prayer on the well-being of another. It examined 1,800 patients undergoing heart-bypass surgery. On the eve of the operations, church groups began two weeks of praying for one set of patients. Each recipient had a praying contingent of about 70, none of whom knew the patient personally. The study found no differences in survival or complication rates compared with those who did not receive prayers. The only statistically significant blip appeared in a subgroup of patients who were prayed for and knew it. They experienced a higher rate of postsurgical heart arrhythmias (59 versus 52 percent of unaware subjects).' Did the knowledge of being prayed for perhaps heighten the apprehension in the latter group of patients?

'I believe in God, even when He is silent' this was a certainty for which they needed no proof. It was the certainty of faith. Their conviction that it was worthwhile to continue believing in him rested on the testimony of countless generations of pious predecessors. Admittedly this is not the same as scientific proof, but it is useful to observe that also scientists work with hypotheses, as Karen Armstrong remarks,

> In science, as in theology, human beings could make progress on unproven ideas, which worked practically even if they had not been demonstrated empirically.[5]

7.2 God's Word in Human Guise

Many people still believe that messages from God must at least be delivered by angels to be true. In 2008 the museum Catharijne Convent in Utrecht, The Netherlands, organized an exhibition called *Allemaal engelen* (All angels). It was a huge success. The public interest was so massive that the exhibition had to be prolongated far into 2009.[6] In the end more than 66.000 people had visited the exhibition. One of its nice features was a stand where visitors could photograph themselves with wings and have their pictures placed on the Internet. Thousands made use of this opportunity to pose as an angel, often adopting pious or hilarious poses. In this way the designer of the exposition, Maarten Spruyt, made clear that if we want, we all can be angels. Among the paintings exposed some depicted angels as normal human beings. Especially the narrative of Abraham's three visitors in Gen. 18 gave rise to paintings in which the 'angels' lack wings, for example by Lambert Jakobsz (1628) and Rembrandt van Rijn (1656). Apparently people realized already long ago that messengers of God can be normal human beings.

We have documented extensively our not too surprising conclusion that whenever deities in the ancient Near East, including the God of Israel, are said to address human beings their word is *mediated*, either by the hearers themselves or by other human beings. This is even the case if a deity or a (semi-)divine messenger

---

[5] Armstrong 2009, 267. See also 286.
[6] Cf. http://www.codart.nl/exhibitions/details/1710.

(angel) is said to speak directly to human beings because it were always reciters or scribes who were relating the divine speech. What are the consequences of this observation?

First of all it means that if we expect God to speak but he remains silent, we as human beings have to ask ourselves if he expects us to speak for him ourselves. Some works we have discussed earlier have proposed similar views. For many people the idea that there is no revelation without the intervention of man is in no way disturbing. They trust the testimony of prophets and biblical writers that they did not merely speak or write their own words, but the word of God. For others the thoroughly human nature of messages attributed to deities meant the end of their faith.

Does this view do justice to the ancient scribes? As we have seen, they themselves ascribed their religious writings to divine revelation.[7] Not necessarily in the sense of verbal inspiration because it has been demonstrated in a conclusive way that to some extent the scribes were free to shape the text according to their own needs and tastes. The divine cannot be separated from the human in religious writings from Antiquity, including the Bible.[8] However, 'inventing revelation' is humanizing it whereas the Ancients saw the deity as the initializing force, but were well aware of the fact that without their own contribution as human servants the word of God would not be heard or would remain incomprehensible.

Believers should acknowledge that if God is silent it is because humans are there not merely for themselves, but also to realize God's plans on earth, including the duty to pass on his word. His silence may be caused by their inertia, even if they have all the means to do what they are praying for and know what he has said in the past. God awaits action from his followers.

---

[7] Cf. Section 5.2.2.3-4.

[8] Second Vatican Council, cf. Rahner 2008; Reformed Churches 1981. For this reason some authors distinguish between divine revelation and its putting into words by the writers of Scripture. So e.g. Wolterstorff 1995, esp. 282-283. Theoretically this may be true, but in practice such a distinction is impossible to maintain.

The young Jewish woman Etty Hillesum expressed this idea poignantly in her diary, 'And if God does not help me to go on, then I shall have to help God'.[9] Later on she would come back to this insight repeatedly and we quote some of her moving thoughts here,

> *Sunday morning prayer* [12 July '42]. Dear God, these are anxious times. Tonight for the first time I lay in the dark with burning eyes as scene after scene of human suffering passed before me. I shall promise You one thing, God, just one very small thing: I shall never burden my today with cares about my tomorrow, although that takes some practice. Each day is sufficient unto itself. I shall try to help You, God, to stop my strength ebbing away, though I cannot vouch for it in advance. But one thing is becoming increasingly clear to me: that You cannot help us, that we must help You, God, in ourselves. And perhaps in others as well. Alas, there doesn't seem to be much You Yourself can do about our circumstances, about our lives. Neither do I hold You responsible. You cannot help us, but we must help You and defend Your dwelling place inside us to the last.[10]

Hillesum was not a sanctimonious woman, but her simple faith, rooted in both Jewish and Christian notions, carried her through the arduous last months before her execution by the Nazis on 30 November 1943. She was fully aware of the fact that her faith would not always be that strong, but she helped many around her to trust in God and often found rest for herself too.

To be sure, one obviously has the choice not to believe in God, but Hillesum's example shows that even in the most difficult circumstances it may help to talk to God as if He exists.[11] Every human being, if she or he is alone, talks to her/himself, or to an absent beloved. Why not talk to God? Why refuse to pray any longer if God does not fulfill an ardent wish? And why feel wronged if God seems unable or unwilling to help? Hillesum's conviction that if God seems unable to help human beings must take the initiative themselves is a message of lasting value.

---

[9] Hillesum 1996, 173. Dutch original: Hillesum 2006, 181.
[10] Hillesum 1996, 178. Dutch original: Hillesum 2006, 187-188.
[11] As Schmitt's Lady in Pink advised Oscar, cf. Section 1.5.

7.3 Synergy

However, does not the concept that human beings can help God detract from God's omnipotence and grace? Especially in churches of the Reformation people have been weary of attributing too much weight to human participation in the work of God. The doctrine of the *sola gratia* (by grace alone) and *sola fide* (in faith alone) excluded cooperation between God and man on an equal footing (Ritschl 1912, 423-455). However, as we have seen,[12] human mediators of the word of deities in the ancient world did not regard themselves as *equals* of their divine masters. They regarded themselves as servants, messengers who merely related the message they believed to have received. They continued to believe that it had been the deity who had taken the initiative, even if they felt obliged to edit the text according to the best of their abilities to bring home its presumed intention.

The idea that human beings should not wait and see if God will do it again but should actively participate in his work on earth is one of the basic concepts of the Hebrew Bible.[13] In the old Deborah Song the town of Meroz is cursed 'because it did not come to the help of the LORD with heroes' (Judg. 5:23). The patriarchs, Moses, Joshua, David and all Israel are regularly designated as 'servants of the LORD'. The prophets as spokesmen of God are described as his servants. Even non-Israelites like the Assyrians, Cyrus and Nebuchadnezzar are supposed to be in his service.

The Book of Ruth is a good example of the initiative human beings have to take even though they are well aware of the fact that God has to bless their efforts.[14] In dire circumstances the Israelites themselves must prepare the way for the LORD (Isa. 40:3), have to climb on a high mountain to espy the arrival of the LORD (Isa. 40:10), have to renew their own 'pinions' to fly back (Isa. 40:31),[15] In spite of the fact that he himself is a 'smoldering wick', the Servant of the LORD will not quench other 'smoldering

---

[12] Section 5.2.2.
[13] Cf. Brueggemann 1997, 413-564.
[14] Korpel 2001; cf. Köhlmoos 2010, XVII.
[15] On the translation of this verse see Korpel & De Moor 1998, 22, n. 14.

wicks', but has to become a light to the nations and free his compatriots suffering in dark dungeons (Isa. 42:1-7). If Zion exhorts God to wake up and clothe his arm with strength as in the days of old (Isa. 51:9) God's answer is that she herself must awake, shake off her chains and restore her own strength (Isa. 51:17; 52:1, 2; cf. 52:7-9 and 40:9). In the Book of Third Isaiah God expresses wonder about the fact that nobody intervenes on his behalf when lawlessness is spreading like wildfire (Isa. 59:16).

In the New Testament too the concept of a certain synergy between God and his human servants is present. The apostle Paul exclaims,

> What then is Apollos? What is Paul? Servants through whom you believed, as the Lord assigned to each.
> I planted, Apollos watered, but God gave the growth.
> So neither he who plants nor he who waters is anything, but only God who gives the growth.
> He who plants and he who waters are equal, and each shall receive his wages according to his labor.
> For we are God's fellow workers; you are God's field, God's building.[16]

The Greek word for 'fellow workers' is συνεργοί (*sunergoi*), 'coworkers'. It is evident that their contribution is not really comparable to what God does, but God has chosen to cooperate with human beings. In this sense also Luther deemed cooperation between God and man absolutely necessary (Seils 1962). We believe that John Locke (1632-1704) was right when he wrote,

> God when he makes the prophet does not unmake the man. He leaves all his faculties in their natural state, to enable him to judge of his inspirations, whether they be of divine origin or not.[17]

In our opinion human participation in the work of God may even go as far as participation in God's work as the Creator. The Bible sees creation not as a finished work of God, but as a continuous process.[18] God calls his servants to partake in his work of creation,

---

[16] 1 Cor. 3:5-9, RSV.
[17] John Locke, *Essay* IV, XIX, 14.
[18] Angerstorfer 1979, 224-225; Van Leeuwen 1996, especially 730; Becking & Korpel 2010, 18, with earlier literature.

> And I put my words in your mouth,
> and cover you with the shadow of my hand,
> to plant the heavens and to found the earth,
> and to say to Zion, "You are my people!"[19]

Under the protection of God's hand the prophet's words become words of the Creator himself who wants to create new things.[20] The Creator of all constantly reveals[21] his ponderings to mankind (Amos 4:13). He does this through his Spirit.[22]

In Ps. 90:17 the Psalmist asks God to use his power as the Creator to give substance to the work of human hands. The Hebrew verb used often designates God's work of creation. We ourselves have to use our hands, but it will actually become something meaningful only if God accepts it as *his* work.

Ken Gire points to the New Testament concept of the body of Christ,[23]

> We are his eyes, so we can see people with the same compassion that Christ would see them with if he were here. We are his ears, so we can listen with the understanding he would have. We are his mouth, so we can speak the words he would speak. We are his hands, so we can reach out to others the way he would if he were here ... (Gire 2005, 153-154).

Believers should not sit still in meek silence when things go awry in this world but should accept their responsibility as God's co-workers, as Nicholas Wolterstorff formulates it,

> We shall join God in doing battle against all that causes early death and all that leads to unredemptive suffering: disease, injustice, warfare, torture, enmity. The self-characterization of the biblical God is not that of a God who passively accepts things going awry with reference to his intent but that of a God who does battle; and is not that of a God who weakly struggles in a

---

[19] Isa. 51:16, with the remarks we made in: Korpel & De Moor 1998, 491-492, 542-543.
[20] See also Isa. 40:28; 42:5-9; 43:19; 48:6-7.
[21] Literally, 'is telling', an active participle in the Hebrew text.
[22] See Section 5.1.2 above and our remarks below.
[23] Rom. 12:4-8; 1 Cor. 12:12-31; Eph. 1:23; 4:4, 12, 16; 5:23, 30; Col. 1:24.

failing cause but that of a God whose cause will triumph. It is in that cause that we shall join, as God's co-workers.[24]

7.4 Is Revelation Still Possible?

In the history of theology the special nature of the revelation in the Bible has been emphasized time and again. Sometimes it is even stated that revelation ended when the last apostle died. This is, however, an unwarranted reduction of the work of God's Spirit in man. Charles Wackenheim states,

> With regard to this point, Christians would do well to familiarize themselves with the Jewish concept of revelation which associates God and man intimately in the act by which the latter appropriates the meaning which the text studied acquires for him here and now. From that moment on, revelation is no longer a one way communication, but a synergy between two agents that are certainly not equal, but are both indispensable for a word of faith to be born. ... Hence this unexpected and yet logical consequence: the activity of the believer is an integral part of revelation. We must, therefore, pass on from a unilateral and direct view of revelation to an interactive, indirect and mediated view.[25]

If God is silent, man must speak.[26] Divine silence is an invitation to speak in his name. The Spirit who guided the writers of the Bible is still at work in our times. Or if one prefers the Jewish approach, the mysterious voice from above (Bath Qol). The Spirit of God certainly did inspire the biblical writers,[27] but to be recognized as revelation, the Spirit must also be at work in the process of understanding Scripture as relevant for the here and now. This is why in many churches a prayer for the enlightenment by the Holy Spirit is said before the Bible is opened.

However, the Bible is a book that in its present form was closed almost two millennia ago. One cannot expect to find an-

---

[24]Wolterstorff 2003, 30.

[25]Our translation. French original: Wackenheim 2002, 71-72; see also 111-112. Wackenheim's thought is in line with Martin Buber's ideas, see Adams 2003, especially 65.

[26]Wackenheim 2002, 179-180.

[27]See Sections 5.1.2 and 5.2.2.2.

swers on all problems of modernity in it. Scripture may give modern believers impulses in the right direction, but it also may lead astray if people do not realize that its ethics and its comprehension of nature reflect a bygone time and culture. This is why it is important to listen to the creative voice of the Spirit which continues to accompany us up to our own times. As Gerhard Lohfink wrote,

> God acts continuously. He grants his Spirit unremittingly, so that Christendom will awake and perform its duty. He wants to act through us in the world. It depends totally on our willingness to listen to God – or do we prefer to close our ears and look away? Therewith the immense responsibility becomes clear, the independence and the freedom which God grants human beings. Ultimately the whole question which has occupied us here ends in the awesomeness of human freedom and responsibility.[28]

In a similar vein Rachel Muers writes,

> The gift of the Holy Spirit is the gift both of the promise that God will hear and of the "capacity for discernment and recognition" that accords with God's own act of discernment and recognition. The possibility of innerworldly transformation depends on both these gifts – being freed for responsible action before God and being enabled to understand the complexity of penultimate reality.[29]

We have seen that in several Psalms the supplicant seems to have reached an inner conviction that God had answered him.[30] Prophets and sages testify to divine illumination that forced them to speak in the name of God.[31] It is easy to dismiss such psychological processes as pure self-delusion. Jewish and Christian believers, however, will not exclude the possibility that in the course of earnest prayer God may suddenly grant them insight in the solution to their problems. From the viewpoint of reason God and his messages may seem illusory, but the Jewish psychiatrist Herman van Praag is right in observing that no human being can live

---

[28] Our translation. Original German: Lohfink 2008, 83-84.
[29] Muers 2004, 99. See also Armstrong 2009, 324.
[30] Cf. Section 6.2.2.2.
[31] Cf. Section 5.2.2.2.

by reason alone. Religious experience has an intrinsic and therapeutic value, especially in situations of severe psychic stress. For that reason he speaks of a 'noble illusion' (Van Praag 2008).

Similarly, the conviction that an outside voice has spoken to a prophet or has shown him or her a vision need not rest on deliberate self-delusion. Trained as we are to distrust such claims to visionary or auditory experiences, we may be inclined to regard them as pure inventions. However, modern social anthropology has established that genuine visionary experience does occur,[32] although in the end this will inevitably remain a verdict based on hearsay.

7.5 Bearing Witness to a Silent God

In a video recording called *Take your god and shove him* (August 21, 2008, on YouTube), the vociferous British atheist Pat Condell demanded from believers proof that will stand up in a court of law. This is exactly what the prophet speaking in Isa. 43:9-12 proposed to do long ago,

> [9] Let all the nations gather together,
>   and let the peoples assemble!
> Who among them will tell what is coming?
>   Let them make us hear first things!
> Let them give their witnesses to be justified,
>   so that one may hear and say: "It is true!"
> [10] You are my witnesses, declares the LORD,
>   and (you are) my Servant, whom I have chosen.
> So that you may know and believe me and will understand,
>   that I am the same One.
> Before me no god was formed,
>   nor will there be one after me.
> [11] I, I am the LORD,
>   and apart from me there is no savior.
> [12] It is I who told and saved and made heard,
>   and not a stranger who was among you.
> And you are my witnesses, declares the LORD,
>   that I am God.[33]

---

[32] Tiemeyer 2008, 574-578; see also Gnuse 1984, 5-10.

[33] See also 44:8. This summons echoes a long tradition of representing dia-

However, it is not easy to bear witness to an invisible God who remains silent. Most of this prophet's contemporaries had given up on God (Isa. 43:22-24).[34] What Condell wanted is a bench of independent, preferably agnostic judges. The problem with faith is that there cannot be a bench of judges, as in a courtroom, because ultimately only God himself is believed to be able to judge the trustworthiness of the witnesses. True, he is often a silent Judge, as capable judges are, most of the time. Unfortunately the case cannot be tried because the prosecutor will refuse to start proceedings since in his opinion there is no judge present.

However, what is certainly possible is to listen to the witnesses with the ears of a prosecutor, counselor or juror – the latter two as delegates of the Supreme Judge. In the case of Judaism and Christianity the testimony stretches over millennia and comprises millions of people. A formidable task indeed. Although in normal cases the number of witnesses declaring basically the same certainly is a factor of considerable importance,[35] the prosecution in this case will no doubt attempt to prove that they all have been 'brainwashed' . . .

As far as we know, no religion in the ancient world has been so acutely aware of the fact that they had (and have) to stand up as witnesses to their God as ancient Israel. The Law of Moses (Torah) is called a testimony,[36] written religious texts can serve as testimony,[37] all Israel is called to bear witness to him (Josh. 24:22; Isa. 43:10, 12; 44:8; 55:4).[38] Commenting on Isa. 43:12, the Tannaitic midrash *Sifre on Deuteronomy* makes God say,

---

logues between God and man in language partially borrowed from court proceedings. See e.g. Boecker 1964; Harvey 1967; Nielsen 1978. See also Josh. 24:22 and Ruth 4:9-11 which both may have been inspired by Second and Third Isaiah. See provisionally Korpel 2001, 232.

[34] For further examples see Korpel 2005b.

[35] Cf. Swinburne 2004, 341: 'The experience of so many people in their moments of religious vision corroborates what nature and history show to be quite likely – that there is a God who made and sustains man and the universe.'

[36] Deut. 4:45; 6:17, 20; Ps. 25:10; 78:56; 93:5 (?); 99:7; 119:2, 22, 24, 46, 59, 79, 95, 119, 125, 138, 146, 152, 167, 168; 132:12.

[37] Deut. 31:19, 21, 26; Isa. 8:16, 20; 30:8

[38] Cf. Korpel & De Moor 1998, 629-630, n. 2.

> When you are my witnesses, then I am God, and when you are not my witnesses, then, as it were, I am not God.[39]

'As it were ... ' – of course the rabbis did not make God's existence dependent on human testimony, but if the testimony would ever come to an end, it would *appear* as if God were non-existent. In the wake of the Hebrew tradition the New Testament emphasizes the importance of witnessing.[40] In Luke 24 Jesus concludes his talks with the two men from Emmaus with the words, 'You are witnesses of these things' (v. 48). The importance of witnessing is expanded in Acts 1:8 and 5:32, where all followers of Jesus are called to bear witness with the help of the Holy Spirit. Finally there is the impressive metaphor of the cloud of male and female witnesses described in the Letter to the Hebrews, Ch. 11.

Karl Barth has a beautiful passage on the difficult task of witnesses to God,

> In his word man hazards himself. And it is demanded of him that in his word he shall continually hazard himself to God's glory, coming out into the open as a partisan of God. ... God as the Lord of this history not only wants man to be the object of His action and the recipient of His blessings, but also to have him as a responsible partner. And the fact that He makes him responsible means also that He calls him to hazard himself to His honour, claiming his word as a word of witness to Him. In order that God's glory may shine forth, the history of the covenant must also be related, proclaimed and therefore imparted. Man is made responsible for this. As God wills man to be free before Him, He always has in view the freedom of those who have something to relate about Him, the freedom of confessors who cannot keep silence but must speak of Him, their freedom to expose themselves to His glory, to commit themselves to His honour with clear and definite words, to be serviceable to Him in and with these words, to be His declared and decided partisans.[41]

---

[39] Sifre on Deuteronomy, § 346, translation Neusner 1987. Original text Horovitz & Finkelstein 1939, 403-404. According to Pes. K., 12:6 (102b), the saying would stem from the 3th generation Tannaite R. Simeon b. Yoḥai.

[40] Cf. Rose 1994; Trites 2004.

[41] *ChD*, vol. 3/4, 75. Original text: Barth, *KD*, Bd. 3/4, 82. Elsewhere however, Barth significantly reduces this human partnership by stating that man is merely an *instrument* by which God speaks. So e.g. *KD*, Bd. 2/1, 221,

Stanley Hauerwas supports Barth's stance with regard to witnessing in contrast to natural theology that seeks to avoid such faith talk (Hauerwas 2002). In a world in which only rational logic is deemed acceptable this inevitably means that tough challenges have to be met by both Jews and Christians.

Walter Brueggemann who has built his *Theology of the Old Testament* around the concept of testimony and counter-testimony ends his book with a similar cautionary statement,

> Which witnesses are believed – concerning Yahweh or the gods 'beyond the River and in Egypt' – will determine the internal shape of the community. Which witnesses are believed – concerning Yahweh or the gods of the empire – will determine the shape of the world. Testimony to this particular, peculiar God, voiced in ways that are as odd as the God to which witness is borne, is characteristically offered from a position of vulnerability. This vulnerability, however, is not evidence against its veracity. The testimony is neither reductionist nor coercive. It is given in all its elusiveness and density, and then the witnesses await the decision of the court, while other testimony is given by other witnesses for other gods. The waiting is long and disconcerting, because witnesses to other gods are sometimes most formidable. And the jury only trickles in – here and there, now and then.[42]

It is the still unbroken chain of witnesses from Antiquity to our own days that makes Judaism and Christianity so special as compared to the far more sophisticated religious systems of ancient Egypt and Mesopotamia that rested on the arcane knowledge of a relatively small group of specialists. However, modernity is eroding the ability and willingness to bear witness to a silent God and ultimately the religions based on this vital testimony may disappear too, so that the words of Amos become true,

> Behold, the days are coming
> – declares the Lord GOD –
>   when I will send a hunger in the land;
> not a hunger for bread,
>   and not a thirst for water,

249-50. Similarly Levinas 2000, 196-197.

[42] Brueggemann 1997, 750. See also Goldingay 2005, 215-249.

> but for hearing the words of the LORD.
> And people will roam from sea to sea,
>   and from north to south,
> they will wander around aimlessly,
>   searching for the word of the LORD,
>   but they will not find it (Amos 8:11-12).

7.6 The Courage to Become a Witness

So it is not easy to speak on behalf of God. The voice of many a witness falters. Witnessing is always taking a risk. Barristers and judges will try to cast doubt on the reliability of the testimony. Especially if the testimony cannot be substantiated by physical evidence and merely rests on what one *believes* to have seen or heard, speaking up in court requires courage.

The prophets of biblical times faced the same opposition and ridicule, especially if they dared to speak up against the ruling class. They too often became tired of having to testify in a hostile world. The prophet known as Second Isaiah observed this apathy among his compatriots who suffered under Babylonian rule,

> The Lord GOD gives me a tongue of disciples
>   to know how to make witnesses those too tired for words.
> Morning by morning he wakens,
>   he wakens my ear
>   to hear like disciples do.
>
> The Lord GOD opens my ear,
>   and I do not resist,
>   I do not move backwards (Isa. 50:4-5).[43]

The prophet hopes that by passing on the message of his divine Teacher he will be able to encourage others to overcome their exhaustion (see also Isa. 40:28-31).

In a world of disbelievers and sometimes fanatic adherents to other religions, believers who testify to their faith have similar experiences. As Barth wrote, 'In his word man hazards himself.'[44]

---

[43] For details on the translation of this passage see Korpel & De Moor 1998, 448.

[44] One does not have to speak in the literal sense of the word. When John

294   CHAPTER SEVEN

It is tempting to escape from confrontation by adopting the doctrine of two separate worlds, the spiritual world of faith, and the ordinary world where 'reason' is said to reign. In the first a person bears witness among his or her fellow believers, in the second he or she keeps silent about faith because of working with a different set of rules.

With Bonhoeffer we reject such a dual system.[45] In this book we have tried to demonstrate that the witnesses who were responsible for the biblical testimony participated in the world in which they lived, often sharing religious views with their neighbors, at other times rebutting them. In our opinion the same courageous attitude befits our times. But nobody should be ashamed if in certain situations words fail to come. Nobody can deny the singer of Psalm 119 piety, but even he, steeped as he was in the teaching of the LORD, feared that at the crucial moment the right words to rebut his opponents would fail him if God would not help him (Ps. 119:32-43). In the New Testament Jesus promises his followers that he will lay the right words in their mouth (through the Holy Spirit) if they themselves feel unsure what to answer under interrogation.[46]

7.7   The Integrity of Witnesses

If making the word of God heard relies on human witnesses, the question of their trustworthiness inevitably crops up. We have seen that from the very beginning there has existed doubt about the truthfulness of those asserting to speak the word of God.[47] Therefore, if in our days someone assumes the role of a spokesman or spokeswoman of God, it is only normal that such a claim generates skepticism. Often the integrity of the person involved is called into question. That this is warranted we want to illustrate with one example.

Paul II (Karol Jósef Woytiła) became unable to speak at the end of his long life his wordless appearance in the window of the apostolic palace was understood as an act of witnessing (Mancini 2008, 7-8).

[45] Cf. Section 1.6.2.1. For a convenient summary of Bonhoeffer's views in this respect, see Dramm 2007, esp. Chapters 6 and 20.

[46] Mt. 10:19-20; Mk 13:11; Lk. 12:11-12; 21:14-15.

[47] Cf. Section 5.2.2.

In 1936 Edwin Erich Dwinger published a book entitled *Und Gott schweigt...? Bericht und Aufruf* ('And God keeps silent...? Report and appeal'). In it he describes the atrocities and the mismanagement of the communist regime under Stalin.

> How can God speak if man keeps silent? Isn't the contemporary Russia a much more convincing proof in favor of God than that it could be proof against him? Because this would never have been possible in a country in which people believe in something divine in man – is all the suffering not also the first punishment for the fact that they cold-heartedly abjured faith? No, his silence is absolutely no evidence against his existence, God had never any other possibility than manifest himself in his human creatures. If they do not make him visible, in what form would he become visible then?[48]

Dwinger was an expert on Russia and one of the few who in the thirties of the twentieth century were warning against the massacres that were taking place under Stalin. Millions of victims did not prompt any serious reaction from the West. At first sight, his appeal to bear witness against this mass murder sounds sympathetic. However, in hindsight it is absolutely clear that his motivation was by no means religious. Dwinger was a Nazi who used religion as a thin varnish over his political conviction that only as a totalitarian state subjected to one national-socialistic will Europe could survive.[49]

This example shows that the decision to speak words of God is a *moral* one. Believers have to ask themselves honestly, 'Is it a word of *God* I am going to speak? Or will I speak what I myself or what others want to hear?' How difficult it is to distinguish the inner voice of God's Spirit from that of one's own spirit was demonstrated by Psalm 51 and the self-doubt of prophets.[50] Isa. 30:21 describes the voice of God instructing the believer to go in the right direction as a voice 'from behind'.[51] The Teacher cannot

---

[48] Our translation. Original German: Dwinger 1936, 150-151. Similar passages on 105, 115, 119.
[49] Unabashedly so Dwinger 1936, 153.
[50] Cf. Section 5.1.2.
[51] *Ibidem.*

be seen at that moment, but in a flash his voice can be recognized – if one is acquainted with him.

But what if people listen more to themselves and manipulate the facts to suit their own goals? Knowingly or unknowingly? We all know this happens. In ordinary life we are prone to embellish accounts of events we witnessed. This also occurs in legal procedures that rest not on forensic evidence, but on the testimony of witnesses. In such cases we have to submit ourselves willingly to the most rigorous tests available. After all, also in the non-religious world provisions against false testimony were severe in Antiquity,[52] and in most countries still are. Mere appeal to illumination by the Spirit is insufficient, as Ezekiel (Ezek. 13:3) and the early Christians realized.[53]

Self-delusion is a risk all who are believing to speak the word of God should be aware of. In his movie *Breaking the Waves* (1996) the controversial Danish film director Lars von Trier tried to demonstrate once again that under circumstances good people can feel compelled to do things that are commonly deemed bad. The main character of the film, Bess McNeill, comes from a strictly orthodox church. She often prays to God, especially for the recovery of her husband Jan who shortly after their marriage has become paralyzed by an accident on an oil rig. In a low voice she herself mutters God's answers to her prayers. Jan, no longer able to have intercourse, asks her to have sex with other men and describe it to him afterwards. He assures Bess this will keep him alive. At first, she adamantly refuses, but when she believes God says the same as Jan, she reluctantly agrees. With each act of promiscuity she performs Jan's health improves. In spite of strong disapproval of her mother and the elders of her church, Bess slowly begins to believe that what she is doing is the will of God. To her sister-in-law she justifies her acceptance of Jan's proposal, 'He is my husband and God has said that I must honor him.' In church she asks God, 'Dear Father, what's going on?' But this time no word of God comes from her lips and in despair

---

[52] Ponchia 2009, 227-228, with earlier literature. For Israel, Exod. 20:16; Deut. 5:20.

[53] Acts 18:24–19:7; 1 Cor. 12:10; 14:29; Gal. 5:16-25; 1 Thess. 5:19-21; 1 Jn 4:1.

she calls out, 'Father, where are you?' On her final trip to a ship offshore which other prostitutes shun because of earlier violent incidents she prays again. This time God does reply, assuring her that He will be with her. But upon arrival she is brutally gang raped and finally dies in hospital. Jan at this point miraculously makes an almost full recovery.

Von Trier deliberately creates the impression that Bess' ultimate sacrifice was approved by God. The spectator, however, knows that Jan's proposal was immoral[54] and that Bess only deluded herself when she muttered God's consent to herself. She should have stood firm by her initial refusal instead of submitting to sexual abuse. But isn't such an act of witnessing against one's mortally ill beloved more than can be expected from a compassionate human being? During her burial at sea heavenly church bells seem to indicate God's approval of her choice. But wasn't God himself implicated in her decision? As in many of his other movies, Von Trier succeeds in demonstrating how difficult it is to choose between good and bad. The case of Bess shows that absolute honesty is imperative if one makes an appeal to divine illumination.

For Levinas bearing witness has everything to do with ethics, with doing justice to one's neighbor.[55] Although we cannot accept his view that God is absent in the relationship with the other and that no dialogue with the Infinite is possible,[56] it is certainly true that in ethical behavior human beings bear witness to God.

'A voice from behind' can also be taken as a voice from the past, the word of God as it was spoken by countless past generations witnessing to the truth of his message. The Word of God, as codified in the Bible, in the form of whatever canon one accepts as authoritative, always has to be explained and actualized for the present. But the wisdom of millennia of believers has to be taken into account. Biblical interpretation is a cumulative process. The role of tradition in the interpretation of Scripture is

---

[54] Jan himself admits that he asked this for his own sake, not for hers.

[55] Levinas 1993, 227-230, quoting Jer. 22:15-16 and Mt. 25:31-40; Levinas 2000, 198-201. On Levinas's problematic, yet promising concept of ethics see Purcell 2006; Perpich 2008.

[56] Cf. Sections 1.3.2.5 and 1.6.2.3.

accepted in Judaism as well as in the Catholic and Eastern Orthodox churches. Protestant churches were always wary of attaching too much weight to tradition, but they too have their heroes of faith and decisions by synods which they regard as authoritative. However, since the Second Vatican Council points of view in this respect are clearly converging.[57]

If we accept that the word of God is usually mediated by human beings, the 'voice from behind' can also be someone looking over your shoulder: a friend, a colleague, a partner. Or even a whole community of believers standing behind you. It has always been the custom, both in Judaism and Christianity, to discuss difficult matters arising from faith together.[58] In the Jewish tradition there is an acute awareness that often such problems cannot be resolved in any definitive way, so that it is better to allow different opinions to exist next to each other than to fix a decision once and for all in a dogma.

Summing up, the integrity of witnesses must always be tested, first of all by critical and honest self-examination, then by observing the witness' attitude towards others, and finally by comparing the testimony to what has been accepted as words of God by previous generations, first of all the Bible itself – but always aware of the danger of a fundamentalist use of Scripture. Exegesis should always remain open-ended, open to new solutions in different times, as Jesus has stated according to the gospel of Matthew,

> Therefore every scribe who has been trained for the kingdom of heaven is like a householder who brings out of his treasure what is new and what is old (Mt. 13:52).

7.8 Theodicy

If it is admissible to challenge human witnesses to the word of God, is it also acceptable to repudiate the Judge himself if he remains silent when innocent people suffer under disasters or violence? Answers to this question differ and did so from Antiquity

---

[57] See, for example, Flesseman-Van Leer 1980, 38-40.

[58] It may be noted that a minimum of two witnesses was required in Antiquity, cf. CAD (Š) 2, 394; Deut. 17:6; 19:15, Mt. 18:16, cf. Num. 35:30. For this reason messengers usually travelled in pairs.

on, both in and outside Israel.⁵⁹ One of the modern answers is that there cannot be an all-powerful good God if he allows so much undeserved suffering in this world. Why did he remain silent during the Shoah,⁶⁰ or at the time of the 2004 Indian Ocean tsunami, or when Haiti was hit by the 2009 earthquake?

It is questionable if the dogmatic concept of God's absolute omnipotence that is at the basis of the argument of people who reject the possibility of theodicy⁶¹ is really found in the Bible. The divine epithet παντοκράτωρ (*Pantocrator*), 'Almighty', is the Septuagint's rendering of Hebrew words that do by no means indicate that God was seen as all-powerful.⁶² The New Testament takes over this epithet from the Septuagint, but outside the Book of Revelation, it occurs only once in the New Testament (2 Cor. 6:18), to underline that the preceding verses are quotations based on the Greek version of the Hebrew Bible.

The texts traditionally cited as supporting the doctrine of the all-powerfulness of God are inconclusive at best. Gen. 18:14; Jer. 32:27 and Zech. 8:6 do state that nothing is impossible with God, but all three texts show that He lets himself be influenced by human wishes and behavior. Surely God is able to kill and make alive,⁶³ can create both light and darkness, peace and evil (Isa. 45:7),⁶⁴ but the context shows that his choice may be influenced by human choices.⁶⁵ Even Job admits grudgingly that God can realize anything he wants (Job 42:2), but the mere fact that according to the canonical version of the Book of Job God has finally responded to Job's complaints proves that eventually he is willing to give in to the power of persistent human argument. When the Psalmists exclaim that their God can do anything that

---

[59] Crenshaw 1983; 2005; Jonas 1984; Oelmüller 1999, 93-104; Laato & De Moor 2003; Dietrich & Link 2004; Ehrman 2008.

[60] We prefer to use this Hebrew word meaning 'Destruction' over the better-known designation 'Holocaust'.

[61] Cf. e.g. Jonas 1984; Kreiner 1997; Baucke-Ruegg 1998.

[62] Cf. Michaelis 1938, 914; Dietrich & Link 2004, 24-25.

[63] Deut. 32:39, etc. Cf. Sanders 1996, 239-240, 420-421.

[64] See on the history of interpretation of this text Laato & De Moor 2003, xxvi, n. 52.

[65] Especially Isa. 45:20-25. See also Gen. 2:17; 3:5; 18:16-33; Deut. 30:15; 32:29, 46; Amos 3, etc.

pleases him (Ps. 115:3; 135:6), their clear presupposition is that he will continue to bless Israel (Ps. 115:9-15; 135:4, 12, 14). He has willingly given up the earth to the human race (Gen. 1:26; Ps. 8:5-7; 115:16). When king Nebuchadnezzar extols God's power both in heaven an on earth (Dan. 4:35), God relents and restores his health (Dan. 4:36). According to Mt. 19:26 Jesus has said 'with God all things are possible'. This is in answer to his disciples' dismay over the difficulty to enter the Kingdom of God, so it has evidently to do with God's grace – he may relent and admit sinners. Indeed Eph. 1:19 speaks of 'the immeasurable greatness of his power' but it is a power that works 'in us who believe' and therefore does not transcend human capabilities. In theory, God *is* all-powerful, but he prefers the good and not the bad. He has willingly given up some of his power to human beings. Especially in the covenant with his people Israel God voluntary committed himself and accepted certain conditional obligations. But in granting humanity the freedom to ignore his conditions, God himself accepted the risk of suffering (Jonas 1984, 25-26).

If according to the biblical testimony God has left room for human initiative, there remains little reason to accuse him of arbitrary silence in the face of suffering. Moreover, it makes a big difference if one realizes that actually an answer must be awaited from those who in any particular era are called upon to act as God's witnesses – to be sure, *God*'s witnesses, i.e. listening to the 'voice from behind', or whatever designation one wants to use for divine guidance.

It is not warranted to apply biblical rules and examples to the present world without realizing that they were meant for a world two, three thousand years ago that admittedly was in many respects practically the same as ours, but in many other respects totally different. Those who nevertheless try to eliminate the latter in order to cling to a set of 'clear' ethical rules inevitably come down to some form of anachronistic fundamentalism. What was a reasonable explanation or even wise solution in the distant past need not be so now anymore.

An example may serve to elucidate this. In biblical times nobody would have understood the mechanism of plate tectonics. It was discovered only about a century ago and even now is not fully understood. So it is unreasonable to expect that the Bible would have explained the origin of earthquakes, volcanic eruptions and tsunamis in rational terms and to demand that *if* God exists he should have prevented these natural phenomena to kill hundreds of thousands of people. In biblical times such natural disasters were explained in terms that were understandable then and there, e.g. as acts of divine wrath because of the depravity of human beings.[66] Within the horizon of its time this may have been a 'logical' explanation. Other peoples in the ancient world explained earthquakes in similar terms. We, however, cannot accept such explanations anymore. Instead we might contemplate the fact that the constant renewal of our planet by the very same mechanism of plate tectonics has been proved to be beneficial to millions of lives on earth because it produces essential minerals and fertile soil.[67] Of course this offers little comfort to the relatives of the hundreds of thousands of victims, but it makes it difficult to accuse God of arbitrariness and unwarranted silence. And certainly it is no conclusive evidence for his non-existence.

If it is inevitable that innocent people suffer, God himself may well be speechless for sorrow and regret, and his inability to do something about it.[68] According to both the Hebrew Bible and the New Testament there are occasions when God suffers because of the sorry fate or the sinful behavior of human beings.[69]

---

[66] Gen. 6:5-6; 2 Sam. 22:8 [= Ps. 18:8]; Isa. 13:13; 24:18; 29:6; 64:1; Jer. 4:23-26; 10:22; 51:29; Ezek. 38:19-20; Joel 4:16[3:16]; Amos 1:1 ('an act of divine judgment', Lessing 2009, 48); 9:5; Mic. 1:4-5; Nah. 1:5; Hab. 3:6; Hag. 2:7; Rev. 11:8-13; 16:17-21. In historical times no volcanic eruptions have taken place in the Holy Land, but people concluded from solidified lava that the rocks must have molten in the past and might melt again.

[67] We leave aside here the question if this is the result of chaotic randomness or intelligent design.

[68] We found that this is one of the reasons why deities in the ancient world might remain silent. Cf. Section 6.2.1.4. The bidirectional nature of the covenantal relation between God and his people implies that he may reconsider a previous decision when he sees the suffering and/or remorse it caused. Cf. Korpel 1990; 180-181; Jeremias 2002; Dietrich & Link 2004, 144-194; Döhling 2009.

[69] For grief on the part of God see e.g. Gen. 6:6; 1 Sam. 15:11, 35 (despite 15:29, on which cf. Tsumura 2007, 407); Isa. 1:14; Lam. 1:5. See on Neh. 9:30, Batten 1913, 370: 'a long-suffering God gave them many years of grace'. For

Several laments in the Book of Jeremiah may be understood as expressions of sorrow not by the prophet, but by God himself, even though it is obviously the prophet who has to put God's lament into words.[70] One of the convincing cases is Jer. 14:17-18,

> And you shall say to them these words:
>   My eyes stream with tears, night and day,
>   and they cannot cease,
>   for the young daughter of my people has been hit
>   with a great affliction,
>   a sickening blow!
>   If I go out into the field,
>   behold, men pierced by the sword,
>   and if I enter the city,
>   behold, men weakened by famine! [71]

According to Jer. 13:17 God may weep in secret. When his chosen people suffers, he suffers with them (Isa. 63:9). This does not mean that those suffering have to bear God's taciturnity in meek silence (Isa. 62:7; 64:11[12]), but there are situations when God's messengers have no divine message to relay that would explain what happened. Human beings are also unable to help God resolve his impossible dilemma with regard to the plate tectonics until one day they will be allowed to predict earthquakes and volcanic eruptions reliably. Modern believers see the discoveries of science as a form of progressive revelation in line with the biblical concept of creation as a continuing process.[72] Meanwhile, however, they can help God by falling back on his earlier commandments with regard to the obligation to show compassion and provide support to the needy. In this respect they will find people entertaining totally different convictions at their side[73]

---

grief of the Holy Spirit see Isa. 63:10; Eph. 4:30.

[70] Roberts 1992; Dietrich & Link 2004, 281-283.

[71] Even rather conservative commentators simply state that the opening line in which the prophet is addressed must be regarded as an inappropriate editorial expansion that should be ignored. This is an unwarranted assumption. Exactly the same introductory formula occurs in Jer. 13:12. Similar cases of divine lament are Jer. 8:18-21; 12:7-9. However, Jer. 4:19-22 is less likely, cf. Korpel 2009b.

[72] Cf. Becking & Korpel 2010.

[73] For example Bart Ehrmann 2008, 277-278.

which demonstrates that one should not wait too long for divine enlightenment in cases of emergency.

If human beings are required to speak the word of God, the tormented question why God remained silent during horrendous crimes like genocide, above all the Shoah, boils down to the question why so few believers protested publicly against such barbarism. No doubt it was partly fear that prevented them from obeying 'the voice from behind', but probably selfishness played a role too, even though that is a vice in all major monotheistic religions.

7.9 Believers and Unbelievers

To state that God is silent amounts to saying that his messengers, angelic or human, are unable to speak in his name. In our era this is increasingly the case. We have seen that also those who dared to speak the word of God in the past often encountered disbelief and ridicule, or felt incapable of assuming the role of spokesmen of God any longer, either temporarily or permanently. If a divine origin is claimed for certain messages or events acceptance of this as true always rests on faith. However, faith is not something one can appropriate. According to the Bible faith is a gift (Eph. 2:8), like the Spirit that compels people to speak the word of God.[74] Others who witness the same phenomena may well maintain that they have seen or heard nothing. Or may reject the testimony of believers. Or interpret it in a totally different way.

This diversity of possible reactions is expressed by the Dutch painter Cornelis Saftleven (*c.* 1607–1681) in his painting of the annunciation of the birth of Christ as narrated in Luke 2.[75] Most adults look up in adoration, but one on the left is fast asleep and another shepherd is starting to run away. One dog sleeps on like his master, another looks up in surprise. One child finds the painter far more interesting than the angels. Another child looks on very skeptically.

---

[74]Num. 11:25, 29; Isa. 42:1; Ezek. 11:19; 36:26; 37:14; Qoh. 12:7; Lk. 11:13; Jn 7:39; 20:22; Acts 2:38; 5:32; 8:18-19; 10:45; 19:2; Rom. 5:5; 2 Cor. 1:22; 5:5; 11:4; Gal. 3:2, 14; Eph. 1:17; 2 Tim. 1:7; 1 Jn 3:24; 4:13.

[75]See for a reproduction in color: http://www.rijksmuseum.nl/assetimage.jsp?id=SK-A-801.

Apparently Saftleven wanted to express the different reactions to angelic manifestations, ranging from disbelief and indifference to adoration. Even if one is an eyewitness to an extraorinary event and hears the words of an 'angel' speaking in the name of God it still requires faith to accept what happens as divine revelation. Saftleven has painted the resulting divergence of opinion with a certain cheerful resignation, as is demonstrated by the naughty little cherub crawling from under the robe of the angel. Such a relaxed attitude might be helpful to mitigate the tension surrounding the debate about the question whether God is forever silent or not. A debate that is not likely to end soon, since believers and unbelievers are quarreling about a speaking or silent God already more than 4000 years ...

Picture on the opposite page: Cornelis Saftleven, The Annunciation to the Shepherds (*c.* 1630, Rijksmuseum, Amsterdam). Most adults look up in adoration, but one on the left is fast asleep, like his dog, and unlike the dog on the right. Another shepherd is starting to run away. One child finds the painter far more interesting than the angels, another child looks on very skeptically.

EPILOGUE

ABBREVIATIONS

All abbreviations of series, handbooks and journals in this book are according to: S.M. Schwertner, *Internationales Abkürzungsverzeichnis für Theologie und Grenzgebiete*, Berlin ²1992 (= S.M. Schwertner, *Theologische Realenzyklopädie: Abkürzungsverzeichnis*, Berlin/New York ²1994). For Judaic literature abbreviations current in English are used. In addition the following abbreviations occur.

ALASP	Abhandlungen zur Literatur Alt-Syrien-Palästinas (Ugarit-Verlag: Münster).
CHANE	Culture and History of the Ancient Near East (Brill: Leiden).
ChD	K. Barth, *The Church Dogmatics*, Vol. 1/1 (§§ 1-12), Edinburgh: T&T Clark, 1975; Vol. 1/2 (§§ 13-24), Edinburgh: T&T Clark, 1956; Vol. 2/1 (§§ 25-31), Edinburgh: T&T Clark, 1957; Vol. 2/2 (§§ 32-39), Edinburgh: T&T Clark, 1957; Vol. 3/1 (§§ 40-42), Edinburgh: T&T Clark, 1958; Vol. 3/2 (§§ 43-47), Edinburgh: T&T Clark, 1960; Vol. 3/3 (§§ 48-51), Edinburgh: T&T Clark, 1960; Vol. 3/4 (§§ 52-56), Edinburgh: T&T Clark, 1961; Vol. 4/1 (§§ 57-63), Edinburgh: T&T Clark, 1956; Vol. 4/2 (§§ 64-68), Edinburgh: T&T Clark, 1958; Vol. 4/3 (§§ 69-73), Edinburgh: T&T Clark, 1961; Vol. 4/4 (Fragment), Edinburgh: T&T Clark, 1969.
CoS	W.W. Hallo (ed.), *The Context of Scripture*, 3 vols, Brill: Leiden, 1997-2002.
ETCSL	The Electronic Text Corpus of Sumerian Literature: http://etcsl.orinst.ox.ac.uk/.
Fs.	*Festschrift.*
HeBSt	Herders Biblische Studien (Herder: Freiburg i.B.).
HCOT	The Historical Commentary on the Old Testament (Kok: Kampen / Peeters: Leuven).
HThK.AT	Herder's Theologische Kommentar: Altes Testament (Herder: Freiburg i.B.).
JHS	The Journal of Hebrew Scriptures (online).

KD	K. Barth, *Die kirchliche Dogmatik*, Bd. 1/1-4/4, Zürich: Theologischer Verlag Zürich, 1980.
KTU	M. Dietrich, O. Loretz & J. Sanmartín, *The Cuneiform Alphabetic Texts from Ugarit, Ras Ibn Hani and Other Places* (KTU: second, enlarged edition), Neukirchen: Ugarit-Verlag, 1995.
NICOT	The New International Commentary on the Old Testament (Grand Rapids: Eerdmans).
NIDOTTE	W.A. van Gemeren (ed.), *New International Dictionary of the Old Testament Theology and Exegesis*, 5 vols, Carlisle: Paternoster Press, 1996.
PredOT	De Prediking van het Oude Testament (Callenbach: Nijkerk).
SAA	State Archives of Assyria (Helsinki: University Press).
SAAS	State Archives of Assyria Studies (Helsinki: University Press).
SBL.WAW	Society of Biblical Literature: Writings from the Ancient World (Atlanta: SBL).
SEL	*Studi Epigrafici e Linguistici sul Vicino Oriente antico* (Verona: CSIC).
SHANE	Studies in the History of the Ancient Near East (Leiden: Brill).
SHCANE	Studies in the History and Culture of the Ancient Near East (Leiden: Brill).
TUAT	O. Kaiser (ed.), *Texte aus der Umwelt des Alten Testaments*, 5 Bde, Gütersloher Verlagshaus: Gütersloh, 1982-2001.
TUAT-NF	B. Janowski & G. Wilhelm (eds), *Texte aus der Umwelt des Alten Testaments: Neue Folge*, Bd. 1– , Gütersloher Verlagshaus: Gütersloh, 2004– .
Univ.	University.
UTR	Utrechtse Theologische Reeks (Utrecht: Universiteit).
WBC	Word Biblical Commentary (Waco: Word Books).

BIBLIOGRAPHY

Aaron 2002 – D.H. Aaron, *Biblical Ambiguities: Metaphor, Semantics, and Divine Imagery*, Boston: Brill (original publication: Leiden: Brill, 2001).

Abusch 1987 – I.T Abusch, *Babylonian Witchcraft Literature* (BJSt, 132), Atlanta: Scholars Press.

Abusch & Van der Toorn 1999 – T. Abusch & K. van der Toorn, *Mesopotamian Magic: Textual, Historical, and Interpretative Perspectives* (Ancient Magioc and Divination, 1), Groningen: Styx.

Achino-Loeb 2006 – M.-L. Achino-Loeb (ed.), *Silence: The Currency of Power*, New York: Berghahn.

Adams 2003 – R.M. Adams, 'The Silence of God in the Thought of Martin Buber', *Philosophia* 30, 50-68.

Aḥituv 2008 – S. Aḥituv, *Echoes from the Past: Hebrew and Cognate Inscriptions from the Biblical Period*, Jerusalem: Carta.

Ahn & Dietrich 1997 – G. Ahn & M. Dietrich (eds), *Engel und Dämonen: Theologische, anthropologische und religionsgeschichtliche Aspekte des Guten und Bösen* (Forschungen zur Anthropologie und Religionsgeschichte, 29), Münster: Ugarit-Verlag.

Ajarai 2008 – H. Ajarai, 'Een plek om even tot rust te komen', *NRC/Handelsblad*, 2 juli 2008, 14.

Albrektson 1967 – B. Albrektson, *History and the Gods: An Essay on the Idea of Historical Events as Divine Manifestations in the Ancient Near East and in Israel*, Lund: CWK Gleerup.

Allen 2005 – J.-A. Allen, *You Only Think God Is Silent: Hearing God in the Defining Moments of our Lives*, Mustang: Tate.

Alkier & Witte 2004 – S. Alkier & M. Witte (eds.), *Die Griechen und das antike Israel: Interdisziplinäre Studien zur Religions- und Kulturgeschichte des Heiligen Landes* (OBO, 201), Fribourg: Academic Press.

Alster 1991 – B. Alster, 'Incantation to Utu', *Acta Sumerologica* 13, 27-96.

Alster 1997 – B. Alster, *Proverbs of Ancient Sumer: The World's Earliest Proverb Collections*, 2 vols, Bethesda: CDL.

Altenmüller 1977 – H. Altenmüller, 'Geheimnis', *LÄ*, Bd. 2, Wiesbaden: Harrassowitz, 510-513.

Altenmüller 2009 – H. Altenmüller, 'Gott und die Götter im alten Ägypten: Gedanken zur persönlichen Frömmigkeit', in: Hartenstein & Rösel 2009, 17-58.

Alter 2007 – R. Alter, *The Book of Psalms*, New York: W.W. Norton & Company.

Anderson 1978 – R. Anderson, *The Silence of God*, Grand Rapids: Kregel (original publication: London: Hodder and Stoughton, 1897).

Andrae 1913 – W. E. Andrae, *Die Stelenreihen in Assur* (WVDOG, 24), Leipzig : Hinrichs.

Angerstorfer 1979 – A. Angerstorfer, *Der Schöpfergott des Alten Testaments: Herkunft und Bedeutungsentwicklung des hebräischen Terminus brʾ (bara) 'schaffen'* (RSTh, 20), Frankfurt a.M.: Lang.

Angier 2006 – T.P.S. Angier, *Either Kierkegaard/Or Nietzsche: Moral Philosophy in a New Key* (Intersections: Continental and Analytic Philosophy), Hants: Ashgate.

Aristotle 1926 – Aristotle, *The 'Art' of Rhetoric*, transl. J.H. Freese ((Loeb Classical Library), Cambridge: Harvard Univ. Press.

Aristotle 1932 – Aristotle, *The Poetics*, transl. W. Hamilton Fyfe (Loeb Classical Library), Cambridge: Harvard Univ. Press.

Armstrong 2009 – K. Armstrong, *The Case for God*, New York: Knopf.

Arnaud 2007 – D. Arnaud, *Corpus des textes de bibliothèque de Ras Shamra-Ougarit (1936-2000) en sumerien, babylonien et assyrien* (Aula Orientalis, Supplements, 23), Sabadell-Barcelona: Ausa.

Assmann 1979 – J. Assmann, 'Primat und Transzendenz: Struktur und Genese der ägyptischen Vorstellung eines "Höchsten Wesens" ', in: W. Westendorf (ed.), *Aspekte der spätägyptischen Religion*, Wiesbaden: Harrassowitz, 7-42.

Assmann 1983 – J. Assmann, 'Die Rubren in der Überlieferung der Sinuhe-Erzählung', in: M. Görg (ed.), *Fontes atque Pontes: Eine Festgabe für H. Brunner* (ÄAT, 5), Wiesbaden: Harrassowitz, 18-41.

Assmann 1984 – J. 'Reden und Schweigen', *LÄ*, Bd. 5, Wiesbaden: Harrassowitz, 195-201.

Assmann 1990 – J. Assmann, *Maʿat: Gerechtigkeit und Unsterblichkeit im Alten Ägypten*, München.

Assmann 1999 – J. Assmann, *Ägyptische Hymnen und Gebete* (OBO), Freiburg: Universitäts-Verlag, 2nd ed.

Bailey 1991 – C. Bailey, *Bedouin Poetry from Sinai and the Negev: A Mirror of Culture*, Oxford: Clarendon Press.

Balentine 1983 – S.E. Balentine, *The Hidden God: The Hiding of the Face of God in the Old Testament*, Oxford: Oxford Univ. Press.

Barr 1993 – J. Barr, *Biblical Faith and Natural Theology: The Gifford Lectures for 1991, Delivered in the University of Edinburgh*, Oxford: Oxford Univ. Press.

Barr 1999 – J. Barr, *The Concept of Biblical Theology: An Old Testament Perspective*, London: SCM Press.

Barrado 1997 – P. Barrado, 'El silencio en el Antiguo Testamento', *EstB* 55, 5-27.

Barta 1971 – W. Barta, 'Zu einigen Textpassagen der Prophezeiung des Neferti', *MDAIK* 27, 35-45.

Barta 1980 – W. Barta, 'Königsberufung', *LÄ*, Bd. 3, Wiesbaden: Harrassowitz, 475-477.

Barth, *The Church Dogmatics*: see Abbreviations.

Barth 1940 – K. Barth, *Der Römerbrief*, Zollikon-Zürich: Evangelischer Verlag, repr. of the sixth edition.

Barth 1968 – K. Barth, *The Epistle to the Romans*, tr. Edwyn C. Hoskyns, Oxford: Oxford Univ. Press, cited after the reprint 1968.

Barthélemy 1982 – D. Barthélemy, *Critique textuelle de l'Ancien Testament*, t. 1 (OBO, 50/1), Fribourg: Éditions universitaires.

Barthélemy 1992 – D. Barthélemy, *Critique textuelle de l'Ancien Testament*, t. 3 (OBO, 50/3), Fribourg: Éditions universitaires.

Basson 2006 – A. Basson, *Divine Metaphors in Selected Hebrew Psalms of Lamentation* (FAT, 215), Tübingen: Mohr Siebeck.

Batten 1913 – L.W. Batten, *The Books of Ezra and Nehemiah* (ICC), Edinburgh: T. & T. Clark.

Batto 1987 – B. F. Batto, 'The Sleeping God: An Ancient Near Eastern Motif of Divine Sovereignty', *Bib* 68, 153-177.

Baucke-Ruegg 1998 – J. Baucke-Ruegg, *Die Allmacht Gottes: Systematisch-theologische Erwägungen zwischen Metaphysik, Postmoderne und Poesie* (TBT, 96), Berlin: De Gruyter.

Bauckham 1993 – R. Bauckham, *The Climax of Prophecy: Studies on the Book of Revelation.* Edinburgh: T&T Clark.

Baumann 1974 – A. Baumann, דמה II / דמם / דום, ThWAT, Bd. 2, Stuttgart: Kohlhammer, 277-83.

Bayer 2001 – O. Bayer, 'Zur Theologie der Klage', *JBTh* 16, 289-301.

Beal 2002 – R. Beal, 'Hittite Oracles', in: L. Ciraolo & J. Seidel (eds), *Magic and Divination in the Ancient World*, Leiden: Brill-Styx, 57-81.

Beckett 1952 – S.[B.] Beckett, *En attendant Godot*, Paris: Les Éditions de Minuit.

Beckett 2004 – S.[B.] Beckett, *Waiting for Godot: A Tragicomedy*, Revised Acting edition (1965), revised edition London: Samuel French.

Becking 1987 – B. Becking, 'A Remark on a Post–Exilic Seal', *UF* 18, 445-6.

Becking 2004 – B. Becking, *Between Fear and Freedom: Essays on the Interpretation of Jeremiah 30–31* (OTS, 51), Leiden: Brill.

Becking 2007 – B. Becking, *From David to Gedaliah: The Book of Kings as Story and History* (OBO, 228), Fribourg: Academic Press.

Becking 2008 – B. Becking, 'Psalm 121: Het verhaal van een ontgoochelde pelgrim,' in: B. Becking & A. Merz (eds), *Verhaal als Identiteits-Code: Opstellen aangeboden aan Geert van Oyen bij zijn afscheid van de Universiteit Utrecht* (UTR, 60), Utrecht: Universiteit, 40-51.

Becking 2009 – B. Becking, 'Means of Revelation in the Book of Jeremiah', in: H.M. Barstad & R.G. Kratz (eds), *Prophecy in the Book of Jeremiah* (BZAW, 388), Berlin: De Gruyter, 33-47.

Becking & Korpel 2010 – B. Becking & M.C.A. Korpel, 'To Create, to Separate or to Construct: An Alternative for a Recent Proposal as to the Interpretration of ברא in Gen 1:1–2:4a', *JHS* 10, Article 3, 1-21.

Becking & Sanders 2010 – B. Becking & P. Sanders, 'De inscriptie uit Khirbet Qeiyafa: een vroege vorm van sociaal besef in oud Israël?', *NedThT* 64, 238-252.

Beeman 2006 – W.O. Beeman, 'Silence in Music', in: Achino-Loeb 2006, 23-34.

Begg 1992 – T. Begg, 'Inquire of God', in: D.N. Freedman (ed.), *The Anchor Bible Dictionary*, vol. 3, New York: Doubleday, 417-418.

Begrich 1934 – J. Begrich, 'Das priesterliche Heilsorakel', *ZAW* 52, 81-92.

Bentz 2007 – J. Bentz, *Silent God: Finding Him When You Can't Hear His Voice*, Kansas City: Beacon Hill Press.

Ben Zvi 2000 – E. Ben Zvi, *Micah* (FOTL, 21B), Grand Rapids: Eerdmans.

Ben Zvi & Floyd 2000 – E. Ben Zvi & M.H. Floyd (eds), *Writings and Speech in Biblical and Ancient Near Eastern Prophecy* (SBL.SymS, 10), Atlanta: SBL.

Berges 2003 – U. Berges, *Schweigen ist Silber – Klagen ist Gold: Das Drama der Gottesbeziehung aus alttestamentlicher Sicht mit einer Auslegung zu Ps 88* (Salzburger Exegetisch-Theologische Vorträge Bd. 1), Münster: Lit.

Berges 2008 – U. Berges, *Jesaja 40–48: Übersetzt und ausgelegt* (HThK.AT), Freiburg: Herder.

Bergmann 2008 – C.D. Bergmann, *Childbirth as a Metaphor for Crisis: Evidence from the Ancient Near East, the Hebrew Bible and 1 QH 11:1-18* (BZAW, 382), Berlin: De Gruyter.

Beuken 1979 – W.A.M. Beuken, *Jesaja: Deel IIa* (PredOT), Nijkerk: Callenbach.

Beuken 1997 – W.A.M. Beuken, 'Isaiah 30: A Prophetic Oracle Transmitted in Two Successive Paradigms', in: C.C. Broyles & C.A. Evans (eds), *Writing and Reading the Scroll of Isaiah: Studies of an Interpretive Tradition*, vol. 1, Leiden: Brill, 369-397.

Beuken 2010 – W.A.M. Beuken, *Jesaja 28–39* (HThK.AT), Freiburg: Herder.

Biese 1893 – A. Biese, *Die Philosophie des Metaphorischen: In Grundlinien dargestellt*, Hamburg: Voss.

Bittner 2009 – W.J. Bittner, *Hören in der Stille: Praxis meditativer Gottesdienste*, Göttingen: Vandenhoeck & Ruprecht.

Black et al. 2004 – J. Black et al., *The Literature of Ancient Sumer*, Oxford: Oxford Univ. Press (paperback edition 2006).

Black 1962 – M. Black, *Models and Metaphors: Studies in Language and Philosophy*, Ithaca: Cornell Univ. Press.

Blans 2000 – G.H.T. Blans, ' "Cloud of Unknowing": An Orientation in Negative Theology from Dionysus the Areopagite, Eckhart, and John of the Cross to Modernity', in: Bulhof & Ten Kate 2000, 58-77.

Blenkinsopp 2002 – J. Blenkinsopp, *Isaiah 40–55* (AncB, 19A), New York: Doubleday.

Blenkinsopp 2003 – J. Blenkinsopp, *Isaiah 56–66* (AncB, 19B), New York: Doubleday.

Block 1997 – D.I. Block, *The Book of Ezekiel: Chapters 1–24* (NICOT), Grand Rapids: Eerdmans.

Blum 2008 – E. Blum, 'Israels Prophetie im altorientalischen Kontext: Anmerkungen zu neueren religionsgeschichtlichen Thesen', in: I. Cornelius & L. Jonker (eds), *"From Ebla to Stellenbosch": Syro-Palestinian Religions and the Hebrew Bible* (ADPV, 37), Wiesbaden: Harrassowitz, 81-115.

Blumenthal 1982 – E. Blumenthal, 'Die Prophezeiung des Neferti', *ZÄS* 109, 1-27.

Boecker 1964 – H.J. Boecker, *Redeformen des Rechtslebens im Alten Testament* (WMANT, 14), Neukirchen-Vluyn: Neukirchener Verlag.

Boehme 2007 – K. Boehme, 'Weltoffen Christ sein: Madeleine Delbrêl', in: Sorace & Zimmerling 2007, 67-76.

Bohak 2008 – G. Bohak, *Ancient Jewish Magic: A History*, Cambridge: Cambridge Univ. Press.

Bonechi & Durand 1992 – M. Bonechi & J.-M. Durand, 'Oniromancie et magie à Mari à l'époque d'Ébla', in: P. Fronzaroli (ed.), *Literature and Literary Language at Ebla* (QS, 18), Firenze: Dipartimento di Linguistica, Università di Firenze, 151-161.

Bonhoeffer 1998 – D. Bonhoeffer, *Widerstand und Ergebung: Briefe und Aufzeichnungen aus der Haft*, ed. Chr. Gremmels *et. al.*, München: Kaiser.

Bonhoeffer 2001 – D. Bonhoeffer, *Letters and Papers from Prison: An Abridged Edition*, tr. John Bowden, London: SCM.

Bons 1994 – E. Bons, שָׁפַט, *ThWAT*, Bd. 8, Lief. 4, Stuttgart: Kohlhammer, 449-454.

Booij 1978 – T. Booij, *Godswoorden in de Psalmen: Hun funktie en achtergronden*, 2 dln, Amsterdam: Rodopi.

Bordeuil & Pardee 2010 – P. Bordreuil & D. Pardee, 'Textes alphabétiques inédits du Musée du Louvre', in: W. van Soldt, *Society and Administration in Ancient Ugarit* (PIHANS, 114), Leiden: NINO, 1-15.

Borger 1979 – R. Borger, *Babylonisch-Assyrische Lesestücke*, Heft 1, Roma: Pontificium Istitutum Biblicum, 2nd ed.

Borghouts 1980 – J. F. Borghouts, 'Magie', *LÄ*, Bd. 3, Wiesbaden: Harrassowitz, 1137-1151.

Boschki 2001 – R. Boschki, 'Schweigen und schreien zugleich: Anklage Gottes im Werk von Elie Wiesel', *JBTh* 16, 109-132.

Bottéro 1987-1990 – J. Bottéro, 'Magie A: In Mesopotamien', *RlA*, Bd. 7, 200-234.

Bottéro & Kramer 1989 – J. Bottéro & S.Kramer, *Lorsque les dieux faisaient l'homme: Mythologie mésopotamienne*, Paris: Gallimard.

Brettler 1989 – M.Z. Brettler, *God is King: Understanding an Israelite Metaphor* (JSOT.S, 76), Sheffield: Sheffield Academic Press.

Brock & Kiraz 2006 – S.P. Brock & G.A. Kiraz, *Ephrem the Syrian: Select Poems*, Provo: Brigham Young Univ. Press.

Brown 1995-2001 – J.P. Brown, *Israel and Hellas* (BZAW, 231; 276; 299), 3 vols, Berlin: De Gruyter.

Brown Taylor 1998 – B. Brown Taylor, *When God Is Silent: The 1997 Lyman Beecher Lectures on Preaching*, Cambridge: Cowley Publications.

Brueggemann 1973 – W. Brueggemann, *In Man We Trust: The Neglected Side of Biblical Faith*, Richmond: John Knox Press.

Brueggemann 1997 – W. Brueggemann, *Theology of the Old Testament: Testimony, Dispute, Advocacy*, Minneapolis: Fortress Press.

Bruneau 2009 – T. Bruneau, 'Silence, Silences, and Silencing', in: St.W. Littlejohn & K.A. Foss (eds), *Encyclopedia of Communication Theory*, vol. 2, London: SAGE, 880-884.

Brunner 1972 – H. Brunner, 'Blindheit', *LÄ*, Bd. 1, Wiesbaden: Harrassowitz, 828-833.

Brunner 1977a – H. Brunner, 'Gebet', *LÄ*, Bd. 2, Wiesbaden: Harrassowitz, 452-459.

Brunner 1977b – H. Brunner, 'Herz', *LÄ*, Bd. 2, Wiesbaden: Harrassowitz, 1158-1168.

Brunner 1988 – H. Brunner, *Altägyptische Weisheit: Lehren für das Leben*, Zürich.

Brunner-Traut 1977 – E. Brunner-Traut, 'Gesten', *LÄ*, Bd. 2, Wiesbaden: Harrassowitz, 573-585.

Brunner-Traut 1979 – E. Brunner-Traut, 'Weiterleben der ägyptischen Lebenslehren in den koptischen Apophtegmata am Beispiel des Schweigens', in: E. Hornung & O. Keel (eds), *Studien zu altägyptischen Lebenslehren* (OBO, 28), Freiburg: Universitätsverlag, 173-316.

Bryden 1998 – M. Bryden, *Samuel Beckett and the Idea of God*, Basingstoke: Macmillan.

Bühlmann 1976 – W. Bühlmann, *Vom rechten Reden und Schweigen: Studien zu Proverbien 10–31* (OBO, 12), Freiburg: Universitätsverlag.

Bulhof & Ten Kate 2000 – I.N. Bulhof & L. ten Kate (eds), *Flight of the Gods: Philosophical Perspectives on Negative Theology* (Perspectives in Continental Philosophy, 11), New York: Fordham Univ. Press.

Burkert 2003 – W. Burkert, *Die Griechen und der Orient: Von Homer bis zu den Magiern*, München: Beck.

Burnett 2005 – J.S. Burnett, 'The Question of Divine Absence in Israelite and West Semitic Religion', *CBQ* 67, 215-235.

Burnett 2010 – J.S. Burnett, *Where Is God? Divine Absence in the Hebrew Bible*. Minneapolis: Fortress.

Butler 1984 – T.C. Butler, *Joshua* (WBC), Nashville: Nelson.

Butler 1998 – S.A.L. Butler, *Mesopotamian Conceptions of Dreams and Dream Rituals* (AOAT, 258), Münster: Ugarit-Verlag.

Cagni 1977 – L. Cagni, *The Poem of Erra*, Malibu.

Caquot 1959 – A. Caquot, Les songes et leur interprétation selon Canaan et Israel', in: Esnoul 1959, 99-124.

Caquot & De Robert 1994 – A. Caquot & P. de Robert, *Les livres de Samuel* (CAT, 6), Genève: Labor et Fides.

Caranfa 2004 – A. Caranfa, 'Silence and Spiritual Experience in Augustine, Pseudo-Dionysius, and Claudel', *JLT* 18, 187-210.

Carroll 2006 – R.P. Carroll, *Jeremiah*, 2 vols, Sheffield: Sheffield Phoenix Press (repr. of the 1986 SCM-edition).

Carse 1995 – J.P. Carse, *The Silence of God: Meditations on Prayer*, San Francisco: Harper.

Černy 1952 – J. Černy. *Paper and Books in Ancient Egypt*, London: Lewis.

Chalupa 2003 – P. Chalupa, 'Gottesschweigen im hebräischen Esterbuch', *Analecta Cracoviensia* 35, 131-8.

Chappaz 1990 – J.-L. Chappaz, 'Un nouveau prophète en Abydos', *Bulletin du Société d'Égyptologie à Genève* 14, 23-31.

Charpin 2002 – D. Charpin, 'Prophètes et rois dans le Proche-Orient amorrite: Nouvelles données, nouvelles perspectives', in: D. Charpin & J.-M. Durand (eds), *Florilegium marianum VI: Recueil d'études à la mémoire d'André Parrot* (Mémoires de N.A.B.U, 4), Paris: SEPOA, 7-38.

Charpin 2008 – D. Charpin, *Lire et écrire à Babylone*, Paris: PUF.

Charpin 2009 – D. Charpin, 'Schreiber (scribe). B. Altbabylonisch', *RLA* 12. 3/4, Berlin: De Gruyter, 266-269.

Childs 1974 – B.S. Childs, *Exodus* (OTL), London: SCM Press.

Childs 2001 – B.S. Childs, *Isaiah* (OTL), Louisville: John Knox Press.

Childs 2005 – B.S. Childs, 'Speech-act Theory and Biblical Interpretation', *SJTh* 58, 375-392.

Choi 2004 – J.H. Choi, 'Protecting the Silence: Exploring Noise and Tranquility in Babylonian Religion', *The Journal of the Association of Graduate Near Eastern Students* 10, 2-22.

Christensen 2001 – D.L. Christensen, *Deuteronomy 1:1–21:9* (WBC, 6A), Nashville: Nelson, 2nd ed.

Clift George 2005 – J. Clift George, *Troubling Deaf Heaven: Assurance in the Silence of God*, B & H Publishing GrOxford Univ. Press.

Clines 1989 – D.J.A. Clines, *Job 1–20* (WBC, 17), Dallas: Word Books.

Clines 2006 – D.J.A. Clines, *Job 21–37* (WBC, 18A), Nashville: Nelson.

Cogan 2001 – M. Cogan, *1 Kings: A New Translation with Introduction and Commentary* (AncB, 10), New York: Doubleday (repr. New Haven: Yale Univ. Press, 2008).

Cohen 1988 – M.E. Cohen, *The Canonical Lamentations of Ancient Mesopotamia*, 2 vols, Potomac: Capital Decisions.

Cole & Machinist 1998 – S.W. Cole & P. Machinist, *Letters from Assyrian and Babylonian Priests to Kings Esarhaddon and Assurbanipal* (SAA, 13), Helsinki: Helsinki Univ. Press.

Collins 2008 – D. Collins, *Magic in the Ancient Greek World* (Blackwell Ancient Religions), Oxford: Blackwell.

Conner 2006 – R. Conner, *Jesus the Sorcerer: Exorcist and Prophet of the Apocalypse*. Oxford: Mandrake.

Coogan 2006 – M.D. Coogan, *The Old Testament: Historical and Literary Introduction to the Hebrew Scriptures*, Oxford: Oxford Univ. Press.

Cooper 1983 – J.S. Cooper, *The Curse of Agade*, Baltimore: Johns Hopkins Univ. Press.

Cooper 1985 – J.S. Cooper, 'Sargon and Joseph: Dreams Come True', in: A. Kort & S. Morschauser (eds.), *Biblical and Related Studies Presented to Samuel Iwry*, Winona Lake: Eisenbrauns, 33-39.

Couroyer 1960 – B. Couroyer, ' "Mettre sa main sur sa bouche" en Égypte et dans la Bible', *RB* 67, 197-209.

Craig 1994 – K.M. Craig, 'Rhetorical Aspects of Questions Answered with Silence in 1 Samuel 14:37 and 28:6', *CBQ* 56, 221-239.

Craigie 1983 – P.C. Craigie, *Psalms 1-50* (WBC, 19), Waco: Word Books.

Crenshaw 1983 – J.L. Crenshaw (ed.), *Theodicy in the Old Testament: Edited with an Introduction* (Issues in Religion and Theology, 4), Philadelphia: Fortess.

Crenshaw 1987 – J.L. Crenshaw, *Ecclesiastes* (OTL), Philadelphia: Westminster.

Cryer 1994 – F.H. Cryer, *Divination in Ancient Israel and its Near Eastern Environment: A Socio-Historical Investigation* (JSOT.S, 142), Sheffield: JSOT Press.

Dahood 1965 – M. Dahood, *Psalms I: 1-50* (AncB), New York: Doubleday.

Dalferth 2006 – I.U. Dalferth, *Becoming Present: An Inquiry into the Christian Sense of the Presence of God*, Leuven: Peeters.

Dalferth 2009 – I.U. Dalferth (ed.), *The Presence and Absence of God: Claremont Studies in the Philosophy of Religion, Conference 2008* (Religion in Philosophy and Theology, 42), Tübingen: Mohr Siebeck.

Dalgish 1962 – E. Dalgish, *Psalm Fifty-one in the Light of Ancient Near Eastern Patternism*, Leiden: Brill.

Dalley 1991 – S.M. Dalley, *Myths from Mesopotamia: Creation, the Flood, Gilgamesh, and Others*, Oxford: Oxford Univ. Press.

Damascius 1967 – *Damascii Vitae Isidori reliquiae*, ed. C. Zintzen (Biblioteca Graeca et Latina suppletoria, 1), Hildesheim: Olms.

Davies & Schofield 1995 – W. V. Davies, & L. Schofield (eds.), *Egypt, the Aegean and the Levant: Interconnections in the Second Millennium BC*, London: The Trustees of the British Museum.

Davis 2009 – S.T. Davis, 'God as Present and God as Absent', in: Dalferth 2009, 147-160.

Dawkins 2007 – R. Dawkins, *The God Delusion*, London: Black Swan.

Day 2003 – J. Day, *Psalms* (T&T Clark Study Guides), repr. Edinburgh: Clark (original publication: Sheffield: Sheffield Academic Press, 1992).

De Halleux 1986 – N. de Halleux. 'Aspects de mise en page des manuscrits de l'Égypte pharaonique', *Communications et Langues, Paris* 69, 66-91.

De Hoop 1999 – R. de Hoop, *Genesis 49 in Its Literary and Historical Context* (OTS, 39), Leiden: Brill.

De Jong 2007 – M.J. de Jong, *Isaiah among the Ancient Near Eastern Prophets: A Comparative Study of the Earliest Stages of the Isaiah Tradition and the Neo-Assyrian Prophecies* (VT.S, 117), Leiden: Brill.

DeJong Ellis 1987 – M. DeJong Ellis, 'The Goddess Kititum Speaks to King Ibal-pi-el: Oracle Texts from Ishchali', *MARI* 5, 235-266.

DeJong Ellis 1989 – M. DeJong Ellis, 'Observations on Mesopotamian Oracles and Prophetic Texts: Literary and Historiographic Considerations', *JCS* 41, 127-86.

Dekker 2008 – W.M. Dekker, *De relationaliteit van God: onafhankelijkheid en relatie in de godsleer en ontologie van Francesco Turrettini en Eberhard Jüngel*, Zoetermeer: Boekencentrum.

Dekker 2009 – J. Dekker, ' "Bind Up the Testimony": Isaiah 8:16 and the Making of the Hebrew Bible', in: R. de Hoop *et al.* (eds), *The Impact of Unit Delimitation on Exegesis* (Pericope, 7), Leiden: Brill, 63-88.

Delcor 1971 – M. Delcor, חרש, *THAT*, Bd. 1, München: Kaiser, 639-41.

Delitzsch 1867 – F. Delitzsch, *Biblischer Commentar über die Psalmen*, Leipzig: Dörfling & Franke.

Del Olmo Lete & Sanmartín 2003 – G. del Olmo Lete & J. Sanmartín, *A Dictionary of the Ugaritic Language in the Alphabetic Tradition*, tr. W.G.E. Watson, 2 vols, Leiden: Brill.

De Moor 1965 – J.C. de Moor, *Mondelinge overlevering in Mesopotamië, Ugarit, en Israël*, Leiden: Brill.

De Moor 1971 – J.C. de Moor, *The Seasonal Pattern in the Ugaritic Myth of Baʿlu According to the Version of Ilimilku* (AOAT, 16), Neukirchen–Vluyn: Butzon & Bercker.

De Moor 1976 – J.C. de Moor, 'Diviners' Oak', *IDB*, Supplementary Volume, Nashville: Abingdon, 243-244.

De Moor 1978 – J.C. de Moor, 'The Art of Versification in Ugarit and Israel: I: The Rhythmical Structure', in: Y. Avishur & J. Blau (eds), *Studies in Bible and the Ancient Near East* (Fs S.E. Loewenstamm), Jerusalem, 119-139.

De Moor 1987 – J.C. de Moor, *An Anthology of Religious Texts from Ugarit* (Nisaba, 16), Leiden: Brill.

De Moor 1988a – J.C. de Moor, ' "O death, where is thy sting" ', in: L. Eslinger & Glen Taylor (eds), *Ascribe to the Lord: Biblical & Other Studies in Memory of Peter C. Craigie* (JSOT.S, 67), Sheffield: Sheffield Academic Press, 99-107.

De Moor 1988b – J.C. de Moor, 'The Seasonal Pattern in the Legend of Aqhatu', *SEL* 5, 61-78.

De Moor 1997 – J.C. de Moor, *The Rise of Yahwism: The Roots of Israelite Monotheism* (BETL, 91A), Leuven: Peeters, 2nd ed.

De Moor 1998a – J.C. de Moor, 'The Duality in God and Man: Gen. 1:26-27 as P's Interpretation of the Yahwistic Creation Account', in: J.C. de Moor (ed.), *Intertextuality in Ugarit and Israel* (OTS, 40), Leiden: Brill, 112-125.

De Moor 1998b – J.C. de Moor, 'Seventy!', in: M. Dietrich & I. Kottsieper (eds), *"Und Mose schrieb dieses Lied auf": Studien zum Alten Testament und zum Alten Orient* (Fs O. Loretz; AOAT, 250), Münster: Ugarit-Verlag, 199-203.

De Moor 2000a – J.C. de Moor, 'Genesis 49 and the Early History of Israel', in: J.C. de Moor & H.F. van Rooy, *The Deuteronomistic History and the Prophets* (OTS,44), Leiden: Brill, 176-198.

De Moor 2000b – J.C. de Moor, 'The Rebel in Bible Lands', in: J.C. Exum & H.G.M. Williamson (eds), *Reading from Right to Left: Essays on the Hebrew Bible in Honour of David J.A. Clines* (JSOT.S, 373), London: Sheffield Academic Press, 329-346.

De Moor 2000c – J.C. de Moor, 'Micah 7:1-13: The Lament of a Disillusioned Prophet', in: Korpel & Oesch 2000, 149-196.

De Moor 2002 – J.C. de Moor, 'The Structure of Micah 2:1-13: The Contribution of the Ancient Witnesses', in: M.C.A. Korpel & J. Oesch (eds), *Studies in Scriptural Unit Division* (Pericope, 3), Assen: Van Gorcum, 90-120.

De Moor 2009 – J.C. de Moor, 'How Ilimilku Lost his Master (RS 92.2016)', *UF* 40, 179-189.
De Moor 2010a – J.C. de Moor, 'Een steuntje in de rug', in: K. Spronk *et al.* (eds). *Studies uit de Kamper School opgedragen aan Willem van der Meer*, Bergambacht: 2VM.
De Moor 2010b – J.C. de Moor, 'The Holy Ones' (in the press).
De Moor & Korpel 2007 – J.C. de Moor & M.C.A. Korpel, 'Paragraphing in a Tibero-Palestinian Manuscript of the Prophets and Writings', in: M.C.A. Korpel *et al.* (eds), *Method in Unit Delimitation* (Pericope, 6), Leiden: Brill, 1-34.
De Waard 1997 – J. de Waard, *A Handbook on Isaiah* (Textual Criticism and the Translator, 1), Winona Lake: Eisenbrauns.
Derrida 1974 – J. Derrida, 'White Mythology: Metaphor in the Text of Philosophy', *New Literary History* 6, 5-74.
Dietrich 1990 – M.Dietrich, 'Die akkadischen Texte der Archive und Bibliotheken von Emar', *UF* 22, 25-48.
Dietrich 2003 – M. Dietrich, *The Babylonian Correspondence of Sargon and Sennacherib* (SAA, 17), Helsinki: Helsinki Univ. Press.
Dietrich 2007 – M. Dietrich, 'Ugarit und seine Beziehungen zu Zypern und zur ägäischen Inselwelt', in: T.R. Kämmerer (ed.), *Studien zu Ritual und Sozialgeschichte im Alten Orient* (BZAW, 374), Berlin: De Gruyter, 55-91.
Dietrich & Loretz 1990 – M. Dietrich & O. Loretz, *Mantik in Ugarit: Keilalphabetische Texte der Opferschau – Omensammlungen, Nekromantie* (AL-ASP, 3), Münster: Ugarit-Verlag.
Dietrich 2004 – W. Dietrich, 'Vom Schweigen Gottes im Alten Testament', in: M. Witte (ed.), *Gott und Mensch im Dialog: Festschrift für Otto Kaiser zum 80. Geburtstag* (BZAW, 345/2), Bd. 2, Berlin: De Gruyter, 997-1014.
Dietrich & Link 2002 – W. Dietrich & C. Link, *Die dunklen Seiten Gottes*, Tl. 1: Willkür und Gewalt, Neukirchen Vluyn: Neukirchener Verlag, 4th ed.
Dietrich & Link 2004 – W. Dietrich & C. Link, *Die dunklen Seiten Gottes*, Tl. 2: Allmacht und Ohnmacht, Neukirchen Vluyn: Neukirchener Verlag, 2nd ed.
Dijkstra 1986 – M. Dijkstra, *Ezechiël I* (Tekst&Toelichting), Kampen: Kok.
Dijkstra 1989 – M. Dijkstra, *Ezechiël II* (Tekst&Toelichting), Kampen: Kok.
Döhling 2009 – J.-D. Döhling, *Der bewegliche Gott: Eine Untersuchung des Motivs der Reue Gottes in der hebräischen Bibel* (HeBSt, 61), Freiburg: Herder.
Dominicus 1994 – B. Dominicus, *Gesten und Gebärden in Darstellungen des Alten und Mittleren Reiches* (SAGA, 10), Heidelberg: Universitätsverlag.
Dorfles 1992 – G. Dorfles, 'Die kreative Stille', in: Kamper & Wulf 1992, 23-26.
Dramm 2007 – S. Dramm, *Dietrich Bonhoeffer: An Introduction to his Thought*, tr. Thomas Rice, Peabody: Hendrickson.
Driver 1954 – G. R. Driver, *Semitic Writing: From Pictograph to Alphabet*, London: Oxford Univ. Press, 2nd ed.

Driver & Miles 1955 – G. R. Driver & J. C. Miles, *The Babylonian Laws*, vol. 2, Oxford: Clarendon Press.

Duguid 1999 – I.M. Duguid, *Ezekiel* (The NIV Application Commentary), Grand Rapids: Zondervan.

Duquesne 2001 – T. Duquesne, 'Concealing and Revealing: The Problem of Ritual Masking in Ancient Egypt', *Discussions in Egyptology* 51, 5-31.

Durand 1988 – J.-M. Durand, *Archives épistolaires de Mari* (ARM, 26), 2 tms, Paris: ERC.

Durand 1997 – J.-M. Durand, *Documents épistolaires du palais de Mari* (LAPO), t. 1, Paris: Éditions du Cerf.

Durand 2000 – J.-M. Durand, *Documents épistolaires du palais de Mari* (LAPO), t. 3, Paris: Éditions du Cerf.

Durand 2002 – J.-M. Durand, 'L'affaire d'Alaḫtum', in: J.-M. Durand (ed.), *Le culte du dieu de l'orage d'Alep et l'affaire d'Alaḫtum* (Florilegium Marianum, 7 / Mémoires de N.A.B.U., 8), Paris: SEPOA, 59-172.

Durand 2008 – J.-M. Durand, 'La religion amorrite en Syrie à l'époque des archives de Mari', in: G. del Olmo Lete (ed.), *Mythologie et religion des Sémites occidentaux*, vol. 1: Ébla, Mari (OLA, 162), Leuven: Peeters 161-716.

Dwinger 1936 – E.E. Dwinger, *Und Gott schweigt ..? Bericht und Aufruf*, Jena: Diederichs.

Ebeling 1953 – E. Ebeling, *Die akkadische Gebetsserie 'Handerhebung' von neuem gesammelt und herausgegeben* (Deutsche Akademie der Wissenschaften zu Berlin: Institut für Orientforschung, Veröffentlichung, 20), Berlin: Akademie-Verlag.

Ehrlich 1953 – E. L. Ehrlich, *Der Traum im Alten Testament* (BZAW, 73), Berlin: Töpelmann.

Ehrman 2008 – B.D. Ehrman, *God's Problem: How the Bible Fails to Answer Our Most Important Question – Why We Suffer*, New York: HarperCollins.

Eidevall 1996 – G. Eidevall, *Grapes in the Desert: Metaphors, Models and Themes in Hosea 4-14* (CB.OT, 43), Stockholm: Almqvist & Wiksell.

Ellermeier 1968 – F. Ellermeier, *Prophetie in Mari und Israel*, Göttingen.

Emmendörffer 1998 – M. Emmendörffer, *Der ferne Gott: Eine Untersuchung der alttestamentlichen Volksklagelieder* (FAT, 21), Tübingen: Mohr Siebeck.

Endo 1976 – S. Endo, *Silence*, tr. W. Johnston, London: P. Owen.

Englund 1987 – G. Englund (ed.), 'The Treatment of Opposites in Temple Thinking and Wisdom Literature', in: G. Englund (ed.), *The Religion of the Ancient Egyptians: Cognitive Structures and Popular Expressions* (Proceedings of Symposia in Uppsala and Bergen 1987 and 1988), Uppsala: [Uppsala Universitet], 77-88.

Enmarch 2008 – R. Enmarch, *A World Upturned: Commentary on and Analysis of The Dialogue of Ipuwer and the Lord of All*, Oxford: Oxford Univ. Press.

Ephratt 2007 – M. Ephratt (ed.), שתיקות: על מקומה של השתיקה בתרבות וביחדים בין־אישים, Tel-Aviv: Resling.
Erickson 2007 – G. Erickson, *The Absence of God in Modernist Literature*, New York: Palgrave.
Esnoul 1959 – A.-M. Esnoul et al. (eds), *Les songes et leur interprétation* (Sources orientales, 20), Paris: Éditions du Seuil.
Everitt 2004 – N. Everitt, *The Non-existence of God*, London: Routledge (repr. 2009).
Fabian 2000 – D. Fabian, 'Prophetic Fulfilment: An Examination of 'True' and 'False' Prophecy in the Deuteronomistic Works', *OTEs* 13, 9-26.
Fales 1991 – F.M. Fales, 'Notes on the Royal Family of Emar', in: D. Charpin & F. Joannès (eds), *Marchands, diplomates et empereurs: Études sur la civilisation mésopotamienne offertes à P. Garelli*, Paris: ERC, 81-90.
Fauconnier & Turner 2003 – G. Fauconnier & M. Turner, *The Way We Think: Conceptual Blending and the Mind's Hidden Complexities*, New York: Basic Books.
Fee 1994 – G. Fee, *God's Empowering Presence: The Holy Sprit in the Letters of Paul*, Peabody: Hendrickson.
Fierro Bardají 1992 – A. Fierro Bardají, 'La conducta del silencio', in: C. Castilla del Pino (ed.), *El silencio*, Madrid: Alianza, 47-78.
Fincke 2001 – A. Fincke, *The Samuel Scroll from Qumran: 4QSam[a] Restored and Compared to the Septuagint and 4QSam[c]* (STDJ, 43), Leiden: Brill.
Fischer-Elfert 2007 – H.-W. Fischer-Elfert, 'Gezeigtes und Verborgenes im Alten Ägypten', in: Streck 2007, 81-102.
Fleming & Milstein 2010 – D.E. & S.J. Milstein, *The Buried Foundation of the Gilgamesh Epic: The Akkadian Huwawa Narrative* (Cuneiform Monographs, 39), Leiden: Brill.
Flesseman-Van Leer 1980 – E. Flesseman-Van Leer, *The Bible: Its Authority and Interpretation in the Ecumenical Movement* (Faith and Order Paper, 99), Geneva: World Council of Churches.
Flew 2008 – A. Flew, *There Is a God: How the World's Most Notorious Atheist Changed His Mind*, New York: Harper Collins, paperback edition.
Flower 2008 – M.A. Flower, *The Seer in Ancient Greece*, Berkeley: UCP.
Fohrer 1963 – G. Fohrer, *Das Buch Hiob* (KAT, 16), Gütersloh: Mohn.
Foreman 2009 – B.A. Foreman, 'Strike the Tongue: Silencing the Prophet in Jeremiah 18:18b', *VT* 59, 653-657.
Foster 1995 – J.L. Foster, *Hymns, Prayers, and Songs: An Anthology of Ancient Egyptian Lyric Poetry* (SBL-WAW, 8), Atlanta: Scholars Press.
Foster 2001 – J.L. Foster, *Ancient Egyptian Literature: An Anthology*, Austin: Univ. of Texas (4th repr. 2005).
Foster 2005 – B.R. Foster, *Before the Muses: An Anthology of Akkadian Literature*, Bethesda: CDL Press, 3rd ed.
Fox 2009 – M.V. Fox, *Proverbs 10–31* (AncB, 18B), New Haven: Yale Univ. Press.
Frahm 2009 – E. Frahm, *Historische und historisch-literarische Texte* (WDOG, 121), Wiesbaden: Harrassowitz.

Frandsen 1998 – P.J. Frandsen, 'On the Avoidance of Certain Forms of Loud Voices and Access to the Sacred', in: W. Clarysse *et al.* (eds), *Egyptian Religion – The Last Thousand Years: Studies Dedicated to the Memory of Jan Quaegebeur*, vol. 2 (OLA, 85), Leuven: Peeters, 975-1000.

Freedman & Frey 2004 – D.N. Freedman & R. Frey, 'False Prophecy Is True', in: Kaltner & Stulman 2004, 82-87.

Freedman & Willoughby 1984 – D.N. Freedman & B.E. Willoughby, 'מָלְאָךְ', *ThWAT*, Bd. 4, Stuttgart: Kohlhammer, 887-904.

Frère Roger 2005 – Frère Roger, *Prier dans le silence du cœur – Cent prières*, Taizée: Les Presses de Taizé.

Frey-Anthes 2007 – H. Frey-Anthes, *Unheilsmächte und Schutzgenien, Antiwesen und Grenzgänger: Vorstellungen von "Dämonen" im alten Israel* (OBO, 227), Fribourg: Academic Press.

Frey-Anthes 2008 – H. Frey-Anthes, 'Concepts of "Demons" in Ancient Israel", *WO* 38, 38-52.

Friebel 1999 – K.G. Friebel, *Jeremiah's and Ezekiel's Sign-Acts* (JSOT.S, 283), Sheffield: Sheffield Academic Press.

Friedrich 1956 – H. Friedrich, *Die Struktur der modernen Lyrik: Von der Mitte des neunzehnten bis zur Mitte des zwanzigsten Jahrhunderts*, erweiterte Neuausgabe (Rowohlts deutsche Enzyklopädie), Hamburg: Rowohlt.

Frood 2007 – E. Frood, *Biographical Texts from Ramessid Egypt*, ed. J. Baines (WAW, 26), Leiden: Brill.

Fuchs & Parpola 2001 – A. Fuchs & S. Parpola, *The Correspondence of Sargon II, Part III: Letters from Babylonia and the Eastern Provinces* (SAA, 15), Helsinki: Helsinki Univ. Press.

Fuchs 1982 – O. Fuchs, *Die Klage als Gebet: Eine theologische Besinnung am Beispiel des Psalms 22*, München: Kösel.

Gardiner 1960 – A. Gardiner, *The Ḳadesh Inscriptions of Ramesses II*, Oxford: Griffith Institute.

Gentili & Schnöller 1986 – A. Gentili & A. Schnöller, *Dio nel silenzio: La meditazione nella vita* (Riscoprire il Centro, 1), Milano: Àncora.

George 2003 – A.R. George, *The Babylonian Gilgamesh Epic: Introduction, Critical Edition and Cuneiform Texts*, 2 vols, Oxford: Oxford Univ. Press.

Gerstenberger 1992 – E.S. Gerstenberger, ' "Where is God?": The Cry of the Psalmists', in: C. Duquoc & C. Floristan (eds), *Where Is God? A Cry of Human Distress*, London: SCM Press, 11-22.

Gibson 1969 – A. Gibson, *The Silence of God: Creative Response to the Films of Ingmar Bergman*, New York: Harper & Row.

Gibson 1978 – J.C.L. Gibson, *Canaanite Myths and Legends*, Edinburgh: T&T Clark, 2nd ed.

Gillmayr-Bucher 2003 – S. Gillmayr-Bucher, 'Wenn die Dichter verstummen: Das Schweigen in den Psalmen', *Theologie und Glaube* 93, 316-332.

Gire 2005 – K. Gire, *The North Face of God: Hope for Times When God Seems Indifferent*, Carol Stream: Tyndale House.

Gnuse 1984 – R.K. Gnuse, *The Dream Theophany of Samuel: Its Structure in Relation to Ancient Near Eastern Dreams and its Theological Significance*,

Lanham: Univ. Press of America.

Görg 2005 – M. Görg, 'Ionien und Kleinasien in früher ausserbiblischer Bezeugung', *BN* 127, 5-10.

Gold 1992 – A. Gold (ed.), *The Complete ArtScroll Selichos – Ashkenaz (Minhag Lita), with a translation by Y. Lavon*, New York: Mesorah.

Goldenstein 2001 – J. Goldenstein, *Das Gebete der Gottesknechte: Jesaja 63,7–64,11 im Jesajabuch* (WMANT, 92), Neukirchen: Neukirchener Verlag.

Goldingay 2005 – J. Goldingay, *The Message of Isaiah 40–55: A Literary-Theological Commentary*, London: T& T Clark.

Goldingay 2007 – J. Goldingay, *Psalms*, vol. 2: Psalms 42–89 (Baker Commentary on the Old Testament), Grand Rapids: Baker Academic.

Goldingay 2008 – J. Goldingay, *Psalms*, vol. 3: Psalms 90–150 (Baker Commentary on the Old Testament), Grand Rapids: Baker Academic.

Goldstein 1988 – J.A. Goldstein, 'The Historical Setting of the Uruk Prophecy' *JNES* 47, 43-46.

Gordis 1968 – R. Gordis, *Koheleth: The Man and his World – A Study of Ecclesiastes*, New York: Schocken, 3rd ed.

Gordis 1978 – R. Gordis, *The Book of Job: Commentary, New Translation and Special Studies*, New York: The Jewish Theological Seminary of America.

Gordon 2007 – R.P. Gordon, 'Standing in the Council: When Prophets Encounter God', in: R.P. Gordon (ed.), *The God of Israel* (UCOP, 64), Cambridge: Cambridge Univ. Press, 190-204.

Graf 2009 – F. Graf, 'Dodona, Dodone', *Brill's New Pauly Online: Antiquity Volumes*, Leiden: Brill, s.v..

Grayson 1975 – A.K. Grayson, *Babylonian Historical-Literary texts* (TSTS, 3), Toronto: Univ. of Toronto Press.

Grayson 2000 – A.K. Grayson, 'Murmuring in Mesopotamia', in: A.R. George & I.L. Finkel (eds), *Wisdom, Gods and Literature: Studies in Assyriology in Honour of W.G. Lambert*, Winona Lake: Eisenbrauns, 301-308.

Greene 1989 – J.T. Greene, *The Role of the Messenger and Message in the Ancient Near East: Oral and Written Communication in the Ancient Near East and in the Hebrew Scriptures – Communicators and Communiques in Context* (BJS, 169), Atlanta: Scholars Press.

Grieshammer 1977 – R. Grieshammer, 'Gott im Menschen', *LÄ*, Bd. 2, Wiesbaden: Harrassowitz, 788.

Groenewald 2005 – A. Groenewald, ' "And please, do not hide your face from your servant!" (Ps 69:18a): The Image of the "Hidden God" ', in: M. Häusl & D. Volgger (eds), *Vom Ausdruck zum Inhalt, vom Inhalt zum Ausdruck: Beiträge zur Exegese und Wirkungsgeschichte alttestamentlicher Texte* (Fs Th. Seidl), St. Ottilien 2005, 121-138.

Guinan 2009 – A. Guinan, 'Schlaf', *RLA* 12. 3/4, Berlin: De Gruyter, 195-202.

Haak 1992 – R.D. Haak, *Habakkuk* (VT.S, 44), Leiden: Brill.

Haas 1987-1990 – V. Haas, 'Magie und Zauberei B. Bei den Hethitern', *RlA*, Bd. 7, Berlin: De Gruyter, 234-255.

Haas 1994 – V. Haas, *Geschichte der hethitischen Religion* (HdO, 1/15), Leiden: Brill.
Haas 2008 – V. Haas, *Hethitische Orakel, Vorzeichen und Abwehrstrategien: Ein Beitrag zur hethitischen Kulturgeschichte*, Berlin: De Gruyter.
Habel 1985 – N.C. Habel, *The Book of Job: A Commentary* (OTL), London: SCM.
Halbmayr & Hoff 2008 – A. Halbmayr & G.M. Hoff (eds), *Negative Theologie heute? Zum aktuellen Stellenwert einer umstrittenen Tradition* (QD, 226), Freiburg: Herder.
Hallo 1966 – W.W. Hallo, 'Akkadian Apocalypses', *IEJ* 16, 231-242.
Hallo 1996 – W.W. Hallo, *Origins: The Ancient Near Eastern Background of Some Modern Western Institutions* (SHCANE, 6), Leiden: Brill.
Handy 1994 – L.K. Handy, *Among the Host of Heaven: The Syro-Palestinian Pantheon as Bureaucracy*, Winona Lake: Eisenbrauns.
Hartenstein & Rösel 2009 – F. Hartenstein & M. Rösel (eds), *JHWH und die Götter der Völker: Symposium zum 80.Geburtstag von Klaus Koch*, Neukirchen-Vluyn: Neukirchener Verlag.
Hartley 1988 – J.E. Hartley, *The Book of Job* (NICOT), Grans Rapids: Eerdmans.
Harvey 1967 – J. Harvey, *Le playdoyer prophétique contre Israël après de la rupture de l'alliance: Étude d'une formule littéraire de l'Ancien Testament* (Studia: Travaux de Recherche, 22), Bruges: Desclée de Brouwer.
Hauerwas 2002 – S. Hauerwas, *With the Grain of the Universe: The Church's Witness and Natural Theology*, London: SCM Press (original edition: Grand Rapids: Baker, 2001).
Heiler 1997 – F. Heiler, *Prayer: A Study in the History and Psychology of Religion*, tr. S. MacComb, Oxford: Oxford Univ. Press (original edition: Oxford: Oxford Univ. Press, 1932).
Heintz 1997 – J.-G. Heintz (ed.), *Oracles et prophéties dans l'Antiquité. Actes du Colloque de Strasbourg 15-17 juin 1995*. (Université des Sciences Humaines de Strasbourg, Travaux du Centre de Recherche sur le Proche-Orient et la Grèce Antiques, 15), Paris: De Boccard.
Herbert 1997 – E.D. Herbert, '4QSam[a] and its Relationship to the LXX: An Exploration in Stemmatological Analysis,' in: B.A. Taylor (ed.), *IX Congress of the International Organisation for Septuagint and Cognate Studies, Cambridge 1995*, Atlanta: Scholars Press, 37-55.
Hieke 2009 – T. Hieke, 'Alles Auslegungssache: Methodisch-hermeneutische Erwägungen zur Kontextualisierung biblischer Auslegung', *BN* 140, 95-110.
High 1967 – D.M. High, *Language, Persons, and Belief*, New York: Oxford Univ. Press.
Hilber 2005 – J. Hilber, *Cultic Prophecy in the Psalms* (BZAW, 352), Berlin: De Gruyter.
Hillesum 1996 – E. Hillesum, *An Interrupted Life: Letters from Westerbork*, tr. A.J. Pommerans, New York: Holt Paperbacks.
Hillesum 2006 – E. Hillesum, *Het verstoorde leven: Dagboek van Etty Hillesum 1941-1943* (Singel Pocket), Amsterdam: Balans, 26th ed.

Himbaza 1997 – I. Himbaza, ' "Se couvriront-ils la moustache?" (Michée 3:7)'. *BN* 88, 27-30.

Hoftijzer & Jongeling 1995 – J. Hoftijzer & K. Jongeling, *Dictionary of the North-West Semitic Inscriptions*, 2 vols, Leiden: Brill.

Holter 1995 – K. Holter, *Second Isaiah's Idol-Fabrication Passages*, Frankfurt a.M.: Lang.

Horn 2009 – P. Horn, 'Simone Weil and Cormac McCarthy's *The Road*: Conditions for the Possibility of Beauty, Justice, and Faith in God', in: Dalferth 2009, 187-199.

Hornung 1971 – E. Hornung, *Der Eine und die Vielen: Ägyptische Gottesvorstellungen*, Darmstadt: Wissenschaftliche Buchgesellschaft.

Hornung 1977 – E. Hornung, 'Gott-Mensch-Beziehung', *LÄ*, Bd. 2, Wiesbaden: Harrassowitz, 788-701.

Hornung 1996 – E. Hornung, 'Götterworte im Alten Ägypten', in: R. Brague & T. Schabert (eds), *Die Macht des Wortes* (Eranos, N.F. 4), München: Fink, 159-186.

Hornung & Keel 1979 – E. Hornung & O. Keel (eds), *Studien zu altägyptischen Lebenslehren* (OBO, 28), Freiburg: Universitätsverlag.

Horovitz & Finkelstein 1939 – H.S. Horovitz & L. Finkelstein, *Siphre ad Deuteronomium* (Corpus Tannaiticum), Berolini: Jüdischer Kulturbund (repr. New York: Jewish Theological Seminary, 1969).

Horowitz & Hurowitz 1992 – W. Horowitz & V. Hurowitz, 'Urim and Thummim in Light of a Psephomancy Ritual from Assur (*LKA* 137)', *JANES* 21, 95-115.

Horowitz & Oshima 2006 – W. Horowitz & T. Oshima (eds), *Cuneiform in Canaan: Cuneiform Sources from the Land of Israel in Ancient Times*, Jerusalem: Israel Exploration Society.

Hossfeld & Zenger 1993 – F.-L. Hossfeld & E. Zenger, *Die Psalmen: Psalm 1–50* (NEB.AT), Würzburg: Echter Verlag.

Hossfeld & Zenger 2008 – F.-L. Hossfeld & E. Zenger, *Psalmen 101–150* (HThK.AT), Freiburg: Herder.

Houtman 1993 – C. Houtman, *Exodus* (HCOT), Vol. 1, Kampen: Kok.

Houtman 2000 – C. Houtman, *Exodus* (HCOT), vol. 3, Leuven: Peeters.

Howells 1981 – C. Howells, 'Sartre and Negative Theology', *MLR* 76, 549-555.

Hunger 1992 – H. Hunger (ed.), *Astrological Reports to Assyrian Kings* (SAA, 8), Helsinki: Helsinki Univ. Press.

Hunger 2009 – H. Hunger, 'Schreiber. C. Im 2. und 1.Jahrtausend', *RLA* 12. 3/4, Berlin: De Gruyter, 269-273.

Husser 1994 – J.-M. Husser, *Le songe et la parole: Étude sur le rêve et sa fonction dans l'ancien Israël* (BZAW, 210), Berlin: De Gruyter.

Husser 1999 – J.-M. Husser, *Dreams and Dream Narratives in the Biblical World* (BiSe, 63), Sheffield: Sheffield Academic Press.

Hyatt 1980 – J.P. Hyatt, *Exodus* (New Century Bible Commentary), Grand Rapids: Eerdmans (original edition: London: Marshall, Morgan & Scott, 1971).

Jablónski et al. 1998 – P. Jablónski, J. van der Lans & C. Hermans, 'Metaphor Theories and Religious Language Understanding', *Metaphor and Symbol* 13, 287-292.

Israelit-Groll 1990 – S. Israelit, 'Chapter Four of the Wisdom Book of Amenemope', in: S Shlomit (ed.), *Studies in Egyptology Presented to Miriam Lichtheim*, Vol. 1, Jerusalem: Magnes Press, 464-484.

Izre'el 2001 – S. Izre'el, *Adapa and the South Wind: Language Has the Power of Life and Death* (Mesopotamian Civilizations, 10), Winona Lake: Eisenbrauns.

Jacobsen 1987 – T. Jacobsen, *The Harps That Once ... Sumerian Poetry in Translation*, New Haven: Yale Univ. Press.

Janowski 2001 – B. Janowski, 'Das verborgene Angesicht Gottes: Psalm 13 als Muster eines Klagelieds des Einzelnen', *JBTh* 16 (2001), 25-53.

Janowski 2003 – B. Janowski, *Konfliktgespräche mit Gott: Eine Anthropologie der Psalmen*, Neukirchen-Vluyn: Neukirchener Verlag.

Janowski 2009 – B. Janowski, 'Der Gott Israels und die Toten: Eine religionsgeschichtliche Skizze', in: Hartenstein & Rösel 2009, 99-138.

Japhet 1993 – S. Japhet, *I & II Chronicles: A Commentary* (OTL), London: SCM Press.

Jaworski 1993 – A. Jaworski, *The Power of Silence: Social and Pragmatic Perspectives* (Language and Language Behaviors Series, 1), Newbury Park: Sage.

Jaworski 1997 – A. Jaworski (ed.), *Silence: Interdisciplinary Perspectives* (Studies in Anthropological Linguistics, 10), Berlin: De Gruyter.

Jean 2006 – C. Jean, *La magie néo-assyrienne en contexte: Recherches sur le métier d'exorciste et le concept d'*ašipūtu (SAAS, 17), Helsinki: The Neo-Assyrian Text Corpus Project.

Jeffers 1996 – A. Jeffers, *Magic and Divination in Ancient Palestine and Syria* (SHANE, 8), Leiden: Brill.

Jeremias 2002 – J. Jeremias, *Die Reue Gottes: Aspekte alttestamentlicher Gottesvorstellung* (Biblisch-theologische Studien, 31), Neukirchen-Vluyn: Verlagsgesellschaft des Erziehungsvereins, 3rd ed.

Jeyes 1989 – U. Jeyes, *Old Babylonian Extispicy: Omen Texts in the British Museum* (UNHAH, 64), Leiden: NINO.

Johnson 1962 – A.R. Johnson, *The Cultic Prophet in Ancient Israel*, Cardiff: Univ. of Wales, 2nd ed.

Johnson 1981 – M. Johnson, 'Introduction: Metaphor in the Philosophical Tradition', in: M. Johnson (ed.), *Philosophical Perspectives on Metaphor*, Minneapolis: Univ. of Minnesota Press, 3-47.

Jonas 1984 – H. Jonas, 'Der Gottesbegriff nach Auschwitz: Eine jüdische Stimme', in: O. Hofius (ed.), *Reflexionen finsterer Zeit*, Tübingen: Mohr (cited after the reprint as Suhrkamp Taschenbuch, 1516, Berlin: Suhrkamp, 1987).

Joüon & Muraoka 2006 – P. Joüon & T. Muraoka, *A Grammar of Biblical Hebrew* (SubBi, 27), Roma: Pontificio Istituto Biblico.

Jüngel 1978 – E. Jüngel, *Gott als Geheimnis der Welt: Zur Begründung der Theologie des Gekreuzigten im Streit zwischen Theismus und Atheismus*, Tübingen: Mohr Siebeck, 3rd ed.

Jüngel 1983 – E. Jüngel, *God as the Mystery of the World: On the Foundation of the Theology of the Crucified One in the Dispute between Theism and Atheism*, Grand Rapids: Eerdmans.

Justice 2006 – W.G. Justice, *When God Seems Silent*, New York: iUniverse.

Kadushin 1952 – M. Kadushin, *The Rabbinic Mind*, New York: The Jewish Theological Seminary of America.

Kaiser 2003 – O. Kaiser, *Zwischen Athen und Jerusalem: Studien zur griechischen und biblischen Theologie* (BZAW, 320), Berlin: De Gruyter.

Kaiser 2008 – O. Kaiser, *Vom offenbaren und verborgenen Gott: Studien zur spätbiblischen Weisheit und Hermeneutik* (BZAW, 392), Berlin: De Gruyter.

Kákosy 1982 – L. Kákosy, 'Orakel', *LÄ*, Bd. 4, Wiesbaden: Harrassowitz, 600-606.

Kaltner & Stulman 2004 – J. Kaltner & L. Stulman (eds), *Inspired Speech: Prophecy in the Ancient Near East – Essays in Honor of Herbert B. Huffmon* (JSOT.S, 378), London: T. & T Clark.

Kammenhuber 1976 – A. Kammenhuber, *Orakelpraxis, Träume und Vorzeichenschau bei den Hethitern* (Texte der Hethiter, 7), Heidelberg : Winter.

Kamper & Wulf 1992 – D. Kamper & C. Wulf (eds), *Schweigen: Unterbrechung und Grenze der menschlichen Wirklichkeit* (Reihe Historische Anthropologie, 18), Berlin: Reimer.

Kaschnitz 1957 – M.L. Kaschnitz, *Neue Gedichte*, Hamburg: Claassen.

Kane 1984 – L. Kane, *The Language of Silence: On the Unspoken and the Unspeakable in Modern Drama*, Rutherford: Fairleigh Dickinson Univ. Press.

Kee 1986 – H.C. Kee, *Medicine, Miracle and Magic in New Testament Times* (MSSNTS, 55), Cambridge: Cambridge Univ. Press.

Kees 1953-1958 – H.A.J. Kees, *Das Priestertum im ägyptischen Staat vom neuem Reich bis zur Spätzeit* (Probleme der Ägyptologie, 1), 2 vols, Leiden: Brill.

Keller 1946 – C.A. Keller, *Das Wort OTH als "Offenbarungszeichen Gottes": Eine philologisch-theologische Begriffsuntersuchung zum Alten Testament*, Basel: Hœnen.

Keller 1991 – S.R. Keller, 'Written Communications Between the Human and Divine Spheres in Mesopotamia and Israel', in: K. L. Younger, Jr. et al. (eds.), *The Biblical Canon in Comparative Perspective* (Scripture in Context, 4), Lewiston: Edwin Mellen, 299-313.

Keown 1995 – G.L. Keown et al., *Jeremiah 26–52* (WBC, 27), Waco: Word Books.

Kessler 2009 – H. Kessler, *Evolution und Schöpfung in neuer Sicht*, Kevelaer: Butzon & Bercker, 3rd ed.

King 1912 – L.W. King, *Babylonian Boundary-Stones and Memorial Tablets in the British Museum*, London: British Museum.

King 1989 – P.J. King, 'The marzēaḥ: Textual and Archaeological Evidence', *ErIs* 20, 98-106.

Kirby 1997 – J.T. Kirby, 'Aristotle on Metaphor', *American Journal of Philology* 118, 517-554.
Kjärgaard 1986 – M.S. Kjärgaard, *Metaphor and Parable: A Systematic Analysis of the Specific Structure and Cognitive Function of the Synoptic Similes and Parables qua Metaphors*, Leiden: Brill.
Klingbeil 2006 – G.A. Klingbeil, ' "Momentaufnahmen" of Israelite Religion: The Importance of the Communal Meal in Narrative Texts in I/II Regum and Their Ritual Dimension', *ZAW* 118, 22-45.
Klutz 2003 – T.E. Klutz (ed.), *Magic in the Biblical World: From the Rod of Aaron to the Ring of Solomon* (JSNT.S, 245), London: T&T Clark.
Knohl 1995 – I. Knohl, *The Sanctuary of Silence*, Minneapolis: Fortress.
Knohl 1996 – I. Knohl, 'Between Voice and Silence: The Relationship between Prayer and Temple Cult', *JBL* 115, 17-30.
Koch-Westenholz 1995 – U. Koch-Westenholz, *Mesopotamian Astrology: An Introduction to Babylonian and Assyrian Celestial Divination* (Carsten Niebuhr Institute Publications, 19), Copenhagen: Museum Tusculanum Press.
Koch-Westenholz 2000 – U. Koch-Westenholz *Babylonian Liver Omens: The Chapters* Manzāzu, Padānu *and* Pān Tâkalti *of the Babylonian Extispicy Series Mainly from Aššurbanipal's Library* (Carsten Niebuhr Institute Publications, 25), Copenhagen: Museum Tusculanum Press.
Köckert 2009 – M. Köckert *et al.*, 'Prophets', in: H. Cançik & H. Schneider (eds), *Brill's New Pauly Online: Antiquity Volumes*, Leiden: Brill. s.v.
Köckert & Nissinen 2003 – M. Köckert & M. Nissinen (eds), *Propheten in Mari, Assyrien und Israel* (FRLANT, 201), Göttingen: Vandenhoeck & Ruprecht.
Köhlmoos 2010 – M. Köhlmoos, *Ruth* (ATD, 9/3), Göttingen: Vandenhoeck & Ruprecht.
Koenig 1994 – Y. Koenig, *Magie et magiciens dans l'Égypte ancienne*, Paris: Pygmalion.
Kövecses 2010 – Z. Kövecses, *Metaphor: A Practical Introduction*, New York: Oxford Univ. Press, 2nd ed.
Kolitz 1999 – Z. Kolitz, *Yosl Rakover Talks to God*, transl. C. Brown Janeway, London: Vintage.
Kolitz 2008 – Z. Kolitz, *Jossel Rakovers Wendung zu Gott: Jiddisch – Deutsch*, ed. P. Badde, Illustrated by Tomi Ungerer (DiogenesTaschenbuch, 23785), Zürich: Diogenes Verlag.
Korpel 1990 – M.C.A. Korpel, *A Rift in the Clouds: Ugaritic and Hebrew Descriptions of the Divine* (UBL, 8), Münster: Ugarit-Verlag.
Korpel 1996a – M.C.A. Korpel, 'Avian Spirits in Ugarit and in Ezekiel 13,' in: N. Wyatt *et al.* (eds), *Ugarit, Religion and Culture. Essays ... John C.L. Gibson*, Münster: Ugarit-Verlag, 99-113.
Korpel 1996b – M.C.A. Korpel, 'Metaphors in Isaiah LV,' *VT* 46, 43-55.
Korpel 1998 – M.C.A. Korpel, 'Exegesis in the Work of Ilimilku of Ugarit', in: J.C. de Moor (ed.), *Intertextuality in Ugarit and Israel* (OTS, 40), Leiden: Brill, 86-111.

Korpel 2000 – M.C.A. Korpel, 'Introduction to the Series Pericope', in: Korpel & Oesch 2000, 1-50.

Korpel 2001 – M.C.A. Korpel, *The Structure of the Book of Ruth* (Pericope, 2), Assen: Van Gorcum.

Korpel 2003 – M.C.A. Korpel, 'Theodicy in the Book of Esther', in: A. Laato & J.C. de Moor 2003, 351-74.

Korpel 2005a – M.C.A. Korpel, 'Unit Delimitation in Ugaritic Cultic Texts and Some Babylonian and Hebrew Parallels', in: M.C.A. Korpel & J.M. Oesch (eds), *Layout Markers in Biblical Manuscripts and Ugaritic Tablets* (Pericope, 5), Assen: Van Gorcum, 141-60.

Korpel 2005b – M.C.A. Korpel, 'Disillusion among Jews in the Postexilic Period', in: R.P. Gordon & J.C. de Moor (eds), *The Old Testament in Its World*, Leiden: Brill, 135-157.

Korpel 2006 – M.C.A. Korpel, 'The Greek Islands and Pontus in the Hebrew Bible', *OTEs* 19/1, 101-117.

Korpel 2007 – M.C.A. Korpel, 'Queen Jezebel's Seal', *UF* 38, 379-398.

Korpel 2008 – M.C.A. Korpel, 'De Ester code', in: B. Becking & A. Merz (eds), *Verhaal als Identiteits-Code: Opstellen aangeboden aan Geert van Oyen bij zijn afscheid van de Universiteit Utrecht* (UTR, 60), Utrecht: Universiteit Utrecht, 189-205.

Korpel 2009a – M.C.A. Korpel, 'Kryptogramme in Ezechiel 19 und im 'Izbet-Ṣarṭa-Ostrakon', *ZAW* 121, 70-86.

Korpel 2009b – M.C.A. Korpel, 'Who Is Speaking in Jeremiah 4:19-22? The Contribution of Unit Delimitation to an Old Problem', *VT* 59, 88-98.

Korpel 2011 – M.C.A. Korpel, 'Symbols of Sainthood and Sin in the Ancient Near East and in the Bible', in: M. Sarot (ed.), *Icons of Sainthood and Sin* (Studies in Theology and Religion), Leiden: Brill (in the press).

Korpel & De Moor 1988 – M.C.A. Korpel & J.C. de Moor, 'Fundamentals of Ugaritic and Hebrew Poetry', in: Van der Meer & De Moor 1988, 1-61.

Korpel & De Moor 1998 – M.C.A. Korpel & J.C. de Moor, *The Structure of Classical Hebrew Poetry: Isaiah 40–55* (OTS, 41), Leiden: Brill.

Korpel & Oesch 2000 – M.C.A Korpel & J.M. Oesch (eds), *Delimitation Criticism: A New Tool in Biblical Scholarship* (Pericope, 1), Assen: Van Gorcum.

Kottsieper 2003 – I. Kottsieper, 'Zu graphischen Abschnittsmarkierungen in nordwestsemitischen Texten', in: M.C.A Korpel & J.M. Oesch (eds), *Unit Delimitation in Biblical Hebrew and Northwest Semitic Literature* (Pericope, 4), Assen: Van Gorcum, 121-61.

Kraus 1978 – H.-J. Kraus, *Psalmen*, 1.Teilband (BKAT,15/1), Neukirchen: Neukirchener Verlag, 5th ed.

Kreiner 1997 – A. Kreiner, *Gott im Leid: Zur Stichhaltigkeit der Theodizee-Argumente* (QD, 168), Freiburg i. B.: Herder.

Kreuzer 1983 – S. Kreuzer, *Der lebendige Gott: Bedeutung, Herkunft und Entwicklung einer alttestamentlichen Gottesbezeichnung* (BWANT, 116), Stuttgart: Kohlhammer.

Kropp & Wagner 1999 – M. Kropp & A. Wagner (eds), *"Schnittpunkt" Ugarit*, Frankfurt: Lang.

Krüger 2008 – A. Krüger (ed.), *Omina, Orakel, Rituale und Beschwörungen* (TUAT-NF, 4), Gütersloh: Gütersloher Verlagshaus.

Krüger 2000 – Th. Krüger, *Kohelet (Prediger)* (BKAT, 19, Sonderband), Neukirchen-Vluyn: Neukirchener Verlag.

Kuhn 1989 – P. Kuhn, *Bat Qol: Die Offenbarungsstimme in der rabbinischen Literatur: Sammlung, Übersetzung und Kurzkommentierung der Texte* (EichM, 13), Regensburg: Pustet.

Kurpershoek 1994-2002 – P.M. Kurpershoek, *Oral Poetry and Narratives from Central Arabia* (Studies in Arabic Literature, 17/1-4), 4 vols, Leiden: Brill.

Kuschel 2001 – K.-J. Kuschel, ' "Ein Gleichgültiger hadert nicht": Zur Funktion der Anklage Gottes bei Joseph Roth und Marie Luise Kaschnitz', *JBTh* 16, 209-231.

Kutsko 2000 – J.F. Kutsko, *Between Heaven and Earth: Divine Presence and Absence in the Book of Ezekiel* (Biblical and Judaic Studies, 6), Winona Lake: Eisenbrauns.

Kwakkel 2003 – G. Kwakkel, *Wonderlijk gewoon: Profeten en profetie in het Oude Testament* (TU-bezinningsreeks, 3), Barneveld: De Vuurbaak.

Laato & De Moor 2003 – A. Laato & J.C. de Moor (eds), *Theodicy in the World of the Bible*, Leiden: Brill.

Labahn & Lietaert Peerbolte 2007 M. Labahn & B.J. Lietaert Peerbolte, *A Kind of Magic: Understanding Magic in the New Testament and Its Religious Environment* (Library of New Testament Studies), London: T&T Clark.

Labuschagne 1990 – C. Labuschagne, *Deuteronomium* (PredOT), dl. 2, Nijkerk: Callenbach.

Lakoff & Johnson 1980 – G. Lakoff & M. Johnson, *Metaphors We Live By*, Chicago: Univ. of Chicago Press.

Lakoff & Turner 1989 – G. Lakoff & M. Turner, *More than Cool Reason: A Field Guide to Poetic Metaphor*, Chicago: Universty of Chicago Press.

Lambert 1960 – W.G. Lambert, *Babylonian Wisdom Literature*, Oxford: Clarendon.

Lambert 1967 – W.G. Lambert, 'Enmeduranki and Related Matters'. *JCS* 21, 126-138.

Lambert 1978 – W.G. Lambert, *The Background of Jewish Apocalyptic*, London: Athlone Press.

Lambert 1989 – W.G. Lambert, 'A Babylonian Prayer to Anūna', in: H. Behrens *et al.* (eds.), DUMU–E$_2$–DUB–BA–A: Studies in Honor of Åke W. Sjöberg (Occasional Publications of the Samuel Noah Kramer Fund, 11), Philadelphia: Univ. Museum, 321-336.

Lambert 2007 – W.G. Lambert, *Babylonian Oracle Questions* (Mesopotamian Civilizations, 13), Winona Lake: Eisenbrauns.

Lambert & Millard 1969 – W.G. Lambert & A.R. Millard, *Atra-ḥasīs: The Babylonian Story of the Flood*, Oxford: Oxford Univ. Press.

Lanczkowski 1955 – G. Lanczkowski, 'Reden und Schweigen im ägyptischen Verständnis, vornehmlich des Mittleren Reiches', in: O. Firchow (ed.), *Ägyptologische Studien* (Fs H. Grapow), Berlin: Akademie-Verlag, 186-196.
Lanfranchi & Parpola 1990 – G.B. Lanfranchi & S. Parpola, *The Correspondence of Sargon II*, Part 2: Letters from the Northern and Northeastern Provinces (SAA, 5), Helsinki: Helsinki Univ. Press.
Leibovici 1959 – M. Leibovici, 'Les songes et leur interprétation à Babylone', in: Esnoul 1959, 63-98.
Leichty 1970 – E. Leichty, *The Omen Series* Šumma izbu (TCS, 4), Locust Valley: Augustin.
Leichty 1991 – E. Leichty, 'Esarhaddon's "Letter to the Gods",' in: M. Cogan & I. Eph'al (eds.), *Ah, Assyria... : Studies in Assyrian History and Ancient Near Eastern Historiography Presented to Hayim Tadmor* (Scripta Hierosolymitana, 33), Jerusalem: Magness Press, 52–57.
Lemaire 1981 – A. Lemaire, *Les écoles et la formation de la Bible dans l'ancien Israël* (OBO. 39), Fribourg: Éditions Universitaires.
Lenzi 2008 – A. Lenzi, *Secrecy and the Gods: Secret Knowledge in Ancient Mesopotamia and Biblical Israel* (SAAS, 19), Helsinki: Univ. of Helsinki.
Lenzi 2009 – A. Lenzi, 'Secrecy, Textual Legitimation, and Intercultural Polemics in the Book of Daniel', *CBQ* 71, 330-348.
Lenzi 2010 – A. Lenzi, 'Invoking the God: Interpreting Invocations in Mesopotamian Prayers and Biblical Laments of the Individual', *JBL* 129, 303-315.
Lessing 2009 – R.R. Lessing, *Amos* (Concordia Commentary), Saint Louis: Concordia Publishing House.
Levin 1982 – S.R. Levin, 'Aristotle's Theory of Metaphor', *Philosophy and Rhetoric* 15, 24-46.
Levinas 1987 – E. Levinas, *Hors sujet*, Cognac: Fata Morgana.
Levinas 1993 – E. Levinas, *Dieu, la Mort et le Temps*, ed. J. Rolland, Paris: Grasset.
Levinas 2000 – E. Levinas, *God, Death, and Time* (Meridian: Crossing Aesthetics), tr. B. Bergo, Stanford: Stanford Univ. Press.
Levine 1989 – B.A. Levine, *Leviticus* (The JPS Torah Commentary), New York.
Levine 1993 – B.A. Levine, 'Silence, Sound, and the Phenomenology of Mourning in Biblical Israel', *JANES* 22, 89-106.
Levine 2000 – B.A. Levine, *Numbers 21–36: A New Translation with Introduction and Commentary* (AncB, 4A), New York: Doubleday.
Levison 2009 – J.R. Levison, *Filled with the Spirit*, Grand Rapids: Eerdmans.
Lewis 1989 – Th.J. Lewis, *Cults of the Dead in Ancient Israel and Ugarit* (HSM, 39), Atlanta: Scholars Press.
Lichtheim 1973 – M. Lichtheim, *Ancient Egyptian Literature*, vol. 1: The Old and Middle Kingdoms, Berkely: UCP.
Lichtheim 1976 – M. Lichtheim, *Ancient Egyptian Literature*, vol. 2: The New Kingdom, Berkely: UCP.

Lichtheim 1980 – M. Lichtheim, *Ancient Egyptian Literature*, vol. 3: The Late Period, Berkely: UCP.

Lindblom 1963 – J. Lindblom, *Prophecy in Ancient Israel*, Oxford: Blackwell.

Lindström 2003 – F. Lindström, 'Theodicy in the Psalms', in: Laato & De Moor 2003, 256-303.

Livingstone 1989 – A. Livingstone, *Court Poetry and Literary Miscellanea* (SAA, 3), Helsinki: Helsinki Univ. Press.

Loevlie 2003 – E.M. Loevlie, *Literary Silences in Pascal, Rousseau, and Beckett* (Oxford Modern Languages and Literature Monographs), Oxford: Clarendon.

Lohfink 1962 – N. Lohfink, 'Enthielten die im AT bezeugten Klageriten eine Phase des Schweigens?', *VT* 12, 260-277.

Lohfink 2008 – G. Lohfink, *Welche Argumente hat der neue Atheismus? Eine kritische Auseinandersetzung*, Bad Tölz: Urfeld.

Loretz 1993 – O. Loretz, '*Marziḫu* im ugaritischen und biblischen Ahnenkult: Zu Ps 23; 133; Am 6,1-7 und Jer 16,5.8," in: M. Dietrich & O. Loretz (eds), *Mesopotamica – Ugaritica – Biblica: Festschrift für Kurt Bergerhof zur Vollendung seines 70. Lebensjahres am 7.Mai 1992*, Neukirchen-Vluyn: Neukirchener Verlag, 94-144.

Loretz 2002 – O. Loretz, 'Die Gefässe *Rdmns* für ein *Marziḫu*-Gelage zu Ehren Baals und der Nestorbecher der Ilias: Zu ugaritisch-griechischen Beziehungen nach KTU 1.3 I 10-15a', in: O. Loretz et al. (eds.), *Ex Mesopotamia et Syria Lux: Festschrift für Manfried Dietrich* (AOAT, 281), Münster: Ugarit-Verlag, 299-324.

Loretz 2003 – O. Loretz, *Götter – Ahnen – Könige als gerechte Richter: Der "Rechtsfall" des Menschen vor Gott nach altorientalischen und biblischen Texten* (AOAT, 290), Münster: Ugarit-Verlag.

Lundbom 1999 – J.R. Lundbom, *Jeremiah 1-20* (AncB, 21A), New York: Doubleday.

Lust 1976 - J. Lust, 'Elia and the Theophany on Mount Horeb (1 Rg 19,11-12)', *BEThL* 41, 91-100.

Lux 2005 – R. Lux, ' "Still alles Fleisch vor JHWH ...": Das Schweigegebot im Dodekapropheton und sein besonderer Ort im Zyklus der Nachtgesichte des Sacharja', *Leqach* 6, 99-113.

Lyons 1995 – M.C. Lyons, *The Arabian Epic: Heroic and Oral Story-Telling*, 3 vols, Cambridge: Cambridge Univ. Press.

Maarsingh 1989 – B. A. Maarsingh, *Leviticus* (PredOT), Nijkerk: Callenbach, 1989.

Mabie 2004 – F.J. Mabie, 'The Syntactical and Structural Function of Horizontal Dividing Lines in the Literary and Religious Texts of the Ugaritic Corpus (KTU 1)', *UF* 36, 291-311.

McAlpine 1987 – T. H. McAlpine, *Sleep, Divine and Human, in the Old Testament* (JSOT.S, 38), Sheffield: Sheffield Univ. Press.

McCarthy 2007 – C. McCarthy, *The Road*, paperback edition, Picador: London.

Mach 1992 – M. Mach, *Entwicklungsstadien des jüdischen Engelglaubens in vorrabbinischer Zeit* (Texte und Studien zum antiken Judentum, 34), Tübingen: Mohr Siebeck.

Macintosh 1997 – A.A. Macintosh, *Hosea* (ICC), Edinburgh: T&T Clark.

McKane 1970 – W. McKane, *Proverbs* (OTL), London: SCM.

McKane 1986 – W. McKane, *A Critical and Exegetical Commentary on Jeremiah*, vol. 1, Edinburgh: T&T Clark.

McKane 1996 – W. McKane, *A Critical and Exegetical Commentary on Jeremiah*, vol. 2, Edinburgh: T&T Clark.

Madl 1977 – H. Madl, 'Die Gottesbefragung mit dem Verb *šā'al*', in: H.J. Fabry (ed.), *Bausteine biblischer Theologie: Festgabe für G. Johannes Botterweck zum 60. Geburtstag dargebracht von seinen Schülern* (BBB, 50), Köln: Peter Hanstein, 37-70.

Mayer 1984 – W. Mayer, *Sargons Feldzug gegen Urartu*, Berlin: Deutsche Orient-Gesellschaft.

Maimonides 1904 – M. Maimonides, *The Guide for the Perplexed*, tr. M. Friedländer, New York: Dover, 2nd ed.

Maitland 2009 – S. Maitland, *A Book of Silence*, paperback edition, London: Granta.

Malamat 1998 – A. Malamat, *Mari and the Bible* (SHCANE, 12), Leiden: Brill.

Malamat 2003 – A. Malamat, 'Musicians from Hazor at Mari', in: P. Marassini (ed.), *Semitic and Assyriological Studies Presented to Pelio Fronzaroli by Pupils and Colleagues*, Wiesbaden: Harrassowitz, 355-357.

Mancini 2008 – R. Mancini, *La lingua degli dei: Il silenzio dall'Antichità al Rinascimento*, Costabissara: Angelo Colla Editore.

Marion 2010 – J.-L. Marion, *Le visible et le révélé* (Philosophie et Théologie), Paris: Éditions du Cerf.

Marquardt 1968 – F.-W. Marquardt, 'Religionskritik und Entmythologisierung: Über einen Beitrag Karl Barths zur Entmythologisierungsfrage', in: W. Dantine & K. Lüthi (eds.), *Theologie zwischen gestern und morgen: Interpretationen und Anfragen zum Werk Karl Barths*, München: Kaiser, 88-123.

Marsman 2003 – H.J. Marsman, *Women in Ugarit and Israel: Their Social and Religious Position in the Context of the Ancient Near East* (OTS, 49), Leiden: Brill.

Martin 2005 – G.T. Martin, *Stelae from Egypt and Nubia in the Fitzwilliam Museum, Cambridge: c. 3000 BC–AD 1150*, Cambridge: Cambridge Univ. Press.

Maul 1988 – S.M. Maul, *'Herzberuhigungsklagen': Die sumerisch-akkadischen Eršaḫunga-Gebete*, Wiesbaden: Harrassowitz.

Maul 2002 – S.M. Maul et al., 'Divination', in: H. Cançik & H. Schneider (eds), *Brill's New Pauly Online: Antiquity Volumes*, vol. 4, Leiden: Brill, 564-577.

Maul 2003-2005 – S.M. Maul, 'Omina und Orakel. A. Mesopotamien', *RlA*, Bd. 10, Berlin: De Gruyter, 45-88.

Mayer 1976 – W.R. Mayer, *Untersuchungen zur Formensprache der babylonischen 'Gebetsbeschwörungen'* (StP, 5), Rome: Biblical Institute Press.
Meier 1937 – G. Meier, *Die assyrische Beschwörungssammlung Maqlû neu bearbeitet* (BAfO, 2), repr. Osnabrück: Biblio-Verlag.
Meier 1988 – S.A. Meier, *The Messenger in the Ancient Semitic World* (HSM, 45), Atlanta: Scholars Press.
Meier 1999a – S.A. Meier, 'Angel I', in: K. van der Toorn et al. (eds), *Dictionary of Deities and Demons in the Bible*, Leiden: Brill, 2nd ed., 45-50.
Meier 1999b – S.A. Meier, 'Angel of Yahweh', in: K. van der Toorn et al. (eds), *Dictionary of Deities and Demons in the Bible*, Leiden: Brill, 2nd ed., 53-59.
Mercier 2006 – P. Mercier, *Nachtzug nach Lissabon*, Random House: München, 32nd ed.
Mercier 2008 – P. Mercier, *Night Train to Lisbon*, tr. Barbara Harshav, London: Atlantic Books.
Mettinger 1988 – T. N.D. Mettinger, *In Search of God: The Meaning and Message of the Everlasting Names*, Philadelphia: Fortress.
Mettinger 1995 – T. N.D. Mettinger, *No Graven Image? Israelite Aniconism in Its Ancient Near Eastern Context* (CB.OT, 42), Stockholm: Almqvist & Wiksell.
Meyer & Smith 1999 – M.V. Meyer & R. Smith (eds), *Ancient Christian Magic: Coptic Texts of Ritual Power*, Princeton: Princeton Univ. Press.
Michaelis 1938 – W. Michaelis, παντοκράτωρ, *ThWNT*, Bd. 3, Stuttgart: Kohlhammer, 913-914.
Migahid 1986 – A.-G. Migahid, *Demotische Briefe an Götter von der Spätbis Römerzeit: Ein Beitrag zur Kenntnis des religiösen Brauchtums im alten Ägypten*, Würzburg: Universitätsverlag.
Migahid & Vittmann 2003 – A.-G Migahid & G. Vittmann, 'Zwei weitere frühdemotische Briefe an Thot', *RdE* 54, 47-65.
Milazzo 1992 – G.T. Milazzo, *The Protest and the Silence: Suffering, Death, and Biblical Theology*, Minneapolis: Fortress.
Milgrom 1990 – J. Milgrom, *The JPS Torah Commentary: Numbers*, Philadelphia: Jewish Publication Society.
Milgrom 1991 – J. Milgrom, *Leviticus 1–16* (AncB, 3), New York: Doubleday.
Miralles Maciá 2007 – L. Miralles Maciá, *Marzeah y thíasos: Una institución convival en el Oriente Próximo Antiguo y el Mediterráneo* (Anejos, 20), Madrid: Publicaciones Universidad Complutense de Madrid.
Mirecki & Meyer 2002 – P. Mirecki & M. Meyer (eds), *Magic and Ritual in the Ancient World* (Religions in the Graeco-Roman World, 141), Leiden: Brill.
Miskotte 1956 – K.H. Miskotte, *Als de goden zwijgen: Over de zin van het Oude Testament*, Haarlem: Uitgeversmaatschappij Holland.
Miskotte 1967 – K.H. Miskotte, *When the Gods Are Silent*, tr. J.W. Doberstein, New York: Harper & Row.
Moltmann 1974 – J. Moltmann, *The Crucified God: The Cross of Christ as the Foundation and Criticism of Christian Theology*, tr. R.A. Wilson & J. Bowden, London: SCM.

Mœller 1958 – C. Mœller, *Littérature du XXe siècle et christianisme*, t. 1: Silence de Dieu, Paris: Casterman, 7th ed.
Montgomery 2002 – E. Montgomery, *When Heaven Is Silent*, Lake Mary: Creation House.
Morgan 2004 – E.E. Morgan, *Untersuchungen zu den Ohrenstelen aus Deir el Medine* (ÄAT, 61), Wiesbaden: Harrassowitz.
Mouton 2007 – A. Mouton, *Rêves hittites: Contribution à une histoire et une anthropologie du rêve en Anatolie ancienne* (CHANE, 28), Brill: Leiden.
Mowinckel 1923 – S. Mowinckel, *The Psalms in Israel's Worship*, tr. D.R. Ap-Thomas, 2 vols in 1, Oxford: Blackwell (repr. as BiSe, 14, Sheffield 1962).
Mrozek & Votto 1999 – A. Mrozek & S. Votto, 'The Motif of the Sleeping Divinity', *Biblica* 80, 414-419.
Muers 2001 – R. Muers, 'Silence and the Patience of God', *Modern Theology* 17, 85-98.
Muers 2004 – R. Muers, *Keeping God's Silence: Towards a Theological Ethics of Communication* (Challenges in Contemporary Theology) Oxford: Blackwell.
Murphy 1992 – R. E. Murphy, *Ecclesiastes* (WBC), Nashville: Nelson.
Murphy 1998 – R. E. Murphy, *Proverbs* (WBC), Nashville: Nelson.
Murphy-O'Connor 2003 – J. Murphy-O'Connor, 'The Prayer of Petition (Matthew 7:7 and par.)', *RB* 110, 399-416
Naveh & Shaked 1985 – J. Naveh & Sh. Shaked, *Amulets and Magic Bowls: Aramaic Incantations of Late Antiquity*, Jerusalem: Magnes.
Naveh & Shaked 1993 – J. Naveh & Sh. Shaked, *Magic Spells and Formulae: Aramaic Incantations of Late Antiquity*, Jerusalem: Magnes.
Neher 1970 – A. Neher, *L'exil de la parole: Du silence biblique au silence d'Auschwitz*, Paris: Éditions du Seuil.
Nel 1996 – P. Nel, שׁקט, NIDOTTE, vol. 4, Carlisle: Paternoster, 1996, 234-235.
Neumann 1990 – P.H.A. Neumann (ed.), *"Religionsloses Christentum" und "Nicht-religiöse Interpretation" bei Dietrich Bonhoeffer* (WdF, 304), Darmstadt: Wissenschaftliche Buchgesellschaft.
Neusner 1987 – J. Neusner, *Sifre on Deuteronomium* (BJSt, 101), Atlanta: Scholars Press.
Niditch 1996 – S. Niditch, *Oral World and Written Word: Ancient Israelite Literature* (Library of Ancient Israel), Louisville: Westminster John Knox Press.
Nielsen 1978 – K. Nielsen, *Yahweh as Prosecutor and Judge: An Investigation of the Prophetic Lawsuit (Rîb-Pattern)*, transl. F. Cryer (JSOT.S, 9), Sheffield: SUP.
Nissinen 1998 – M. Nissinen, *References to Prophecy in Neo-Assyrian Sources* (SAAS, 7), Helsinki: Univ. of Helsinki.
Nissinen 2000a – M. Nissinen (ed.), *Prophecy in its Ancient Near Eastern Context: Mesopotamian, Biblical, and Arabian Perspectives* (SBL.SS, 13), Atlanta: SBL.

Nissinen 2000b – M. Nisssinen, 'Spoken, Written, Quoted and Invented: Orality and Writtenness in Ancient Near Eastern Prophecy', in: Ben Zvi & Floyd 2000, 235-271.

Nissinen 2003 – M. Nisssinen et al. (eds), *Prophets and Prophecy in the Ancient Near East* (SBL.WAW, 12), Atlanta: SBL.

Nissinen 2004 – M. Nisssinen, 'What Is Prophecy? An Ancient Near Eastern Perspective', in: Kaltner & Stulman 2004, 17-37.

Noegel 2007 – S.B. Noegel, *Nocturnal Ciphers: The Allusive Language of Dreams in the Ancient Near East* (AOS, 89), New Haven: American Oriental Society.

Noll 1996 – S.F. Noll, 'מַלְאָךְ', NIDOTTE, vol. 2, Carlisle: Paternoster Press, 941-943.

Noort 1977 – E. Noort, *Untersuchungen zum Gottesbescheid in Mari: Die "Mariprophetie" in der alttestamentlichen Forschung* (AOAT, 202), Neukirchen: Neukirchener Verlag.

Noth 1988 – M. Noth, *Das 2. Buch Mose: Exodus* (ATD, 5), Göttingen: Vandenhoeck & Ruprecht, 8th ed.

Oelmüller 1999 – W. Oelmüller, *Negative Theologie heute: Die Lage der Menschen vor Gott*, München: Fink.

Oesch 1979 – J.M. Oesch, *Petucha und Setuma: Untersuchungen zu einer überlieferten Gliederung im hebräischen Text des Alten Testaments* (OBO, 27), Freiburg: Universitätsverlag.

Ogden & Richards 1946 – C.K. Ogden & I.A. Richards, *The Meaning of Meaning*, New York: Harcourt, Brace & World, 8th ed.

Olley 1998 – J.W. Olley, 'Texts Have Paragraphs Too – A Plea for Inclusion in Critical Editions', *Textus* 19, 111-25.

Oppenheim 1956 – A.L. Oppenheim, *The Interpretation of Dreams in the Ancient Near East*, Philadelphia: The American Philosophical Society (repr. Piscataway: Gorgias Press, 2007).

Oswalt 1986 – J.N. Oswalt, *The Book of Isaiah: Chapters 1–39* (NICOT), Grand Rapids: Eerdmans.

Oswalt 1996a – J.N. Oswalt, דמה, NIDOTTE, vol. 1, Carlisle: Paternoster, 1996, 970-971.

Oswalt 1996b – J.N. Oswalt, דמם, NIDOTTE, vol. 1, Carlisle: Paternoster, 1996, 972-973.

Oswalt 1998 – J.N. Oswalt, *The Book of Isaiah: Chapters 40–66* (NICOT), Grand Rapids: Eerdmans.

Oswalt 2003 – J.N. Oswalt, *Isaiah* (The NIV Application Commentary), Grand Rapids: Zondervan.

Oswalt 2009 – J.N. Oswalt, *The Bible among the Myths: Unique Revelation or Just Ancient Literature?*, Grand Rapids: Zondervan.

Patterson 1991 – B. Patterson, *Waiting: Finding Hope When God is Silent*, Downers Grove: InterVarsity Press.

Pardee 2000 – D. Pardee, *Les textes rituels* (Ras Shamra-Ougarit, 12), 2 vols., Paris: ERC.

Pardee 2002 – D. Pardee, *Ritual and Cult at Ugarit* (WAW, 10), Atlanta: SBL.

Pardee 2009 – D. Pardee, 'A New Aramaic Inscription from Zincirli', *BASOR* 356, 51-71.
Parpola 1987 – S. Parpola, *The Correspondence of Sargon II*, Part I: Letters from Assyria and the West (SAA, 1), Helsinki: Helsinki Univ. Press.
Parpola 1993 – S. Parpola, *Letters from Assyrian and Babylonian Scholars* (SAA, 10), Helsinki: Helsinki Univ. Press.
Parpola 1997 – S. Parpola, *Assyrian Prophecies* (SAA, 9), Helsinki: Helsinki Univ. Press.
Paul 1804 – J. Paul, *Vorschule der Ästhetik*, Berlin: Perthes.
Pelsy 1995 – L. Pelsy, *Le silence dans la Bible* (Les Cahiers de "Christ seul", 2), Montbéliard: Editions Mennonites.
Pentiuc 2001 – E. J. Pentiuc, *West Semitic Vocabulary in the Akkadian Texts from Emar* (HSS, 49), Winona Lake: Eisenbrauns.
Perlitt 1971 – L. Perlitt, 'Die Verborgenheit Gottes', in: H.-W. Wolff (ed.), *Probleme biblischer Theologie* (Fs G. von Rad), München: Kaiser, 367-382.
Perpich 2008 – D. Perpich, *The Ethics of Emmanuel Levinas*, Stanford: Stanford Univ. Press.
Pettinato 1966 – G. Pettinato, *Die Ölwahrsagung bei den Babyloniern* (SS, 21-22), 2 vols, Roma: Instituto di Studi del Vicino Oriente.
Phillips 2004 – W.G. Phillips, *Judges, Ruth* (Holman Old Testament Commentary), Nashville: Broadman & Holman.
Plöger 1965 – O. Plöger, *Das Buch Daniel* (KAT, 18), Gütersloh: Gerd Mohn.
Pöhlmann 1990 – H.G. Pöhlmann, 'Leben wir in einem religionslosen Zeitalter? Zur Religionslosigkeitsthese von Dietrich Bonhoeffer', in: P.H.A. Neumann (ed.), *'Religionsloses Christentum' und 'nicht-religiöse Interpretation' bei Dietrich Bonhoeffer* (Wege der Forschung 304), Darmstadt: Wissenschaftliche Buchgesellschaft, 370-386.
Poirier 2010 – J.C. Poirier, *The Tongue of Angels: The Concept of Angelic Languages in Classical Jewish and Christian Texts* (WUNT, 2.Reihe, 287), Tübingen: Mohr Siebeck.
Ponchia 2009 – S. Ponchia, 'Witnessing Procedures in the Ancient Near East: Problems and Perspectives of Research', in: N. Bellotto & S. Ponchia (eds), *Witnessing in the Ancient Near East* (Acta Sileni, 2), Padova: S.A.R.G.O.N., 225-251.
Pongratz-Leisten 1999 – B. Pongratz-Leisten, *Herrschaftswissen in Mesopotamien: Formen der Kommunikation zwischen Gott und König im 2. und 1. Jahrtausend v. Chr.* (SAAS, 10), Helsinki: The Neo-Assyrian Text Corpus Project.
Posener 1960 – G. Posener, 'Une nouvelle histoire de revenant (Recherches littéraires, VII)', *RdE* 12, 75-82.
Prechel 2008 – D. Prechel, ' "Gottesmänner", "Gottesfrauen" und die hethitische Prophetie', *WO* 38, 211-220.
Prinsloo 2009 – G.T.M. Prinsloo, 'Petuḥot/Setumot and the Stucture of Habakkuk: Evaluating the Evidence', in: R. de Hoop *et al.* (eds), *The Impact of Unit Delimitation on Exegesis* (Pericope, 7), Leiden: Brill, 196-227.

Propp 1999 – W.H.C. Propp, *Exodus 1–18: A New Translation with Introduction and Commentary* (AncB, 2), New York: Doubleday.

Propp 2006 – W.H.C. Propp, *Exodus 19–40: A New Translation with Introduction and Commentary* (AncB, 2A), New York: Doubleday.

Puech 2010 – E. Puech, 'L'ostracon de Khirbet Qeyafa et les debuts de la royauté en Israël', *RB* 117, 162-184.

Purcell 2006 – M. Purcell, *Levinas and Theology*, Cambridge: Cambridge Univ. Press.

Rahner 2008 – J. Rahner, 'Gotteswort in Menschenwort: Die Bibel als Urkunde des Glaubens', in: S. Gilmayr-Bucher *et al.* (eds), *Bibel verstehen: Schriftverständnis und Schriftauslegung* (Herder Theologische Module, 4), Freiburg: Herder, 7-36.

Rahner 1994 – K. 'Erfahrungen eines katholischen Theologen', in: A. Raffelt (ed.), *Karl Rahner in Erinnerung*, Düsseldorff: Patmos, 134-148.

Reformed Churches 1981 – *God with Us: On the Nature of the Authority of Scripture*, tr. Secretariat of the Reformed Ecumenical Synod, Grand Rapids [n.y.] (Dutch original: *God met ons: Over de aard van het Schriftgezag* (Kerkinformatie, 113), Leusden: Informatiedienst, 1981).

Reiner 1958 – E. Reiner, *Šurpu: A Collection of Sumerian and Akkadian Incantations* (BAfO, 11), Graz: Weidner.

Reiterer 2007 – F.V. Reiterer *et al.* (eds.), *Angels: The Concept of Celestial Beings – Origins, Development and Reception*, Berlin: De Gruyter.

Renaud 1977 – B. Renaud, *La formation du livre de Michée: Tradition et actualisation* (Études Bibliques), Paris: Gabalda.

Renkema 1983 – J. Renkema, *"Misschien is er hoop ...": De theologische vooronderstellingen van het boek Klaagliederen*, Franeker: Wever.

Renkema 1998 – J. Renkema, *Lamentations* (HCOT), Leuven: Peeters.

Ricoeur 1978 – P. Ricoeur, *The Rule of Metaphor*, London: Routledge & Kegan Paul.

Richards 1936 – I.A. Richards, *The Philosophy of Rhetoric*, Oxford: Oxford Univ. Press.

Ridderbos 1972 – N. H. Ridderbos, *Die Psalmen: Stilistische Verfahren und Aufbau mit besondere Berücksichtigung von Ps 1–41* (BZAW, 191), Berlin: De Gruyter.

Ringgren 1983 – H. Ringgren, 'Akkadian Apocalypticism', in: D. Hellholm, *Apocalypticism in the Mediterranean World and the Near East: Proceedings of the International Colloquium on Apocalypticism, Uppsala, August 12-17, 1979*, Tübingen: Mohr Siebeck, 379-386.

Ritner 2001 – R.K. Ritner, 'Dream Books', in: D.B. Redford (ed.), *The Oxford Encyclopedia of Ancient Egypt*, vol. 1, Oxford: Oxford Univ. Press, 410-411.

Ritschl 1912 – O. Ritschl, *Dogmengeschichte des Protestantismus*, Bd. 2, Leipzig: Hinrichs.

Rittig 1989 – D. Rittig, 'Maske', *RlA*, Bd. 7, Lief. 5./6., Berlin: De Gruyter, 448-449.

Robbins 2007 – J.W. Robbins (ed.), *After the Death of God: John D. Caputo & Gianni Vattimo* (Insurrections: Critical Studies in Religion, Politics, and Culture), New York: Columbia Univ. Press.

Roberts 1991 – J.J.M. Roberts, *Nahum, Habakkuk, and Zephaniah: A Commentary*, Louisville: Westminster/John Knox.

Roberts 1992 – J.J.M. Roberts, 'The Motiv of the Weeping God in Jeremiah and Its Background in the Lament Tradition of the Ancient Near East', *OTE* 5, 361-374.

Rochberg 2004 – F. Rochberg, *The Heavenly Writing: Divination, Horoscopy, and Astronomy in Mesopotamian Culture*, Cambridge: Cambridge Univ. Press.

Rockwood 2004 – E. Rockwood, *When Prayers Are Not Answered: Finding Peace When God Seems Silent*, Peabody: Hendrickson, 3rd edition.

Römer 2004 – W.H.Ph. Römer, *Die Klage über die Zerstörung von Ur* (AOAT, 309), Münster: Ugarit-Verlag.

Römer 2009 – T. Römer, 'Das Verbot magischer und mantischer Praktiken im Buch Deuteronomium (Dtn 18,9-13)', in: T. Naumann & R. Hunziker-Rodewald (eds), *Diasynchron: Beiträge zur Exegese, Theologie und Rezeption der hebräischen Bibel* (Fs W. Dietrich), Stuttgart: Kohlhammer, 311-327.

Rose 1994 – C. Rose, *Die Wolke der Zeugen: Eine exegetisch-traditionsgeschichtliche Untersuchung zu Hebräer 10,32–12,3* (WUNT, 2.Reihe, 60), Tübingen: Mohr Siebeck.

Rosenberg 1986 – A. Rosenberg, *Engel und Dämonen: Gestaltwandel eines Urbildes*, München: Kösel.

Rousseau 1966 – J.J. Rousseau, 'Essay on the Origin of Languages', in: *On the Origin of Language*, transl. J.H. Moran & A. Code, New York: F. Ungan (repr. Chicago: Univ. of Chicago Press, 1986).

Rowley 1970 – H.H. Rowley, *The Book of Job* (NCB), London: Nelson.

Ruf 2010 – M.G. Ruf, *Die heiligen Propheten, Eure Apostel und Ich: Metatextuelle Studien zum zweiten Petrusbrief*, Ridderkerk: Ridderprint (also: Utrecht: M.G. Ruf).

Runze 1889 – G. Runze, *Studien zur vergleichenden Religionswissenschaft*, vol. 1, Berlin: R. Gaertners Verlagsbuchhandlung.

Ryken *et al.* 1998 – L. Ryken *et al.* (eds), *Dictionary of Biblical Imagery*, Downers Grove: InterVarsity.

Saiko 2008 – M. Saiko, 'Noise', in: H. Cançik & H. Schneider (eds), *Brill's New Pauly Online*, Leiden: Brill, s.v.

Sanders 1996 – P. Sanders, *The Provenance of Deuteronomy 32* (OTS, 37), Leiden: Brill.

Sanders 2007 – P. Sanders, '*Argumenta ad Deum* in the Plague Prayers of Mursili II and in the Book of Psalms', in: B. Becking & E. Peels (eds), *Psalms and Prayers: Papers Read at the Joint Meeting of the Society of Old Testament Study and Het Oudtestamentisch Werkgezelschap in Nederland en België, Apeldoorn August 2006* (OTS, 55), Leiden: Brill, 181-217.

Sarraute 1998 – N. Sarraute, *Le silence* (Collection Folio/Théâtre), ed. A. Rykner, Paris: Gallimard, 2nd ed.

Sartre 1951 – J.-P. Sartre, *Le diable et le bon Dieu: Trois actes et onze tableaux* (Collection Folio, 869), Paris: Gallimard.

Sauneron 1959 – S. Sauneron, 'Les songes et leur interprétation dans l'Égypte ancienne', in: Esnoul 1959, 17-61.

Sauneron 1988 – S. Sauneron, *Les prêtres de l'ancienne Égypte*, rev. edition, Paris: Perséa (Eng. tr. by D. Lorton: *The Priests of Ancient Egypt*, London: Cornell Univ. Press, 2000).

Schaap-Jonker 2008 – J. Schaap-Jonker, *Before the Face of God: An Interdisciplinary Study of the Meaning of the Sermon and the Hearer's God Image, Personality and Affective State*, Zürich: LIT-Verlag.

Schäfer 1972 – P. Schäfer, *Die Vorstellung vom Heiligen Geist in der rabbinischen Literatur* (StANT, 28), München: Kösel.

Schäfer 1990 – P. Schäfer, 'Jewish Magic Literature in Late Antiquity and Early Middle Ages', *JJS* 41, 75-91.

Schäfer & Shaked 1994 – P. Schäfer & S. Shaked (eds.), *Magische Texte aus der Kairoer Geniza*, Bd. 1 (TSAJ, 42), Tübingen: Mohr.

Schäfer et al. 1998 – P. Schäfer et al. (eds.), *Magische Texte aus der Kairoer Geniza*, Bd. 2 (TSAJ, 64). Tübingen: Mohr.

Scheepers 1960 – J.H. Scheepers, *Die Gees van God en dies gees van die mens in die Ou Testament*. Kampen: Kok.

Schellenberg 2009 – A. Schellenberg, 'Abwesenheit Gottes', *WiBiLex.de: Das wissenschaftliche Bibellexikon am Internet*, 2009 (http://www.bibelwissenschaft.de/nc/wibilex/das-bibellexikon/details/quelle/WIBI/referenz/12312/)

Scherf 2009 – J. Scherf, 'Pythia', in: H. Cançik & H. Schneider (eds), *Brill's New Pauly Online: Antiquity Volumes*, Leiden: Brill, s.v.

Schlichting 1977 – R. Schlichting, 'Hören', *LÄ*, Bd. 2, Wiesbaden: Harrassowitz, 1232-1235.

Schlichting 1982a – R. Schlichting, 'Ohrenstelen', *LÄ*, vol. 4, Wiesbaden: Harrasowitz, 562-566.

Schlichting 1982b – R. Schlichting, 'Prophetie', *LÄ*, Bd. 4, Wiesbaden: Harrassowitz, 1122-1125.

Schmidt 2007 – W.H. Schmidt, *Alttestamentlicher Glaube*, Neukirchen: Neukirchener Verlag, 10th ed.

Schloen et. al. 2009 – J.D. Schloen et al., 'The New Excavations at Zincirli and the Stele of KTMW', *BASOR* 356, 1-80.

Schmitt 1999 – É.-E. Schmitt, *Théâtre: La Nuit de Valogness; Le Visiteur; Le Bâillon; L'École du diable*, Paris: Albin Michel.

Schmitt 2002 – É.-E. Schmitt, *Plays: 1: Don Juan on Trial; The Visitor; Enigma Variations; Between Worlds*, tr. Jeremy Sams and John Clifford, London: Methuen Publishing.

Schmitt 2004a – É.-E. Schmitt, *Oscar et la dame rose*, ed. W. Adler & G. Krüger, Stuttgart: Reclam (original publication: Paris: Albin, 2002).

Schmitt 2004b – R. Schmitt, *Magie im Alten Testament* (AOAT, 313), Münster: Ugarit-Verlag.

Schmitt 2005 – É.-E. Schmitt, *Oscar and the Lady in Pink*, tr. Adriana Hunter, London: Atlantic Books.

Schoors 2003 – A. Schoors, 'Theodicy in Qohelet', in: Laato & De Moor 2003, 375-409.

Schulte & Schneider 2009 – "The Absence of the Deity in Rape Scenes of the Hebrew Bible", in: Dalferth 2009, 21-33.

Schulz 2008 – P. Schulz, *Atheistischer Glaube: Eine Lebensphilosophie ohne Gott*, Wiesbaden: marixverlag.

Schwemer 2007 – D. Schwemer, *Abwehrzauber und Behexung: Studien zum Schadenzauberglauben im Alten Mesopotamien*, Wiesbaden: Harrassowitz.

Scott 1965 – R.B.Y. Scott, *Proverbs, Ecclesiastes: A New Translation with Introduction and Commentary* (AncB), New York: Doubleday, 2nd ed.

Seifert 1996 – B.Seifert, *Metaphorisches Reden von Gott im Hoseabuch* (FRLANT, 166), Vandenhoeck & Ruprecht.

Seils 1962 – M. Seils, *Der Gedanke vom Zusammenwirken Gottes und des Menschen in Luthers Theologie* (BFChTh, 2.Reihe, 50), Gütersloh: Mohn.

Seow 1997 – C.L. Seow, *Ecclesiastes: A New Translation with Introduction and Commentary* (AncB, 18C), New York: Doubleday.

Seux 1976 – M.-J. Seux, *Hymnes et prières aux dieux de Babylonie et d'Assyrie: Introduction, traduction et notes* (LAPO, 8), Paris: Éditions du Cerf.

Seybold 1996 – K. Seybold, *Die Psalmen* (HAT, 1/15), Tübingen: Mohr Siebeck.

Seybold 2003 – K. Seybold, *Poetik der Psalmen*, Stuttgart: Kohlhammer.

Shelley 1962 – P.B. Shelley, 'A Defense of Poetry', reprinted in: G.W. Allen & H.H. Clark (eds.), *Literary Criticism: Pope to Croce*, Detroit: Wayne State Univ. Press.

Shupak 1989-1990 – N. Shupak, ''Egyptian "Prophecy" and Biblical Prophecy: Did the Phenomenon of Prophecy, in Biblical Sense, Exist in Ancient Egypt?', *JEOL* 31, 1-040.

Shupak 1993 – N. Shupak, *Where Can Wisdom Be Found? The Sage's Language in the Bible and in Ancient Egyptian Literature* (OBO, 130), Fribourg: Univ. Press.

Simons 2000 – A. Simons, 'The Author's Silence: Transcendence and Representation in Mikhail Bakhtin', in: Bulhof & Ten Kate 2000, 354-374.

Simpson 1972 – W.K. Simpson (ed.), *The Literature of Ancient Egypt*, New Haven: Yale Univ. Press.

Singer 2002 – I. Singer, *Hittite Prayers* (SBL.WAW,11), Leiden: Brill.

Sittser 2007 – J. Sittser, *When God Doesn't Answer Your Prayer: Insights to Keep You Praying with Greater Faith and Deeper Hope*, Grand-Rapids: Zondervan.

Smith 1979 – G.H. Smith, *The Case against God*, New York: Prometheus.

Smith 1990 – M.S. Smith, *The Early History of God: Yahweh and the Other Deities in Ancient Israel*, San Francisco: Harper & Row.

Smith 2001 – M.S. Smith, *The Origins of Biblical Monotheism: Israel's Polytheistic Background and the Ugaritic Texts*, Oxford: Oxford Univ. Press.

Smith & Pitard 2009 – M.S. Smith & W.T. Pitard, *The Ugaritic Baal Cycle*, vol. 2 (VT.S, 55), Leiden: Brill.

Sneller 2000 – R. Sneller, 'Crisis in Our Speaking about God: Derrida and Barth's *Epistle to the Romans*', in: Bulhof & Ten Kate 2000, 223-249.

Soares 2006 – C. Soares, 'No Prayer Prescription: Send Good Vibrations, but Keep It to Yourself', *Scientific American* 294/6, 12.

Sollberger & Kupper 1971 – E. & J.-R. Kupper, *Inscriptions royales sumériennes et akkadiennes* (LAPO, 3), Paris: Éditions du Cerf.

Sorace & Zimmerling 2007 – M.A. Sorace & P. Zimmerling (eds), *Das Schweigens Gottes in der Welt* (Jahresschriften der "Gesellschaft der Freunde christlicher Mystik e.V.", 2), Nordhausen: Traugott Baitz.

Soskice 1987 – J.M. Soskice, *Metaphor and Religious Language*, Oxford: Clarendon (original publication: Oxford: Clarendon, 1985).

Sowayan 1985 – S.A. Sowayan, *Nabṭi Poetry: The Oral Poetry of Arabia*, Berkeley: Univ. of California Press.

Sparks 2008 – K.L. Sparks, *God's Word in Human Words: An Evangelical Appropriation of Critical Biblical Scholarship*, Grand Rapids: Baker.

Spieckermann 2004 – H. Spieckermann, 'Schweigen und Beten: Von stillem Lobgesang und zerbrechender Rede im Psalter', in: F.-L. Hossfeld & L. Schwienhorst-Schönberger (eds), *Das Manna fällt auch heute noch: Beiträge zur Geschichte und Theologie des Alten, Ersten Testaments* (Fs E. Zenger) (HBS, 44), Freiburg: Herder, 567-584.

Spieckermann 2008 – H. Spieckermann, 'Wenn Gott schweigt: Jüdische Gedanken zu Schicksal und Vorsehung aus hellenistischer Zeit', in: R.G. Kratz & H. Spieckermann (eds), *Vorsehung, Schicksal und göttliche Macht*, Tübingen: Mohr Siebeck, 104-124.

Spronk 1986 – K. Spronk, *Beatific Afterlife in Ancient Israel and in the Near East* (AOAT, 219), Neukirchener Verlag: Neukirchen.

Spronk 1997 – K. Spronk, *Nahum* (HCOT), Kampen: Kok Pharos.

Spronk 2010 – K. Spronk, 'De stilte van God', *Schrift* 248, 41-44.

Spykerboer 1976 – H. Spykerboer, *The Structure and Composition of Deutero-Isaiah*, Meppel: Krips Repro.

Stachel 1989 – G. Stachel, *Gebet – Meditation – Schweigen: Schritte der Spiritualität*, Freiburg i.B: Herder Taschenbuch Verlag.

Starbuck 1999 – S.R.A. Starbuck, *Court Oracles in the Psalms: The So-Called Royal Psalms in their Ancient Near Eastern Context* (SBL.DS, 172), Atlanta: SBL.

Starr 1990 – I. Starr, *Queries to the Sungod: Divination and Politics in Sargonid Assyria* (SAA, 4), Helsinki: Helsinki Univ. Press.

Steck 1998 – O.H. Steck, *Die erste Jesajarolle von Qumran (1QIs[a]): Schreibweise als Leseanleitung für ein Prophetenbuch* (Stuttgarter Bibelstudien, 173/1-2), 2 vols, Stuttgart: Katholisches Bibelwerk.

Stemberger 2003 – G. ' "Ich habe nichts Besseres für den Menschen gefunden als Schweigen" (mAv 1,17)', In: I. Fischer *et al.* (eds), *Auf den Spuren der schriftgelehrten Weisen (Fs Johannes Marböck)* (BZAW, 331), Berlin: De Gruyter, 401-10.

Stenger 2009 – J. Stenger, 'Somnus', in: H. Cançik & H. Schneider (eds), *Brill's New Pauly Online: Antiquity Volumes*, Leiden: Brill, s.v.

Stiver 1996 – D. Stiver, *The Philosophy of Religious Language: Sign, Symbol and Story*, Oxford: Blackwell.

Stoebe 1973 – H.J. Stoebe, *Das erste Buch Samuelis* (KAT, 8/1), Gütersloh: Mohn.

Stott 2008 – K.M. Stott, *Why Did They Write This Way? Reflections on References to Written Documents in the Hebrew Bible and Ancient Literature*, London: T & T Clark International.

Strauß 2000 – H. Strauß, *Hiob: 2. Teilband 19,1–42,17* (BKAT, 16/2), Neukirchen: Neukirchener Verlag.

Streck 2007 – B. Streck (ed.), *Die gezeigte und die verborgene Kultur*, Wiesbaden: Harrassowitz.

Stuart 1987 – D. Stuart, *Hosea – Jonah* (WBC, 31), Waco: Word Books.

Stulman 2004 – L. Stulman, 'Jeremiah as a Polyphonic Response to Suffering', in: Kaltner & Stulman 2004, 302-318.

Sweeney 2005 – M.A.C. Sweeney, *Form and Intertextuality in Prophetic and Apocalyptic Literature* (FAT, 45), Tübingen: Mohr Siebeck.

Sweeney 2007 – M.A.C. Sweeney, *I & II Kings: A Commentary* (OTL), Westminster John Knox: London.

Swinburne 2004 – R. Swinburne, *The Existence of God*, Oxford: Clarendon Press, 2nd ed.

Szpakowska 2001 – K. Szpakowska, 'Through the Looking Glass: Dreams in Ancient Egypt', in: K. Bulkeley (ed.), *Dreams: A Reader on Religious, Cultural, and Psychological Dimensions of Dreaming*, New York: Palgrave, 29-43.

Szpakowska 2006 – K. Szpakowska (ed.), *Through a Glass Darkly: Magic, Dreams and Prophecy in Ancient Egypt*, Swansea: Classical Press of Wales.

Talon 2005 – Ph. Talon, *The Standard Babylonian Creation Myth* Enūma eliš (SAA.CT, 4), Helsinki: Helsinki Univ. Press.

Tam 2002 – E.P.C. Tam, 'Silence of God and God of Silence', *Asia Journal of Theology* 16, 152-163.

Taracha 2000 – P. Taracha, *Ersetzen und Entsühnen: Das mittelhethitische Ersatzritual für den Großkönig Tuthalija (CTH*448,4) und verwandte Texte* (CHANE, 5), Leiden: Brill.

Tate 1990 – M.E. Tate, *Psalms 51–100* (WBC, 20), Dallas, Word Books.

Tavanti 2008 – P. Tavanti, *Das Schweigen Gottes* (Tanztheater – Regie: P. Tavanti/Choreographie: B.J. Lins), St. Blasien.
(http://www.tavanti.de/schweigengottestext.html)

Taylor 1984 – M.C. Taylor, *Erring: A Postmodern A/theology*, Chicago: Univ. of Chicago.

Taylor 2007 – M.C. Taylor, *After God* (Religion and Postmodernism), Chicago: Univ. of Chicago Press.

Terrien 1978 – S.L. Terrien, *The Elusive Presence: Toward a New Biblical Theology*, San Francisco: Harper & Row.

Terrien 2003 – S.L. Terrien, *The Psalms: Strophic Structure and Theological Commentary*, Grand Rapids: Eerdmans.

Tertel 1994 – H.J. Tertel, *Text and Transmission: An Empirical Model for the Literary Development of Old Testament Narratives* (BZAW, 221), Berlin: De Gruyter.

Thelle 2002 – R.I. Thelle, *Ask God: Divine Consultation in the Literature of the Hebrew Bible*, Frankfurt a. M.: Lang.

Thiel 2009 – W. Thiel, *Könige* (BKAT, 11/2-4), Neukirchen: Neukirchener Verlag.

Thibon 1959 – G. Thibon, *Vous serez comme des dieux*, Paris: Fayard.

Thomas 1989 – R. Thomas, *Oral Tradition and Written Record in Classical Athens* (Cambridge Studies in Oral and Literate Culture, 18), Cambridge: Cambridge Univ. Press.

Thomas 1992 – R. Thomas, *Literacy and Orality in Ancient Greece*, Cambridge: Cambridge Univ. Press.

Tiemeyer 2008 – L.-S. Tiemeyer, 'Through a Glass Darkly: Zechariah's Unprocessed Visionary Experience', *VT* 58, 573-594.

Tigay 1982 – J. H. Tigay, *The Evolution of the Gilgamesh Epic*, Philadelphia: Univ. of Pennsylvania Press.

Tigay 1996 – J.H. Tigay, *The JPS Torah Commentary: Deuteronomy*, Philadelphia: Jewish Publication Society.

Tov 2004 – E. Tov, *Scribal Practices and Approaches Reflected in the Texts Found in the Judean Desert* (StTDJ, 54), Leiden: Brill.

Trachtenberg 1939 – J. Trachtenberg, *Jewish Magic and Superstition: A Study in Folk Religion*, New York: Behrman's Jewish Book House [several reprints].

Trites 2004 – A.A. Trites, *The New Testament Concept of Witness* (MSSNTS, 31), Cambridge: Cambridge Univ. Press (original edition: 1977).

Tropper & Hayajneh 2003 – J. Tropper & H. Hayajneh, 'El, der scharfsinnige und verständige Gott: Ugaritisch *ltpn 'il dp'id* im Lichte der arabischen Lexeme *laṭīf* und *fu'ād*', *Or* 72, 159-182.

Tsukimoto 1990 – A. Tsukimoto, 'Akkadian Tablets in the Hirayama Collection (I)', *Acta Sumerologica* 12, 177-259.

Tsumura 2007 – D.T. Tsumura, *The First Book of Samuel* (NICOT), Grand Rapids: Eerdmans.

Ulrich 2003 – E. Ulrich, 'Impressions and Intuition: Sense Divisions in Ancient Manuscripts of Isaiah', in: Korpel & Oesch (eds) 2003, 279-307.

Urbach 1975 – E.E. Urbach, *The Sages: Their Concepts and Beliefs*, tr. I. Abrahams, Jerusalem: Magnes.

Van Dam 1997 – C. van Dam, *The Urim and Thummim: A Means of Revelation in Ancient Israel*, Winona Lake: Eisenbrauns.

Van den Hout 2009 – Th. van den Hout, 'Schreiber. D. Bei den Hethitern', *RLA* 12. 3/4, Berlin: De Gruyter, 273-280.

Van der Lans 2001 – J. van der Lans, 'Empirical Research into the Human Images of God', in: H.G. Ziebertz, *et al.* (eds), *The Human Image of God* (Fs. A. van der Ven), Leiden: Brill, 347-360.

Van Leeuwen 1985 –C. van Leeuwen, *Amos* (PredOT), Nijkerk: Callenbach.

Van der Lugt 2006 – P. van der Lugt, *Cantos and Strophes in Biblical Hebrew Poetry with Special Reference to the First Book of the Psalter* (OTS, 53), Leiden: Brill.

Van der Meer 1987 – L.B. Van der Meer, *The Bronze Liver of Piacenza: Analysis of a Polytheistic Structure* (Dutch Monographs on Ancient History and Archaeology, 2), Amsterdam: Gieben.

Van der Toorn 1985 – K. van der Toorn, *Sin and Sanction in Israel and Mesopotamia: A Comparative Study*, Assen: Van Gorcum.

Van der Toorn 2003 – K. van der Toorn, 'Theodicy in Akkadian Literature', in: A. Laato & J.C. de Moor 2003, 57-89.

Van der Toorn 2007 – K. van der Toorn, *Scribal Culture and the Making of the Hebrew Bible*, Cambridge: Harvard Univ. Press.

Van Dijk 2000 – J.J.A. van Dijk, 'Inanna, le bon augure de Samsu'iluna', in: A.R. George & I.L. Finkel (eds), *Wisdom, Gods and Literature: Studies in Assyriology in Honour of W.G. Lambert*, Winona Lake: Eisenbrauns, 119-129.

Van Dijk 2006 – Y. van Dijk, *Leegte, leegte die ademt: Het typografisch wit in de moderne poëzie*, Nijmegen: Vantilt.

Van Hecke 2005 – P. van Hecke (ed.), *Metaphor in the Hebrew Bible*, Leuven: Peeters.

Van Henten 1999 – J.W. Van Henten, 'Angel II', in: K. van der Toorn *et al.* (eds), *Dictionary of Deities and Demons in the Bible*, Leiden: Brill, 2nd ed., 50-53.

Van Leeuwen 1996 – R.C. Van Leeuwen, ברא, NIDOTTE, vol. 1, Carlisle: Paternoster Press, 728-735.

Van Praag 2008 – H.M. van Praag. *God en psyche: De redelijkheid van het geloven – Visies van een Jood*, Amsterdam: Boom.

Vanstiphout 2003 – L.J. Vanstiphout, *Epics of Sumerian Kings: The Matter of Aratta*, ed. J.S. Cooper, Atlanta: SBL.

Viberg 1992 – Å. Viberg, *Symbols of Law: A Contextual Analysis of Legal Symbolic Acts in the Old Testament* (CB.OT, 34), Stockholm: Almqvist & Wiksell.

Viberg 2007 – Å. Viberg, *Prophets in Action: An Analysis of Prophetic Symbolic Acts in the Old Testament* (CB.OT, 55), Stockholm: Almqvist &Wiksell.

Vieyra 1959 – M. Vieyra, 'Les songes et leur interprétation chez les Hittites', in: Esnoul 1959, 87-98.

Villamil Touriño 2006 – A. Villamil Touriño, 'Metaphor in Scientific Language: A Study on Medical Texts', in: M.J. Luzón Marco *et al.* (eds), *Metaphor, Blending and their Application to Semantic Analysis: Actas del congreso AELCO (mayo 2004)*, Zaragoza: Anubar, 171-189.

Villanueva 2008 – F. G. Villanueva, *The 'Uncertainty of a Hearing': A Study of the Sudden Change of Mood in the Psalms of Lament* (VT.S, 121), Leiden: Brill.

Villing 2006 – A. Villing (ed.), *The Greeks in the East*, (BMP Research Paper, 157), London: British Museum.

Vittmann 1995 – G. Vittmann, 'Zwei demotische Briefe an den Gott Thot', *Zeitschrift für Demotistik und Koptologie* 22, 169-181.

Vlaardingerbroek 1999 – J. Vlaardingerbroek, *Zephaniah* (HCOT), Leuven: Peeters.

Von Beckenrath 1992 – J. von Beckenrath, 'Die Geschichte von Chonsemḥab und dem Geist', *ZÄS* 119, 90-107.

Wackenheim 2002 – Ch. Wackenheim, *Quand Dieu se tait*, Paris: Éditions du Cerf.

Wächter 1984 – L. Wächter, 'Prophetie in der Umwelt des Alten Testaments', in: G. Wallis (ed.), *Von Bileam bis Jesaja: Studien zur alttestamentlichen Prophetie von ihren Anfängen bis zum 8. Jahrhundert v. Chr.*, Berlin: Evangelische Verlagsanstalt, 9-31.

Waetzoldt 2009 – H. Waetzoldt, 'Schreiber. A. Im 3. Jahrtausend', *RLA* 12. 3/4, Berlin: De Gruyter, 250-266.

Wagner-Hasel 2010 – B. Wagner-Hasel, 'Adultery', in: H. Cançik & H. Schneider (eds), *Der Neue Pauly Online*, Leiden: Brill, s.v.

Walde 2009 – Chr. Walde, 'Dreams; Interpretation of Dreams', in: H. Cançik & H. Schneider (eds), *Brill's New Pauly Online*, Leiden: Brill, s.v.

Watanabe 1987 – K. Watanabe, *Die adê-Vereidigung anlässlich der Thronfolgeregelung Asarhaddons* (BaghM, Beiheft 3), Berlin: Mann.

Watts 1985 – J.D.W. Watts, *Isaiah 1–3* (WBC, 24), Waco: Word Books.

Weinfeld 1972 – M. Weinfeld, *Deuteronomy and the Deuteronomic School*, Oxford: Clarendon.

Weinfeld 1991 – M. Weinfeld, *Deuteronomy 1–11: A New Translation with Introduction and Commentary* (AncB, 5), New York: Doubleday.

Weippert 1997 – M. Weippert, *Jahwe und die anderen Götter: Studien zur Religionsgeschichte des antiken Israel in ihrem syrisch-palästinischen Kontext* (FAT, 18), Tübingen: Mohr.

Weippert 2001 – M. Weippert, ' "Ich bin Jahwe" – "Ich bin Ištar von Arbela": Deuterojesaja im Lichte der neuassyrischen Prophetie', in: B. Huwyler *et al.* (eds), *Prophetie und Psalmen* (Fs. K. Seybold) (AOAT, 280), Münster: Ugarit Verlag, 31-60.

Weippert 2002a – H. Weippert, 'Der Lärm und die Stille: Etno-archäologische Annäherung an das biblische Alltagsleben', in: A. Lemaire (ed.), *Congress Volume Basel 2001* (VT.S. 92), Leiden: Brill, 163-184.

Weippert 2002b – M. Weippert, ' "König, fürchte dich nicht!": Assyrische Prophetie im 7.Jahrhundert v.Chr.', *Or* 71, 1-54.

Wenham 1994 – G. Wenham, *Genesis 16–50* (WBC, 2), Dallas: Word Books.

Westermann 1960 – C. Westermann, *Grundformen prophetischer Rede* (BEvTh, 31), München: Kaiser.

Westermann 1981 – C. Westermann, *Genesis* (BKAT, 1/2), Neukirchen: Neukirchener Verlag.

Westermann 1986 – K. Westermann, *Das Buch Jesaja* (ATD, 19), Göttingen: Vandenhoeck & Ruprecht, 5th ed.

Westermann 1990 – C. Westermann, *Die Klagelieder: Forschungsgeschichte und Auslegung*, Neukirchen-Vluyn: Neukirchener Verlag.

White 2010 – R. White, *Talking about God: The Concept of Analogy and the Problem of Religious Language* (Transcending Boundaries in Philosophy and Theology), Farnham: Ashgate.

Whybray 1975 – R.N. Whybray, *Isaiah 40-66* (NCBC), Grand Rapids: Eerdmans (repr. 1996).

Wick 1998 – P. Wick, 'There Was Silence in Heaven (Revelation 8:1): An Annotation to Israel Knohl's "Between Voice and Silence" ', *JBL* 117, 512-4.

Widengren 1969 – G. Widengren, *Religionsphänomenologie*, Berlin: De Gruyter.

Wiesel 1979 – E. Wiesel, *Le procès de Shamgorod tel qu'il se déroula le 25 février 1649*, Paris: Éditions du Seuil.

Wiesel 1986 – E. Wiesel, *The Trial of God (as it was held on February 25, 1649, in Shamgorod*, tr. Marion Wiesel, New York: Schocken Books.

Wiesel 1987 – E. Wiesel, 'Die politisch-moralische Aufgabe des Schriftstellers heute', in: O. Schwenke (ed.), *Erinnerung als Gegenwart: Elie Wiesel in Loccum*, Rehburg-Loccum: Evangelische Akademie, 103-126.

Wiesel 2006 – *Night*, tr. Marion Wiesel, London: Hill & Wang (original publication: Paris: Les Éditions de Minuit, 1958).

Wiesel 2007 – E. Wiesel, *La nuit*, Paris: Les Éditions de Minuit, revised edition (original publication: Paris: Les Éditions de Minuit, 1958).

Wildberger 1982 – H. Wildberger, *Jesaja*, 3.Teilband: Jesaja 28–39 – Das Buch, der Prophet und seine Botschaft (BKAT, 10/3), Neukirchen-Vluyn: Neukirchener Verlag.

Williamson 1985 – H.G.M. Williamson, *Ezra–Nehemiah* (WBC, 16), Waco: Word Books.

Wimmer 2008 – St.J. Wimmer, 'A New Hieratic Ostracon from Ashkelon', *Tel Aviv* 35, 65-72.

Wolff 1985 – H.W. Wolff, *Dodekapropheton 2; Joel und Amos* (BKAT14/2), Neukirchen-Vluyn: Neukirchener Verlag, 3rd ed.

Wolterstorff 1995 – N. Wolterstorff, *Divine Discourse: Philosophical Reflections on the Claim that God Speaks*, Cambridge: Cambridge Univ. Press.

Wolterstorff 2003 – N. Wolterstorff, 'The Silence of the God Who Speaks', *Philosophia* 30, 13-32.

Wood 2008 – A. Wood, *Of Wings and Wheels: A Synthetic Study of the Biblical Cherubim* (BZAW, 385), Berlin: De Gruyter.

Wulf 1992 – C. Wulf, 'Präsenz des Schweigens', in: Kamper & Wulf 1992, 7-16.

Wyatt 1998 – N. Wyatt, *Religious Texts from Ugarit: The Words of Ilimilku and his Colleagues* (The Biblical Seminar, 53), Sheffield: Sheffield Academic Press. 2006

Young 1972 – *The Book of Isaiah: A Commentary*, vol. 3, Grand Rapids: Eerdmans (reprint 1996).

Younger 2002 – K.L. Younger, *Judges, Ruth* (The NIV Application Commentary), Grand Rapids: Zondervan.

Yu 2008 – N. Yu, 'Metaphor from Body and Culture', in: R.W. Gibbs, Jr. (ed.), *The Cambridge Handbook of Metaphor and Thought*, Cambridge: Cambridge Univ. Press, 247-261.

Zandee 1960 – J. Zandee, *Death as an Enemy according to Ancient Egyptian Conceptions* (Supplements to Numen, 5), Leiden: Brill.

Zgoll 2002 –A. Zgoll, 'Die Welt im Schlaf sehen: Inkubation von Träumen im antiken Mesopotamien', *WO* 32, 74-101.

Zgoll 2006 – A. Zgoll, *Traum und Welterleben im antiken Mesopotamien: Traumtheorie und Traumpraxis im 3.-1. Jt. v.Chr. als Horizont einer Kulturgeschichte des Träumens* (AOAT, 333), Münster: Ugarit Verlag.

Zgoll 2007 – A. Zgoll, 'Schauseite, verborgene Seite und geheime Deutung des babylonischen Neujahrsfestes: Entwurf einer Handlungstheorie von "Zeigen und Verbergen"', in: Streck 2007, 165-190.

Zimmerli 1969 – W. Zimmerli, *Ezechiel*, 2.Teilband: Ezechiel 25–48 (BKAT, 13/2), Neukirchen: Neukirchener Verlag.

INDEX OF SUBJECTS

Aaron 118, 125f., 148, 191f.
Abraham 27, 76, 112, 124f., 281
Absalom 83, 86
absurdity 31, 49; see also: rationality
abyss 24, 105, 172, 232
Adad 102, 142. 145, 168f., 217, 239; see also: Hadad
Adam 82
Adapa 247
adversity, see: suffering
afterlife 113, 143; see also: death, Nether World
Agamemnon 179
agnosticism xi, 26, 32, 33f., 49, 54, 290
Ahab 126
Aḫat-abiša 175
Aleppo 87, 168
Allani 143
alliance, see: covenant
Amaziah (priest) 93, 186f.
ambiguity 24, 26, 34, 40, 42, 44, 49, 60, 118, 233
Amenemhet I 160, 172
ʿAmmurapi 174
Amnon 83
Amos (prophet) 93, 186f., 228
Amun(-Re) 48, 57, 68, 111f., 114, 117, 124, 145, 171, 231f., 256-258
analogy 60f., 65, 69, 106, 122; see also: metaphor
ʿAnatu 81, 147, 160, 247
ancestors 116, 136, 142, 160-162, 174, 221, 226, 229
anchorite 18
androgyny 262
angel, see: deity – angel
Anshar 245
answer 2-10, 16, 22, 27-30, 32-34, 40f., 53, 67, 73, 77, 82, 86f., 89, 94f., 97, 100-102, 104, 108, 112, 114, 116f., 119, 125-127, 129f., 134f., 139f., 143-145, 147, 149, 154, 158, 163f., 168, 173, 175, 178, 185 , 189, 193, 217-219, 224, 236f., 239-241, 243, 246, 250, 252-254, 257, 259, 261-276, 280, 285, 288, 294, 296f., 300
anti-Semitism 54
Anu 48, 141, 247
Anunnaki 245
Anzû 250
apocalyptic 149, 164, 171-173, 216
Apollo 179f.
apophatic 19, 68
apostasy 10, 249
apprehension, see: fear
Apsû 130, 238, 245
Apšukka f161
Aqhatu 81, 122, 144, 146
Arbela 175, 262
Aristotle 61
Asarluḫi 113
Ashkelon 180
assembly, see: deity – council
Assur (city) 140f.
Assur (god) 48, 138, 262
Assurbanipal 82, 142, 196, 214, 245
astrology 48, 111, 151, 158, 210, 212, 219, 229
Aten 103
atheism xi, 26, 30-32, 34, 48-53, 289
Athiratu 146
ʿAthtartu 257
Attanu 146f., 162, 197-199, 207
Atum 172
Augustine 18
authenticity 185
author, see: scribe
automata 32, 44
awe, see: fear

Baal, see: Baʿlu
bad, see: evil
Balaam 150, 173, 178, 182, 204, 216f., 220
Baʿlshamayn 173

Baʿlu 73, 146f., 160, 174, 197f., 219, 247, 252f., 257
Bar Hadad 173
Barth, K. 20-22, 36-38, 40, 42-44, 55, 57, 193, 291-293
Bashan 48
Bath Qol 165, 287
Bayâ 262
beauty 3, 67, 235
Beckett, S. 5f.
Bel 262
belief, see: faith
Belshazzar 151
Benedict XVI 23f., 49, 70
Bergman, I. 8-10
biblical theology 36, 57, 75, 237
Black, M. 62f.
blank, see: space (blank)
blasphemy 30, 96, 100, 129. 241
blessing 29, 69, 103, 123, 126, 128, 146, 175, 205, 217, 265, 284, 291, 300
Boatman 177
book 98, 182f., 188, 206, 209f., 228
brontoscopy 147; see also: thunder
Buddhism 10, 50
Byblos 97f., 170f., 203

calamity, see: death, destruction, evil, nature
canon 37f., 75, 101,116, 135, 165, 182, 193, 197, 199, 211, 221, 224, 226, 228, 233, 237, 241, 246, 275f., 297, 299
Carmel 253
Carthusians 19, 45
Cassandra 179
cherub, see: angel
Christianity 10, 19, 24, 26, 29f., 36-43, 46, 49, 51, 53f., 68, 74, 118, 158, 165, 224, 224, 226, 280, 283, 287f., 290, 292, 296, 298, 303
Cistercians 18
clamor 123, 126f., 130, 238f.; see also: noise

communication 1, 10, 18-20, 27, 29, 41, 45, 47. 50, 54, 56, 58-60, 66, 71f., 76, 79, 119, 135-238, 245, 271, 287; see also: deity – speech
complaint 22, 28, 30, 80, 100f., 129, 175, 177, 189, 207, 211, 234, 236f., 250f., 259, 261, 263f., 272-274, 299; see also: lamentation, prayer
Condell, P. 289f.
conversion 23, 44
Coptic 18, 37
cosmology 31, 49, 148, 231-235, 280
Costanzo, S. 45f.
covenant 39, 44, 53, 151, 161, 237, 274, 291, 300f.
creation, see: deity – creator, nature
crime, see: offenses
crisis 27, 46, 51, 76, 199f., 202
criticism 21, 34, 54
– historical 21, 36
– literary 187, 198, 207
– redaction 58, 96, 116, 164, 182, 185, 187, 190, 227, 248f., 254
cryptography 185
cult 82, 112, 132f., 140, 171, 173-175, 181, 199f., 217, 221, 223f., 226f., 245, 248, 254, 267
curse 12, 99, 118, 126, 128, 217, 263, 284
Cyrus 122, 284

Dachau xii; see also: Shoah
Dagan 169f., 218
Damgalnunna 130
Daniel 29, 99, 122, 151, 189f., 206, 228
Daniʾilu 122, 126, 134, 144, 146, 226, 253
David 82, 86f., 91, 111, 150, 164, 221f., 236f., 240f., 270f., 284
Dawkins, R. 26, 31, 50
deafness 11, 31, 90, 98f., 108, 128, 140, 144, 190, 238; see also: dumbness

INDEX OF SUBJECTS

death 6, 8, 10, 20, 22-26, 30-33, 37-40, 42, 49, 51, 67, 73, 84, 97, 100, 102-108, 114f., 125, 130-133, 135, 153, 158-163, 165, 172, 174, 179, 188, 197f., 211, 217, 220, 223, 252, 256, 263, 268, 271f., 275f., 286
death, see also: Motu, Osiris
death, see also: deity – death
Deber 164
Deborah 284
defeat 116, 133, 219, 238, 245, 247
deification 30, 67, 116, 136, 161, 226, 260
Deism xi, 50
deity *passim*
- absence xi, 1, 4f., 22-26, 34, 39-42, 47-49, 55, 237, 244, 297
- acting 25, 36, 40, 50, 57f., 63, 69, 76, 113, 121, 127, 139f., 154, 181, 217, 231, 234, 236f., 241, 259, 263, 268-270, 276, 287f., 291, 301
- almighty, see: – omnipotence
- angel 11, 29, 102, 106, 151f., 154, 157-159, 162-167, 190f., 216, 226, 229, 233, 241, 243f., 281f., 303f.
- anthropomorphism 57-60, 68, 75f., 134, 151, 159-161, 226, 235, 260
- benevolent, see: – goodness
- character 39f.
- commandment, Law 17, 24, 48, 127, 149f., 151f., 155f., 179f., 181, 183, 186, 188, 205, 210, 224, 231, 234, 290, 299, 302
- compassion 40, 249, 259, 286; see also: – emotions, – grace, – mercy
- council – 142, 144, 150, 164f., 251f.
- creator 21f., 40, 46, 53, 56, 66f., 97, 101, 103, 111, 127, 134, 153, 172, 201, 231-238, 245f., 251f., 255, 257, 260, 262f., 274, 276, 285f., 288, 299, 302
- death 20, 22-25, 30-32, 39, 47-49, 51, 67, 73, 248, 252, 275
- demon 96, 99, 102, 117f., 162-164
- emotions 247
- essence 39f., 291
- existence xi, 1, 5, 9, 23, 26, 31-34, 40, 50, 65, 114, 162, 280, 283, 291, 295, 301
- fear 245-247, 275-277
- forbearance 247-250, 275f.
- forgiveness 7, 11, 84, 120; see also: – grace, – mercy
- freedom 21, 27, 32, 40, 53, 55, 154, 236, 274
- goodness xi, 3, 27, 34, 39f., 66, 117, 120, 128f., 132, 157, 225, 231, 233, 257, 272, 299f.
- grace 21, 36, 40, 44, 154, 249, 275, 284, 300f.
- helper 105, 114, 117, 119f., 154, 173, 193, 211, 233, 240f., 251, 253f., 259, 268, 270, 283f., 291, 294
- hiddenness 8, 23f., 68f., 116, 123, 155-157, 232-234, 237, 259
- Holy Ones 163f., 165f., 243
- image 38, 45, 66-68, 70, 111, 117, 124, 135, 154f., 171, 215, 217, 226, 232, 254f.
- immanence 19, 84, 105, 112, 146, 152-154, 165f., 266-268, 270-274
- immortal, see: – living
- incapacity 250-255, 275-278
- indifference 1, 3
- inscrutability, see: – hiddenness, – remoteness
- inspiration 53, 146, 151, 156, 170, 192, 194, 201f., 207, 211, 226-229, 271, 282, 285, 287
- intelligence 49f., 301
- jealousy 247
- justice 23, 26f., 94, 129, 236f., 249
- law, see: – commandment
- listening, see: listening below
- living 38-40, 49, 98, 132, 276
- love 3, 7, 9, 23f., 40, 124, 250f.

352	INDEX OF SUBJECTS

- mercy 6f., 11, 20, 27, 114, 129, 233, 269
- monotheism 48, 51, 114, 232, 247, 303
- omnipotence 32, 34, 40, 53f., 100f., 129, 194, 210, 216, 235, 237, 240, 274, 284, 299f.
- omnipresence 50
- omniscience 32, 50, 54; see also: – providence
- *opus alienum* 40
- patience 25, 44f., 250
- plan 46, 123, 139, 238, 245, 264, 282; see also: – providence
- power 26, 28f., 34, 40, 66, 105, 134f., 158-160, 223, 232, 250, 256, 261, 275f., 286, 299f.
- presence 4, 9, 19, 22, 25, 28f., 39f., 49f., 55, 126, 155, 157
- providence 32, 52, 139
- remoteness 2f., 231-237; see also – transcendence
- representation by humans 67, 99, 117, 158, 190f., 262, 275
- representation by images 68, 160, 226, 229, 254f.
- righteousness, see: justice
- silence *passim*
- sleep 102f., 108, 134f., 238, 251, 255-261, 269, 275-277
- speech xii, 3, 5, 10f., 13-17, 19-22, 26, 30, 34f., 39f., 42-45, 52f., 55, 59, 64-70, 74-77, 121, 131, 139-150, 156-163, 166-229, 231, 234, 236, 244, 249, 254f., 262, 268, 270f., 276, 280, 282, 286-289, 291, 293-296, 303f.
- Spirit/spirit 21, 24, 29, 36, 38, 41-44, 48, 50f., 54, 92, 111, 115, 141, 150-154, 156-159, 161-166, 178f., 186, 190, 192-195, 210f., 220, 222, 225-227, 233f., 240, 249, 253f., 263f., 266, 271, 286-288, 291, 294-296, 302f.
- suffering 76, 100, 103, 112, 114, 154, 211, 232f., 244, 251f., 255,

265, 268, 272, 300-302
- theriomorphic 68, 159, 159-161, 226
- transcendence 1, 18, 25-26, 47f., 68, 232, 270, 274, 276, 300
- unicity, see: – monotheism
- weakness 36-38, 46, 256, 275, 286
- will, see: – freedom
- wrath 3, 40, 211, 241, 243f., 246f., 268, 275, 301

deliverance, see: salvation
Delphi 180
Deluge, see: Flood
demon 96, 99, 102, 117f., 162-164
demon, see: deity – demon
destiny, fate 48, 52, 87, 93, 115, 125, 169, 194, 215, 242, 251, 262, 272, 301
destruction 1, 12, 30, 39f., 43, 47f., 52, 81, 97, 112, 119, 121, 131, 133, 140, 157, 164, 171f., 176, 178, 185, 193f., 196, 211f., 225, 238f., 242, 249, 251, 256, 261, 272, 298f.
deus absconditus, see: deity – hiddenness
Deutero-Isaiah, see: Second Isaiah
devastation, see: destruction
devil 3, 27f.
devil, see also: Satan
dialectic 3, 21, 39, 40, 44, 250
dialogue 2, 4f., 10, 25, 31, 34, 47, 55, 88, 94, 140, 144, 150, 162, 179, 225, 250, 297
Dinah 83
disaster, see: death, destruction, doom, nature
disease, see: illness
distress. see: suffering
divination 81, 85, 112, 141-143, 147f., 158f., 167, 173, 176, 178, 193, 197, 202, 210f., 213, 218-226, 228, 264
doom 86, 93, 107, 176, 178f., 182f., 185-188, 207, 209, 227, 272

INDEX OF SUBJECTS

dream 11, 121, 134-136, 142-144, 159, 167, 178, 210-216, 228, 236, 257, 264, 266
dumbness 22, 90f., 93, 96f., 99, 102, 104, 108, 121, 128, 133, 188-190, 250f., 254-256, 260
Dumuzi 251
dynasty 117, 141, 169, 174, 217, 226, 240

Ea 102, 219, 238, 245, 247, 263
ear 2, 96, 99, 111f., 116, 141, 143, 155, 163, 188, 236, 239, 241, 249, 286, 288, 290, 293
earthquake 19, 210, 250, 299, 301f.
ecstasy 168, 170, 176-179, 184
Ekur 141
Eli 150
Elijah 106, 126, 166, 182, 250, 253, 257
Eliphaz 163f., 243
Elihu 92f., 194f., 236f., 240
Elisha 86, 104, 182, 241
Emar 170, 218f.
embarassment, see: incapacity
Endor 266
enemy 63f., 81f., 84, 96, 99, 104, 107, 118, 133, 136, 144, 211, 219, 244, 248, 253, 259, 262, 268f.
Enki 130, 245, 251, 255
Enkidu 84, 131, 145, 256, 263
Enlightenment 25, 52
Enlil 140, 176, 263
Enmeduranki 142, 148
Ephrem the Syrian 69
Erra 201f., 239, 246, 255, 263
Esarhaddon 82, 122, 175, 214, 262
Eshnunna 168
Esther 244
ethics 50-52, 79f., 106f., 288, 295, 297, 300
Evagrius of Pontus 18
evil xi, 3f., 27-29, 44, 47, 66, 88, 93, 96, 99, 101, 104, 117, 129, 139, 144, 179, 227, 239, 246, 251, 257, 263, 270, 299

exegesis, see: interpretation
experience 2, 16, 18f., 24, 27, 29, 33, 39-40, 42, 51, 56, 59, 61, 65, 67f., 70-72, 81, 116, 130, 139, 187, 189, 209, 212, 215f., 227, 237, 246, 256, 261, 266, 279f., 289f., 293
Ezekiel 99, 134, 149, 185, 187, 189, 223, 241, 296
Ezra 134

faith, belief 1, 3, 5, 7-9, 11, 14-16, 20, 22-42, 45f., 48f., 52f., 56f., 65f., 68-70, 74, 76, 115, 119, 135f., 143, 167, 171, 177, 186, 195, 199, 201f., 208, 212-215, 220, 225, 228, 231, 242, 244, 273f., 279-290, 292-298, 300, 302-305
fasting 7, 126, 241, 269
fatalism 237, 274; see also: destiny
fate, see: destiny
fear 9, 15, 20, 59, 81f., 84-87, 92, 107, 109, 117, 121-137, 152, 167, 175, 179, 187, 233, 237, 241, 243, 245-247, 249, 251, 254, 260-262, 275-277, 280, 294, 303; see also: – fear
Feuerbach, L. 66
figurine, see: idolatry, image
Flood, deluge 97, 147, 172, 210, 238f., 250, 275; see also: tsunami.
forbearance 47, 59, 87-95, 107-109, 122-137; see also: deity – forbearance
free will 32, 41, 52f., 55, 132, 146, 152, 154, 158, 170, 176, 186, 199, 206f., 225, 228, 266, 282, 288, 291, 300; see also: deity – freedom
Freud, S. 32f., 66
fundamentalism 30, 44, 54, 298, 300
future 13, 32, 70, 99, 115, 130, 139, 160, 171f., 178, 201, 205, 210-213, 228, 262f., 271

Gad 164, 182
Gedaliah 244
genocide 53, 303; see also: death, Shoah

Gera 148, 161f., 178
ghost 162, 243; see also: deity – spirit
Gilgamesh 57, 84, 131, 145, 226, 247, 256, 263
God/god/goddess, see: deity
Greece/Greek 38, 56, 60, 76, 80, 87, 108, 124, 132, 148, 150, 154f., 160, 167, 173, 179f., 195, 202-204, 214, 219-221, 226, 256, 285, 299
Gregory of Nazianze 18
Gröning, Ph. 19, 45

Habakkuk 184
Hadad 160; see also: Adad
Hagar 151
Haggai 165, 167
Hamath 173
Ḥammurapi 97
hand 4, 8f., 23, 32, 81, 84f., 87, 89, 91, 94f., 100, 103, 106f., 112, 134, 141f., 145, 151, 161, 164, 170, 173, 177, 187, 189, 198, 201, 209, 233, 235, 237, 251, 254, 265, 270, 286
Hannah 27, 128
hardship, see: suffering
Hathor 142f.
Hazael 173
Hazrach 173
hearing, see: listening
heaven 5, 17, 23, 29, 42, 56, 102, 105, 111, 115, 127, 130, 144-147, 149, 151f., 160, 164f., 210, 225, 233, 235, 244f., 247, 249, 257, 264, 275, 286, 297f., 300
Hebrew Bible 75 et passim
Heka 246
Heliopolis 231
hepatoscopy 142f., 176, 217-220, 223, 228
Hera 246
Hermes 162
Hezekiah 100, 112, 117, 203, 253
Hillesum, E. 283
Holocaust, see: Shoah

Holy Ones, see: deity – Holy Ones
Homer 80, 103, 124, 147, 162, 203, 214, 220
Horeb 48, 166
Horus 144, 258
Huldah 182
human endeavour, see: 'free' will, morality, obedience, piety, righteousness
humanism 25
humbleness 80, 89, 127, 133, 233
hymn 3, 20, 45, 56, 58, 68, 105, 113f., 135, 173, 175, 181, 203, 210, 223, 231f., 242f., 245, 249, 256, 258, 267, 270

Ibalpiel II 140f., 213
iconography 56, 85, 160
idolatry 28, 149, 254f., 270, 275; see also: images
Igigi 245
Ilimilku 146f., 197-199, 207
illness 8, 20, 49, 63f., 90, 96, 99, 108, 128, 142, 144, 161, 211, 238, 252, 286, 292f.
image, see: deity – image; idolatry
Imhotep 115
Inanna 176, 212, 251, 256
incapacity (human) 59, 72, 96-102, 108f., 130-134, 136
inspiration, see: deity – inspiration, spirit
integrity 294-298
intelligent design, see: deity – intelligence
intercession 81, 112, 116, 135f., 151, 159, 213, 280; see also: intermediaries, mediation
intermediaries 58, 111f., 116, 130, 135f., 141. 149f., 158-207, 217, 225, 229, 243, 271; see also: intercession, mediation
interpretation 21, 25-27, 36, 40, 43-45, 55f., 58f., 64-66, 69, 72, 75, 77, 80, 82, 90, 92, 125, 143f., 145, 147, 149, 152f., 162f., 176, 180,

INDEX OF SUBJECTS

190, 200, 205, 211-214, 216-221, 225, 228f., 240, 237, 249f., 297, 299, 303
Ipuwer 172, 196f., 232, 237, 257, 261
Irḫanta 161
Isaac 124
Isaiah 68, 104, 112, 120-122, 154-156, 182f., 188, 190, 192, 206, 228, 234, 248f., 253f., 275, 285, 290, 293
Isis 144
Ishum 246
Ishtar 102, 175, 247, 256, 262
Islam 51
Išme-Dagan 140f.
Israel *passim*

Jacob 83, 121, 193, 215, 265
Jakobsz, L. 281
Jeremiah 83, 100, 112, 153, 184, 187f., 190, 195, 206f., 215, 244, 270, 302
Jeroboam 112, 186
Jesus 11, 29, 38f., 49, 102, 118, 152, 267, 291, 294, 298, 300
Jews 6f., 18, 24, 30, 38f., 47, 51, 54, 68, 74, 101f., 134, 152, 155, 173, 190, 205, 225, 244, 279, 283, 287f., 292, 298; see also: Judaism
Jezebel 106
Job 12, 27, 30, 41, 52f., 82, 92-94, 100f., 106, 129, 133f., 163f., 194, 235-237, 240, 243, 247, 274, 299
John Paul II 23
Johnson, M. 63
Joram 241
Joseph 27, 86, 215, 228
Joshua 90, 96, 150, 208, 225, 250, 284
Judaism 18, 36, 39, 53, 75, 93, 118, 152, 164f., 224, 226, 229, 290, 292, 298; see also: Jews

Kadesh 145
Kallassu 168f.
Kaschnitz, M.L. 2f.
Kemosh 57, 148

killing, see: death
kingship, see: royalty
Kirtu 90, 131f., 144, 214, 251
Kititum 141
Kolitz, Z. 24, 279
Kotharu 73
Kraut, M. ii, xii
Kubaba 160

Lachish 98, 180, 208
Lakoff, G. 63f., 66
lamentation 7, 30, 53, 58, 86, 89, 101, 113-116, 119, 130-135, 157, 175f., 185, 188, 239, 244, 250, 263, 266-268, 269-271, 275, 302
law 24, 32, 48f., 50, 53, 97, 122, 127, 152, 155f., 181, 183, 188, 205, 210, 234, 256, 285, 289f.
law, see also: God, – commandment, Torah
letter 33, 58, 70, 97f., 116f., 136, 142f., 168-170, 180, 184., 208, 215
Leviathan 237, 247
Levinas, E. 24, 47f.
lightning 146f., 149, 152
listening (hearing) 1, 4f., 7-10, 13-17, 21, 25, 27, 30, 40-42, 45f., 50, 55, 71f., 79, 83, 87f., 93f., 97-99, 105, 108, 111-115, 119f., 122-124, 126-129, 134f., 139f., 143-146, 148, 152, 154f., 158, 161, 163, 165, 167, 169, 174, 176f., 185f., 188-190, 192, 201-207, 211, 209, 216, 223, 225, 231-234, 239, 240f., 243, 245, 247f., 253-255, 261, 263, 270f., 274, 281f., 286, 288, 290, 293-296, 300, 303f.
literacy 169, 180, 200, 208f.
liver, see: hepatoscopy
logic 52, 61, 72, 134, 204, 210, 238, 267, 280, 287. 292, 301; see also: absurdity, rationality
love (human) 3, 8f., 17, 32, 52, 130, 132f., 158, 215, 279f., 283, 278f.
Lugalbanda 255
Luther 285

McCarthy, C. 12f.
magic 58, 86, 96, 100, 104, 111, 117f., 136, 151, 149, 151, 158, 196f., 212, 224, 252
Malachi 165
Malik-Dagan 169
mantic 178; see also: prophecy
Marduk 48, 57, 81, 171f., 201, 245f., 262-264
Mari 117, 143, 168-170, 176, 178, 203, 215, 218
marzeaḥ 148, 161, 178
mediation 45, 67, 69, 118, 151, 155f., 158f., 174, 189, 195, 202, 204, 207, 225, 229, 231, 244, 247f., 257, 274, 276, 281, 284, 287, 298; see also: intercession, intermediaries
mediator, see: intermediaries
meditation 19, 24, 41
medium 111, 158, 161, 171, 226, 266
Meister Eckhart 18
Memphis 232
Menippus 179
Merikare 80, 231
message 5, 39, 53, 58, 67, 73, 77, 98, 119, 139, 143, 147, 153, 166, 169-171, 176-180, 182-188, 200, 205f., 208f., 215, 227f., 231f., 240, 248, 254, 260, 271, 281-284, 288, 293, 297, 302f.
messenger 5f., 98, 118, 130, 142, 151f., 154, 158, 160f., 163-170, 172f., 177f., 187, 189f., 196, 210, 229, 238, 240f., 252, 272, 281, 284, 298, 302f.
metaphor 41, 56, 59-71, 79, 93, 103f., 108, 256, 259, 269, 276, 291
Micah 91, 133, 182, 192-194, 209, 222, 240
might (human), see: power (human)
mirror 183
Miskotte, K.H. 21f., 37
modernity 1-53, 274, 288, 292
moon 56, 102, 142, 235, 262
morality, see: ethics

Mordecai 244
Moses 59, 72, 83, 99, 112, 118, 125f., 128, 134, 148-153, 155f., 181, 183, 189-192, 208, 225, 227, 239, 250, 284
mountains 259f.
mourning 95, 126, 128, 130-134, 136, 242, 252f., 269
mouth 22, 80, 85-87, 90f., 93-96, 99f., 106f., 114, 120, 124, 126, 128f., 134, 140f., 145, 149f., 156, 169, 175, 188-192, 201, 206, 213, 216f., 243, 255f., 262, 286, 294
Muers, R. 25, 44f., 288
Mursili II 211, 265
Music, Z. ii, xii
Muslims, see: Islam
Muwatalli 143
mysticism 18, 25, 41f., 46f., 68, 124, 280
myth 57, 66, 97, 118, 146f., 164, 247, 250

Nabal 91
Nabû 142, 201, 262
nakedness 170, 181
Nammu 255
Namtar 246
Nanaya 177
Naomi 27, 100, 121
Nathan 87, 169, 182
natural theology 31f., 36, 292
nature 31, 53, 298, 301
Nebuchadnezzar 152, 180, 284, 300
negative theology 19, 42, 68f., 94, 280
Nehemiah 101, 192
Neferty 85, 172
Nergal 117, 246, 258, 263
Nether World 104-106, 135, 143, 160-162, 172, 215, 240, 246, 252, 256, 263f., 270
New Testament 22, 35, 41, 75, 102, 118, 152, 165, 195, 216, 225, 285f., 291, 294, 299, 301; see also:

INDEX OF SUBJECTS

Christianity; Index of Biblical Texts
Nietzsche, F. 20, 61, 69
Ninmaḫ 245, 251, 255
Ninurta 48, 121
Nippur 140-142
noise 19, 71, 87, 90, 102, 107, 123, 126, 129f., 136, 238f., 256, 275; see also: clamor
Nur-Sin 168
Nuth 144

offenses 24, 29, 37, 40, 44, 53, 59-84, 103, 106f., 109, 114, 119-121, 128f., 133, 136f., 140, 143, 153f.,165, 167, 178, 187, 193f., 205, 238-243, 247, 249f., 259, 265, 268, 275-277, 296, 298, 300f., 303
oil 142, 211, 219, 257
'Old' Testament, see: Hebrew Bible
omen 5, 27, 58, 125, 139, 141-143, 144, 147, 167, 173, 183, 197, 210f., 213, 218, 220, 222f., 229, 244, 268
oracle 117, 134, 141f., 144, 149f., 168f., 173-175, 178, 180-187, 190, 209-214, 216-224, 227, 240, 265-267, 270-272, 276
oral tradition 72, 98, 168, 180, 182-184, 197-204, 206f., 208-210, 227f.
Osiris 142, 172, 256

paganism 22, 36f., 48, 119, 260
Paheri 143
paradox 18, 23, 48, 68, 233
parallels 56, 82, 100-104, 108, 113, 122, 126, 129, 135, 145f., 151-154, 156f., 163-166, 168, 170, 174f., 181, 183, 200, 202, 221, 238, 248f., 255, 265, 270
Paul 30, 118, 152, 154, 158, 195, 285
Peshiṭta 104, 155, 273
pessimism 88, 232, 257, 264
Philo Alexandrinus 68
philosophy xi, 1, 3-5, 18, 20-26, 30, 32, 35, 38, 47-51, 59-68, 93, 148

Pidrayu 257
piety 18, 20, 26, 30, 36, 46, 70, 89f., 91f., 103f., 107, 111-113, 119, 121-129, 136, 139, 148, 150, 165, 201, 232, 259, 263f., 269, 281, 294
plagiarism 228
Plato 68, 124, 148, 219
poet 2, 56, 61, 105, 126, 203, 235f., 259f., 268; see also: singers
poetry 7, 43, 51, 61, 67, 168, 174f., 184, 200, 202, 237
poorness, see: poverty
poverty 9, 41, 83, 87-89, 93, 95, 104, 107, 232, 264
power (human) 9, 24, 37, 41, 64, 67, 79, 88f., 79, 92f., 99, 103f., 118, 130, 175, 193-197, 199f., 212, 215, 217, 221, 227, 235, 249, 286, 299f.
power, see also: deity – power
praise 7, 94, 104f., 108, 126-128, 135, 143, 185, 196f., 201f., 223, 243-245, 256f., 262, 267-269, 270f.; see also: hymn
prayer 1, 7, 9f., 13, 19, 22, 27-29, 31, 42, 45-47, 53, 58, 67, 77, 83f, 102f., 105,108, 111-117, 119f., 122-125,127-130, 132, 134f., 139f., 142-149, 154, 158, 160f., 164, 168, 173-175, 178, 181, 185, 191, 201, 210f., 217, 224, 227, 232f., 236-239, 241-244, 246, 253f., 258-276, 280, 282f., 287f., 296
Preᶜ-Harakhty 113f.
priest 4, 8, 30, 46, 52, 67, 73, 80, 82, 84, 93, 96, 102, 107f., 111f., 119, 124, 126f., 135, 141f., 146f., 156, 158f., 161f., 167, 172, 175, 186, 191f., 196-199, 207, 211f., 215, 217f., 220f., 225f., 260, 264, 267, 270f., 276
prince, princess, see: royalty
proleptic perfect 268
prophecy 4, 13, 21, 30, 56, 59, 69, 74, 84-87, 91, 93, 100, 104, 106f., 111f., 114, 117, 119f., 130, 133, 135, 141, 143f., 150f., 153,

156-159, 164-195, 202f., 205-208, 210f., 215f., 221-223, 225-228, 234, 240-244, 248f., 253, 257, 259, 262f., 265-268, 270-276, 282, 284-286, 288-290, 293, 295, 302
prosperity 52, 112, 123, 127f., 137, 260
prudence, see: forbearance
Pseudo-Dionysius 18
Pseudo-Philo 234
psychology 41, 59, 107, 184, 267, 269, 276, 284f.
Ptah 111, 196, 232
Ptahhotep 89, 96
Puduḫepa 115
punishment 29, 44, 53, 82, 85, 96, 119, 125, 128, 132f., 136, 138, 146, 203, 225, 235f., 238, 242f., 267, 29143
Pythia 180

queen, see: royalty
quiet 19, 82, 90, 92, 96, 100, 106, 113, 120-122, 127f., 131, 244, 257, 264f.
Qumran 104, 118, 155, 165, 183, 206, 244, 273

rain 19, 146f., 149, 198, 257
Ramesses II 145
rape 83, 240, 293
Rashi 156, 250
rationality 25f., 43, 50, 275f., 288, 297
rationality, see also: absurdity, paradox
raven 141
Re 48, 57, 68, 114, 117, 122, 142, 168f, 210, 227f. 252-254; see also: sun
reading (Antiquity) 84, 93, 97f., 107f., 117, 127, 135, 140, 149, 176, 180, 181f., 190, 193, 196f., 199-201, 204-207, 216, 269
Rebekah 124
rebellion 81, 84, 86, 120f., 167, 191, 235, 239, 250f., 262

reciprocity 139f., 239, 268
relationship 9f., 24, 39f., 55, 60, 67, 72, 77, 189, 197, 202, 264, 293, 297
Rembrandt van Rijn 281
Rensi 97
repentance 7, 44, 92, 126, 187, 214, 262
reply, see: answer
resignation xii, 52, 92, 101, 120, 126, 133, 242, 268f., 274, 304
rethoric 61f., 72-74, 101, 188, 201f., 243f., 246, 249, 271
revelation 21, 23, 30f., 40-43, 48f., 53, 56f., 64f., 69, 76, 134, 145f., 150, 156, 158, 163f., 169, 174, 176, 185f., 192-195, 199, 202-204, 207, 209, 211f., 214, 217, 221, 227, 272, 278, 282-285, 299f.
Richards, I. 61
rock 269-271
Rosh Hashanah 7
Rousseau, J.-J. 61
royalty 31, 66f., 73, 80-88, 90f., 94f., 97-100, 107, 111f., 115-117, 122f., 126, 132, 135f., 140-146, 148, 150f., 157, 160f., 164, 166, 168-176, 178, 180, 182, 184f., 188, 192, 196, 199, 200f., 203, 205-207, 211-219, 221, 224, 226, 239-241, 245f., 251, 253f., 257f., 262f., 265f., 270-272, 300
rule 66f., 95, 103, 128, 140-142, 169, 211, 221, 235, 246, 256, 264, 265, 293f., 300; see also: royalty
Ruth 27, 100, 121, 284

Saftleven, C. xii, 303f.
sainthood, see: ancestors, holy ones
salvation 6, 11, 27, 52, 68f., 71, 77, 81, 97, 114, 120, 125, 127-129, 133-135, 139, 144, 149, 153f.,172-175, 182, 184-186, 219, 221, 228, 232-234, 236, 238, 253f., 259, 264f., 267-272, 277, 289
Samson 96

INDEX OF SUBJECTS

Samuel 90f., 112, 116, 150f., 165, 182, 226, 240, 266
sanctuary 81, 107, 111f., 117, 119, 121-124, 127, 129-134, 136, 140f., 157, 168f., 174, 177f., 181f., 185, 188, 194, 196, 198f., 203, 206f., 219, 225, 231, 241f., 244, 253
Sarah 27
Sarraute, N. 10-12
Sargon I 212
Sargon II 84
Sartre, J.-P. 3-5
Satan 28
Saul 82, 90f., 150, 221, 226, 265f., 271
save, see: salvation
Saul 82, 90f., 150, 221, 226, 265f., 271
school 181
scribes 38, 73f., 85, 98, 108, 111, 135, 141f., 146f., 158f., 170, 172, 178, 184, 196-210, 213, 219, 225., 227f., 262, 282, 298; see also: writing
scroll 104, 155, 183, 188f., 206f., 209
Second Isaiah 68, 120, 122, 188, 234, 248f., 254, 290, 293
secret 3, 80-82, 85, 90, 107, 130, 141f., 147, 159, 171, 188, 196-198, 204-206, 232, 302
secularization 48, 51
seer, see: visionary
Selah 84, 103
selfishness 53, 158, 303
Selichos 7
Sennacherib 100, 112, 203, 254
Septuagint 155. 273
servant 81f., 85, 87, 91f., 104, 121, 125, 141f., 163, 180, 187, 210, 218, 248, 253, 273, 282, 284f., 289
Seth 144, 251
shadow 105, 160, 174, 226, 235, 286
Shamash 102, 142, 145, 160, 217, 262
Shapshu 145; see also: sun
Shelley 61

shepherd 64, 66, 156-158, 225, 254, 257, 268, 303
Shiloh 150, 182
Shoah xii, 6f., 299, 303
Shu 231
Shulgi 171f., 196
Shūsaku, E. 10
sign, see: omen
silence *passim*
similarity, see: parallels
simile 65f., 164, 260
sin, see: offenses
Sin (god) 102, 142, 262
Sinai 48, 151
singers 100, 105f., 111, 135, 142, 203, 210, 235, 243, 267, 271, 294
Sinuhe 85, 114
Sippar 142
skepticism xi, 52, 75, 115, 130, 196, 237, 294, 303
sleep 59, 96, 102-106, 108f., 121, 134f., 137, 163, 213, 236; see also: deity – sleep
smoke 149, 211, 219, 226
Snefru 172
Socrates 124, 148
Solomon 112, 150, 164
soothsaying, see: divination
sorcery 117f., 136, 252
sorrow, see also: suffering
soul 4, 12, 17, 30f., 105, 160, 223, 258, 273
space (blank) 72-74, 79, 83, 86f., 91, 101, 108, 125-127, 204, 241, 243f., 247f., 250, 272, 275
speech *passim*
sphinx 159, 213
Spruyt, M. 281
star 2, 56, 102, 147, 235
stele 97, 111, 135, 160
stone 98, 122, 147f., 151, 160, 182f., 220-222, 226, 229, 254f., 263, 270
stylus 142, 183, 201, 262
suffering xii, 10, 20, 22, 27. 29, 30f., 33, 38f., 87, 89, 99, 101, 118f., 122, 128, 136, 189, 207, 233,

242-244, 255, 257, 259, 263f., 272, 283, 285f., 293, 295, 298-302
sun 6, 56, 81, 102, 113, 115, 142-145, 213, 217, 225, 231f., 249, 255, 262f., 279
supplication, see: lamentation, prayer
symbolic acts 170, 181, 183, 223
synergy 283-287

tablet 57, 72f., 79, 98, 142, 147, 151, 178, 182-184, 196f., 201, 204, 212, 215, 238, 247, 256, 262
Taizé 20
Tamar 83
Targum 95, 155f., 190f.
Tavanti, P. xii, 13-17
teacher 93, 155-158, 188, 194-196, 222, 293, 295
Teiresias 179, 203
Tell Deir 'Alla' 178
temple, see: sanctuary
Terqa 169
terror 48, 84, 121f., 144, 163, 246; see also: fear
testifying, see: witness
testimony, see: witness
Tharrumannu 162
Tharyelli 174
Thebes 145, 179, 203, 232
theism xi, 22, 30, 34, 47-50, 53
theodicy xi, 26-33, 298-303
theomorphousness 66f.
theophany 22, 111, 127, 212, 249
Third Isaiah 120, 275, 285, 290
Thomas Aquinas 18
throne 31, 141, 168f., 213, 244, 246, 252
Thucydides 180
thunder 19, 30, 66, 116, 145-149, 152, 225, 250, 254
Tiâmat 201, 238, 245, 250
Tobijah 180
tongue 2f., 40f., 84, 86, 88, 96, 99f., 108, 129, 188, 190, 243, 267, 271, 293

Torah 24, 148, 205, 290
Torah, see also: law, Pentateuch
transcendence, see: deity – transcendence
Trappists 19
tree 19, 147, 220, 222, 226, 229
Trito-Isaiah, see: Third Isaiah
tsunami 299, 301

unbeliever 9, 303f.
universalism 48, 249
Uriah 182
Utanapishti 97
Utu 255

Van der Toorn, K. 117, 129, 142, 148, 159, 168, 170, 197-202, 208-210, 219, 238, 264
vaticinium ex eventu 171, 173, 185
victory 16, 39, 86, 144f., 170f., 231
visions 134-136, 163, 165, 184, 210-216, 236, 246, 273, 289
visionary 104, 112, 143, 150, 167, 173, 178-180, 192f., 216, 215f., 246, 289; see also: visions
voice 4, 7f., 14, 41, 45, 50, 54, 66, 88, 91, 98, 111f., 116, 123f., 128, 132, 140, 144f., 146, 148-150, 152, 156, 158, 163, 165f., 180f., 189, 192, 225f., 232, 234, 239, 241, 244, 253f., 271, 287-289, 292f., 295-298, 300, 303
volcanic eruptions 301f.
Von Trier, L. 296f.
Vulgate 104, 155, 183

Wenamun 97f., 170f.
Wiesel, E. 6f., 27f.
wind 160f., 163, 165, 226, 247; see also: spirit
wings 86, 159, 247, 281
wisdom 18, 66, 80, 88, 91-95, 101f., 105, 107, 122-124, 129, 130f., 140, 151, 159, 164, 172, 175, 177, 179, 192, 194-197, 219, 231-233, 240, 245, 251, 255, 263, 264, 274, 288, 297, 300

witches 96, 252

witness 6, 9, 21, 29, 34, 43, 45, 65, 70, 82, 122, 144, 149f., 153f., 168, 174, 183-185, 188, 194, 199, 215, 221, 229, 228, 273, 289-298, 300, 303f.

writing 27, 33, 56, 58f., 68, 72, 74, 76f., 79, 81, 89!, 96!, 97-99, 108, 111, 116f., 136, 139, 142, 148, 151, 158f., 168, 170, 172, 182-186, 188, 193, 196, 198-203, 206-209, 211, 217, 225-229, 271, 273, 282, 287, 290; see also: scribes

Yaminite 169f.
Yammu 73
Yarragib 162
Yašmaḫ-Addu 117
Yom Kippur 7

Zakkur 173
Zechariah 102, 165
Zedekiah 83, 112, 188
Zeus 147, 246
Zimrilim 81, 117, 168-170., 218
Zion 48, 87, 99, 120, 126f., 133, 154, 234, 249, 261, 285f.
Zophar 93

INDEX OF TEXTS
Ancient Near Eastern Texts

AKKADIAN TEXTS
Adapa and the South Wind: 247
AGH, 11:3-6: 261f.
AGH, 13:8: 262
AGH, 22:20-21: 262
AGH, 27:19: 262
ANET, 288: 96
Anzû OBV II.2-3: 250
Anzû OBV II.23: 251
ARM 26, No. 192-194: 170
ARM 26, No. 233:9-39: 169f.
ARM 26, No. 414:29-35: 170
Assyr. Dreambook, 327f.: 144
Atraḫasis Ep., I.352-359 par.: 238
Bab. Theodicy: 88, 233, 264
BWL, 33: 233
BWL, 39: 263f.
BWL, 41: 264
BWL, 47-52: 264
BWL, 75-77: 264
BWL, 79: 264
BWL, 87: 233
BWL, 89: 88, 233
BWL, 112-113, line 16: 80
BWL, 146-147, lines 2'-6': 88
BWL, 266: 264
CAD (A) 2, 162a: 219
CAD (L) 2, 210-211: 96
CAD (M) 2, 38-39: 262
CAD (N) 1, 382: 203
CAD (Q), 72-73: 97
CAD (Q), 72b: 97
CAD (Q), 73b-75b: 87

CAD (Q), 75b: 123
CAD (R), 322-333: 145
CAD (S), 75: 81
CAD (S), 75a: 97
CAD (Ṣ) 67b: 256
CAD (Ṣ) 68a: 258
CAD (Ṣ), 69: 103
CAD (Š) 1, 108a: 84
CAD (Š) 1, 490-491: 80
CAD (Š) 1, 491: 84
CAD (Š) 2, 135: 161
CAD (Š) 2, 149a: 262
CAD (Š) 2, 231b: 217
CAD (Š) 2, 326: 102
CAD (Š) 2, 394: 298
CAD (Š) 2, 445: 96
CAD (Š) 3, 332: 246
CAD (T), 374b: 219
CAD (T), 457: 145
Chronogr. Text: 177
CoS 1, 390-402: 238
CoS 1, 402: 201
CoS 1, 404-416: 239
CoS 1, 406: 247
CoS 1, 415: 202, 243
CoS 1, 420: 131
CoS 1, 476-477: 251
CoS 1, 481-482: 171
CoS 1, 481: 131
CoS 1, 487: 90
CoS 1, 488: 131
CoS 3, 328-329: 250
CoS 3, 332: 250
Dialogue of Pessimism, 2'-6': 88
Dream Oracle from Ebla: 212
Emar Tablet: 218f.
En. Elish I.26: 238
En. Elish I.40: 238
En. Elish I.58: 245
En. Elish I.114: 245

En. Elish II.6: 245
En. Elish II.122-126: 245
En. Elish II.139-142: 245
En. Elish III.1: 245
En. Elish VII.42: 245
En. Elish VII.145: 201
En. Elish VII.157-158: 201
En. Elish VII.161-162: 201
Enmeduranki: 142
Erra Ep. I.15-20: 255
Erra Ep. I.41: 239
Erra Ep. I.81: 239
Erra Ep. I.95: 246
Erra Ep. II. Fragm. C, 23: 263
Erra Ep. IV.68: 239
Erra Ep. V.42-47: 202
Gilg. Ep. I.118: 84
Gilg. Ep. IV.194-195: 145
Gilg. Ep. VI.22-79: 247
Gilg. Ep. VII.132-133: 145
Gilg. Ep. VII.192: 256
Gilg. Ep. X.67: 131
Gilg. Ep. XI.106: 239
Gilg. Ep. XI.130-135: 239
Gilg. Ep. XI.134-135: 97
Gilg. Ep. XII.55-71: 263
Gilg. Ep. XII.73-153: 263
Ḫammurapi Stele: 97
Ibalpiel and Kititum: 141, 213
Išme-Dagan and Enlil: 140f.

KAR 1:8: 256
Kudurru, BM 90850, III.42-44: 263
LAPO 18, No. 931: 117
Ludlul I.43-46: 233
Ludlul, II.4-5: 263
Ludlul, II.6-9: 264
Ludlul, II.23-24: 264
Ludlul, II.34-38: 264
Ludlul, III: 264
Malamat 1998, 107f.: 168f.
Maqlû I.56-60: 263
Maqlû I.56-59: 253
Maqlû VII.38: 96
Marduk Prophecy: 171
Prayer to the gods of the night: 102
SAA 1, No. 29, r. 14: 80
SAA 1, No. 32, 14: 84
SAA 1, No. 244, r. 13: 82
SAA 3, No. 2, 26-27: 84, 246
SAA 3, No. 32, r. 13: 246
SAA 3, No. 40:3: 245
SAA 3, No. 40:5: 245
SAA 4, XVI: 217
SAA 4, XXXVI-LV: 218
SAA 5, No. 149, r. 5: 82
SAA 9: 168
SAA 9, LXXIII: 173
SAA 9, LXXIV: 214
SAA 9, No. 1, II, 16'-40': 262
SAA 9, No. 2, iii.11': 122f.
SAA 9, No. 1, v.12-25: 175
SAA 9, No. 1, VI.1-32: 263
SAA 9, No. 2, III, 11': 81

SAA 9, No. 9: 175
SAA 9, No. 294, 12-13: 96
SAA 10, No. 107, r.e. 12-13: 80
SAA 10, No. 294, 12-13: 96
SAA 10, No. 294, 32: 177
SAA 13, No. 134, r. 16: 119
SAA 13, No. 21:2-6: 81
SAA 13, No. 21:11-16: 81
SAA 15, No. 288, 4-8: 97
SAA 17, No. 21, r. 2-6: 81
SAA 17, No. 21, r. 11-16: 81
SAA 17, No. 22, 17-18: 84
SAAS 17: 117f., 168
SAAS 19: 159, 197
SAAS 19, 43: 81
SAAS 19, 221: 204
SAAS 19, 223-224: 205
Seux 1976, 102: 205
Seux 1976, 169f.: 262
Seux 1976, 243: 256
Seux 1976, 313: 262
Shulgi Prophecy: 171
Šurpu V-VI.3-4: 96
Šurpu V-VI.15-16: 96
Šurpu VII.17-18: 96
Šurpu VII.33-34: 96
TUAT 2, 257: 102
TUAT 2, 719: 102
TUAT 2, 766: 245
TUAT 3, 118: 90
TUAT 3, 120:100: 131
TUAT 3, 120:106: 131
TUAT 3, 169: 121
TUAT 3, 172: 80
Uruk Prophecy: 171

EGYPTIAN TEXTS
Admon. of Ipuwer, 5.9: 232
Admon. of Ipuwer, 6.6-7: 196f.
Admon. of Ipuwer, 12:1-5: 257
Admon. of Ipuwer, 12:5: 261
ANET, 449: 213
Ashkelon Ostracon: 180
Biographical Text: 141
Book of the Dead, 175: 172, 256
Coffin Texts Spell 1130: 172, 231
CoS 1, 8-9: 231
CoS 1, 24: 231
CoS 1, 25: 232
CoS 1, 26: 231f.
CoS 1, 27: 172
CoS 1, 28: 172, 256
CoS 1, 35: 257
CoS 1, 38-39: 114
CoS 1, 39: 256
CoS 1, 45: 103
CoS 1, 47: 113f.
CoS 1, 49: 115
CoS 1, 52-54: 213
CoS 1, 54: 144
CoS 1, 65: 80
CoS 1, 66-68: 160
CoS 1, 481-482: 171
CoS 1, 80: 114f.
CoS 1, 81-82: 85
CoS 1, 84: 160
CoS 1, 86: 160
CoS 1, 88: 160
CoS 1, 91-92: 98
CoS 1, 93-110: 177
CoS 1, 93-98: 172
CoS 1, 95: 237
CoS 1, 91: 97
CoS 1, 100: 97, 256
CoS 1, 105: 256

CoS 1, 106: 81, 131
CoS 1, 108: 81
CoS 1, 111: 124
CoS 1, 117: 88
CoS 1, 120: 123
CoS 1, 134-136: 161
CoS 2, 43: 80
CoS 2, 58: 80, 246
CoS 2, 65: 256
Demotic Egyptian Handbook: 218
Dream Book: 144, 210, 213
Eloquent Peasant: 80, 97
Harpers' Songs: 142f., 256
Assmann 1999, No. 32:15-20: 231
Assmann 1999, No. 136:15-19: 231
Assmann 1999, No. 136:21-22: 231
Hymns to Amun-Re: 114, 231-233, 256, 258
Instr. of Amenemhet: 160f.
Instr. of Amenemope: 123, 196
Instr. of Any, IV. 1: 123f.
Instr. of Merikare: 80, 231
Instr. of Ptahhotep 116: 88f., 96
Kadesh Inscr. Ramesses II: 145f., 156
Laments: 114f.
Shipwrecked Sailor: 160
Sinuhe Tale: 85
Sphinx Stele: 213
Pap. Boulaq, 17: 233, 256
Pap. Cairo 58032: 232

Pap. Chester Beatty, VI, verso 5, 1: 124
Pap. Chester Beatty, VI, verso 5, 8: 124
Pap. Insinger: 80, 89, 124
Pap. Leiden: 231, 258
Potter's Oracle: 173
Prayers: 103, 112ff., 117, 148
Prophecy of Neferty: 85, 172
Pyramid Text, 573: 258
Report of Wenamun: 97f., 170f.
Stele of Suty and Hor, BM 826: 258
Tale of the Two Brothers: 160
Theban Eulogy: 232
TUAT 1, 539: 130
TUAT 1, 561: 80
TUAT 2, 104: 80
TUAT 2, 849: 103
TUAT 2, 873: 88
TUAT 2, 878: 88
TUAT 2, 883: 88
TUAT 2, 907: 256
TUAT 3, 223-224: 88
TUAT 3, 226: 88
TUAT 3, 229-230: 88
TUAT 3, 234: 88
TUAT 3, 283: 80
TUAT 3, 317: 124

HITTITE TEXTS
Dreams: 213
Prayers: 115, 143, 177f., 211, 264
TUAT 1, 125: 81f.

NORTH-WEST SEMITIC TEXTS
Arslan Tash amulet: 216

Balaam Text: 173, 178, 180, 182, 204, 216
CoS 2, 137-138: 148
CoS 2, 140-145: 178
CoS 2, 155: 173f.
CoS 3, 102-103: 85
Hazor stele: 160
Hazor liver models: 219
KAI 222B:8-9: 98
Karatepe: 74
Khirbet Qeiyafa Inscription: 83, 209
Lachish Ostracon No. 3: 98
Lachish Ostracon No. 16: 180
Marzeaḥ Papyrus: 148, 161f., 176
Mesha Inscription: 148
Stele of KTMW (Zinçirli): 160
Syriac Menander, 311-313: 92
TUAT 2, 433: 96
Zakkur Inscription: 173f.

SUMERIAN TEXTS
Account of the Rise and Power of Sargon I: 212, 215
Balbale to Inana: 251
CoS 1, 516-517: 255
CoS 1, 518: 245, 251
CoS 1, 538: 131
CoS 1, 589: 98
ETCSL 1.6.2, 281-299: 121
ETCSL 1.8.2.1, 240-263: 255
ETCSL 2.2.3, 58-68: 131
ETCSL 2.2.3, 303-317: 131
ETCSL 4.8.4: 251
Incantations: 113, 261

Lamentations: 176
Lugalbanda in the
 Wilderness: 214,
 255
Enki and
 Ninhursag/Ninmaḫ:
 130f., 251, 255
Sum. Proverbs, 1.96:
 88
Sum. Proverbs, 1.185:
 85
Sum. Proverbs, 2.32:
 89
Sum. Proverbs, 2.40:
 201
Sum. Proverbs, 2.85:
 80
Sum. Proverbs, 13.42:
 175f.
TUAT 2, 28: 121
TUAT 2, 685: 84
TUAT 2, 706: 131
TUAT 3, 71: 85
TUAT 3, 470-471: 256
TUAT 3, 565-593: 238

UGARITIC TEXTS
KTU 1.2:I.3-38: 252
KTU 1.2:IV.9-10: 73
KTU 1.3: 147
KTU 1.3:II.8: 81
KTU 1.3:II.44: 81
KTU 1.3:III.20-28: 147
KTU 1.4:V.6-9: 146
KTU 1.4:VII.29-34:
 146f.
KTU 1.5:I.1-8: 247
KTU 1.5:I.25: 73f.
KTU 1.5:II.7: 73
KTU 1.5:II.9: 73
KTU 1.5:II.12: 73
KTU 1.5:V.16-17: 256
KTU 1.6: III.10f.: 257
KTU 1.6:VI.23: 145
KTU 1.6: VI.58: 162
KTU 1.12:II.46-47: 252
KTU 1.14–1.16: 214
KTU 1.14:III.10: 90
KTU 1.15:II-III: 144
KTU 1.15:II.13-16: 265
KTU 1.15:V.10-28: 252

KTU 1.16:I.25-35: 90
KTU 1.16:I.25-30: 131
KTU 1.16:II.33-44: 132
KTU 1.17:I.1-19: 122,
 146
KTU 1.17:I.28-29: 81
KTU 1.17:II: 146
KTU 1.19:I.34-35: 131
KTU 1.19:III.45: 103
KTU 1.20–1.22: 144
KTU 1.82:6: 145
KTU 1.82:36-43: 220
KTU 1.90:1: 215
KTU 1.114:28: 257
KTU 1.119: 253
KTU 1.119:26'-36': 171
KTU 1.132:25-26: 257
KTU 1.161:31-34: 174f.
KTU 1.168:8: 215
KTU 3.9: 161
RS 24.266:26'-36': 171f.
RS 92.2016: 159, 198,
 215

ELEPHANTINE TEXTS
Aḥiqar: 74

Early Jewish Texts

2 BARUCH

3:6-7   234
13:1   150
22:1   150

4 EZRA

3-14   233f.
6:39   234
7:30   234
7:32   106
10:22   133

QUMRAN
4QSamª 91
4Q405, Fragm. 20 244

4Q405, Fragm. 21 244
4Q405, Fragm. 22 244
11Q17:VII 244

WISDOM OF BEN SIRA
5:12   94
13:23   95
17:27-28   105
20:5-7   95
31:1-8   215
38:24-39   210
38:34   210
39:1   210
39:5-6   210
39:6   210
39:8   210

40:5-7   215

WISDOM OF SOLOMON
8:11-12   91
8:12   95

1 ENOCH
13:8   150
65:4   150

PSEUDO-ARISTEAS
213-216   215

PSEUDO-PHILO
60:2   234

Rabbinic Texts

MISHNA
Sanh. VII.4 118
Sanh. VII.11 118
Soṭa IX.15 165

TOSEFTA
Soṭa XIII.4 165

BABYLONIAN TALMUD
Pes.K. 12:6 (102b) 291
Sanh. 67a-68a 118
Zev. 115b 95

JERUSALEM TALMUD
Sanh. VII.19 [25d] 118

MIDRASH
Exod. R. XXIX.9 165
Qoh. R. 3:9 95
Sifre Deut. §346 291

TARG. QOHELET
3:7   95

Greek and Latin Texts

AESCHYLUS
Agamemnon,
    1130-1135: 179
Agamemnon, 1197: 179
Agamemnon,
    1240-1241: 179

ANONYMOUS
Homeric Hymns,
    III.172: 203

CICERO
De Divinatione, I.72: 147

HOMER
Iliad, I.62-67: 214
Iliad, I.69-70: 179
Iliad, I.69: 220
Iliad, I.92-100: 179
Iliad, I.511-512: 246
Iliad, I.518-519: 246
Iliad, I.568-569: 246

Iliad, V.144-151: 214
Iliad, VI. 76: 220
Iliad, VII.194-195: 124
Iliad, VII.427-428: 132
Iliad, VIII.28-29: 124
Iliad, IX.695: 132
Iliad, XIV.160-181: 217
Iliad, XIV.231-233: 103
Iliad, XVI.233-235: 220
Iliad, XVI.454: 103
Iliad, XVI.672: 103
Iliad, XVI.682: 103
Iliad, XXIV.667-678: 256
Odys., II.182: 220
Odys., VIII.43-47: 203
Odys., VIII.62-83: 203
Odys., VIII.261-369: 203
Odys., VIII.482-521: 203
Odys., X.490-495: 179
Odys., XI.37: 162
Odys., XI.90-151: 179

Odys., XV.160-181: 220
Odys., XV.430: 80
Odys., XX.98-121: 147
Odys., XXII.445: 80
Odys., XXIV.1: 162
Odys., XXIV.15: 162
Odys., XXIV.35: 162

LUCIAN
Dialogues of the Dead,
    9 (29): 179

NONNUS
Dionysiaca, XIV, 269-283: 220

PLATO
Apology, 31:148
Phaedrus, 15: 124
Phaedrus, 20: 148
Phaedrus, 244c: 219

VITA PROPHETARUM
7:1-2 93

INDEX OF BIBLICAL TEXTS
Hebrew Bible

GENESIS
1	67
1:26	66, 300
1:28	67
2:2-3	260
2:7	194
2:17	299
3:5	299
3:8-10	82
3:23	181
6	239
6:3	153
6:5-6	301
6:6	301
6:7	40
6:8	194
12:1-9	76
12:6	222
16:7-14	163, 166
16:7	152
16:13	164
16:18-19	166
18–19	164
18	281
18:14	299
18:16-33	299
19:12	24
19:15	163
20:17	112
21:13	237
21:17	151, 163, 165
22:2-3	124
22:11	163
22:12-18	164
22:18	139
22:23	125
24	125
24:10	124
24:13-14	125
24:21	125
24:22	125
24:24-27	125
24:30	125
24:50	134
26:5	139
28:11	181
31:3	165
31:11	163
32:22-32	265
32:39	295
34:5	83
37:8-10	215
37:19-20	215
41:49	100
45:3	86

EXODUS
3–4	190f.
3:4ff.	190
3:4	190
3:7-10	190
3:11	189f.
4:1	190
4:8	167
4:9	167
4:10-16	189
4:10	99, 190
4:11	99, 190
4:13-16	67
4:13	191
4:14-16	191
5:1-3	191
5:2	167
6:9	167
6:12	167, 190
6:30	130
7:1	181, 191
7:9-10	118
7:4	167
7:13	167
7:16	167
7:19-20	118
7:22	167, 197
8:15	167
8:19	167
9:12	167
10:14	260
11:9	167
14:9-14	125
14:9-10	125
14:10-12	125
14:10	125
14:11-12	125
14:14	125
14:15	125
14:19	158
15:14-15	121
15:16	122
15:20	181
15:26	139
16:20	167
17:1-7	83
18:17-26	156
19:9	167
20:11	260
20:16	296
20:18-21	149
20:19	167
21:2-11	101
22:17	118
22:24-26	101
22:27	100
23:12	260
23:14	260
23:20-23	167
23:20-21	158
24:4	151
24:7	139
24:12	151, 180
28:3	157
31:3	157
31:15	260
31:17	260
31:18	151
32:15-16	151
32:19	151
33:12-16	250

INDEX OF TEXTS

34:1	151	1:26-27	239	18:9-12	223
34:27-28	151	1:32	239	18:15-20	167
35:31	157	1:43-45	140	18:15-19	150

LEVITICUS

		1:43	239	18:19	167
5:1	82	1:45	239	18:21-22	186
10:1-2	126	3:23-28	83	18:22	186
10:3	126	3:26	83, 140, 167	19:15	298
13:45	100	4:12	149	23:4-5	178
19:18	17	4:13	151, 183	24:8	156
19:26	118	4:15	149	24:10-13	101
20:6	118	4:28	149, 254	26:17	139
24:15-16	100	4:33	149	27:8	183
25	101	4:36	149	27:9-10	126, 139
26:14	139	4:45	290	27:9	127
26:18	139	5:4-5	149	27:10	126
26:21	139	5:5	149	28	139
26:27	139	5:4	149	28:14	155

NUMBERS

		5:14	260	29:6	112
		5:20	296	29:17-27	205
11:2	112	5:22-23	149	29:19-20	205
11:15	250	5:22	151, 153, 183	29:28	205
11:17	156	5:23-31	167	30	139
11:22	250	5:23-27	149	30:10	181
11:25-29	153, 156, 181	5:32-33	155	30:11	181
11:25	153, 303	6:4	14	30:13-14	181
11:29	153, 192, 303	6:5	17	30:14	152, 181
11:30	153	6:17	290	30:15	299
12:1-15	148	6:20	290	31:12	152
14:45	239	8:20	167	31:19	290
20:2-13	83	9:10	151	31:21	128, 290
21:7	112	9:23	167	31:26	290
22–24	150, 167, 178	10:1-5	151	32:20	259
22:22-35	4	11:26-28	167	32:39	299
22:22	164	13:2-6	186	32:46	299
23–24	216	13:2	215	34:9	192
23:9	76	13:4	215	34:10	151, 156, 192
23:18-19	217	13:6	215		

JOSHUA

23:23	220	15:1-18	101	1:7	155
24:3-4	215	15:5	139	1:17-18	167
27:28	192	16:22	222	2:1	90
30	90	17:6	298	5:6	167
31:8	178	17:8-13	156	6:5	90, 95f.
31:16	178	17:11	156	6:10	96
35:30	298	17:20	155	6:16	90

DEUTERONOMY

		18	159	6:20	90
1	239	18:9-13	118	7:9	250

INDEX OF TEXTS

7:19-22	90	7:1	116	28:7	162
8:30-32	183	7:5-11	112	28:13	165
13:22	178	7:5	112	28:15	266
18	222	7:7-14	116	28:16-19	266
21:45	150	7:8	116		
23:6	155	7:9	116	2 Samuel	
23:14	150	7:10	116, 149	1:12	241
24:9-10	178	8:6	112	2:26	82
24:22	290	8:18	239f.	3:11	86
24:24	139	9	112	5:24	222
		9:9	216	7	150, 169, 271
Judges		10:6	150, 153	7:7	248
2:1-5	164	10:7	223	12:1-4	87
2:1	163	10:9	223	12:5-6	87
2:17	167	10:11-12	271	12:16	269
3:12-30	205	10:10-12	150, 153	12:18	91
3:19	94, 205	10:16	91	12:21-22	241
3:20	205	10:25	182	12:21	269
5:23	284	10:27	91	12:22	269
6:11-24	166	12:9	259	13:20	83
6:12	163	12:19	112	13:22	83
6:14-18	164	14:24-45	261f.	14:17	164
6:23	164	14:24-30	265f.	14:20	164
8:14	208	14:24	82	16:14	260
9:23	154, 165	14:37	265	19:10	86
9:37	222	14:38-39	265f.	19:11	86
10:7	259	14:39	82, 266	19:12	86
13:3-23	163, 167	14:40-45	266	19:27	164
13:3-21	166	14:41	221	22:3	270
13:22	164	15	167	22:7	112
16:2	96	15:11	301	22:8	301
17–18	82	15:28-29	266	22:14	149
18:19	82, 91	15:29	301	22:32	270
18:20	82	15:30-31	266	22:42	241
19:28	104	15:35	301	22:47	270
20:26	241	16:1	266	23:1	271
		18:10	150, 271	23:2-3	150, 271
1 Samuel		19:20	153, 181	24	164
1:13	127	19:22-24	150	24:11	216
2:9	106	19:24	181, 216, 271	24:16	164
2:34	223	20:26	91	24:17	164
3	150	23:20-21	153	24:18	164
3:1	242	25:36	91		
3:8-9	150	28	165, 226	1 Kings	
3:19-21	150	28:3	266	1:31	132
3:20	181	28:6	221, 243, 266	1:47-48	169
3:21–4:1	151			3	164

370   INDEX OF TEXTS

3:5-15	150	4:29-31	104	8:16-18	183
8	112	4:31	101, 104	8:16	156, 181, 290
8:35	112	4:38	181	8:18	223
8:39	112	6	241	8:20	156, 290
8:42	112	6:9	180	9:15	156
8:44	112	6:33	241	10:10-11	156
8:49	112	7:9	82	10:14	86
8:56	150f.	10:10	150	13:13	301
13	186	12:3	156	14:7	121
13:6	112	17:13	216	15:1	106, 133
14:4	203	17:27-28	156	15:2-3	132
18–19	253	18:34	253	15:8	132
18	167, 198	18:36	100	16:7	132
18:26	253	19	253	16:11	101
18:27	257	19:1-5	253	16:12	253
18:29	253	19:6-7	253	16:14	127
19	250	19:7	163	17:7	156
19:4	106	19:8-37	254	17:12-14	126
19:5-8	166	19:14-19	112	18:4	242
19:5	163	19:14	117	19:19-20	221
19:7	163	19:16	112	20	181
19:11-14	250	19:20-34	112	21:6	242
19:11-13	19, 66	20:8-9	223	21:8	242
19:11	250	22:2	155	23:1	130
19:12	244, 250	22:13	188	23:2	130
20:35	181	23:24	222	23:6	130
21:27	126	25:22-26	244	24:18	301
21:28-29	126			25:5	126
22	150, 186	Isaiah		28–31	190
22:3	82	1:14	140, 301	28:7-11	193
22:15	186	1:15	181, 241	28:7-10	192
22:19-24	165	1:18-19	139	28:9	156
22:19-23	186	1:19-20	140	28:21-22	40
22:21-23	154	2:3	154	29:6	301
22:21ff.	165	3:23	183	29:9-10	192
22:21	163	5:14	126	29:10	193, 216
22:27	155	6	150	29:11	183
22:28	205, 209	6:5-7	190	29:13-16	192
2 Kings		6:8	165	29:17	99
1:3	163	6:9-10	140	29:18	99
2:3-5	86	6:14	126	30:8	183f., 290
2:3	181	7:2	121	30:10	86, 216
2:5	181	7:4	121	30:11	156
2:7	181	7:10-17	223	30:15	121, 128
2:15	181	8:1	183	30:16	128
4:1	181	8:2	183	30:17	121
		8:3-4	13		

INDEX OF TEXTS

30:19-21	154-158	42:1-4	188	51:9	259, 261, 285
30:20-21	155	42:1	157, 303	51:16	286
30:20	155, 157	42:2	91	51:17	261, 285
30:21	158, 295	42:5-9	286	52:1-2	261
30:26	157	42:5	157	52:1	285
30:30	149	42:13-15	249	52:2	285
32:3-4	99	42:13-14	248	52:3	259
32:9	121	42:13	248	52:7-9	261, 285
32:10	121	42:14	248f.	52:8	91, 156, 242
32:14	121	42:18-21	240	52:10	261
32:15	157	42:18-19	248	52:15	87
32:17	121	42:22	241	53:7	91
33:17	156	42:23-25	248	54:8	259
35:2-4	99	43:9-21	249	54:13	181
35:5-6	99	43:9-12	289	55:4	290
36:19	253	43:10-11	249	56:10	104, 242
36:21	100	43:10	290	57:11	249
37:7	163	43:12	290	57:15-16	157
37:8-37	254	43:19	286	57:20	12
37:14-20	112	43:22-24	290	58:1	91
37:17	112	43:23-24	249	58:4	241
37:30	223	44:3	157	58:5-12	241
38:7	223	44:7-8	249	58:9	40
38:18	104	44:8	290	59:1-3	241
40:2	120	44:11	454	59:16	285
40:3	284	45:6	249	59:21	157
40:9	261, 285	45:7	299	61:1	157
40:10-11	64, 157, 280	45:8	249	61:3	157
40:10	249, 284	45:15-17	68	61:10	120
40:16	249	45:15	69, 157, 234	62	242
40:18	249	45:19	69	62:1	120, 242
40:25	249	45:20-25	299	62:4	120
40:27	250	45:21-22	249	62:6-7	242
40:28-31	293	46:1-7	254	62:7	302
40:28	286	46:5	249	62:11-12	157
40:31	284	46:7	254	63:9	157, 302
41:1	122, 249	46:9	245	63:10-11	157
41:2-6	122	47:5	106, 133	63:10	157, 302
41:6	122	48:6-7	205, 286	63:11	157, 192
41:17	40	48:16	153, 155	63:14	157
41:20	234	48:17	156	63:15	101
41:21-29	249	49:15	234	63:17	156
41:26	234	50:1	259	64	242
41:28	255	50:4-5	188, 293	64:1	301
42	240	50:4	181	64:4	242
42:1-7	285	51	295	64:6	242

64:8	243	14:23	186	36:20	207
64:11	157, 242f., 302	14:27-28	186	36:21	207
65:6	243	15:16	188	37:3	112
65:12	140	15:19	190	38:16	188
65:24	40, 139f.	18:18	100, 205	38:17-18	221
66:3-4	119	19:14	112	38:20	181
		20:9	187	38:24-27	83, 188
JEREMIAH		20:18	266	38:27	83
1:6-10	190	22:15-16	297	40:6	244
1:9	190	23:3	64	40:7–41:18	244
3:23	126	23:18	150	42:2	112
4:8	133	23:22	150	42:4	112, 188
4:19-22	302	23:25-32	215	42:7	153
4:19	87, 101	23:33-34	178	43:1-3	207
4:23–26	301	23:36	178	45	207
6:2	106, 133	25:34	132	45:1	206f.
6:10	140	25:37	106, 133	46:27	121
6:11	140, 187	26:2	112	47:5	106, 133
6:13-14	175	26:17-19	194, 209	48:2	106, 133
6:17	242	26:17	209	49:23	121
7:6	112	27–28	86	49:26	106
7:16	140	27:9-10	215	50:30	106
7:22	248	28:9	186	50:42	126
7:23-28	140	28:15-17	186	51:29	301
8:7	222	29	184	51:39	106
8:8	156, 207	29:7	112	51:55	126
8:10-11	175	29:8-9	215	51:57	106
8:14	101, 106	29:11-13	139	51:60	204
8:18-21	302	29:12-14	40		
9:11	195	30:10	121	EZEKIEL	
10	254f.	31:15	133	1–2	150
10:1	254	31:26	103	1:24-25	149
10:5	254f.	31:31-34	153	1:28–2:2	189
10:13	254	32:10	184, 204	1:28	149
10:14	254	32:25	184	2:2	157
10:22	301	32:27	299	2:5	189
11:7-10	140	32:44	184	2:7	189
11:11	140	33:3	40	2:9	188
11:14	112, 140	36:2	207	3:1	188
12:7-9	302	36:4	207	3:2	188
13:1-3	157	36:6	207	3:3	188
13:12	302	36:8	207	3:7	189
13:17	302	36:10	207	3:11	189
14:8-9	266	36:13-14	207	3:12-14	157, 189
14:13-16	186	36:14-19	207	3:14	188f.
14:17-18	302	36:18	206	3:17-21	187
14:17	23			3:17	242

INDEX OF TEXTS

3:18	187	37:5-6	157	MICAH	
3:24-27	189	37:9-10	157, 165	1:1	209
3:24	157, 188	37:14	157, 303	1:2	209
3:26-27	189	38:11	121	1:3–4	111
3:26	99, 180	38:19-20	301	1:4-5	301
5:7	126	39:11	126	1:8-9	133
7:11-14	126	39:19	157	1:8	181
7:26	242	43:2	149	1:10	133
8:3	157, 189	43:5	157, 189	2:1	104
8:18	241	44:23	156	2:5	222
11:1	157, 189	HOSEA		2:6	86
11:5	153, 157	2:23-24	148	2:7	157, 194
11:19	153, 157, 303	3:4	221	2:11	190, 194
11:24	153, 157, 189	4:12	222	3	240
12–13	186	9:7	153, 157	3:4-7	239
13	223	9:8	242	3:4	193, 240
13:3	296			3:5-8	192
13:10	175	JOEL		3:5-7	193
13:16	175	2:12-16	269	3:5	175
14:14	122	2:17	266	3:6-7	193, 243
14:20	122	3:1-2	157, 181	3:7	100, 216
16:42	242	4:16	301	3:8	157, 193
16:63	120	AMOS		3:11	156, 181
19	185	1:1	301	3:12	194, 209
21:26	223	3	299	4:2	156
23:42	126	3:7-8	187	5:12-14	222
24:15-27	189	3:7	150	6:5	178
24:17	100	4:13	286	7	240
24:22	100	5:13-15	93	7:1-6	209
24:27	99	5:13	93, 126	7:4	242
28:3	122	5:23	126, 181	7:5	91
31:18	126	6:5	126	7:7	242
32:16	126	6:10	133	7:16	91
33:1-6	187	7:9	186	NAHUM	
33:2	242	7:10	93, 187	1:5	301
33:6-7	242	7:12	216	2:14	98
33:7	242	7:17	93, 222	HABAKKUK	
33:22	99, 189	8:3	133	1	272
34:4	157	8:11-12	292f.	1:4	272
34:8	64	8:12	243	1:5-11	272
34:14	64	9:5	301	1:12	272
34:16	157	9:2	105	1:13	272
34:18	64	JONAH		1:17	273
36:26-27	157	3:5	269	2	272f.
36:26	153, 303	3:9	269	2:1-4	273
37:1	153, 157				

374   INDEX OF TEXTS

2:1-3	273	3:5	271	22:32	268
2:1	242	3:6	135	23:4	64
2:2	184	4:5	18, 103	25:10	290
2:4	273	4:9	104, 135	25:13	129
2:11	254	6:6	105	27:7	271
2:18-19	255	6:9-10	271	28	269ff.
2:20	127	7:7	258	28:1	269f.
3:6	301	8	235	28:2	270
3:10	148	8:5-7	235, 300	28:3-5	270
		10:1	266	28:4-5	270

ZEPHANIAH

		10:4	52	28:4	270
1:7	127	13	272	28:5	270
3:17	250	13:2	272	28:6	270

HAGGAI

		13:4	104, 271f.	28:8-9	270
1:13	167	13:6	271f.	28:8	270f.
2:5	157	14:1	52	28:9	270f.
2:7	301	16:5-6	222	29:3-9	149
		17:6	271	30:6	135

ZECHARIAH

		18:3	270	30:10	105
1:9	163	18:7	112	30:13	105, 128
1:11	121	18:8	301	31:3	270
1:14	163	18:14	149	31:18	106
1:18	216	18:32	270	32	84
2:1	216	18:42	237	32:3	84
2:17	56	18:47	270	32:4	84
3	150	18:51	271	32:5	84
4:1-2	216	19:2-5	127	34:5	271
4:1	163	19:2-4	56	35	268f.
4:4	163	19:2	148	35:1-21	268
4:6	157	19:15	270	35:3	269
5:1	216	20:2	271	35:9-10	268
5:5	163	20:7	271	35:13	128, 268f.
6:1	216	20:10	271	35:14	269
7:7	140	22	262ff.	35:18	268
7:12	157, 192, 249	22:1-3	267	35:20	127, 268
7:13	140	22:2-3	267	35:21	128
8:6	295	22:2	234	35:22	269
10:2	215, 221f.	22:3	103, 267, 271	35:23	258, 269
12:10	157	22:4	267	35:24	268
13:2	187	22:5-6	267	35:28	268
13:9	40	22:10	268	37:7	128

MALACHI

		22:12	234, 267	38:14-15	99, 128
2:7	1677	22:16	267	38:15	273
		22:20	234, 267	38:16	100, 271

PSALMS

		22:22	267, 271	38:22	234
2:7	132	22:23-32	267	39	119, 128f.

INDEX OF TEXTS

39:2-3	119, 128	50:21	249	78:56	290
39:2	129	51	151f.	78:63-64	260
39:3	128f.	51:12-14	153	78:65	258, 260
39:3-4	119, 129	51:12	153f.	81:6	149
39:5-7	128	51:13	153, 157	81:8	40, 149
39:5-6	1289	51:14	153f.	81:7-17	149
39:8	129	51:15	154	83:2	127, 242, 269
39:9	119, 129	51:17	154	83:3	126
39:10	119, 127, 129	51:19	154	86:1	271
39:11-12	128	53:1	52	86:7	139, 271
39:12	119, 128	55:2-3	115	86:17	223
39:13-14	128	55:2	269	88	105f.
39:13	119, 269	55:3	270f.	88:6	106
39:14	128	55:10-24	270	88:7	106
40:7-11	267	59:6	258	88:11-12	105
40:10	128	59:7	126	89:20	150
41:12	126	59:15	126	89:27-28	132
42:8	148	60:7-10	270	89:27	270
42:10	266	60:7	271	89:39	271
43:2	266	62	2213	89:47	157
44	258f.	62:2	128	89:52	271
44:2-4	259	62:3	270	90	235
44:2	259	62:6	128	90:14	135
44:10	259, 262	62:7-8	270	90:17	286
44:12	259	62:12-13	223	91:15	40, 265
44:13	259	63:12	106	92:3	135
44:18-22	259	65:2	127	93:5	290
44:23-24	267	65:3	127	94:9	99
44:24	258f.	65:6	127, 271	94:12-15	121
44:25	259	65:8	127	94:17	105
44:27	259	65:10-14	127	95:6-11	239
45:7	132	65:14	127	96:12	148
46:6	135	66	239	99:7	290
46:7	126	66:16-19	242	104:30	165, 194
50	248f.	69:14	271	107:42	106
50:1	249	69:17-18	271	108:7-10	270
50:3	249	71:3	270	108:7	271
50:4-6	249	72:12	234	109	269
50:4	249	74	244	109:1	269
50:5	248	74:1	244	109:2-3	269
50:6	249	74:4	223, 244, 269	109:4	269
50:7-23	249	74:9	243f., 269	109:6-19	269
50:8-13	249	74:23	126	109:20	269
50:14	249	77	100	109:25	269
50:16-22	249	77:2-3	100	109:30	269
50:16-20	248	77:3-5	100	110:1	271

114:3-4	235	144:1	270	32:3	100
115	22	147:2-3	157	32:5	100
115:3	300	JOB		32:6-7	92
115:5	255			32:8	194
115:7	255	1:21	169	32:11	92
115:9-15	300	2:12-13	133	32:12	92, 100
115:16	300	3:13	106, 121	32:15-16	92, 100
115:17	105	3:17	106	32:16	92
119	294	3:18	106	32:17-19	194
119:2	290	3:26	121, 132	32:19-20	92
119:22	280	4:12–5:1	163, 243	33:4	194
119:24	290	4:17-18	163	33:13-17	236
119:32-43	294	5:16	106	33:31-33	93f.
119:46	290	6:24	94	34:14	194
119:59	290	7:11-12	235	34:29	236, 272
119:79	290	7:17-19	235	35:9-14	240
119:95	290	7:21	235	35:11	223, 236
119:119	290	9	101	35:12	239
119:125	290	9:3	101	35:13-16	242
119:138	290	9:14-15	101	36:22	156
119:146	290	9:16	40	37:2-5	149
119:152	290	9:21	101	38–39	134
119:167	290	9:32	101	39:26	223
119:168	290	10:12-13	237	39:37-38	40
121	259f.	11:3	93	40:1-5	100f.
121:1	259	11:5	236	40:2	101
121:2	259	13:5	94	40:4-5	134
121:3-4	260	13:13	94	40:4	91, 101
127:2	103	13:17	94	40:5	101
130:5-6	273	13:19	94	40:9	149
131:2	128	17:3	237	40:25–41:26	247
132:12	290	19:7	236	40:28	237
135:2	112	21	52	41:4	247
135:4	300	21:5	91	41:17	247
135:6	300	21:14-15	52	41:25	247
135:12	300	23:4	273	42:2	299
135:14	300	27:3	194	42:6	40, 101
135:15-17	255	29:9-10	94	PROVERBS	
137:3	203	29:21-22	94	1:24-25	140
137:6	99	29:22	94	1:28	140
138:3	271	30	101	3:24	103
139:7	157	30:20	101, 232	7:11	126
139:8	105	30:26	101	10:19	92
143:1	271	30:27	101	11:12-13	92
143:7	271	31:33-34	82	13:2	91
143:8	135	32	194f.	15:18	121
		32:1–37:24	92		

INDEX OF TEXTS

17:1	126	1:16	133	10:15-19	99, 190
17:27-28	92	2:9	243	10:15	189
17:28	94	2:10	120, 133	10:16	189
19:23	103	3:8	120	10:17	189
20:12	99	3:26-29	120.		
21:13	140	3:26	133	**Ezra**	
21:23	91	3:28	133	9:1-2	134
27:2	94	3:33	40	9:4-5	134
29:24	82	5:20	267	9:6-15	134
30:32	91, 94				
31:8-9	83	**Esther**		**Nehemiah**	
31:8	93	4:1	132	1:4	241
		4:3	269	5:7	101
Ruth		4:11-14	87	5:8	101
1:18	100	4:16	269	8:9-10	128
3:18	121	7:4	87, 255	8:11	127
4:9-11	290			9:30-31	245
		Daniel		9:30	192, 301
Qohelet		3:29	100	13:2	178
3:7	95	4:28	152, 165		
4:17–5:1	130	4:29	152	**1 Chronicles**	
5:1-6	127	4:31	149	12:18	173
5:5	130	4:35	300	21:16	164
5:6	215	4:36	300	22:9	121
7:14	130	5	151	25:8	181
8:17	130	5:5	151		
9:1	130	5:11	151	**2 Chronicles**	
12:7	153, 303	5:24	151	15:3	156
		9:28	153	20:5	112
Lamentations		10:10	189	24:19-20	192, 249
1:5	301				

New Testament

Matthew		17:5	152, 165	1:23-27	195
3:17	152, 165	18:16	298	3:11	195
7:7-8	40	19:26	300	3:30	195
7:11	40	20:30-31	11	4:9	17
8:8	11	22:37-39	17	5:2	195
9:27	11	22:46	102	5:8	195
9:32-34	102	23:16-19	11	5:13	195
10:19-20	294	25:31-40	297	5:39	132
12:22-24	102	27:46	267	9:7	152, 165
12:43-45	195			9:38-40	118
13:13-17	11	**Mark**		13:11	294
13:52	298	1:11	152, 165	15:34	267

INDEX OF TEXTS

LUKE
1:18   102
1:19   102
1:63-64 102
2   303
9:35   152, 165
11:13   303
11:14-15 102
12:11-12 294
14:4   102
14:6   102
20:26   102
21:14-15 294
23:34   11
24   291
24:48   291

JOHN
1:18   65
5:37   65
6:46   65
7:39   303
9:31   40
12:28   152
12:29   152
14:8ff. 65
17:21-22 15
20:22   303

ACTS
1:8   291
2:38   303
5:32   291, 303
8:18-19 303
9:3-6   152, 165
10:45   303
13:2-6   118
18:24–19:7 296
19:2   303
22:9   152

ROMANS
4:3-5   20
5:2-4   27
5:5   303
8:2   43
8:9   154
8:11   154
8:14   154
8:16   158
8:19   148
8:22   148
8:24-25 27
8:26   154
12:4-8   286
18:18-23 27

1 CORINTHIANS
2:9   65
3:5-9   285
9:16   193
12:10   296
12:12-31 286
13:12   8, 65
14:29   296

2 CORINTHIANS
1:22   303
5:5   303
6:18   299
11:4   303

GALATIANS
3:2   303
3:14   303
5:13   158
5:16-25 158, 296
5:25   158

EPHESIANS
1:17   303
1:19   300
1:23   286
2:8   303
4:4   286
4:12   286
4:16   286
4:30   302
5:14   106
5:23   286
5:30   286

PHILIPPIANS
2   38

COLOSSIANS
1:24   286

1 THESSALONIANS
5:19-21 296

2 TIMOTHY
1:7   303

HEBREWS
11   291
11:1   70
11:2   70
11:4   70
11:5   70
11:39   70
12:1   70

2 PETER
1:17-18 152
1:19-20 195
1:21   195

1 JOHN
3:24   303
4:1   296
4:12   65
4:13   303

REVELATION
1:10   158
1:12   158
8:1   8, 244, 275
8:3-4   244
10:4   149
10:8   149
11:8-13 301
11:12   149
14:13   149
16:17-21 301